W9-AXY-669

Personal Encryption Clearly Explained

Pete Loshin

AP PROFESSIONAL

AP PROFESSIONAL is a division of Academic Press

San Diego   London   Boston
New York   Sydney   Tokyo   Toronto

AP Professional
1300 Boylston Street, Chestnut Hill, MA 02167, USA
An Imprint of Academic Press
A Division of Harcourt Brace & Company
http://www.apnet.com

United Kingdom Edition published by
ACADEMIC PRESS LIMITED
24–28 Oval Road, London NW1 7DX
http://www.hbuk.co.uk/ao/

Library of Congress Cataloging-in-Publication Data
Loshin, Peter
      Personal encryption clearly explained / Peter Loshin.
            p.   cm.
      Includes index.
      ISBN 0-12-455837-2 (alk. paper)
      1.   Microcomputers—Access control.   2.   Data encryption (Computer
science)   I.   Title.
QA76.9.A25L67   1998
005.8—dc21   98-19661
                                                                                CIP

Printed in the United States of America
98 99 00 01 02 IP 9 8 7 6 5 4 3 2 1

Contents

Acknowledgments

Although my name is on the front cover, a lot of other people made this book possible—all of whom deserve to be mentioned. Most important were Lisa and Jacy, my wife and son, who put up with my unavailability while feverishly writing away in my office.

Many thanks to both Ed Amoroso and Peter Wayner, who, in addition to both being best-selling authors, were willing to read my early drafts and help keep me from making too many egregious errors.

Acquisitions editor Ken Morton, who did a terrific job of supplying ideas as well as help in turning an idea into a book, gets my deepest appreciation for his contributions as well as his patience. The other people at AP Professional, including Samantha Libby, Shawn Brown, and Thomas Park, who helped move this book through the production process, also deserve many thanks for making the process relatively painless.

Finally, thanks to everyone at Microsoft, Netscape, RSA, Verisign, Symantec, and all the other vendors and industry workers who helped make it possible for me to write about their products.

Introduction

One of the most startling revelations to people just learning about the Internet is that the Internet is an open network. There is no privacy on the Internet. Anything you send over the Internet is accessible to practically anyone. And there is no way you can even know that your data transmissions are being monitored. There are no telltale opened envelopes, or odd clicking noises on a tapped phone, or suspicious-looking characters dogging your steps to tip you off to the fact that you are being watched.

On the Internet, there is no privacy by design. Data can be transmitted over any number of public, semi-public, or private connections, and at any given point can be intercepted by listeners, authorized or unauthorized. This means your e-mail, your terminal sessions, your credit card payment numbers, are all accessible to anyone with the skills, determination, and a little bit of access.

Encryption, and its cryptographic partner function, the digital signature, offer the one best hope for maintaining privacy in your digital doings on-line. If you buy or sell on-line, chances are good you have used application software that uses encryption and digital signatures. However, your e-mail is most likely still susceptible to interception and even counterfeiting by the bad guys.

This book lays out everything you need to know in order to use and understand how encryption and digital signatures work, how they can be used to protect your personal interests, and how you can use popular software products like Netscape's Navigator and Microsoft's Internet Explorer, to protect your data through encryption and digital signatures.

Organization

The first half of this book is largely theoretical. Just as you don't need to understand how a transmission works to effectively and safely drive a car, you don't need to know how encryption and digital signatures work to use them effectively and safely. However, understanding the theory will help you to choose the most appropriate encryption and digital signature solutions as well as to use those solutions most effectively.

Chapter 1 examines the risks you run when you send or receive data over the Internet, as well as the privacy threats that we are increasingly facing. In it, I present the various types of risk you face, as well as how to place value on your personal data. In addition to spelling out some of the techniques criminals use to steal your data, I also introduce the most important cryptographic functions.

Chapter 2 is a primer on modern cryptography. In it, I guide the reader through the basics of cryptography, working up from simple ciphers through symmetric and asymmetric algorithms up to the most important of the popular secret key encryption, public key encryption, and digital signature functions. Also discussed in this chapter are certification authorities and secure hashing techniques.

Chapter 3 examines the social and political issues relating to the use of encryption. Encryption-enabled software is one of the most controversial products on the market today, and in this chapter I present some of the key points raised in arguments over the dissemination, use, and export, of cryptographic technologies.

Chapter 4 examines how encryption is incorporated into systems, both hardware and software—and both on stand-alone systems and in networked environments. If you are not sure of what data needs to be protected, or how it is best protected, this chapter will help put it all in perspective for you.

The second half of this book is very, very practical. It offers hands-on guidance to using the most popular encryption and digital signature products for browsing the web, securing e-mail, and securing data on your desktop.

Chapter 5 discusses not only what type of encryption-enabled products are now generally available, but also how to use these products to get started using encryption and digital signatures for your own communications.

Chapter 6 provides an introduction to using Netscape Navigator and Microsoft Internet Explorer to securely browse the web. Here you'll learn how you can make browsing safter by configuring security options and monitoring the certification of web sites you visit. You'll also learn about anonymous browsing and controlling web cookies with the leading web client software in this chapter.

Chapter 7 presents secure e-mail, using Netscape's Communicator, Microsoft's Outlook Express, and Qualcomm's Eudora with Pretty Good Privacy's PGP for Personal Privacy. If you're connected to the Internet, chances are you've already got at least one of these products. This chapter will help you take advantage of the power of software you've already got to secure your e-mail messages.

Encryption is important to Internet communication, but you don't have to be connected to want to encrypt data for protection. Chapter 8 shows you how you can use PGP for Personal Privacy or SecurPC from RSA Data Security, Inc., to encrypt data on your desktop system.

Chapter 9 examines one of the applications that most often uses encryption: digital commerce. Here, I explain how on-line transactions work, and what products and protocols are available.

Finally, Chapter 10 revisits PGP for Personal Privacy, showing how the PGP web of trust functions, and how to administer and manage interactions with other PGP users.

With Chapter 2, Appendix A provides all the mathematics you need to really understand public key cryptography. Appendix B offers a handful of Internet resources for the interested reader, while Appendix C includes four Internet documents that highlight how security and encryption concerns have been addressed by the Internet Engineering Task Force (IETF).

Using This Book

If you are in a hurry to use encryption and digital signatures to protect your data and transmissions, you can skip to the appropriate chapter and find the function and product most appropriate to your needs. If you already use encryption or digital signatures, but want to understand how they work, the first five chapters will give you what you need.

MIS, IT, and systems managers unfamiliar with encryption technologies will want to work through the entire book to both understand the basics and to understand how the most popular products work and what they can do for users.

Tell Me What You Think

If you find this book useful, please let me know (and recommend it to your friends and colleagues). In any case, I always enjoy reader comments, so feel free to e-mail me at *pete@loshin.com*. Thanks, and enjoy!

1

It's a Dangerous World

The average citizen would never walk down a city street with a wad of currency in a see-through plastic bag, or leave an expensive camera on the dashboard of an unlocked, parked car, or leave a townhouse full of luxury items with the windows open and the front door unlocked. You will get little sympathy when you find yourself the victim of theft in such situations, and yet most citizens exercise even less caution in their digital lives, leaving themselves open to victimization in many forms from assailants unlikely to leave fingerprints or be identified in any criminal lineup.

VOCABULARY NOTE: The term *computer criminal* (or just *criminal*) refers to an individual who breaks the law through the use of computers and networks. In particular, computer crimes may include activities like these:

- Accessing other computers without authorization.
- Stealing information from a computer without prior authorization.
- Deleting or modifying information without authorization.
- Intercepting network transmissions.
- Impersonating another person for fraudulent purposes.
- Denying authorized users access to their networks or systems.
- Coercing or extorting individuals based on information gathered improperly from computers or networks.
- Committing fraud with computers or networks.

Although the term *hacker* is often used to refer to computer criminals, the term originated with positive connotations of technical expertise and even in its negative meaning implies (at least to some) a certain amount of swashbuckling and cleverness. Likewise, the term *cracker* has been suggested, and often used, as an alternative to describe computer criminals. However, neither term is as accurate or as clear as *computer criminal.*

The fact that you have purchased this book means you have recognized the need to protect yourself, a crucially important first step. The next step is understanding what you need to protect yourself against, and what might happen if you fail to take precautions.

 This book includes explanations of security hazards. This information could be as easily used by criminals to pursue their activities—vandalizing computers or stealing goods or services—as it can be used by law-abiding citizens to secure their own, perfectly legitimate, business activities. This information should be considered no more (or less) dangerous than instructions for driving an automobile, using a telephone, or using a pen or pencil to write a message—all tools used by criminals and law-abiding citizens alike.

This chapter outlines the various threats to privacy and security that exist in the Internet and the digital world at large. It begins with a brief introduction to the digital world we are increasingly immersed in, our increasing reliance on digital and networked devices, and how this reliance brings increased risks. The next section discusses how criminals can use computers to attack the average law-abiding citizen (though anyone, even other computer criminals, might like to protect themselves from attack); the following section explains some of the defenses available to the law-abiding citizen to avoid becoming a victim. The last section introduces very briefly some of the technical concepts relating to personal encryption; for those who cannot wait, the most important terms are defined in the accompanying note. The less-technical reader will be able to skip the technical discussion of these concepts in Chapter 2 while still understanding the terms when they are used elsewhere throughout the book.

 Certain conventions exist for referring to the things or people that communicate using encryption. In this book I use the term *entity* to refer to a person, organization, or system that uses encryption. This emphasizes the use of encryption to protect information communicated by people, systems, or organizations. When discussing encryption protocols, Alice and Bob are the two preferred names given entities sending and receiving encrypted information, though there are other standard names assigned when the protocols require more than two entities.

ESSENTIAL SECURITY TERMS

Access Control: A mechanism by which use of computer or network resources is limited depending on the security policy; this will take into account such factors as the entity using the resource.

Authentication: The use of some mechanism by which one entity offers some data that proves its authorization to use a computer or network resource. This usually and traditionally entails a user ID and passphrase, although it can be based on a physical characteristic (fingerprint or retinal scan), a token (a key, for example), or some combination of all three.

Ciphertext: Data that has been encrypted.

Decryption: Any procedure that takes as its input a stream of apparently random or meaningless information and produces as output a stream of recognizable information that is the same as the original plaintext.

Digital signature: This is a (usually) short string of data that can be associated with any other type of data, and that is used to certify that the communication has been sent by the signing entity and that it has not been tampered with in any way.

Encryption: Any procedure that takes as its input a stream of (usually) usable, recognizable, or understandable information and produces as output a stream of data that appears to be random and/or meaningless to anyone who does not have the proper key with which to decrypt it.

Key: A sequence of data used to encrypt a transmission or data file. Knowledge of the correct key will allow an entity to decrypt an encrypted message or file.

Plaintext: Data in recognizable format. This refers to information that has not yet been encrypted or that has already been decrypted.

Information at Risk

There are those who believe the life of all citizens should be an open book—after all, what could you be hiding? There are legal and moral precedents that tend to support the right of the individual to keep personal matters private. However, differentiating between personal and public information in practice is not so simple a matter—nor is differentiating valuable and worthless information. In both cases there is a broad spectrum to which can be assigned any individual instance of information.

Sensitive and Valuable Information

We are increasingly awash—in many cases overwhelmed—with information. One way to look at this ocean of data is to split it into information that belongs to a private entity or to the public. Private entity information could be personal information that refers to or is owned by individuals, or it could be information owned by an organization or a corporate entity. Public information is about public entities or is owned by public entities—or it can be information owned or about a private entity which that entity wishes to make public. A more complete modeling breaks down private information into personal, organizational, and governmental information. Information owned by a particular person tends to be treated differently than information owned by an organization or corporate entity, while governmental information tends to be handled with a more formal hierarchy.

Another dimension across which to categorize information is by its value. Information that can be sold or used to achieve a material advantage, whether owned by an individual, a corporate entity, or the public, is treated differently than information that does not confer a material advantage. A graphical representation combining these two dimensions is shown in Figure 1.1.

Public Information

The array of information that can be considered to be public is vast. It includes virtually everything ever published in print, broadcast over the electronic media, or made public in any form. It can

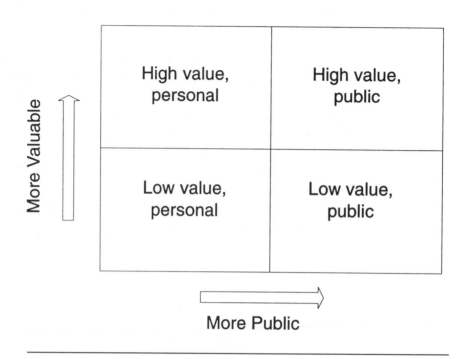

Figure 1.1. One way to view the world's data is to categorize it by its relative value and the degree to which it is personal or public.

include the fact that someone in your neighborhood is selling a refrigerator, or the telephone number of a government office, or the sale price on a pound of carrots. Other information in this category might include

- The names of candidates for a public office over time.
- The retail sale price of a bottle of shampoo at a supermarket.
- The ingredients of a bottle of a soft drink.
- Operating specifications of an automobile.
- Instructions for filing income taxes.

The owners or generators of this information may not only not care that other people or organizations find it out, but they may in fact be eager to disseminate it and have it become well-known—in some cases they may be required by law to make the information available to the public.

Each bit of this information, individually and by itself, usually has relatively low value, at least on average. In other words, the fact that your neighbor is selling a refrigerator has no value to you unless you actually want to buy a refrigerator, and your neighbor is offering a good deal. Likewise, getting any individual telephone listing in the published directory is free, but your telephone company may charge some small amount to provide the service of looking it up for you.

There are other types of information that can be public but that may have much higher values attached to them. For example, any publisher—whether it publishes books, music, or software—depends on other entities paying something for its information.

The magnitude of the volume of public information can be sensed by imagining how much information there is stored in public libraries; available for sale in book, music, and software stores; and published daily in books, periodicals, electronic media, and the World Wide Web. All of that information is intended to be shared more or less openly, depending on how much the owners charge their customers to access the data.

Private Information

Private information is information whose distribution is meant to be limited—in other words, information that the owner would not like seen (or would not expect to be seen) in a stranger's hands. The information that falls into this category is probably as varied as can be imagined: anything from a consultant's report on a corporation's operations to love letters to medical records to classified government files.

Understanding what is, and what is not, private information is central to understanding why you would need the rest of the information in this book. If you do not want your private information to find its way into a stranger's hands, you need to protect it somehow. Protection may be by keeping the information physically isolated, by destroying copies of the information (which probably means losing it entirely even for your own personal use), or by encrypting it.

The next sections discuss the differences between organizational information and personal information, with a special section examining how governments approach the task of protecting their private information.

Personal Information

This is the stuff that you own completely. If someone else has it, either you gave it to them, or they took it from you. Your personal diary, your love letters, your address book, the recipes you created, and your appointment calendar qualify. You may want to keep some or all of this information totally private for any number of reasons, ranging from avoiding the humiliation of having someone read personal revelations in your diary to keeping your sister-in-law from being able to use your recipe for brownies to protecting your client list.

There is a much larger category of personal information that includes information that is about you, or that you generated with the aid of another person or entity. This includes your medical history, your personal tax returns, your financial records, and details of your employment history.

You can protect some of your most personal information yourself through judicious distribution and the use of encryption. But for information like that contained in medical, personnel, and financial records, you must rely on the discretion of the providers and maintainers of these records. While you may not be able to encrypt your medical records, knowing that they should be protected may help you select medical service providers who are capable of protecting them.

Organizational Information

Considering that both a person and a corporation are legal entities, it should be far from surprising that a corporate entity might have information that it would like to remain "personal." As with individuals, corporations have information that they generate themselves and would like to maintain as private— things like internal memos, personnel records, employee salary information, and accounting reports. Likewise, organizations can generate information in tandem with other entities that they might like to maintain as confidential. This includes reports from consultants, tax returns and audits, and plans for corporate activities.

The discussion of encryption to protect personal information can, in large part, be extended to apply to the protection of corporate information. And just as individuals may feel the need to qualify that their service providers are able to keep their records private, people working within organizations will also want to ensure that the entities they deal with know how to protect their mutual secrets.

Governmental Model of Securing Information

One approach to securing organizational information is that used by governments. While organizations may be treated in some senses like monolithic entities, in fact an organization is composed of (often many) individual humans who also can behave like independent entities.

Governments (and other organizations) often secure information in two different ways: one hierarchical and the other nonhierarchical. The hierarchical framework assigns different levels of access to individuals based on their position. In the hierarchy, all employees—no matter what their rank—may have access to certain basic organizational information—for example, the name of the organization for which they work. As individuals gain rank within the hierarchy, they also gain access to more information— for example, a midlevel manager might have access to an employee directory that includes name, work telephone number, and office, while a higher-level manager might have additional access to the home telephone numbers and addresses of all employees.

As one moves up the hierarchy, one also gains access to more information. If you get a promotion, you will get greater access to information simply by virtue of your rank. This works adequately for certain information, but is inadequate for certain tasks that require access to sensitive data. For example, in the example just given, while only a high-level manager may have approval to see employees' home telephone numbers, that manager may not want to actually do the calling when employees must be summoned for an emergency meeting. Other, lower-level, employees may be given clearance to see sensitive data on a need-to-know basis; they are given all (and only) the information they need to know to complete their tasks.

In either case, there is an assumption that the organization can trust the individual. When a person gets a promotion, part of the promotion process may include additional security background checks (or other processes intended to ensure that the person can be trusted with the additional responsibilities of the position). When a person is accepted for employment in a position that requires access to sensitive information on a need-to-know basis, part of the hiring process will also include sufficient security background checks to satisfy the organization's security policies.

Security policies like these are most evident in government and military organizations, but can also be found in nongovernmental organizations that work closely with the government and in organizations whose activities require a great deal of security: financial institutions, communications and transportation providers (who may be carrying valuable information and cargo), and other organizations whose activities generate sensitive information.

Determining the Value of Personal Information

Most of us would prefer to keep the sordid details of our personal lives private—yet others are more than happy to share them in the pages of tell-all books or magazines. Likewise for personal career information—some people find it distasteful to even answer questions about what they do for a living, while others do not mind telling you exactly how much they made last year and what they paid for their house. Answers to some personal questions are appropriate depending on who is doing the asking—I will only tell my accountant how much I make each year, and I will discuss the true current state of my health only with my physician.

However, whether you are a private person or not, some value can almost always be assigned to any of your personal information. Personal information can sometimes confer a competitive advantage, most obviously and often measured in financial terms. Here are examples of personal information that might confer competitive advantage:

- ◆ Knowledge of a seller's target price for a piece of real estate, as distinct from an asking price, would be quite useful to anyone bidding for that property.
- ◆ A person's medical history, particularly if that history includes substance abuse or psychiatric treatment, could affect that person's ability to secure and keep a job, get approval for insurance, or adopt a child.
- ◆ Employers or business partners who are aware of a person's financial difficulties could take advantage of that information when negotiating contracts.
- ◆ Blackmailers can use almost any bit of personal information that a person would prefer to keep personal.

As can be most readily seen by the last example, the relative value and sensitivity of a piece of personal information can vary wildly from individual to individual. While some people might not care if the world knows about their personal affairs, however messy, there are others whose personal lives, if exposed, could hurt them— including politicians, executives, health care providers, and married people.

It is important to keep in mind, however, that most people probably have some personal information that they would rather keep private. It goes without saying that there are things most of us would prefer to keep to ourselves that would not necessarily cause us any financial loss or permit anyone else to gain. These vary from person to person, but can include anything from quirky personal habits to whether or not someone wears a wig or uses hair color.

Personal versus Public Information

It is not always immediately clear what information is personal and what information is public. Even ownership and access to information that belongs to an organization can be categorized as either public or corporate. Corporations, which act as artificial people, usually have every bit as much incentive to keep their own "personal" information private as real people do.

Developing Demographic Information

A piece of personal information may be perfectly innocuous and still have considerable value to an organization. As shown in Figure 1.2, an organization can collect very simple information about individuals and aggregate it in a database to generate valuable demographic data. The idea is not new and has been used for years in building demographic data about consumer populations as well as to build competitive marketing profiles. The format may be a random telephone call, a personal interview with a data collector in a shopping mall, or a supervised focus group for consumers or professionals, but usually the information provider is made aware, by the sponsor, that the information solicited will be used for market research.

The providers of this type of information may not always be aware that they are actually giving away information when marketers begin combining with computing and networking technologies. Users routinely fill out forms to gain access to various Web sites, and once they are connected, it is possible for the Web site sponsor to track their browsing habits. The results can be correlated across relatively large populations, with conclusions that may link interest in, say, Elvis Presley, with age, gender, income level, or geographic location.

Developing a Personal Profile

Organizations of all types store information about the individuals they are concerned with (whether customers, employees, or com-

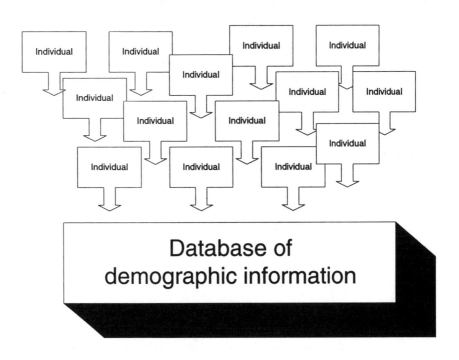

Figure 1.2. Collecting a little bit of information from members of a large population can be useful in building valuable demographic or market demographics information.

petitors). While any single organization may have only certain bits of information—for example, a dry cleaner might keep records of exactly what laundry its customers have brought in—there are enough different organizations with enough different bits of information that a determined snoop could collect a fairly detailed profile of any individual based on the information in all these different databases. This is illustrated in Figure 1.3, showing the collector hitting many different databases and integrating the results in the collector's database, from which a detailed personal profile can be built. This process is known as *aggregation* in database circles, and can be a powerful source of information.

To give an example, in the United States a taxpayer identification number (e.g., one's Social Security number) was originally meant to be a fairly personal piece of information. In the United States, people are legally obligated to provide their Social Security number only to entities that will pay them taxable income. This includes employers, banks, and brokerage firms. (Again, this characterization is something of an oversimplification.) However, many other organizations have seized upon the Social Security number because it is a largely (though not entirely) universal and largely (though not entirely) unique identifier for everyone in the United States.

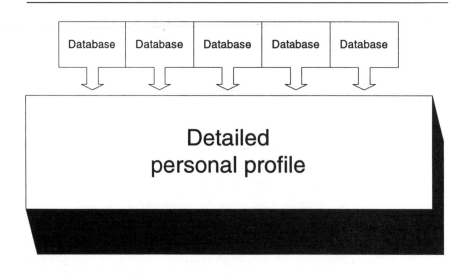

Figure 1.3. Gathering information about an individual from disparate databases—aggregation—can result in a fairly detailed and comprehensive personal profile.

Entities that request this number include schools, health insurance companies, mortgage companies, real estate sellers, credit card companies, rental agents, and even travel agencies. In addition to being conveniently universal and unique, these entities (and others) can use Social Security numbers to run credit checks on consumers and potential customers.

UNIVERSAL IDENTIFIERS AND THE SOCIAL SECURITY NUMBER: The United States does not require its residents to carry identity papers of any kind, nor is there an official universal identifier to which identity records are attached. Whether or not this is a good thing will be discussed later, in Chapter 3, but as of the end of the 20th century, for all practical purposes the Social Security number in the United States acts very much like such a universal identifier.

Because the Social Security number is used as an identifier for so many systems and organizations, it is possible to find out a lot more about me once you have my Social Security number—including my credit, educational, and medical histories. Information about medical treatment, which at one time would have been known only to the patient and the physician, can now be accessed by health plan employees and others; information about personal net worth, salary, and education may also be at risk. Any of that information may properly be considered personal, but by providing your Social Security number you may be making any or all of that information available.

The greatest risk you run by revealing your Social Security number to a criminal is that the number will be used improperly to provide an identity to someone else, possibly even to the extent of using the number to collect unemployment insurance benefits or Social Security benefits intended for you, and also possibly adversely affecting your credit rating.

So, although one's Social Security number may seem as if it should be classified as a piece of public information—after all, it is issued by the government of the United States and used by many prestigious institutions to keep track of people—it should be treated as a fairly private piece of information.

Valuable versus Valueless Information

The precise value of certain information can be hard to determine, and not only because there are relatively few open markets for raw information. For example, a provider of stock market tips may not want to let potential customers look at current tips before deciding whether or not to buy them; likewise, the charge for the information is largely determined by the seller, particularly in the case of specialized newsletters and information services. Similarly, while Coca-Cola protects its recipe for Coke, you would need a huge marketing, advertising, and manufacturing budget to take advantage of that recipe if you could somehow manage to acquire it. While Pepsi might be interested in knowing what goes into its competitor's product, other potential buyers would probably be limited to companies interested in actually making (counterfeiting?) Coca-Cola.

Adding Value to Valueless Information

The high degree to which our lives are tracked on various computers produces another category of valuable information, one that often overlaps with information that many of us assume to be personal. For example, you might assume that an itinerary of a vacation trip falls under the category of personal information with little or no value. Likewise, your supermarket purchasing habits might also fall into this category. This is not the case. This information is of considerable value to a wide range of marketing organizations, and is readily available to them in some form or another through the use of airline frequent flier mileage programs, supermarket membership discount cards, and many other similar programs sponsored by credit card issuers, travel service providers, and a host of other companies. While most of these programs pay the consumer for this information by offering free airline services or extra discounts on groceries, most consumers are probably unaware of the volume of information being stored, tracked, and manipulated.

The stated purpose of such affinity programs is to make sure that the marketers can target appropriate promotions to the appropriate consumers—for example, sending discount coupons for diapers to consumers who buy baby food or sending premium goods catalogs to executives who spend a lot of time traveling first class. What may be more troubling to consumers, however, is the ability to store this information electronically and keep it instantly accessible indefinitely. It is repugnant to some that somewhere, someone can track your every move, as expressed in the form of receipts for air travel, restaurant meals, hotel stays, rental cars, and taxis. There is a strong feeling in the United States that freedom of movement is an important right for those living in a free country, and once a government has the means to keep track of your movements, it may be tempted to use that data.

Thus it becomes apparent that small bits of seemingly innocuous information, if they are easily accessible and can be indexed on a single identifier across multiple databases, can be gleaned and put together to create something menacing to the individual who would prefer to keep a low profile.

 Some people actually *like* to be targeted by marketers. They are willing to sell their souls for cents-off coupons and free samples of diapers and detergent. For these people, such affinity programs are definitely positive developments and anything but sinister. However, knowing how these programs work allows consumers to decide for themselves how and whether to take advantage of them.

Your Vulnerable Digital Side

The term *security through obscurity* refers to a situation in which the security of a system depends in whole or in part on keeping some aspect of the system secret. One common example is the hidden house key. If you keep it under the doormat or on top of the door lintel, it is not very safe.

Security in this case derives solely from the assumption that any attackers would know nothing about the system. That assumption may, in some cases, be a valid one. For example, if you lived among chimpanzees you could reasonably expect privacy for your information if you keep it on a removable disk cartridge, stored in an unlocked box next to your computer. The chimps might be bright enough to figure out how to power up the computer, locate the cartridge, insert it into the proper hole in the computer, and even access the files—but even if they could decipher the writing, only the best-trained of them would even have a shot at telling any humans about the contents.

 Privacy in the chimp example is not necessarily equivalent to security. The chimps may not be able to understand what's on the disk cartridge, but they could certainly destroy it. This information could not be considered secured unless a backup copy had been stored in a place the chimps cannot reach.

This approach to securing information may sound ridiculously trivial, even dangerous, yet it is probably also the most prevalent approach to security. The fact is, most people still consider computers, even their friendly personal computers, to be relatively obscure devices. We convince ourselves that storing our important bits of information in a subdirectory of a subdirectory, which is in turn a subdirectory of a subdirectory, will somehow hide it from the casual snoop. This attitude is not restricted to nonprofessionals; at a recent software vendor conference, one MIS professional claimed that the obscurity of the terminal emulation protocols being used by users at one location to access a mainframe application across the Internet rendered the sessions reasonably secure. The fact is, those protocols are widely known and understood (which means that anyone who understands them can get at the information they are carrying), and those sessions were being conducted across various public Internet service providers (which means that anyone who can access those providers can also access any of the data they are carrying). The bottom line is that if there is any valuable information on those systems, those unprotected sessions unnecessarily and recklesslessly expose the MIS veteran's company's data.

The security-through-obscurity approach may or may not be appropriate for all cases, but it also tends to force us to consider (or is it to hope?) that the casual snoop is the most likely attacker—particularly since we know that the slightly less casual snoop is very likely to be able to find those sensitive documents in moments with simple disk management tools.

As personal computers increasingly penetrate the home after blanketing most offices, users are learning that their system security can be compared to their home security: If your [home | computer] is in a safe [neighborhood | environment], then you are less likely to be the victim of a [burglary | data theft | vandalism]. In other words, if your computer sits in an open space where many people might pass by in the course of a day, you have probably learned to use some sort of passphrase utility to control access—just as you would be more likely to lock all doors and windows if you lived in the center of a large city than if you lived on a remote farm.

This also means that if you are storing something very valuable in your [home | computer] like [a world-class stamp collection | passphrases for systems controlling a telecommunications network], living in a safe neighborhood will not necessarily save you if a criminal is aware of the prize and has targeted it for theft.

Two trends make the security-through-obscurity approach increasingly unviable—if it ever was a viable method for dealing with security within an organization. The first is the growing use of portable computers, which are increasingly vulnerable to theft while they are in transit from home to office to remote site—as well as to theft at each of those destinations simply by virtue of their high value and portability. However, by itself, the threat of laptop theft can be countered to some extent by using removable media to store sensitive information. The trend with far greater impact, of course, is the tremendous growth in the use of networks, particularly the Internet.

Stealing a laptop or sitting down at someone else's desktop system is bad. Any and all information stored on such systems is at risk. (There have been numerous reports about industrial spies carrying on a brisk trade in stolen laptops, for example.) However, stealing a laptop or getting unauthorized access to a desktop system that is used to connect to organizational networks, network service providers, or the Internet puts much more information and many more systems at risk.

Security versus Usability

The more secure something is, the harder it usually is to get at so you can use it. You may hide the television remote control to keep your spouse off the couch over the weekend, put the cookies behind the canned squash to keep your kids' hands off them, or keep your office personal computer keyboard unplugged to discourage the casual snooper. However, in each of these cases, while the action you take may have the desired effect, that same action makes it far less convenient for *you* too.

An Object Lesson in Security versus Usability

The preceding observation applies to computer and network security as well. You may want to use a passphrase to limit access to a computer or network resource, but once you decide to do so you have committed yourself to remembering that passphrase. The mere fact of having a passphrase will deter some, probably large, portion of the individuals who might potentially want to gain access to your system—no matter what passphrase you choose, even if you choose to have *no* passphrase! However, this group will probably also include most of the people who will assume that since you have used a passphrase to control access, you have something private there that is none of their business.

There is a more determined group of individuals who may attempt to guess your passphrase to gain access to your system. These are the people who pose a far greater threat to your information. They know enough about passphrases to guess yours. It may be your name (first, last, or middle), initials, name of your [spouse | significant other | offspring | pet], favorite catch phrase from a television show, movie, or book, or some other easily guessed sequence like a birthday or favorite movie. If it is not one of those, there are a number of other fairly common passphrases selected for the ease with which they can be remembered. Finally, if those all fail, the determined snoop might look around your desk for the passphrase engraved on a desktop or written on a PostIt™ note stuck to the side of your monitor.

To make a passphrase authentication system work, you must choose a passphrase that is not easily guessed and then keep it strictly inside your head—never write it down or tell it to anyone. That is difficult. However, that is the only way to make the system work. Should you decide to take the easier way to security, you are likely to have a less secure system.

There are ways to make things easier, like keeping your passphrase hidden away inside a corner of your wallet, or camouflaging it as a name in your address book. However, these tricks still ultimately leave the system that much weaker, as they give attackers that many more avenues to successfully breaking your security.

More Lessons in Security and Usability

Security can be achieved with personal computers and ubiquitous networks, but it requires great attention to details. The dominant operating system, Microsoft Windows, tends to grab passphrases and remember them, so you don't have to—doing so, however, makes it more convenient for snoops and thieves to connect to the same systems you connect to. Likewise, personal or sensitive information can be kept more securely if you are willing to work with it on a removable disk and store that disk securely except when you are working with it.

Even if you choose to use all the security tools described in this book, you must constantly keep that software up-to-date. Criminals are constantly attacking security products in order to steal or damage your information, while there are others who do so for the purpose of testing the products or simply for the notoriety that comes with announcing that they have broken a product that had been generally presumed secure.

Having an out-of-date version of a security product can be worse than having no security product at all. The old product, just like any product that does not quite work, will generate a false sense of security that often leads to carelessness, while having no product can help keep you on your toes by being aware that your system is not secured.

And having the most up-to-date product can also be worse than having no security at all. Software patches, upgrades, and new releases of products often add new bugs and security holes as well as new features. Your vendor may be touting that new product as the solution to all your problems, but until it has gone through rigorous testing to make sure it does not add any new security problems, it should be kept off production systems.

In all these cases, it is clear that achieving security means a reduction in ease of use. However, just because something is difficult to use does not mean it is secure. An array of the most expensive and impregnable locks on your doors may do nothing more than cause a burglar to break in through the window.

The message here is twofold: Not only will security cost you, but it requires eternal vigilance. An important corollary is that because security comes at a high price, you should keep in mind that not all systems and resources require the same degree of security. A single computer, unconnected to any network and with little or no important data, does not require the same degree of security as the system that runs your company's payroll system. You can keep your resume secure from coworkers by storing it on a floppy diskette, but a brokerage firm will keep a much tighter hold on data files detailing mergers or initial public stock offerings.

The bottom line is that you must decide how much security you are willing to pay for or, to put it another way, how little security you can get away with. Once you can attach a dollar value to the resource and to the cost of protecting that resource, you can come up with a reasonable plan for security.

Watch Your Data

The problem with networks is that everything is connected. That this also happens to be the primary benefit of networks is beside the point. The fact that your system can "leak" information out over a network, some of it potentially sensitive, is cause for real concern.

Internet applications—things like the World Wide Web and Internet-based e-mail are perhaps the two most important—are still quite novel to most of their users, which means that many of them do not really understand what is happening to the data they send and receive over the wires. There is a great deal of mis-understanding about expectations for data being transmitted across the Internet:

- ◆ What is the legal expectation for privacy of information transmitted over the Internet?
- ◆ How, and how much, can technology protect these com-munications?
- ◆ What are threats to communications?
- ◆ How secure can you make these communications?
- ◆ How do these new modes of communication compare with traditional channels such as postal mail, voice tele-phone and in-person interactions?

It is not necessary to understand all the underlying technological issues of providing security over an open network like the Internet any more than it is necessary to have a deep understanding of the technology of voice telephony to understand that conversations conducted over cordless and cellular telephones are more easily monitored by casual eavesdroppers than conversations conducted through traditionally wired instruments—because the wireless phones transmit by radio waves, which anyone with a radio can listen to. This does demonstrate the need to be aware of the channels by which your data is being transmitted and to understand how your data might be exposed to security threats before, during, and after transmission.

Computers and networks definitely present a security problem, but they are not the only security problem. In fact, the better your computer and network security, the more likely criminals are to resort to other means of theft or vandalism. A strong door alone is unlikely to deter a criminal, particularly if there is a weakly defended window nearby. Your personal data can be at risk from the moment you generate it:

- Prior to entering it into a computer or network.
- During its tenure on your personal computer.
- Enroute from one computer to another over a network.
- Subsequent to its arrival at its destination.

This section discusses how your data may be vulnerable before, during, and after you enter it into a computer.

Data Not Yet Entered into a System

If a criminal can convince you to divulge a piece of valuable information, you have saved her the trouble of breaking into your computer—in fact, she may be able to get your data into her database before you have entered the data into your own database. This might happen as the result of subterfuge on the part of the criminal, or it might be the result of surveillance: using binoculars or telescope to watch you enter your calling card number at a public payphone, looking over your shoulder at your bank's automatic teller machine, or eavesdropping at the doctor's office as you give your insurance account number (which is quite often the same as your Social Security number).

Eavesdropping on telephone conversations, whether in person at the home, office, or payphone, is another threat. More aggressive attackers may use scanners to listen to your cellular or cordless telephone conversations, while wiretaps and other bugging techniques (although largely illegal) have been known to be used to gather competitive intelligence through industrial espionage.

Data on a Personal Computer

Most personal computers act as repositories for many different types of information, usually in the form of discrete data files or documents: letters, memos, reports, databases, spreadsheets and graphical images that contain information readily viewable with standard application software. Depending on your operating system and your inclination, you might put access controls on personal files to protect them from prying eyes, but these controls will only be as strong as the passphrases you choose; forgoing such controls (which may be required by your employer) makes your personal data vulnerable to anyone with physical access to your system.

Operating systems permit you to delete data files to make room for other data, but in most instances this does not physically remove the actual data, but simply removes a file's entry in a directory table and permits the operating system to use the former file's space on disk when it next needs to write data. Undelete programs have long been central to the popular utility software market, and even for-matting a disk does not remove the data so much as destroy the directory table itself, allowing unformat programs to recover data from disks that held data and were subsequently formatted. This means that simply formatting a disk drive may not be sufficient when, for example, you donate obsolete equipment to charities— particularly if you stored your company's business plan on the hard drive.

Information artifacts are also constantly being deposited throughout your system, whether you realize it or not. One example is the Microsoft Windows operating system. As a convenience to users, many passphrase prompts include an option to remember the pass-phrase. This is doubly problematic. It may cause you to forget strategic passphrases, and it makes those passphrases available to the unscrupulous intruder to your office or the criminal who has stolen your laptop.

Other sensitive data artifacts enter through the process of application configuration, particularly when configuring communications services. It is convenient to program the computer to enter a passphrase and user ID combination when setting up a connectivity service, but also less secure. Likewise, personal information including your name, contact information, user ID, and passphrase, is often stored on your system after setting up Internet access and Internet e-mail programs.

Data Transmitted over a Network

Networks as we know them (local area networks running over Ethernet) and internetworks as we know them (in other words, the Internet) are by their nature open systems. Systems connected to an Ethernet network are by definition able to listen to all transmissions, but are supposed to ignore all transmissions intended for other systems.

Attackers with access to a LAN, if they are able to program their system to interpret all Ethernet transmissions, and not just the ones intended for that system, can monitor the LAN and listen for interesting data—things like

♦ Credit card numbers.
♦ Personal e-mail.
♦ Mainframe login user IDs and passphrases.

In fact, such *sniffing devices*, whether in the form of dedicated hardware or simply software programs running on standard personal computers, are widely available and are extensively used for legitimate purposes of network management (as well as for the illegitimate purposes described here). One way to reduce (but not eliminate) the risk of unauthorized use of sniffing, or protocol analysis, software and hardware is to use switched Ethernets. (See the accompanying note.)

Internet transmissions must also use standardized protocols to format and send data, all those transmissions could be inter-

SWITCHING ETHERNETS: Traditional Ethernet uses a cable to which all systems on the LAN are connected. When data is transmitted, it is packaged into a unit called an Ethernet frame. The frame has a destination address and a source address associated with it—each connected system is constantly listening for frames addressed to it, meaning that the frame's destination address is the same as the listening system's address. The only thing keeping the user of one system from listening in on transmissions intended for another user is that the network cards and software are programmed to behave themselves.

Increasingly, however, switched Ethernet is becoming the norm for new installations and upgrades. In these networks, all frames are transmitted through a network backplane that sits inside a box called an Ethernet switch. Every connected system is cabled directly to the box, and when one system sends data to another system, the transmission is switched directly, by the box, to the cable port associated with the destination system. These switched Ethernets make it more difficult for anyone to attach a sniffer to the network simply because such a device would have to be attached directly to the switch; attaching it to the network through a remote cable would not produce the desired result.

preted by anyone able to intercept them. The fact that the Internet makes use of many different intermediary and backbone networks points up the Internet's inherent lack of security. You may be able to secure your computers and your own corporate networks, but once you connect to the Internet, you must rely on the security not only of your Internet service provider but also of every intermediary network that forwards your packets to their destinations.

It has long been known that there is a serious potential for the automated theft of credit card numbers through the use of network sniffers placed on an Internet service provider's network. It would be a relatively simple matter for a criminal to somehow get inside the provider's site (determining the best method is left as an exercise to the reader) and install the protocol analysis device or software in an out-of-the way corner of the site. The sniffer is programmed to analyze all packets for sequences of numbers that match the format used by credit card numbers, store those numbers, and then either forward them to the criminal over the Internet or simply save them for eventual retrieval of the device.

Not until the late spring of 1997 did such a case of network data theft came to light. A criminal had extracted as many as 100,000 credit card numbers and stored them on a system that had been monitoring an Internet service provider's network. Considering that at the start of 1997 there were well over 3,000 Internet service providers operating in the United States, all competing for resources such as knowledgeable network engineers as well as for customers, this theft is not likely to be an isolated incident. There are tools and protocols available to protect against this kind of attack, but, like seatbelts, they will only protect you if you use them.

Data Taken off the Network

You can keep your personal sensitive information private before you enter it into any computer, and you can use the various tools and techniques described later in this book to protect it once you do enter it into a computer and transmit it across a network, but once it has arrived at its destination—whether that is a bank, an on-line merchant, your physician or your educational institution—it may be as vulnerable as it ever was. Unless you can control how data is handled at the other end of your data transmissions, you must rely on the security expertise of the recipient to keep it safe.

For example, keeping data secure while it is in transit between two systems only protects it from interception during that transmission. Once the data arrives at its destination, the recipient must protect the data or risk losing it. As shown in Figure 1.4, if the data is not protected on the recipient system, it may be vulnerable to theft. This type of situation probably occurred far more frequently than would

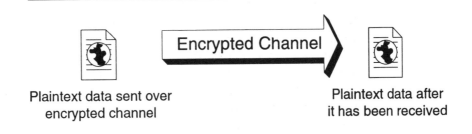

Figure 1.4:. Securing a channel for transmitting sensitive information does not relieve the recipient of the responsibility for protecting that data once it has been received.

make the credit card issuers comfortable, and it arose from the mechanism by which Netscape introduced the first widely used secure Web browsers and servers. Security for web transactions at that time was based entirely on the use of Secure Sockets Layer (SSL), a network protocol (set of rules that govern how data is transmitted across a network) that permits the client (Web browser being used to access an on-line store) and the server (Web server hosting the on-line store) to communicate through an encrypted (scrambled so that only the server and client can understand) stream of data.

The approach to security over the Internet, sometimes referred to as a secure channel, is fine but limited. On-line merchants with limited expertise or funds often tended to assume that a secure channel was sufficient to provide security—which it is, as long as you are only concerned with security of data being transmitted. However, the data, once received and unscrambled, very often was stored on the same Web server that received it, but in plain text. Once data is stored in plain text on a server connected to the Internet, the only protection against theft of that data is to secure it through access control, something that often is beyond the ken of novice system administrators. In other words, in some case sensitive data collected over the Internet—often including consumers' credit card numbers, addresses, and contact information—has been protected only by the fact that its presence on the server is not publicly advertised or directly referenced by a hyperlink.

Compromise of systems in that way have not, to my knowledge, been made public on a large scale, but there are other ways in which data is at risk after it has been transmitted over the Internet. One particularly prominent case occurred in 1995, when a criminal managed to steal thousands of credit card numbers from a network provider simply by dialing, over a telephone line, into a computer (not connected to the Internet).

Digital Threats

So far, we have discussed some of the types of information that can be at risk on computers and networks and some of the situations and circumstances in which that information is placed at risk. This section introduces more specifically some of the methods used by criminals to attack information stored on computers or transmitted over networks. These include

- ◆ Eavesdropping.
- ◆ Theft and digital trespassing.
- ◆ Spoofing.
- ◆ Man-in-the-middle attacks.
- ◆ Repudiation and nonrepudiation.
- ◆ Assorted on-line fraud and mischief.
- ◆ Social engineering.

Some of the techniques discussed in this section may seem to be extreme, and you may think that only the most paranoid of computer users would be concerned with them. For many or most users, this is true, particularly if the most important secrets you have stored on your computer are your grandmother's pie recipes or your tax deductions for last year. However, the rapidly growing populations of telecommuters, independent consultants, and highly mobile executives will all, sooner or later, find themselves in a situation where they must keep fairly sensitive information secure in an unfriendly environment.

The author is not a lawyer, and this warning should not be construed as legal advice, but the techniques described here are either immoral, illegal or both; in any case, they are not nice things to do. Please do not do them.

Eavesdropping

Just as in real life, digital eavesdropping can be either passive or active. Passive eavesdropping is the kind that goes on in restaurants, bars, buses, and public spaces of all kinds, and tends to be opportunistic rather than planned. For the same reasons that people are interested in watching dramatic portrayals of human interactions on a movie screen or on the television screen, many will also pay the same attention to small dramas happening around them—including those happening to others in public spaces. The lovers' quarrel and the high-pressure business negotiation are just two situations that commonly unfold in public, and may be subject to uninvited spectators. Even reading a newspaper or magazine over someone's shoulder in a bus or train qualifies as a form of passive eavesdropping. The point is that in most cases, passive eavesdropping can be thought of as mostly innocent (but not in all cases, particularly in cases where a criminal follows someone with the intention of listening to a conversation). It should be remembered that activity occurring in a public place has no expectation of privacy. If you do not want others to hear your conversations, you should carry them on in private.

Active eavesdropping is usually much less innocent, and occurs any time someone takes steps to listen or detect activity that would not otherwise be detectable. Active eavesdropping techniques include telephone wiretaps and hidden microphones. However, as with most things in life, the lines separating active from passive eavesdropping are fuzzy. One might argue that using a telescope and a lip reader is a passive means of "listening" to a conversation. However, the people whose conversation is being eavesdropped may have an expectation of privacy because they are talking in an open, but empty, public place—or because they are inside a house with the shades up. Although the people conversing may feel they have a reasonable expectation of privacy, they have taken no steps (other than removing themselves from other people) to keep their conversation private.

How does this relate to digital eavesdropping? Simply this: There are far fewer opportunities for digital eavesdroppers to claim their activity was innocent. Put another way, there are many opportunities for eavesdroppers to use what might seem to be passive mechanisms (in that they do not impact directly on the eavesdroppee), but there are fewer innocent explanations for them in the digital arena.

Turnabout can be fair play, and it should be mentioned that some of the active eavesdropping techniques described here have been used by the good guys who are doing intrusion detection work.

Passive Eavesdropping

A few of the more common types of passive digital eavesdropping are illustrated in Figure 1.5 and include

- ♦ "Shoulder surfing" (simple surveillance).
- ♦ Enhanced visual surveillance.
- ♦ Electromagnetic surveillance.

Perhaps the most common form of passive digital eavesdropping, shoulder surfing refers to the practice of looking over someone's shoulder at the input or display device as they work with any sort of computer or terminal. The target may include your long-distance telephone calling card numbers, your ATM personal identification number, your network passphrase, or a document you are working with on a laptop on the plane. There are relatively simple remedies to reduce this type of eavesdropping. The most obvious is to be aware that there may be prying eyes and to avoid exposing your information to those prying eyes. This includes simply covering keypads at public telephones and cash-dispensing machines, ask-

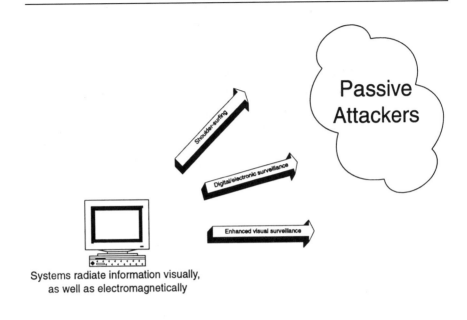

Figure 1.5. Visual and electromagnetic signals can be used by passive digital eavesdroppers.

ing office visitors to turn their heads when you enter your network or system passphrases, and simply saving work on sensitive documents for after your flight.

Criminals eager to get your information will use every tool at their disposal, and this includes telescopes or binoculars to steal your calling card number or to read the contents of your computer screen from across the street—if that information is sufficiently important. The same type of shielding strategies that keep your ATM PIN private work for military secrets. Classified computing in military or government-funded installations takes place inside sealed rooms with no windows. Individuals with sensitive information and smaller organizations attempting to protect their secrets would do well to emulate this approach, even if it means simply facing all computer monitors away from windows.

Electromagnetic surveillance takes advantage of the fact that all electronic devices, including microprocessors, emit electromagnetic signals. Special computers designed to be used for secure computing include special shielding to block these emissions. This type of eavesdropping attack would tend to be directed against targets of extremely high value, and the organizations responsible for such data (usually government or military organizations) would be most likely to guard against such attacks. Most of the criminals the average citizen needs to guard against would be unlikely to use such techniques against personal computers.

However, another form of electromagnetic surveillance is fairly common: that of scanning cordless and cellular telephone transmissions. As these are transmissions over the radio spectrum, listening to these communications may be limited through legislation, but in practice there is little technological difficulty standing in the way of the person who wants to listen to them.

Active Eavesdropping

Just as a bug can be inserted into a telephone or a tap placed on a telephone line where it enters a house, so too can mechanisms be inserted into computers and networks to permit active eavesdropping. The two most likely methods used to actively eavesdrop, as illustrated in Figure 1.6, are

♦ Network protocol analyzers (sniffers).
♦ Trojan horse programs.

Network Sniffing

As mentioned earlier, a network protocol analyzer, also known as a sniffer, can be programmed to listen to all network traffic and to detect and store data that meets certain requirements. Typical legitimate uses of sniffers include detecting transmissions from systems that have been improperly configured and analyzing network traffic. Criminals are more likely to put sniffers to use to monitor the network for user ID and passphrase combinations, credit card numbers, and e-mail sent to or from particular individuals.

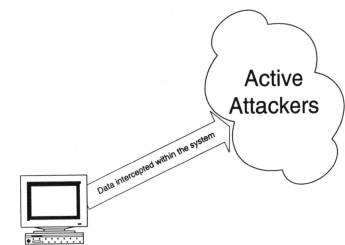

A system with a trojan horse program on it may be
transmitting data without the user's knowledge.

**Figure 1.6. A trojan horse program may be used to actively eavesdrop on a comput-
er, while a network sniffer can be used to actively scan all network data traffic.**

In some ways, network sniffing is completely passive. There is no
external way to determine that a system connected to a network is
sniffing that network. Thus, if a system is legitimately connected to
a network, the only way to detect that it is running sniffer software
would be to actually sit down in front of the system and identify all
the programs running on it. In other words, while it may be possible to keep outsiders from eavesdropping on your network, you
still must provide access to insiders—who may not be as loyal as
you would prefer. Security against internal attackers like this can be
provided by upgrading the network (see the note on page 27) or by
implementing secure computing inside the organization, often by
using the same approaches as those detailed in this book for personal security.

Unauthorized systems connected to a network, especially any systems connected directly to network devices (switches, routers, hubs, or bridges) should receive immediate attention. Network devices should be kept in locked, secure rooms or closets, and all authorized network-connected systems should be clearly marked. (Corporate inventory tags are recommended.) While this will not protect against insider attacks, it will help keep outsiders on the outside.

Trojan Monitoring

A trojan horse program is any program that outwardly acts in a useful way, but in fact is intended for harmful purposes. For example, a trojan horse program might outwardly appear to act as a passphrase and user ID database, simplifying the task of remembering which passphrase and use ID to use for all the different accounts that the user owns. However, the writer of the program might actually have included a routine in the program that sends all of the stored data to the writer, thus giving access to all those accounts to the trojan program writer.

Monitoring software can be written to listen to network transmissions, or to scan all keyboard input for particular data strings, or to monitor information displayed on screen, printed out on a printer, or stored in a disk drive. Software can also be written to search hard drives for particular files, types of files, or files containing data matching certain criteria.

Theoretically, such attacks could be targeted to particular individuals, with the criminal specifically installing the monitoring software (or causing it to be installed) on the target's computer. The objective might be some particular bit of information, or merely to monitor data entered into a database or log file. Alternatively, trojan horse monitoring software could also be widely disseminated with the intention of gathering more general information. The objective in that case might be to monitor keyboard entries searching for credit card numbers, and then forward those numbers to the trojan author.

Thwarting Eavesdroppers

There are two basic approaches to thwarting eavesdroppers. The first is to remove the temptation, or to simply not expose sensitive information to prying eyes. This means, as suggested above, blocking views to telephone keypads or ATM touchpads, keeping monitors turned away from the window, and avoiding the use of laptops in public places. The second approach is to make sure that any data the eavesdropper can gather is worthless. This includes the use of various authentication techniques, mostly beyond the scope of this book, to keep intruders out of your networks and systems. It also includes the use of encryption, very much within the scope of this book, to render any data intercepted worthless to the eavesdropper.

Theft and Digital Trespassing

If a criminal can get physical access to your computers, your data will also be at risk—unless you take steps to protect it. A criminal can steal your data without stealing your system, as long as the system is in an accessible location. This section discusses both these risks, which are largely nontechnological in their nature, as well as a technological strategy for protecting against such thefts.

System Theft

Thieves who can steal your computer are, by extension, stealing the data stored on that computer. Most vulnerable are laptop computers—the fact that they are so portable adds to their susceptibility to theft. However, desktop, server, and other multiuser systems can also be stolen, and their thefts will also expose the data stored on them.

To the criminal, the advantage of stealing a computer is that data can be extracted from it in private at the criminal's leisure, without fear of discovery by the owner of the system and data. This prospect is particularly worrisome to the owner of the data because it means that simple-minded approaches to security (like deceptive naming of sensitive documents, use of layers of subdirectories, or even just deleting a sensitive file from a hard drive) are more likely to be easily defeated. Even user-level access controls may be relatively easily defeated by removing the stolen system's hard drive and reading it with a different system.

Digital Trespassing

Snoops view unattended and unprotected systems as an open invitation to see what is inside. System snooping causes many of the same problems that arise from system thefts, with some frightening differences. When your laptop is stolen, you know it and can take steps to minimize the harm done by the stolen data; when the same data is stolen from your desktop system by someone who leaves no trace of the theft, you can not take any action—you have no reason to.

On the other hand, relatively simple security tools can be used to record all attempts to boot up a system, and may alert the user to such attempts. However, these work only when they are installed and the resulting logs are regularly monitored for unauthorized activities.

Protecting against Data Theft

The best defense against data thieves is to make certain that what they steal is of no value. As mentioned before, passphrase access protection can be easily defeated by a data thief, so it is safe to assume that whatever you have stored on your hard drive will be accessible to a determined criminal. However, if you can render that data unintelligible to the unauthorized user—through encryption—your confidence level in the encryption technique you use will determine your confidence in the safety of your data. As long as your data is properly backed up, a laptop theft should not be cause for concern, other than for the inconvenience and cost of losing a piece of hardware.

Protection against theft by most petty criminals is relatively easy; there are others who will not be so easily deterred. If certain large organizations with access to lots of resources—like the National Security Agency (NSA) or the successors to the KGB—decide to target your data, you must use more extreme methods to protect your data.

Spoofing and Misrepresentation

Most individuals have, at times in their nondigital lives, been asked for some kind of proof of identity. You may be asked to prove your identity in some form or another for any number of different reasons:

- For check-cashing purposes at a grocery store, you may be required to show a check-cashing card.
- Other merchants may request to see a driver's license and a major credit card before accepting payment by personal check.
- An airline employee may request to see a valid driver's license or passport prior to allowing you to board an airliner.
- When crossing an international border, you may be required to show a passport.
- When applying for a passport, you may be requested to present proof of your birth as well as a valid driver's license, or some other combination of proof of identity.

While far from foolproof and certainly vulnerable to attack by determined criminals, for most purposes a photo ID (like a driver's license or passport) is usually sufficient proof of identity. The person checking your identity can compare a photograph and a signature with the appearance and signature of the person presenting the credentials. If they substantially match, the identification is successful.

Digital Misrepresentations

In the digital world, things are different. Because interactions take place between entities connected across vast distances with no other link than a relatively tenuous virtual circuit, it can be difficult to ascertain identity. Particularly vexing is the fact that the data actually received must somehow include its own certification of identity. There is no obvious trusted method to communicate credentials, at least not in the traditional sense. A customer can order a pizza over the Internet and then transmit a scanned copy of a signed personal check along with a scanned image of a driver's license, but such digitized documents can easily be doctored undetectably.

Such misrepresentations of identity take several forms over the Internet:

- Individuals may take on fictional personalities (also known as avatars or personas, which in of and themselves may be used for noncriminal purposes), which they use to misrepresent themselves for criminal gain.
- Individuals may fraudulently use someone else's identity, for example, sending e-mail that appears to be from someone other than the actual sender.
- Individuals can generate Internet traffic that appears to be from a system other than the actual source system.

Avoiding Digital Misrepresentation

Although scanned images showing driver's licenses, birth certificates, major credit cards, and passports cannot be trusted as digital credentials, there are mechanisms by which individuals can prove they are who they say they are. Modern cryptography has produced functions that can generate a *digital signature*, simply a small amount of data that, when checked by the recipient, will certify that the data being sent originated with the entity claiming to be the originator. (Again, this tends to simplify the case. In fact, the digital signature simply links the signed data with the entity holding a particular key.) Digital signatures are vitally important to issues of personal digital security, and actually derive from the same functions that are used for encryption.

The details of digital signatures will be presented at much greater length, with a brief introduction of the concept later in this chapter, technical background and explanation in Chapter 2, and hands-on discussion throughout the book. In view of the issue of digital misrepresentation, it is worthwhile to introduce the three key benefits of using digital signatures:

- Digital signatures link the data to the signer of the data— if you receive a digitally signed message, you know that it originated with the entity doing the signing.

- Digital signatures allow recipients of data to certify that the data was received in the exact same form that it was sent by the originating entity.
- Digital signatures provide nonrepudiation. The sender cannot later claim not to have sent the data if the message has been signed by the sender.

Man-in-the-Middle Attacks

Identity is a major issue for personal digital security. Being secure in communication with some entity over a public network requires being secure in the knowledge that you know the identity of the entity you are communicating with. If this knowledge is missing, you may be susceptible to a man-in-the-middle attack.

A Sophisticated Threat

The man-in-the-middle attack occurs when a criminal attacker manages to insert herself between two end-points of a channel. Figure 1.7 illustrates how this works. The attacker, through misrepresentation, convinces entity A that she is entity B. Entity A sends a stream of data to the attacker, who turns around and then forwards that information to entity B, pretending to be entity A. When entity B receives the data, it responds with a transmission to the attacker, which it believes to be the actual source of the data—and which it also believes to be entity A.

The attacker's object may be to intercept and use the data being sent between A and B. This might be the case if A is an end-user connected to a mainframe host (entity B) over the Internet. The target data could be the user's passphrase and user ID, or it might be e-mail or some proprietary data stored on the mainframe.

The attacker may also modify the information being sent between the two entities. For example, entity A might be a consumer attempting to access banking services, and entity B might be the bank's on-line presence. The attacker may attempt to take control of funds in the account

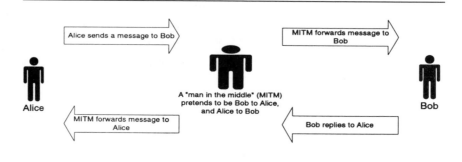

Figure 1.7. If an attacker manages to insert herself between two communicating entities, she may be able to make each believe that they are communicating directly.

by acting as a conduit for the user's login information. Once the session is initiated with the user's passphrase, the attacker might instead forward an error message to the user indicating that the system is unavailable. The attacker would then be able to take over the properly negotiated session in an attempt to manipulate the user's funds.

Thwarting the Man-in-the-Middle

This attack may seem to be tough to guard against and prevent, but it requires a comprehensive approach to security that uses a combination of encryption, digital signatures, and secure authentication procedures, as discussed throughout this book. Central to defeating the man-in-the-middle attack is to be able to confidently link entities with their keys.

Repudiation and Nonrepudiation

It is very important to carefully review credit card bills each month for billing errors. Incorrect charges often appear mysteriously; sometimes a merchant double-bills in error or due to some other relatively innocent cause—or the incorrect charge may be due to fraud, on the part of either a merchant attempting to get away with something or a criminal who has misappropriated your credit card number. In any case, the consumer has the right to repudiate a charge. Unless the merchant can prove that the charge was a proper one—for example by presenting a signed charge receipt—the charge is usually dropped. Merchants, however, take on the greatest risk in these transactions because if they make a sale that is later repudiated, they are liable to lose the product as well as the payment.

Credit card issuers permit consumers as much as three months to contest charges, a right that has in the past been used against the credit card issuers for criminal gain. Despite the best efforts of the issuers, thieves have found ways to use credit cards to purchase valuable items and then claim that they did not actually make the purchase. This scenario is particularly frightening to Internet merchants, who fear criminals who submit credit card numbers to pay for digital goods or services. If the account is bad or the charge is later repudiated, the merchant loses. The rate of loss in other types of *card-not-present* transactions (including mail orders and telephone orders) is much higher than that of in-person transactions because the merchant has no way to verify identity.

The good news for Internet merchants and consumers, however, is that one of the benefits of using digital signatures on transmissions is to actually provide a higher degree of trust in those transactions than is even possible in most face-to-face transactions.

The concept of *nonrepudiation* is central to personal encryption. As we will see later in this chapter and in Chapter 2, when a piece of data has been digitally signed, the entity that owns the key used to sign that data cannot repudiate the data. In other words, only the owner of the key used to sign a piece of data could possibly have signed the data—as long as the owner of the key keeps that key secure.

By including digital signatures in digital commerce architectures, merchants are theoretically able to minimize the risk that customers will repudiate their orders when doing business over the Internet.

Traffic Analysis

Entities communicating over an open channel need to be aware that even if they attempt to disguise their messages, their opponents may be able to figure out what a signal means if it is transmitted often enough. The situation is the same whether the entities are the third-base coach communicating instructions to batters and runners during a baseball game or a consumer sending credit card data to an on-line merchant. This type of attack is called *traffic analysis*, and it is a well-known method for attackers to determine your data even if you have taken steps to hide it.

In baseball, an opponent may be able to determine that every time the coach scratches her nose, a baserunner attempts to steal a base. On the Internet, an attacker may determine that every time a credit card transaction is carried out, a certain series of characters or words is encrypted and transmitted between the consumer and the merchant. Such data is called a *known plaintext* either because it is known (because it is part of a protocol specification, for example) or because it can be inferred in some way (when a baserunner steals a base after the coach sends some particular signal).

The thing to remember about traffic analysis is that even if you take measures to secure your channels of communication, an interceptor may be able to break your security over a long period of time by analyzing the data you send. As with other security threats, answering this one requires constant vigilance and the use of security principles. Traffic analysis can often be countered by frequent changes of encryption keys, as well as by reducing the volume of the transmissions that can be associated with known plaintexts. Under some circumstances you might even be encouraged to fill out the volume of transmissions with nonsensical or random data so that the actual target data will be interspersed and thus much harder to even identify, let alone intercept.

Assorted On-Line Fraud and Mischief

The same type of mentality that drives people to try to steal from others through shady propositions operates in the digital world as well. Just as the perpetrators of frauds like three-card monte games, pyramid scams, and insider trading schemes depend on the greed of the victims, the on-line versions of these frauds require willing victims in order to succeed.

Protecting against the on-line versions of these scams requires common sense: if an on-line deal is too good to be true, it probably is. Critical questioning of the propriety of any deal offered on-line is necessary, as is confirmation of credentials and identities of anyone offering a deal on-line. While there are no technologies that can help you differentiate an on-line scam from a legitimate business offering, working with reputable entities and using digital signatures can help reduce the risks.

Social Engineering

Technological fixes to security problems will only protect against attackers who stick to technology. The term *social engineering* originated among computer criminals who use it to refer to methods of attack that rely on interpersonal interaction rather than any technical expertise or device—in other words, telling a good story to any person who can provide the criminal with access to a restricted resource.

One common social engineering technique is for a criminal to call a user posing as a system manager. The criminal's objective is to get the user to give out her user ID and passphrase. The technique is to alarm the user into divulging the information, often by telling her that her account has been compromised and the system administrator needs to reset her passphrase.

Another technique for gaining unauthorized access through social engineering is for the criminal, posing as an irate executive, to contact a system manager. In this case, the criminal attempts to convince the system manager that her job may be in jeopardy if she does not help the "executive" to finish a vital corporate report that requires access to some restricted system. By convincing the system manager that the executive (criminal) has simply forgotten a passphrase, the criminal may be able to gain access to the system with the help of the person most interested in keeping it secure.

Social engineering has been documented elsewhere, notably in books covering the exploits of computer criminals. The average citizen should be aware that this type of attack can occur, and you should keep the following guidelines in mind when someone calls with a plausible explanation of why you should divulge sensitive data:

♦ Never tell anyone your passphrase, personal identification number, or other access code. Authorized system managers can access your system without asking you for this information.

♦ When you receive a call from someone who identifies herself as a system manager or security person, confirm her identity. A good technique is to ask for her name and number and tell her you will call back; calling her organization directly to confirm her identity is even better.

♦ Report social engineering attacks to the appropriate authorities. Even if you got stung, you may be able to educate others in your organization so they can avoid future problems.

Introduction to Cryptographic Concepts

This section introduces some of the most basic concepts relating to encryption and personal cryptography in general, starting with a brief definition of cryptography. It introduces the ideas of encryption, secret key encryption and public key encryption, digital signatures, shared secret authentication, digest functions, and cryptographic hashes. This section is strictly introductory; these concepts will be defined in greater detail in Chapter 2 (as well as discussed throughout the book), but this section provides a set of basic definitions as a foundation for later discussions.

As should now be clear, it is vital that we be able to perform two basic functions with data we send over open networks. We must be able to

♦ Prevent unauthorized people from accessing our data.

♦ Provide a method by which our data can be certified as ours to its recipients.

This section introduces five mechanisms by which these goals can be met. The functions include

◆ Encryption of all sorts.
◆ Public key encryption.
◆ Digital signatures.
◆ Cryptographic hashes and digests.
◆ Steganography.

Each of these functions will be introduced in this section, with all but steganography discussed at greater length in Chapter 2. Because these are the basic building blocks of all personal encryption tools, it is nice to be able to understand how they actually work as well as what they do. The difference, of course, is the same as the difference between knowing how to drive—step on the "go pedal" to make the car go, step on the "stop pedal" to make the car stop—and knowing how fuel injectors and antilock braking systems work. This introduction explains what each cryptographic function does, while Chapter 2 explains in greater depth and detail how these functions actually work.

WHAT IS CRYPTOGRAPHY? *Cryptography*, from Greek roots, literally means "hidden writing" and currently refers to the art and science of developing and using mechanisms by which to render data unreadable to anyone but the intended recipient. Because digital signatures have been developed as a direct result of cryptographic research, they are typically included when discussing modern cryptography.

Encryption

Encryption is any function or mechanism by which a plaintext can be converted into a *ciphertext* (encrypted data stream or file). The description of the mechanism is usually called an *algorithm*.

A successful encryption algorithm should produce ciphertexts that

- ◆ Can be returned to their plaintexts only by the holder of a key.
- ◆ Cannot be easily returned to plaintext by anyone who does not hold the key.
- ◆ Are secure even when the attacker knows the algorithm. (The security of the algorithm depends solely on the secrecy of the key, not the details of the algorithm being used.)
- ◆ Simulate a random data stream.

The algorithm itself should be relatively simple to implement on a computer program (whether in software or in a hardware device), and should also provide high performance. The faster the encryption and *decryption* (the process of turning a ciphertext into plaintext) processes, the more valuable it is to its users.

A very simple example of an encryption algorithm is replacement. The key is a number x with a value of anywhere from 1 to 25, and the algorithm works by replacing each letter of the message with the letter that comes x letters after the plaintext letter. In other words, using 1 as the key, the plaintext

Longfellow

becomes this ciphertext

Mpohgfmmpx

With this algorithm, it is very easy to decrypt a ciphertext as long as you know the key. However, if you know that a substitution algorithm is being used, with a computer (or even without one) it is not that much more difficult to decrypt the ciphertext even if you do not know the key—simply try all 25 possibilities (a *brute force attack*, see the accompanying note) and see which one makes sense. Thus, by the four criteria mentioned in the preceding list, this algorithm fails on the second (not hard to decrypt without the key) and the third (easy to break when you know the algorithm being used). On the fourth criteria, a random-looking data stream, this algorithm fares only slightly better. While the data stream does not look like a sequence of words, it does look like a sequence of letters, and those letters will have a frequency distribution pattern (representing how frequently each character occurs) similar to normal English. (For example, if the letter *q* replaces the letter *e*, *q* will tend to occur most frequently in ciphertext, on average.) Truly random data would include a variety of nonalphabetic as well as nonprinting characters; when using simple encryption algorithms like this one, spaces between words as well as punctuation are usually removed to reduce the cues an attacker might take advantage of to guess the contents of the message.

BRUTE FORCE ATTACKS : When the encryption algorithm used to encrypt any given ciphertext is known, an attacker can use a technique called *brute force* to decrypt the ciphertext. This simply means using every possible key combination on the ciphertext and looking at the result to see if it appears to be the correct plaintext.

Computers are instrumental in making brute force attacks possible. Although a simple encryption algorithm with a very short key may be susceptible to an individual in a reasonable length of time, as key length increases the amount of work required to successfully brute force a ciphertext increases even more rapidly.

To illustrate, take the simplest possible example of a key that is one bit long. The key is either 1 or it is 0; running the possibilities requires trying a maximum of two different keys. Now, increase the key size by a factor of 10, to a 10-bit key, and there are 2^{10} (1,024) different keys possible. This is roughly the situation faced by the thief who has taken a briefcase with a three-digit combination lock—while with a little patience she may attempt every combination over the course of an hour or two, but she is more likely to apply some other tool, like a crowbar, to break in.

As you continue to increase the key length, the difficulty of applying a brute force solution will continue to increase more rapidly. Increase the number of bits in the key by x, and the number of available keys (the key space) increases by a factor of 2^x.

This means you should consider very closely key length when choosing keys for encrypting important data. While longer keys tend to reduce overall performance of the algorithm—they make the encryption and decryption processes go slower—they also tend to reduce the risk that someone with plenty of computer time will be able to try all the possible combinations against your data and come up with the original plaintext.

As will be explained in Chapter 2, encryption algorithms use a variety of techniques to create secure ciphertexts. Suffice it to say that a good encryption algorithm will turn your data into what appears to be random noise to anyone who attempts to decrypt it without the key.

Secret Key and Public Key Encryption

Throughout history, until relatively recently, all encryption relied on secrets. You used the secret to generate a key to encrypt the plaintext and to decrypt the ciphertext. If someone learns the secret you use to generate a key with which to encrypt your data, she can decrypt any data you encrypted using the same secret. The function that describes the processes of encrypting and decrypting in this way can be referred to as a *symmetric encryption function* because it is symmetric—it works the same way in both directions.

More recently, developments in the fields of mathematics and computer science have produced a technology called *public key encryption* that uses an *asymmetric encryption function*. Rather than deriving a key from the same secret for both encryption and decryption, entities use pairs of keys: one to encrypt information and the other to decrypt it. This means that one key can be kept public and used to encrypt data by entities wishing to send encrypted messages. The only entity that can decrypt such a ciphertext is the holder of the private key of the pair. As we will see, this is a hugely powerful tool for data encryption in a world that relies increasingly on open channels of communication.

Secret Key Encryption

Secret key encryption has many benefits. Usually it

- ◆ Is easy to implement on a computer.
- ◆ Performs well enough to encrypt data streams on the fly.
- ◆ Is secure enough against brute force attacks when used with a sufficiently long key.

However, secret key encryption presents some problems when it is used to communicate between more than two people. One approach is to use a single key to encrypt all communications with a large number of entities. Disadvantages to this approach include the need to trust every entity to keep the key secret, the problem of delivering the secret key to all users in such a way that it is not vulnerable to interception, and the generation of a large volume of traffic all encrypted with the same key—a valuable resource for the attacker using a traffic analysis approach to breaking your encryption.

Another approach to using secret keys when communicating among a large number of entities is to assign a single key to be used by every pair of communicators. As shown in Figure 1.8, the number of keys each entity must maintain securely soon becomes unmanageable, and the problem of delivering the keys to each entity remains.

The problem of key distribution and key management in the military or government realms is limited both by a smaller possible number of entities that need to communicate directly, and by remedies that use strict procedures. Mechanisms for secret key distribution are often used in corporate or government implementations, and are often based on Kerberos, a solution for secure key distribution developed at MIT for protecting network resources. Outside of organizations able to use Kerberos or similar solutions, secure key distribution is a significant hurdle to using symmetric encryption for personal encryption.

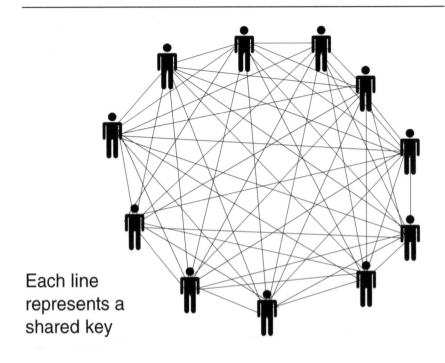

Each line
represents a
shared key

Figure 1.8. As the number of communicating entities increases, so does the number of keys that each must manage to communicate securely.

Public Key Encryption

Public key encryption helps solve the problems of usability and scalability by providing each entity with a pair of keys: one is a public key, the other a private key. Unlike in secret key encryption where the key must always be kept secret from everyone but authorized entities, public key encryption encourages the publication of the public key. If you know an entity's public key, you can use that to encrypt a message for that entity. The public key encryption process is illustrated in Figure 1.9. Attempting to decrypt that message with the entity's public key will yield only a ciphertext version of the first ciphertext. In order to decrypt a ciphertext encrypted with a public key, you must use the private key associated with the public key— a key that the owner entity will guard very closely.

The result is that once you have the entity's public key, you can send a message to that entity that can only be decrypted by the entity itself using the private key of the original public-private key pairing.

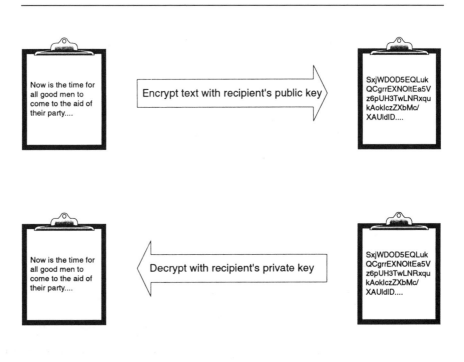

Figure 1.9. A plaintext encrypted with the recipient's public key can only be decrypted with the recipient's private key.

Public key encryption thus appears to solve several of the problems of secret key encryption:

- ◆ All communications to any given entity use that entity's public key, reducing the number of keys any given entity must maintain.
- ◆ Entities need not worry about securing their public keys; on the contrary, they will be more concerned about making them public.
- ◆ Assuming that each entity can keep its own private key secret, the danger of a key falling into the wrong hands is reduced drastically. (The best way to keep a secret is not to tell anyone.)

Implications of the public key asymmetry will be discussed further in the context of digital signatures. Details of how these asymmetric functions actually work will be addressed in Chapter 2.

Digital Signatures

Public key pairs are interchangeable in a way. If you use the public key to encrypt a message, the private key is the only way to decrypt it—by the same token, if you encrypt the message with the private key, anyone could decrypt that message using your public key. This is the basis for digital signatures. If you encrypt a piece of data with your private key, anyone who has access to your public key can decrypt it, but you (the holder of the private key) are the only entity that could have done the encryption in the first place.

To be practical, digital signatures should not really interfere with the process of actually reading the message, so they do not in fact require the sender to encrypt the message with the sender's private key nor do they require the recipient to decrypt the entire message with the sender's public key. What happens is illustrated in Figure 1.10. The sender takes the data to be signed and uses a special function to digitally summarize the data (a digest or hash function, introduced in the next section). The data generated as a result of that process is then encrypted with the sender's private key, and

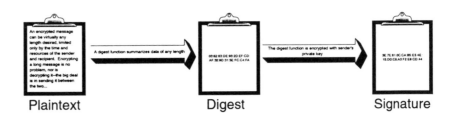

Plaintext   Digest   Signature

Figure 1.10. The sender creates a digest of the message to be signed and then encrypts that with the sender's private key.

appended to the original message—the recipient is able to certify the signed data by using the same hashing function and encrypting the result with the sender's public key.

If the result matches the digital signature attached to the message, then the recipient can be certain the message originated from the owner of the public key and that it arrived unchanged from the way it was sent. If the two results do not match, all the recipient can be certain of is that the message may have been tampered with, that it may have originated from someone other than the owner of the public key, or that something may have gone wrong during the process of signing, sending, or certifying the message. However, that is sufficient to alert the recipient that the message should not be trusted.

Ideally, digital signatures are both generated and certified automatically; unfortunately, software implementations that are secure to date have often been hard to use, while those that are easy to use are not always secure. The result has been that prior to 1998 digital signatures have not routinely been used outside of certain special-purpose applications, nor have they been routinely used by the general population. However, new software products as well as a heightened awareness of the issues should soon result in the routine use of digital signatures—as should reading the rest of this book.

Digest Functions and Cryptographic Hashes

With computers, whether networked or not, there is always the possibility that an error can creep into data. A stray cosmic ray might hit the hard drive and knock a bit from one to zero, or a stray bit might be added in the course of transmission across a network. In any case, it is always useful to have some method of error detection. The simplest method is to use something like a check digit or a parity check.

Adding up all bits in a data file or transmission and then recording the result, when compared to the result provided by the sender, will often flag a problem. However, the accuracy and dependability of such a check depend directly on how it is calculated and how long the resulting value is. For example, using a single-bit check digit (either 1 or 0) means that if an error has occurred, there is a 50% probability that the check digit will *not* reveal it—assuming that the check digit will be some random number, it has one chance in two that it will be the same as the correct check digit. Increasing the length of the number you use to summarize the data file or transmission will decrease the likelihood that an incorrect but random result will match the real result.

Although there is much more to digest or hash functions than that, in practice this is precisely their purpose. A cryptographic hash function accepts any set of data as its input and generates as its output a result of fixed length (almost always smaller than the original data) that meets the following criteria:

- ♦ The digest result will be as unique to the source data as is possible within the constraints of its length. This means that it should not be easy to create two or more messages that produce the same hash value.
- ♦ When the source data changes incrementally, the resulting digest will be significantly different. This means that changing a message by a small amount (for example,

changing a letter grade on a school report card from "B" to "A") should mean that the hash value will change by much more than a single byte or character.

♦ It should not be possible to use the digest result to reconstruct the source data. This means that the hash function will operate as a one-way function, eliminating any meaning from the result that could be used to infer the data originally being hashed.

♦ The digest result should approximate a random set of data. This means that the hash results can be appended to encrypted data in such a way that an attacker would not be able to determine where the ciphertext ended and the hash value began.

Hashes, also known as *message digests*, are frequently used to verify the integrity of a data transmission—particularly when used with public key encryption to create digital signatures. If a digest function works well, the statistical likelihood of generating duplicate digest values for any two random sets of data will be astronomically remote.

Steganography

When using encryption, it can be hard to hide that fact, particularly when you are using Internet applications and protocols that may require that you identify whether the data stream is being encrypted; data encrypted to the desktop often is identified by a particular file type extension. Whether you are sending streams of apparently random data across the Internet, or saving files full of apparently random bits, what you are doing is quite obviously using encryption. If you really, *really* wanted to keep your data private, you would not want anyone to know that you have even got anything to keep private. If you could somehow hide the fact that you are encrypting data, you would be less likely to attract the attention of anyone who might attempt to break your encryption scheme.

The use of technologies or mechanisms to hide the existence of a message is called *steganography,* a word derived from Greek roots meaning "hidden writing." Steganography covers a wide range of techniques, with a long history that predates computerized cryptography. Steganographic methods include invisible ink, false-bottomed boxes, and messages swallowed by the messenger and somehow retrieved later at their destination. One impractical technique once suggested involved tattooing a message on the shaved head of the messenger and allowing enough time for the hair to regrow: once the messenger arrives, one more application of the razor reveals the message.

The fact that steganography will hide the actual message means that the sender must somehow notify the recipient of the impending arrival of a message as well as somehow indicate how to identify that message. There are ways of applying steganographic techniques to digital communications, but such techniques are beyond the scope of this book. If your adversaries cannot be thwarted through use of more straightforward techniques like public key encryption and digital signatures, you are likely to require more help than I can offer.

Using Personal Encryption

Formerly the domain of governments and big business, the combination of computers, the Internet, and public key cryptography make it possible for individuals and small businesses to protect their own interests by taking advantage of security tools like encryption and digital signatures. Such tools, when properly used, can keep your personal and business data private, can facilitate secure communication over open networks, can enable secure digital commercial transactions, and can help you maintain a competitive edge in a fast-moving world. The key, however, is to use these technologies properly—using them incorrectly can lead to a false sense of security and worse.

This book provides an introduction to the theory as well as the use of encryption and digital signature technologies. The reader interested in cryptography theory should read Chapters 2 through 4 to get a better idea of how modern encryption works and why. If you prefer to skip the theory, Chapters 5 through 10 offer all the hands-on guidance you need to actually start protecting your personal information with the most popular web, e-mail, and desktop security software now available.

2

Modern Cryptography Primer

This chapter introduces the basic concepts of cryptography, including ciphers, codes, computerized encryption, symmetric and asymmetric algorithms, public key encryption, digital signatures, and message digests. Those who want to understand the mathematics of cryptography can find the basics in Appendix A—this section is purely optional, for those interested in the way things work.

 You can use encryption and digital signature products without understanding the theory behind them. If you don't want to get too technical, or if you just want to get started with protecting your data and come back later for the details, skip ahead to Chapter 5!

Although the basic mathematics underlying most modern cryptography is surprisingly simple, it is not necessary to understand how encryption works to be able to use encryption any more than it is necessary to understand how an internal combustion engine works to drive an automobile. However, just as some basic understanding of your automobile will help you to use it properly (for example, to make sure that you keep the engine properly lubricated, avoid driving with the parking brake on, and use the windshield wiper to keep the windshield clear of rain or snow), so will a basic understanding of cryptography help you to use encryption properly (for example, to avoid giving away secret keys, or to distrust any message whose digital signature cannot be certified).

Topics to be covered in this chapter include

- Codes, ciphers and encryption.
- Computerized encryption.
- Secret key (symmetric) encryption.
- Cryptographic hashes and messsage digests.
- Public key (asymmetric) encryption.
- Digital signatures.
- Certification authorities.

Although this chapter provides an in-depth introduction to issues of implementing and using various types of encryption and other cryptographic tools, it is only an introduction. Those interested in understanding more about the theory of public key cryptography can see Appendix A. For more details about how applying and implementing cryptography, as well as for a lively historical account of cryptography and *cryptanalysis*, the art of breaking ciphers and codes (collectively referred to as *cryptology*), see the books described in the accompanying box.

FOR MORE SERIOUS STUDENTS OF CRYPTOLOGY: The field of cryptology is a subject of serious academic study and research, as well as the subject of many books, chapters, and articles in the popular, trade, and academic presses. Good resources for the interested reader include

- *Applied Cryptography: Protocols, Algorithms, and Source Code in C*, 2nd ed., by Bruce Schneier (John Wiley & Sons, 1996). This is a comprehensive sourcebook for programmers and developers implementing cryptographic algorithms. Although some sections will be accessible to the general reader, this book is a tool for software developers interested in building applications that use the cryptographic algorithms described.
- *The Codebreakers: The Story of Secret Writing* by David Kahn (Scribner, 1996). This is a thorough history of cryptography, focusing on cryptographic activities during the 20th century (but also offering a fascinating description of the evolution of cryptography through the centuries), providing a complete historical and political context for the use of cryptography and related pursuits. Although historically relevant encryption and cryptographic techniques are described, there is little discussion of more modern public key technologies including public key encryption and digital signatures.
- *Network Security: Private Communication in a Public World* by Charlie Kaufman, Radia Perlman, and Mike Speciner (Prentice Hall 1995). This is an excellent introduction to the technical aspects of network security, with detailed coverage of encryption, digital signatures, public and secret key algorithms, strong authentication over networks, and much more. The technically inclined reader will get a solid introduction to the technologies, while other readers should still benefit from many of the clear descriptions of network security issues.

Codes, Ciphers, and Encryption

Strictly speaking, a *code* usually refers to a complete system of informational representation; for example, Samuel Morse's eponymous system for turning characters into series of dots and dashes is referred to as a code. Codes use a one-to-one mapping between

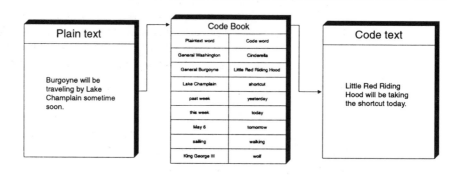

Figure 2.1. Codes represent words or symbols with other assigned words or symbols.

symbols (or representations) and characters (or words)—in other words, they require code books or lists to keep track of what information is being transmitted, and there is no algorithmic consistency in the way data is represented. There is no reason that the letter *s* should be represented by the sequence *dot dot dot*, nor is there any reason that a military codebook might (or might not) use the word *grandmother* to refer to the president. Codes, as illustrated in Figure 2.1, tend to define some mapping of meaning from one representation (the underlying meaning of a word) onto some other representation (the code representation of that word); to decode a message you would need to know the underlying representations and the corresponding code words. Also characteristic of codes is a limitation. If you have not put a particular word or symbol into your code book, you cannot encode that word.

 Perhaps the best known code, at least for most Americans, is the familiar "One if by land, two if by sea" system worked out to warn of the mode by which the British would invade Boston. This particular system also nicely illustrates the limitations of codes. First, the signals could easily have been confused if the recipient had misheard the signal mapping. Second, had the British chosen to attack by both land and sea, or had they attacked by air (or through mines or telepathy, for that matter), the patriots would have had no predetermined way to represent those eventualities—they could only communicate those events they had the foresight to think of in advance.

A *cipher*, on the other hand, refers to a method of manipulating data in such a way that (it is hoped) it will not easily be understood by anyone but the intended recipient (or anyone who has the correct key to decrypt it). A cipher tends to use some kind of repetitive operations, as are used in mathematics, to take a plaintext character and turn it into a ciphertext character. There may or may not be a one-to-one correspondence between a character as it appears in plaintext and ciphertext representations. In other words, the letter *A* may be turned into the letter *f* in one part of a message and the character $ in another part of the message, or it may always be represented by the letter *Q*.

A cipher describes a process by which any plaintext can be turned into ciphertext (and vice versa). Unlike a code, which can handle only those symbols or words that have been predefined, a cipher can usually handle any data at all, whether it has been anticipated or not. The process that describes how the cipher actually transforms a piece of the plaintext into the corresponding ciphertext is referred to as the cipher's *algorithm*. If you know a cipher's algorithm, a ciphertext and the key associated with that ciphertext, you can decrypt that ciphertext.

Encryption is the process by which a cipher's algorithm is implemented on a particular plaintext. There is no need to understand the semantics of the message in order to encode it, which, along with the mechanical nature of encryption algorithms, makes ciphers the hands-down favorite for computer implementation.

 Codes tend not to be implemented on computers to provide data security— ciphers are more commonly used for that. As a result, the distinction in meanings between code and cipher, and between encryption/decryption and encoding/decoding, often are blurred. Although this text is consistent in its use of the terms, the reader may find that other sources are less consistent and may sometimes refer to coded text when what is meant is *ciphertext*.

It is a truism of cryptography and security that any security mechanism is susceptible to a determined adversary with sufficient resources. However, some mechanisms are more susceptible than others. Just because a cipher is complicated to implement does not mean that it is secure, and just because a code system is comprehensive does not mean that an adversary cannot guess message contents by their context and timing. Cryptography, both an art and a science, is in any case a very difficult profession. Both amateur and professional cryptographers have devised many flawed systems. Relatively few systems have withstood the test of time and attempts by rivals to demonstrate flaws and weaknesses. The rest of this section discusses some of the ciphering principles underlying modern cryptography.

Cryptanalysis

The term *cryptanalysis* refers to the pursuit of breaking ciphers. The purpose is, of course, to figure out the contents of an encrypted message. There are several different approaches to such attacks, but the most basic techniques (particularly when used against the simpler types of cipher) rely on a knowledge of the language of the plaintext. What this means is that an attacker may have little or no problem deciphering a message, as long as the following information is available (although other clues may help break the cipher without this information):

- ◆ Letter frequency. If the attacker knows which letters are common (in English, letters like *e*, *s*, and *t*) and which are uncommon (*x*, *q*), the attacker can make certain guesses about the contents of the ciphertext.
- ◆ Letter distribution. Some two- and three-letter combinations occur frequently, particularly at certain parts of words (for example, *io*, *ing*, and *th*), while others occur rarely or never (for example, *iy*, *tp*, and *pk*).

◆ Word length. One-letter words will be either *I* or *a*; two-letter words are drawn from a limited stock.

◆ Context. Having some idea as to the contents of a message will help the attacker. This includes any knowledge of names of recipient or sender, or even whether the content is largely numeric or alphabetic.

Cryptanalysis is not just for spies, counterspies and criminals. Law enforcement agencies commonly use cryptanalysis to decrypt ciphertexts generated by criminals. There is even a large audience of amateurs who enjoy cryptographic puzzles, which are often published in daily newspapers. Researchers and consultants also attack ciphers for the purpose of verifying whether or not the cipher actually is resistant to such attacks.

There are other methods and approaches to breaking encryption algorithms, but these tend to require the collection of various different pieces of information. While it is possible to break relatively simple ciphers (such as most of those discussed in the next section, especially when they are used improperly) simply by knowing or guessing the language of the plaintext, other types of cipher require more. While one might imagine that attacks against a cipher might most commonly have only the ciphertext itself, this is not always the case. Common classes of attacks include

◆ Ciphertext-only. The attacker has access only to one or more ciphertexts, with no additional information. For example, an encrypted data file or a portion of a data stream being transmitted across a network might be instances where a ciphertext-only attack is employed. (The owner of the data file or the source and destination of the network transmission may provide some hints about the content, however.)

◆ Known-plaintext. The attacker has access to one or more ciphertexts, as well as to some or all of the associated plaintext. For example, for a ciphertext that contained a user ID and passphrase when logging into a network resource, the attacker might deduce that the first portion of the ciphertext is your user ID. Many protocols that use encryption also use standard formats and data for their headers, which can also provide a known-plaintext.

♦ Chosen-plaintext. There are times when an attacker may be able to access not only ciphertexts, but may be able to actually choose some particular plaintext to be encrypted. For example, an attacker might break into an office to gain access to and encrypt with a computer used for encryption; alternatively, an attacker might co-opt an operator to send an encrypted message, or even plant information that would trigger a transmission. A chosen-plaintext attack against a commercial enterprise might be engineered as simply as becoming a client of the firm and providing them with the chosen-plaintext as part of a business transaction. There are other methods that involve manipulating the target to encrypt and send a message that contains one of a small number of possibilities, for example, the answer to a yes or no question, or the name of a member of the board of directors.

When the attacker already has some or all of plaintext associated with a ciphertext, the purpose of the attack may be to determine the keys and algorithms being used to encrypt the plaintext and, in particular, to enable the attacker to decrypt any future messages.

Ciphers and Encryption

The objective of encryption is to keep something secret, and the success of any given cipher is directly related to two factors: how hard it is to decipher any given ciphertext without the key, and how easy it is to encipher (or decipher) texts with a key. If the cipher is very difficult to break, but also very difficult to use, it may not be as useful as it could be; if it is very easy to use, but also very easy to break, then its usefulness will be even more limited.

Most ciphers make use of one form or another of a handful of approaches. These approaches, each discussed next, include

♦ Substitution ciphers.
♦ Transposition ciphers.
♦ Rotor or multiple substitution ciphers.

Substitution Ciphers

The simplest type of cipher, the basic substitution cipher, has also served as the precursor for some of the most successful ciphers. Substitution ciphers are exactly that. They replace (or substitute) each character of a plaintext with some other character. Even a very short message of a few words, when encrpyted with the simplest substitution ciphers, can often be broken in minutes—in fact, such ciphertexts often appear as puzzles in daily newspapers. However, more sophisticated versions of the substitution cipher can be more difficult to break.

Simple Substitution

The simple substitution cipher is familiar even to many schoolchildren: Write down the alphabet, from a to z on a sheet of paper. Choose some offset number between 1 and 25 (0 and 26 won't produce any changes), count out the offset, and make another copy of the alphabet underneath the first as shown in Figure 2.2, wrapping around to the start of the first alphabet. That figure shows an offset of 3, so the word *cat* becomes *zxq*.

A simple substitution cipher may use an alphabet, but they are generally fairly easy to attack. The frequency of letter distribution in even the shortest message tends to produce a susceptibility, while letter combinations also tend to give the ciphertext away.

One common computer implementation of a simple substitution cipher is called ROT13. This cipher is most often found in e-mail and Internet news readers, and is not intended so much as a data

A	B	C	D	E	F	G	H	I	J	K	L	M	N	O	P	Q	R	S	T	U	V	W	X	Y	Z
x	y	z	a	b	c	d	e	f	g	h	i	j	k	l	m	n	o	p	q	r	s	t	u	v	w

Figure 2.2. With an offset of 3, a simple substitution cipher is simple to implement without computers—and is simple to break without computers as well.

protection mechanism as a means to protect readers from inadvertently reading off-color jokes, movie spoilers, or puzzle solutions. ROT13 "rotates" the characters of a message by 13—the offset for the simple substitution cipher is 13, so A becomes N, B becomes O, and so on. The objective is to provide a simple mechanism for instantly (or almost instantly) converting apparent gibberish into readable text.

The simple substitution cipher with an offset of 3 is also known as the Caesar cipher because it has been reported as being used by Julius Caesar. Although the Caesar cipher and other examples cited here are simple offset ciphers (the substitution alphabets run in alphabetical order, but start at some letter other than A and wrap around once they hit Z), scrambling the substitution alphabet helps improve security. Simple offset substitutions need only yield one mapping of plaintext to ciphertext to yield the complete ciphertext. If you know that C replaces A, you also know that B replaces Z, D replaces B, and so on. Producing a more random substitution alphabet, like that in Figure 2.3, eliminates this attack—although it still retains the weaknesses of any other substitution cipher, most important of which is frequency analysis.

Even simple substitution ciphers can be made slightly more secure by removing as many clues from the message as possible. These methods include things like removing word spacing and punctuation. The result is that attackers cannot make any inferences about letters by their location within a word or the size of the words they are in. Removing punctuation also takes away semantic cues.

A	B	C	D	E	F	G	H	I	J	K	L	M	N	O	P	Q	R	S	T	U	V	W	X	Y	Z
k	f	x	t	a	i	u	l	q	w	p	n	b	g	c	m	h	y	e	z	d	j	o	r	v	s

Figure 2.3. Randomly replacing plaintext with ciphertext characters improves the simple substitution cipher slightly.

To make the substitution cipher any more secure requires taking away the cues that attackers can use to infer the contents. One-for-one substitutions, as in simple substitution ciphers, do not modify the distribution of symbols, but rather shift the distribution. Whereas in normal text, the letter *e* will most likely be the most frequent, ciphertexts generated by simple substitution ciphers will have some other character that appears more frequently than any other. This character can reliably be mapped to the letter *e* by the attacker.

Homophonic Substitution

One elaboration of the substitution cipher uses two or more homophones, or sound-alike characters, for each plaintext character. In *homophonic substitution* ciphers a set of symbols for each plaintext character is used, each one in turn, for each instance of the plaintext character. Figure 2.4 shows how one such cipher might be structured.

The result of using a group of different characters or symbols for each plaintext is that the ciphertext will look slightly more random than it would with a simple substitution cipher. The symbols representing the letter *e* will still predominate, but since there is no clear relationship between the plaintext characters and ciphertext characters,

Plaintext character		A	B	C	. . .
Homophones		1	25	5	. . .
		17	88	9	
		3	41	11	
		31	54	12	
		28	90	76	

Figure 2.4. Homophonic substitution ciphers use more than one ciphertext character for each plaintext character.

translating the ciphertext becomes less easy. However, the task is still not necessarily hard, particularly when the ciphertext is long enough. Applying computer analysis to such ciphertexts using brute force techniques will translate most in moments.

Polygram Substitution

Another alternative to the simple substitution cipher is to group letters together and encrypt them as blocks. Rather than simply replace the letter *a* with some other letter, polygram substitution ciphers encrypt two or more letters together as a block, so the letter pair *aa* might be encrypted as *qr* while the pair *ab* might be encrypted as *et*. The larger the encryption blocks are, the more effective this approach is—but also more difficult to use. It is also susceptible to alphabetic distribution attacks, particularly as the volume of ciphertext grows. Although analysis is more difficult due to the larger number of possible combinations of letters, there is still a set distribution of character pairings (e.g., *th* is more common than *qx*).

Polyalphabetic Substitution

A simple improvement to the simple substitution cipher is to use multiple keys to encrypt the plaintext. Figure 2.5 shows how such a scheme works with five different keys; the first letter of the plaintext is encrypted with the first of the keys, the second letter of the plaintext with the second key, and so on. Once you reach the sixth letter of the plaintext, the first key is re-used. The key to a polyalphabetic substitution cipher can be expressed as a series of letters, with each letter referring to the place in the alphabet at which the substitution begins.

The cipher represented in Figure 2.5 uses the letters of the author's last name. If the first character of the plaintext were an *A*, it would be encrypted as *L*; if the second letter of the plaintext were *A*, it would be encrypted as *O*; if the third letter of the plaintext were *A*, it would be encrypted as *S*, and so on. To encrypt a plaintext, look in the first column of the table to find the first plaintext character. Then, look to the right, for the corresponding ciphertext character

	L	O	S	H	I	N
a	l	o	s	h	i	n
b	m	p	t	i	j	o
c	n	q	u	j	k	p
d	o	r	v	k	l	q
e	p	s	w	l	m	r
f	q	t	x	m	n	s
g	r	u	y	n	o	t
h	s	v	z	o	p	u
i	t	w	a	p	q	v
j	u	x	b	q	r	w
k	v	y	c	r	s	x
l	w	z	d	s	t	y
m	x	a	e	t	u	z
n	y	b	f	u	v	a
o	z	c	g	v	w	b
p	a	d	h	w	x	c
q	b	e	I	x	y	d
r	c	f	j	y	z	e
s	d	g	k	z	a	f
t	e	h	l	a	b	g
u	f	i	m	b	c	h
v	g	j	n	c	d	i
w	h	k	o	d	e	j
x	i	l	p	e	f	k
y	j	m	q	f	g	l
z	k	n	r	g	h	m

Figure 2.5. A polyalphabetic substitution cipher using a key based on the author's last name.

in the first substitution alphabet. Continue with the second character of the plaintext by looking in the second substitution alphabet column, and so on until the fifth character; at the sixth character, start over with the first substitution alphabet. To illustrate, a plaintext consisting of *AAAAA* would be encrypted as *LOSHIN*. The plaintext *LOSHIN* would be encrypted as *WCKPA*.

The polyalphabetic substitution cipher is an improvement over the simple substitution cipher, and longer keys make it more difficult to solve—but, like other substitution ciphers, while it may be difficult for a human to solve, ciphertexts generated by a polyalphabetic substitution cipher can be relatively easily decrypted when a computer is used.

Transposition Ciphers

Unlike substitution ciphers, transposition ciphers do not make any changes to the characters of a text but rather jumble them up so they are not recognizable. In other words, the ciphertext is actually an anagram of the plaintext. A very simple form of this type of cipher would simply take the plaintext and turn it backwards, turning *Now is the time* into *emit eht si woN*. Figure 2.6 shows a slightly more complicated transposition cipher, the simple columnar transposition cipher. The plaintext is written out horizontally onto a grid, and the ciphertext is produced by reading words vertically from the same grid. The plaintext in Figure 2.6 is

```
Now is the time for all good men to come to the
aid of their party
```

while the ciphertext is

```
Nmdtt oemoh wfete ionhi srter taoap hlcia elodr
tgmot ioefy.
```

Note that the first and last letters of the transposed message (in this case, at least) are the same as the plaintext. Padding the message, by adding characters at the start or end of the ciphertext, is one approach that can be used to eliminate this problem. Transposition

N	o	w	i	s	t	h	e	t	i
m	e	f	o	r	a	l	l	g	o
d	m	e	n	t	o	c	o	m	e
t	o	t	h	e	a	i	d	o	f
t	h	e	i	r	p	a	r	t	y

Figure 2.6. The simple columnar transposition cipher takes every nth letter of the plaintext, and groups the ciphertext into words, usually five characters long.

ciphers become more secure as the length increases, and they are also strengthened by *superencryption* or the application of a second cipher to the ciphertext generated by a first cipher.

Rotor (Multiple Substitution) Ciphers

The most sophisticated incarnation of substitution cipher is the multiple substitution cipher, also known as the rotor type of cipher because it was often implemented in a machine using rotors. Each rotor has the 26 characters of the alphabet arranged in an arbitrary order. The first rotor is connected to a keyboard for the entry of the plaintext. Pressing a key corresponding to a plaintext character then activates a connection to one of the characters on the first rotor. In other words, the rotor takes a plaintext character as input and generates some output character depending on its position. (Remember, it acts as a simple substitution cipher, but each time it is rotated, it produces a different substitution.)

The output of the first rotor is then sent to the next rotor, which uses a different arbitrary ordering of the alphabet. It too acts as a simple substitution cipher, taking its input from the first rotor and generating another output. This process continues until all the rotors have been traversed and a final ciphertext character is produced as output.

The Enigma, a German rotor device used during World War II, represented the state of the art in cryptography, but was broken by Allied forces who actually had to reverse-engineer the device in order to break its encryption. The actual devices added complications in the form of special plugboard wiring between the keyboard and the first rotors, and used interchangeable rotors.

Figure 2.7 shows how a very simple rotor device might work. The first column in the figure shows the plaintext alphabet, with the letter *e* shown linked with the letter *B* in the first rotor. This means that the first rotor takes *e* as its input and produces *B* as its output, which is aligned with *R* on the next rotor, which in turn is aligned with *A* on the final rotor. After each plaintext letter is encrypted, all the rotors rotate—and not necessarily in the same direction or even at the same rate. In the example shown in Figure 2.7 this means that the first rotor rotates down two positions after each plaintext letter, the second rotor rotates up three positions and the third rotor rotates down one position.

Plaintext	Rotor 1 (rotate down 2 positions)	Rotor 2 (rotate up three positions)	Rotor 3 (rotate down 1 position)
a	X	M	Q
b	R	A	T
c	G	U	I
d	A	L	C
e	B	R	A
f	J	F	C
g	E	S	V
h	C	N	U
i	Z	X	E

and so on

Figure 2.7. Part of a simple rotor cipher.

The figure shows the process of encrypting a single letter; if the next letter to be encrypted were also *e*, then the first rotor (after moving down two positions) would produce *G* as its output to rotor 2, which would produce *N* as its output to rotor 3, which would produce *C* as the ciphertext for the original letter.

PERFECT CIPHER SECURITY WITH ONE-TIME PADS : There is a simple type of cipher that is unbreakable: the one-time pad cipher. The one-time pad itself is simply a sequence of random characters. The one-time pad is also simple to use. The first step is to take the first character of the plaintext, and use the first character of the one-time pad as the key for a simple offset substitution cipher. (In other words, if the first character of the pad is C, the first character of the plaintext is encrypted using the Caesar cipher.) Each succeeding character is encrypted in the same way, using the corresponding character of the one-time pad as a key.

This approach, as long as it is used properly, is unbreakable because it generates a ciphertext that can be decrypted to literally any plaintext. The randomness of the one-time pad ensures that there are no cues to the content of the plaintext.

The sender and recipient both have copies of the same one-time pad, and both destroy the used portions of the pad after it has been used. Re-using any part of the pad turns it into a very long polyalphabetic substitution cipher, which is relatively easily broken.

The one-time pad approach has several problems that make it impractical for most uses, particularly for computerized encryption:

♦ It must be truly random. This means pseudo-random sequences generated by computers cannot be used because they can be easily recreated and also because they tend to contain detectable regularities that can aid attackers.

> ◆ The one-time pad must be used only once. This means that the total length of all messages sent cannot exceed the size of the one-time pad itself. If more data is to be sent, another one-time pad must be generated and distributed.
>
> ◆ One-time pad distribution must be secure. If an attacker could acquire the one-time pad, all messages sent with the pad could be read.

Automating Encryption

The preceding section covered the basic elements of encryption, which are the same whether they are used to encrypt data by hand or with a computer. However, when these elements are combined correctly and implemented with computers, they can be used to generate ciphertext that is much more difficult to decrypt than anything that could be done manually. For example, rotor ciphers are susceptible to determined adversaries, as the Germans discovered after World War II. However, the rotor devices demonstrated that computers would inalterably affect the way encryption was used. First, it provided an excellent tool for creating stronger methods of encryption, and second, it provided attackers a new tool for breaking other people's encryption methods.

Three of the most important issues relating to encryption, as it relates to computerization, are

- ◆ Encryption algorithms.
- ◆ Key lengths and security.
- ◆ Judging algorithm security.

The most vital strength (and also a weakness) of using computers to encrypt and decrypt data is that computers can perform repetitive tasks extremely quickly. The simple ciphers we have already discussed should have made clear that the encryption of a plaintext is simply a matter of performing a very simple function (or set of functions) on each and every character of the plaintext. People are not as well equipped for the mindlessly repetitive task of doing encryption and decryption as computers are, and making ciphers more secure requires using the power of the computer to transform plaintexts in ways that would be impossible for an individual to reproduce.

Just as the computerization of encryption makes it simpler to implement strong encryption methods, so the computerization of cryptographic attacks makes it easier to defeat ciphers that are not strong, through brute force attacks.

Computer Encryption Algorithms

The challenge of encryption is to create a cipher or algorithm that is sufficiently simple in its implementation to make it reasonably easy to use, yet at the same time produces ciphertext output that is sufficiently impervious to attacks. Computers expand the concept of simplicity of implementation. If a cipher were to require hundreds of operations to encrypt and decrypt each character of a plaintext, that cipher would be deemed far too difficult to use for unaided encryption by a human. It would take far too long to encrypt or decrypt even a very short message, reducing the usefulness of the cipher. In effect, the cipher would require massive amounts of labor to use—the effort would be comparable to that required to attack the cipher.

On the other hand, computers are able to execute many hundreds of operations in fractions of a second, reliably and perfectly reproducibly. The result is that highly complex algorithms can be devised to be implemented on computers—thus making it possible to use them easily and securely. The most important computer encryption algorithms include

- ◆ Data Encryption Standard (DES).
- ◆ International Data Encryption Algorithm (IDEA).

- ◆ RSA Public Key Encryption.
- ◆ Digital Signature Algorithm (DSA).
- ◆ Proprietary Algorithms.

DES and IDEA, both symmetric algorithms, will be discussed in the next section, as will be proprietary algorithms. Public key encryption algorithms RSA (owned by RSA Data Security, Inc., also known as RSADSI) and the Digital Signature Standard (DSS is the specification for DSA, specified by the National Institute of Standards and Technology, or NIST) will be discussed later in this chapter.

Key Length and Large Numbers

With all other things being equal, for example, using a polyalphabetic substitution cipher, a longer key will provide more security than a shorter one. However, it is important to remember that all things are usually not equal, and it is especially important to consider that an insecure encryption algorithm will not suddenly become secure because it uses a very long key.

It should also be remembered that the large numbers of possible configurations, keys or alphabetic combinations do not necessarily impart any added security. An obvious example is the use of the simple substitution cipher. Theoretically, there are many different ways to uniquely map the 26 letters of the alphabet onto each other. While the simplest ciphers just offset the alphabet anywhere from 1 to 25 letters, more complicated ciphers randomly map plaintext letters to ciphertext letters, with no conscious effort to create any relationship between plaintext and ciphertext characters. In other words, every permutation of the 26 characters A through Z (other than the well-known one) could conceivably be used as a substitution alphabet.

Some of these substitution alphabets would be useless, such as the ones in which only one or a handful of letters actually shifts. However, there are a total of 26! (see the accompanying box) or roughly 400 million billion billion (over 400,000,000,000,000,000,000,000,000) different combinations of the 26 characters of the alphabet. The odds against someone guessing the exact substitution ordering of any given substitution alphabet is very small—but breaking any given substitution cipher is relatively easy nonetheless.

PERMUTATIONS AND FACTORIALS : The exclamation mark represents the *factorial* function. The factorial of any number n is equal to the product of n and all the integers less than n down to 1. In symbols:

$$n! = n * (n-1) * (n-2) * ... * 2 * 1$$

As it happens, the number of permutations of a set of n symbols is equal to n!. Consider an unmatched pair of socks, one white and one black. There are exactly two permutations of that set of socks. One starts with the black sock, the other starts with the white sock. Add a red sock to those two, and there are now six different combinations:

```
whitered      black
whiteblack    red
redwhite      black
redblack      white
blackwhite    red
blackred      white
```

◆ Permuting the 26 characters of the alphabet produces 26!, or 26 * 25 * 24 * ... * 2 * 1, possible different substitution alphabets. The actual value is 403,291,461,126, 605,635,584,000,000.

Taking Advantage of Large Numbers

As is apparent even from the simplest encryption algorithms, in general a longer key will help keep the ciphertext more secure. Computer encryption algorithms take advantage of their ability to rapidly perform many simple transformations on data to securely encrypt data. The same algorithms, if used with very short keys, might not be terribly secure—it would be a simple matter to just use another computer to attempt to decrypt a ciphertext with all the possible keys. This type of brute force attack takes much longer to successfully complete as the key length increases.

For example, if the key length is only 8 bits (about the same as a single character, and in practice a binary value between 0 and 255), and it takes 0.001 seconds to decrypt with the correct key, an attacker could have plaintext without the correct key in no more than about a quarter of a second and probably faster. On average, the attacker will hit the correct key after searching about half the possible keyspace, meaning in this case the key will be found in about 0.0128 seconds.

Double the length of the key to 16 bits (about two characters), and the attacker now has to deal with 2^{16} (65,536) different possibilities. This is still fairly vulnerable to computer attack. If it still takes 0.001 seconds to decrypt with the correct key (you can try 1000 keys per second, a rate that can be vastly improved by a determined attacker), a 16-bit key can be broken in no more than a little over a minute. Double it again to 32 bits, and the attacker must consider that the key is one of 2^{32}—over four billion different possibilities, but still breakable in less than two months at 1000 tries per second. Obviously, a simple doubling of the key length returns a far more considerable increase in the difficulty of attempting a brute force attack against the encrpyted data.

 No matter how long the key is, if the algorithm being used is susceptible to non-brute force attacks, the algorithm itself is not strong. The ciphertext can also be susceptible if the attacker successfully uses a noncryptographic approach—such as blackmailing or extorting the holder of the key into decrypting the data.

Determining Ideal Key Lengths

As should by now be apparent, achieving security requires a balance of ease of use with difficulty of penetration. This balance applies to key lengths as well. Different computer encryption algorithms have different requirements to ensure safety, but only a handful are generally accepted to be breakable only through brute force attacks. However, determining whether a key is long enough depends on various factors, including

- ♦ How long must the ciphertext remain private?
- ♦ How valuable is the ciphertext?
- ♦ How many resources can the attacker apply, and for how long?

Taking the last item first, the determination of the attacker is best gauged by the number of processor cycles that can be applied to the problem of decrypting your cyphertext. This changes over time. As computer processors improve in speed, the number of cycles that a single computer can perform per second increases. Likewise, as the cost of computers drops over time, the number of computers that can be applied to any particular brute force attack can also increase. Finally, the amount of time necessary for any given attack will also decrease as the number of computers and their relative performance increase.

The resources that the potential attacker can throw into the attempt, therefore, will determine how valuable a ciphertext must be before it is worthwhile to attempt to break the encryption. Likewise, how long that secret is valuable also limits the attacker.

When encrypting a secret worth, for example, $1000, the cost of successfully breaking the encryption should be at least $1000 in computer time and attacker effort. If that secret has a lifetime of months, a key length that would fall to a brute force attack in less than months would be insufficient. This is roughly the situation encountered with credit card payment information, and despite the recent successful brute force attack against the standard DES encryption algorithm used for many commercial transactions, in general it is still much easier for a criminal to acquire credit card numbers in other ways as of 1998—but that will almost certainly change.

On the other hand, consider a secret worth $10 billion that retains its value over decades. This could be a state secret of the sort that might be used by an evil mastermind, or it could be a trade secret of some sort. In any event, such a piece of information would surely require a far longer key than more ordinary types of data.

Finally, consider much-lower-value information, such as the contents of your personal e-mail. Encrypting this information may not even be strictly necessary, but if it is, the key length should probably be as long as possible without causing inconvenience to the authorized users of the data. In practice, this may mean a similar level of protection for almost all your data because a reasonable level of security is possible with relatively low impact. There is no need to resort to 40-bit encryption for low-value data, for example, if 128-bit encryption is readily available and will not affect performance because there is no added cost to using the longer key and using the shorter key offers no advantages.

MOORE'S LAW AND CRYPTOGRAPHY: Remarkably accurate for most of the past 25 years but still more a rule of thumb, Moore's law states that the computing power of available microprocessors doubles roughly every 18 months. This has a critical impact on cryptography: A brute force attack against a set-length key that today takes a year will 18 months from now likely take only six months. In six years (four 18-month cycles), the same key will likely be breakable through a brute force attack in a bit more than three weeks.

The relationship between key length and brute force attacks is discussed elsewhere, in particular in Schneier's *Applied Cryptography*. More up-to-date calculations are readily available through Internet resources but for end-users, available key lengths are limited by the software or hardware being used and by the performance of the systems being used to encrypt and decrypt the data.

Judging Encryption Technologies

Cryptography is like chess, in a way. It takes a special kind of mind, and there are very few people who can really do it well. You can play chess for the enjoyment of it, and you can also do cryptography for its own sake—but amateur cryptographers tend not to be able to build usable algorithms that can withstand concerted attacks and that can be relied upon to secure valuable information.

Proprietary Algorithms and Snake Oil

Among those conversant about the issues of modern cryptography, anyone who sells products that implement proprietary encryption algorithms should be willing to make those algorithms available for review. The justification is that any encryption product that relies on obscuring the algorithm being used is unlikely to be very secure. All it would take to break it, in fact, would be to discover the algorithm. Whether through illegal break-ins or simply by bribing an employee, such disclosure does not present an insurmountable problem. For example, one fairly important proprietary algorithm, RC4 (devised by Ron Rivest of RSA fame; see the section later in this chapter on public key encryption) was published over the Internet a few years ago.

The term *snake oil* when applied to cryptography usually refers to a product or approach to cryptography that violates all known precepts. Snake oil usually pours forth from an individual or small company not otherwise known for cryptographic expertise, and often makes promises that contradict generally accepted cryptographic science. Snake oil can usually be identified by extravagant claims and a reluctance to disclose the algorithms being used. (The perpetrators often claim that since the algorithms have been submitted for patent protection, they cannot be made public.)

In general, serious encryption algorithms are published in peer-reviewed journals, which means that other cryptographers will attempt to determine whether the algorithm is strong or weak. Alternatively, a vendor that wants to prove a new algorithm is strong would hire professional cryptographers to analyze the algorithm; vendors of snake oil generally have less incentive to pay good money to prove that their product is worthless. Snake oil vendors may offer anyone the opportunity to examine their algorithm under a nondisclosure agreement, or offer some token fee to anyone who can break their algorithm—however, these arrangements usually cost the vendor little or nothing, and since most expert cryptographers currently have more highly-paid consulting work than they can handle, there is little incentive for them to examine these products. One vendor even offered to sign over the company to anyone who could prove that their algorithm was insecure. Of course, once the algorithm was proven worthless, so would the company.

Experts and Market Forces

As of the late 1990s, the accepted choices for encryption are focused on the handful of algorithms that have proven themselves over many years of attack by academics, as well as in general use in business applications. This makes a lot of sense. Why should any business use a new, unproven algorithm when there are alternatives that have been reliably in use for many years? This tendency to employ proven solutions for encryption provides a high degree of confidence over time, because the high concentration of users of any particular algorithm will draw additional resources devoted to continually testing and attacking the algorithm.

In other words, cryptographers are more likely to attack the most well-known and impervious algorithms, rather than wasting their time on less well-known algorithms that do not have a long and successful track record. This tends to strengthen existing algorithms that can continue to withstand attacks; other and newer algorithms that are introduced through peer-reviewed publications can also be brought on track as they are studied, without trusting them prematurely by implementing them in commercial systems. As existing algorithms are weakened, the newer algorithms that prove themselves stronger and more efficient than existing algorithms can be brought on line in commercial products.

Secret Key (Symmetric) Encryption

As its names imply, secret key or symmetric encryption uses secret keys and is symmetric. In other words, the same key is used to encrypt as well as to decrypt the ciphertext—and in all cases, the key must remain a secret to all but those entities authorized to encrypt or decrypt data.

Secret key encryption tends to be relatively easy to implement either in dedicated hardware or as software (although some algorithms are easier to implement in hardware), and in either case will run reasonably efficiently. In fact, many protocols that use public key encryption use it only to encrypt a secret key, which is used in turn to encrypt an entire data stream because the secret key encryption is more efficient than public key encryption.

Secret Key Encryption Mechanics

Successful secret key encryption algorithms use a fairly simple set of functions and procedures in the attempt to take identifiable plaintexts and turn them into what appear to be random bits of ciphertext. The concept of *block encryption* is central to most secret key algorithms. Rather than taking one byte or character at a time, a group of bytes is grouped together into blocks for encryption. Each block may be operated on with any combination of the following processes:

- substitution
- permutation
- encryption functions

Each of these processes is discussed at greater length next. The combined processes can be applied repeatedly for some number of encryption *rounds* before the final ciphertext is generated. Finally, the ciphertext can be re-encrypted with the same algorithm but with any number of additional keys for even greater security.

Block Encryption

Encrypting one character at a time means that ciphertext and plaintext characters are related one-to-one, and can be therefore susceptible to various types of attacks. Encrypting in blocks several bytes long is very much like using a polygram substitution cipher. Each block of several bytes is encrypted together, resulting in a very different ciphertext for similar plaintexts. For example, the plaintext "Mary had a little lamb . . . ," if encrypted as a block, might be rendered very differently from the plaintext "Mary had a little lamp . . ." If those two plaintexts were encrypted character by character with the same key, however, the ciphertexts would look very similar.

In practice, the weakest form of block encryption is to simply split a message into blocks of the same length and encrypt each block with the same key. In an extreme example, we have encrypting a database (or spreadsheet report) with fields and records that break evenly with the encryption block size. When fields within each record are duplicated, the same ciphertext will be generated. If an attacker has an idea of what the underlying plaintext represents (for example, if the attacker knows that an encrypted file contains regional sales figures), then the actual contents may be estimated with a fair degree of accuracy by the attacker.

To avoid this problem, most block encryption algorithms are implemented with some form of *block chaining*. Using some random or pseudo-random number to initialize with, all blocks are *XORed* (*exclusive OR* is a simple binary operation used often in encryption; see the accompanying box) with a changing value before being encrypted. For example, a simple form of block chaining uses a random value, which is XORed with the first block; from then on, each succeeding block is XORed with the previous encryption block. This means that if a block were to repeat, it would still be encrypted differently even when using the same key.

To illustrate, consider that I begin all my correspondence the same way, with my full name, address, and telephone number—after all, that is what is at the top of my letterhead. If I encrypt all my correspondence, then every ciphertext provides attackers with a known plaintext. If an attacker intercepts enough of my messages, they may more easily be able to succeed in breaking my encryption. However, if I use block chaining, every time I generate a ciphertext I also generate a short sequence of random data that is appended to the beginning of my messages. Every time I send a message, I generate a different random sequence. This means that every message starts out differently. To begin with, the random sequence is encrypted and produces a ciphertext of a random sequence; more importantly, the real start of each message (which is always the same plaintext—my name and contact information) is also always different because its value changes (because it is being XORed with the random sequence) every time.

Substitution

As discussed earlier in this chapter, substitution is one strategy used by many encryption algorithms. Simply replacing one character for another, however, tends to let in a bit too much light on the ciphertext, so substitution is often used on blocks of characters instead. The effect is to have a one-to-one mapping between blocks of characters of plaintext and blocks of ciphertexts that are the same size but that do not have any discernable relation to one another. This concept of having a small change in the plaintext cause a large change in the ciphertext helps to improve algorithm security.

Encryption substitutions usually use some form of easily reversed function that takes as input a plaintext block and the key, and produces as output a random-appearing ciphertext. That function can be anything from some sort of lookup table to a simple binary operation like the XOR function.

THE EXCLUSIVE OR : In normal conversation, the word or has a special meaning when used with two or more statements in this form: "Condition A or condition B is true." If either of those two conditions are correct (or if both are correct), the statement will be true. When put into mathematical terms, this is considered the *inclusive* or function. In other words, given the conditions (A, B), when either one is true (for binary functions, true is the same as equal to 1; false being equal to 0), the inclusive or function of those two conditions is also true (equal to 1). In other words,

```
inclusive OR (1, 1) = 1
inclusive OR (1, 0) = 1
inclusive OR (0, 1) = 1
inclusive OR (0, 0) = 0
```

A different use of the word or is called the *exclusive* or (also sometimes expressed as XOR). The exclusive or is used to indicate that either one condition or the other is true, but not both conditions. In other words, given two conditions (A, B), when one of those (but not both) is equal to 1, the value of the exclusive or function on those two values is also equal to 1. The complete set of possibilities for two values being XORed is

```
exclusive OR (1, 1) = 0
exclusive OR (1, 0) = 1
exclusive OR (0, 1) = 1
exclusive OR (0, 0) = 0
```

The interesting thing about the XOR function is that it can be used to reverse itself.

```
Take the value A =    101011
XOR it with B =       101010
The result is C =     000001
XOR with B again:     101010
The result is A:      101011
```

This turns out to be a very useful function with which to build encryption algorithms.

Permutation

Simply jumbling up the characters of a plaintext, as discussed earlier in this chapter, tends to turn the the plaintext into an anagram if used alone. Even if the function used to do the permutation appears to be random, the problem to attackers is not so much figuring out what that function is as it is to figure out what the plaintext is—and that can be done without necessarily knowing how the characters were mixed up in the first place.

When combined with a good substitution process, permutation can be a useful ingredient to be used when building an encryption algorithm. For example, most text messages consist of 7-bit ASCII characters. If you have a method of scrambling up the bits in the message so that they do not appear to be ASCII characters but rather look like random bits evenly distributed across 8-bit bytes, you remove a potential avenue of attack from your encryption algorithm.

Encryption Functions

The strongest encryption algorithms use only a handful of actual functions to operate on plaintexts using ciphertexts to produce ciphertexts. One, the exclusive or, has already been discussed; there are others that use some form of binary additions or multiplications, as well as some that use modular arithmetic functions (to be discussed later in this chapter).

Plaintext bits can also be permuted as part of the encryption function, and although permutation is not thought to always be a necessary part of a successful encryption algorithm, it is an important part of some encryption algorithms.

One way to implement a substitution function is through the use of a construct referred to as a *substitution box* or *S-box*. The S-box function takes some bit or sets of bits as input, and spits out some other bit or set of bits as output according to some replacement table. The replacement table may actually map more than one input to a single output, so that faced with a particular piece of output from an S-box, one could not determine which of the several possible inputs had been used to produce the result.

When there are more than one inputs that can produce the same output from an S-box, another function, known as *expansion permutation*, may be used. An expansion permutation takes a block of data and expands it, perhaps by breaking it up into smaller groups, but a set of overlapping groups. In other words, a block of 48 bits can be expansion permuted into a block of 64 bits by breaking the 48 bits into eight groups of six bits. Add to each group the bit that precedes it and the bit that follows it, and you now have eight groups of eight bits each. If the S-boxes are properly designed, and if the data overlaps enough, it will be possible to recreate the original, unexpanded, 48 bits, even if the expanded pieces get replaced in the S-boxes from shorter sequences. (Two or more different pieces are mapped to a single replacement.)

These are some of the ingredients of an encryption algorithm. Some or all of them may be combined in different ways to produce the actual algorithm. However, simply mixing and matching some set of encryption functions will not necessarily produce a secure algorithm.

Encryption Rounds

Part of the complexity of encryption algorithms comes from the use of multiple rounds. Consider the simple substitution cipher. Once you have used it to encrypt a plaintext, using it again (even with a different substitution alphabet) will not make it any more secure. You could re-encrypt the ciphertext thousands of times, using thousands of different substitution alphabets, but it will still be susceptible to the same type of frequency attacks as the ciphertext encrypted only once, because the ciphertext characters will always be directly mapped to the original plaintext characters.

On the other hand, using a more complicated encryption algorithm to begin with (for example, one that uses a combination of substitutions and permutations), actually can improve the security of the algorithm by using multiple *rounds* of encryption. If you are shifting as well as replacing bits of plaintexts, additional apparent randomness can be added to the resulting ciphertexts. As will become apparent as specific symmetric encryption algorithms are discussed, as many as 8 or 16 different encryption rounds are commonly used.

Risks and Benefits

Secret key encryption algorithms have some very important benefits:

- ♦ The most important algorithms are reasonably well understood and seem to be safe from all but brute force attacks.
- ♦ The most important algorithms are old enough to have been subjected to many years of review and have been found most secure against most attacks.
- ♦ Secret key algorithms are relatively simple to implement in either software or hardware.
- ♦ Secret key algorithm implementations are efficient enough to be used to encrypt large volumes of data, or to be used for data stream encryption, with minimal impact on system resources.
- ♦ Secret key algorithms are conceptually relatively easy to understand, and users feel comfortable with the concepts involved.

Secret key encryption simplicity is a major benefit. As long as two parties (and only those two parties) know the secret key, they can communicate securely. However, some of the disadvantages of secret key encryptions derive from this quality. Secret key encryption disadvantages, which tend to manifest themselves as risks, include

- ♦ Use of secret key encryption to protect data being shared by more than two users is risky if all communicants share the same key, because the more individuals know the key, the more likely it is to be stolen, lost, or given up.

◆ Use of secret key encryption to protect data being shared by more than two users is unwieldy if each individual maintains a separate key to be used to communicate with each other individual. When all recipients must receive a copy of an encrypted message, the message must be encrypted (and transmitted) separately for each recipient.

◆ Disclosure of a secret key exposes all communications and data that have been encrypted with that key, through all the time the key was in use.

◆ Disclosure of a secret key exposes all communications and data that will be encrypted with that key in the future unless the user becomes aware of the loss of the key, or unless the key is changed frequently.

◆ A secret key stored in any form, whether human- or machine-readable, is susceptible to theft or loss.

As long as the risks and benefits of secret key encryption are considered during implementation of a data security architecture, advantage can be taken of the benefits, while avoiding the riskier features. For example, assuming that there is a mechanism for easily and securely sharing a secret key between two parties, that shared key can be used to encrypt a message or a short series of messages, and then discarded, thus avoiding some of the problems that arise from the distribution of static keys.

Important Secret Key Encryption Algorithms

Computer product consumers, even corporate customers, rarely have much say over how specific aspects of the product are implemented, nor is it common for them to be able to look under the hood at the inner workings of the implementation. Even if we could take a peak at how encryption were implemented in commercial products, most of us would have little or no idea of what algorithms were being used or whether those algorithms were implemented correctly and securely.

In this not uncommon situation, consumers tend to rely on the use of brand names. When ordering a hamburger, we hope that the meat in it is wholesome and free of contamination. When purchasing computer products that incorporate encryption, we generally have little more to go on beyond the vendor's word that a certain type of algorithm has been used. When the vendor assures us that the algorithm is a proprietary one, brewed up by one of the vendor's own engineers working in her spare time, the chances are good that the algorithm is a flawed one. However, most of the products incorporating encryption features that are achieving any degree of success and market penetration also happen to use reasonably well known and well understood algorithms.

Some of the more important of these algorithms include

- ◆ Data Encryption Standard (DES).
- ◆ International Data Encryption Algorithm (IDEA).
- ◆ RC2, RC4, and RC5.

These are not the only symmetric encryption algorithms in general use, but they are the most important ones. They provide a starting point. If a vendor indicates that one or more of these algorithms have been incorporated into a product, there is a much better chance that the product will do encryption securely and effectively than if the vendor claims to have built a proprietary algorithm.

Data Encryption Standard (DES)

At almost precisely the same time that the United States government gave permission to vendors Netscape and Microsoft, among others, to export software that uses strong encryption (keys as long as 128 bits), an informal group sharing spare computer cycles through the Internet had successfully employed a brute force attack against 56-bit key Data Encryption Standard (DES). The United States National Bureau of Standards (now the NIST, National Institute of Standards and Technology) published DES in 1977 as a standard for commercial encryption and for use by government agencies to encrypt nonclassified data.

Since then, DES has become an important component of security for business computing in large part because, despite recent successes, it has still proven over the years to be resistant to all known attacks. Used with a longer key, or implemented with some refinements, DES will probably continue to enjoy widespread acceptance, at least for a few years, despite its age.

DES was derived from work done by IBM, as well as having considerable input from the supersecret NSA (the National Security Agency, the organization responsible for monitoring—and interpreting—plaintext and ciphertext communications for the United States). DES is important because it was the first time that the precise specification of a strong encryption algorithm was made public, and as such it is worth taking a somewhat more detailed look at that algorithm.

DES uses 16 rounds of encryption, with each round consisting of several steps. Before the first round, each 64-bit plaintext block gets an initial permutation that jumbles up the bits; this permutation is reversed after the last round. Each of the 16 rounds consists of the following steps:

◆ A round sub-key is created from the 56-bit DES key. Each round uses a different key generated from the main key by splitting the key, permuting the results, and selecting a 48-bit round key. This is called a compression permutation.

◆ The 64-bit input plaintext block is split into two halves: the right and the left.

◆ The 32-bit piece of the input block on the right passes along to the next round, but as the left side. At the same time, the right half of the data is processed with some encryption functions as well.

◆ The right half of the data is expanded from 32 bits to 48 bits. This makes it the same length as the round key.

◆ The expanded right half of the data is XORed with the round key.

◆ The results of that exclusive OR are fed into DES S-boxes, with each 6-bit input substituted with a 4-bit output. The result is a 32-bit value.

♦ That 32-bit value is run through another permutation function.

♦ The result of that permutation function is exclusive ORed with the leftmost 32-bit portion of the original 64-bit input block, and that result becomes the right half of the block to be used for the next round. (The right half of the original 64-bit input block becomes the left half of the block to be used for the next round.)

Figure 2.8 shows how a DES round works.

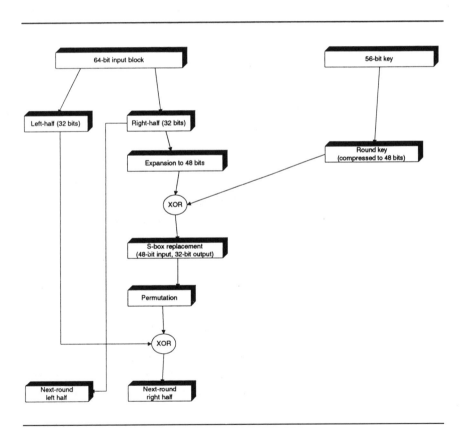

Figure 2.8. The DES encryption round uses several steps, repeated a total of 16 times, to encrypt a plaintext.

DES decryption and encryption use the exact same process, the only difference between them being the order in which the round keys are used. In other words, to encrypt a plaintext, you would generate a series of 16 different 48-bit round keys from the 56-bit secret key. These can be referred to as key_1, key_2, key_3, and so on through to key_{16}. The first encryption round uses key_1, and so on. Decrypting the resultant ciphertext requires simply that the last round key used to encrypt the plaintext be the first round key used to decrypt the ciphertext. Thus, decryption uses key_{16} for the first round, followed by key_{15}, key_{14}, and so on down to key_1 for the last round.

FOR GREATER SECURITY, TRIPLE DES : DES is no longer as invulnerable as it once was. The successful Internet-based brute force attack, while representing an impractical way to steal a credit card number, does seem to toll a death knell for the usable life of the algorithm. However, one approach to extending DES's life is called triple DES.

If running a plaintext through DES with a single 56-bit key provides almost enough security, running the plaintext through DES three times, with three 56-bit keys, produces a much higher expectation of security. Because the input to the second DES pass is the ciphertext output from the first pass, and the input to the third DES pass is the ciphertext output from the second pass, attempting a brute force attack against triple DES is far more difficult than simply doing three brute force attacks against the final ciphertext. This is because it is hard to tell when the brute force attack against the intermediate ciphertext is successful. The "plaintext" input to the last DES pass is, itself, ciphertext and as such it will appear to be random data.

Triple DES is attractive because of its interoperability with single DES—triple DES is no more and no less than single DES, repeated three times.

Consumers wishing to protect relatively transient data from individuals or small organizations will find that DES should still be sufficient. However, DES should not be considered sufficient to protect data from large organizations or governments. Estimates of the cost of building a DES-breaking machine capable of using brute force methods to decrypt DES ciphertexts range from the tens of thousands of dollars to the millions, although the cost of such a machine drops considerably with every improvement in processor price and performance.

International Data Encryption Algorithm (IDEA)

Rolled out publicly in 1991, the International Data Encryption Algorithm (IDEA) is considered by expert cryptographers to be one of the most secure algorithms currently available for secret key block encryption. IDEA employs 128-bit keys and 16 rounds of encryption that use a handful of fairly simple functions to encrypt 64-bit blocks of plaintext. The 128-bit key is expanded into a total of 52 16-bit keys, which are used differently in odd and even encryption rounds. Encryption rounds employ the XOR function as well as modular addition and multiplication. Unlike DES, IDEA was designed to be easy to implement in software.

Although IDEA is an important algorithm, and despite its long record of relative invulnerability, it has not been implemented as widely as DES. This may be due to its status as a patented design, which must be licensed for use—unlike DES, which does not need to be licensed.

RC2, RC4, and RC5

Ron Rivest, one of the world's leading cryptographers working for RSA Data Security, Inc. (bought out by Security Dynamics in 1997), developed a series of eponymous ciphers. Rivest's Codes 2, 4, and 5, also known as RC2, RC4, and RC5, are all the products of RSA and all are available to be licensed for use in a variety of products. RSA considers the details of RC2 and RC4 to be trade secrets, while RC5 has been submitted for patent protection.

RC2 is a block cipher that supports the use of variable length keys, but that operates on 64-bit blocks of plaintext. It was intended to be a replacement for DES that would operate efficiently in software.

RC4, unlike the algorithms already discussed, is a stream cipher. This means that the algorithm operates on 8-bit bytes rather than larger blocks of data. First developed in 1987, the details of RC4 were published anonymously in 1994 on the cypherpunks mailing list and eventually made their way to Usenet newsgroups. RC4 is used in a variety of products, most notably Lotus Notes.

RC5 is another block cipher developed by Rivest at RSA. It allows the implementer or user to decide the size of the blocks to be encrypted, the length of the keys, and the number of encryption rounds to be used.

Prior to 1997, RC2 and RC4 were accorded special export status by the U.S. government, allowing them both to be exported in implementations supporting keys no longer than 40 bits.

Cryptographic Hashes and Message Digests

While the ability to turn a plaintext into a ciphertext that can be easily turned back into the plaintext is clearly valuable, so is the ability to take a plaintext and apply a function to it that will return some value that has the following features:

- It is easy to calculate, given any particular message.
- It is hard to reconstruct the original message using the calculated value.
- It is hard to find another message that will generate the same result as your message.
- It is hard to find any two messages that will generate the same result.

These functions are known as one-way hash functions, also often referred to as message digest functions. They are extremely useful in cryptography to provide some means of checking that the message that was sent is identical to the message being received. In this they function much like a decimal check digit (which has a 1 in 10 chance of being reproduced by chance) or a checksum function (which has a 1 in 2n chance of being reproduced by chance where n is equal to the number of bits in the checksum). However, unlike check digits or checksums, cryptographic hashes are intended to provide a higher degree of assurance on the integrity of the message.

Hash functions are used to generate what amounts to a digital fingerprint of a message. The reason they are sometimes called digest functions is that instead of taking the original message and creating an output of the same length, the hash function produces an output of some fixed, and usually shorter, length than the original message. The most commonly used hash functions generate 128-bit outputs; shorter outputs would tend to make it too easy for sometime to use a brute force approach to find messages that produce the same hash as your message, while longer outputs are unnecessarily long.

 Cryptographers have come to use the names *Alice* and *Bob* to refer to two entities wishing to communicate securely.

To understand the requirements just listed, we can consider how someone might use a hash function: to verify that a message received is indeed the message that was sent. The message itself need not even have been encrypted, but could have been sent in plaintext over an open network (though hashes have added value when dealing with encrypted data and other secrets). Taking each requirement one by one, we can examine how a hash function is meant to work:

- ♦ The hash function should be easy to calculate because it must be calculated on every message sent and received.
- ♦ If it were easy to reconstruct the original message from the hash, the value of the hash is reduced. For example,

Bob and Alice can use the same hash function to prove to each other that they share the same secret. Both of them hash their secret and exchange the values; if the hashed values match, they can each assume that the other has the same secret. If the hash can be used to arrive at the value of the message being hashed, this use of the function is eliminated.

◆ If it were easy to find a message that produces the same value as some target message, then the security of the hash is eliminated. For example, Alice might send Bob the message "buy 100 shares of Acme," but if Bob were able to come up with an alternate message that produces the same hash as Alice's message, Bob could claim that was the message he received. By manipulating the precise wording, punctuation, and various other options, Bob might be able to generate a message with a totally different meaning (for example, "Bob, this is Alice. I'd like you to liquidate all my accounts and just do whatever you want with the money. Thanks for everything. Love, Alice"). This is why it must be hard to find a message that produces the same hash value as your message.

◆ If it were easy to find two random messages that produce the same hash, then digital fraud would be a simple matter of the criminal generating two messages, both relevant, but with radically different meanings. To build on the previous example, the difficult of finding two random messages with the same hash value means that Bob could not send a message to Alice that said something like "Alice, respond with a yes if you want me to sell your 100 shares of Acme" and then later claim that Alice's assent was to a different message, like "Alice, please confirm that you want me to liquidate all your assets and retire on them."

Important cryptographic hashes include MD4 and MD5 (Message Digest 4 and 5) from RSADSI and the Secure Hash Algorithm (SHA) specified by the NIST with the NSA. Cryptographic hashes use a variety of manipulations that are similar to those used for other cryptographic functions. Hashes are of vital importance as applied to modern cryptography, particularly as they apply to the implementation of public key cryptography and especially digital signatures, as discussed in the next sections.

Public Key (Asymmetric) Encryption

Secret key encryption has been with us for centuries in one form or another. Although they may not be totally intuitive, the basic concepts of secret key encryption are certainly accessible to the layperson, without any requirement to understand any complicated mathematics or computer science. The biggest problem with secret key encryption is the necessity to securely convey the secret key to both ends of a communications channel. The encryption method may be safe, but if the key cannot be passed from one user to the other securely, the data encrypted with it cannot be considered safe.

The discovery of an asymmetric function that allows data to be securely encrypted using one key while using a different key to decrypt the ciphertext is an invaluable adjunct to secure data communications. The asymmetric function means that not only is it no longer necessary to keep an encryption key private, it is possible (and in many cases desirable) to publicize the public encryption key. This enables anyone with access to the key to originate encrypted data that can only be decrypted by the holder of the private key. Whereas before, the only way for two individuals to exchange encrypted data was to have one choose a key and pass it to the other, with public key encryption anyone can encrypt data with an entity's key—with no prior contact and no worry about a compromised secret key.

Public key cryptography, while not quite as intuitive or familiar as secret key cryptography, is still surprisingly accessible to the layperson. A detailed discussion of the mathematics behind public key cryptography is included below and in Appendix A. For now, after this section is a brief description of how public key cryptography works, followed by discussion of the more important public key algorithms: Diffie-Hellman and RSA. The section ends with a discussion of how public key pairs are generated.

Public Key Principles

One of the basic problems of cryptography is this: How can two entities that can communicate only over an open channel do so privately? In other words, cryptographers want to make it possible for two people to somehow connect with each other, make each participant aware of a key to be used to encrypt messages for the other, and transmit it all across a medium open to anyone: a crowded room, classified advertisements, or the Internet.

One way to accomplish this type of communication is through the use of asymmetric encryption algorithms, or public key encryption. These functions, which use one key to encrypt a plaintext and another key to decrypt the resulting ciphertext, are proving themselves very useful in many different applications. However, there is another approach to the problem, and that is to create some mechanism that will allow two entities to exchange enough information over an open channel to generate a secret key (to be used with any desired secret key algorithm), but not enough information for anyone but those two entities to figure out what that key is.

Diffie-Hellman Key Exchange

The Diffie-Hellman key exchange algorithm was invented in 1976, and provides a mechanism for two or more parties to exchange just enough information to allow them to share a secret key, which only those parties know, for encrypting a session. However, Diffie-Hellman is for key exchange only. It does not do encryption or decryption. Once two entities have done Diffie-Hellman key exchange, they can then go ahead and use the key with some other encryption algorithm.

The Modulo Function

The mathematics of the Diffie-Hellman key exchange algorithm is fairly simple; the only complication is the use of the *modulo* or mod function (explained in much greater detail in Appendix A). For now, knowing that when evaluating the expression

    $X \bmod Y = Z$

Z is equal to the remainder when dividing X into Y. In other words, 3 mod 7 is equal to 4, and 5 mod 1021 is equal to 1. In all cases, the numbers involved must be integers (no fractional or irrational numbers allowed).

Secure Key Exchange

What cryptographers Whitfield Diffie and Martin Hellman realized was that entities could agree on two numbers (these numbers could even be made public) that provide the basis for secure key exchange. These two numbers have to meet certain requirements. One of the numbers must be a very large (at least around 512 bits long) prime number (a number divisible only by itself and 1). The other number is less restricted, but must be less than the large prime. (There are other conditions, but these are beyond the scope of this discussion.)

Given these two numbers, two entities, Alice and Bob, can now securely exchange enough information to generate a secret key.

How is this possible? First, Alice and Bob each choose a secret number at random; these numbers they keep to themselves. These numbers should be about the same length as the large prime, which we can call P. We'll call Alice's random number A and Bob's random number B. That other number that was chosen at the same time as P but that is shorter than P, we can call N.

The next step is to have both Bob and Alice calculate a value using their random numbers (which they keep secret) and the public values P and N. Each raises the value N to the power of his or her random number, and calculates the value of that power modulo the large prime, to get values a and b. Bob transmits his b value to Alice, and Alice transmits her a value to Bob.

At this point, there are six different values, of which all but two have been sent over a public medium. The only two values that are actually private are

```
A = a random, secret number chosen by Alice
```

B = a random, secret number chosen by Bob

The public values are

P = a large (512-bit) prime
N = an integer smaller than P
a = (N^A) MOD P
b = (N^B) MOD P

Once Bob and Alice have these values, they can each compute one more value, which becomes their shared secret. Bob computes a value X such that

$$X = (a^B) \text{ MOD } P$$

Alice computes a value Y such that

$$Y = (b^A) \text{ MOD } P$$

The two resulting values Y and X are equivalent. This is because

$X = (a^B)$ MOD P
$(a^B) = (N^A)^B$
$(N^A)^B = N^{AB}$
$X = N^{AB}$ MOD P

The same holds true for Y:

$Y = (b^A)$ MOD P
$(b^A) = (N^B)^A$
$(N^B)^A = N^{BA}$
$= N^{BA}$ MOD P

Because the following is true:

$$N^{AB} = N^{BA}$$

the following is also true:

$$X = N^{AB} \text{ MOD } P = N^{BA} \text{ MOD } P = Y$$

This value can then be used as a key to whatever type of algorithm Bob and Alice want to use to encrypt the rest of their dialogue. The reason it works is that anyone listening in would have to do some prodigious feats of calculation to figure out Bob's and Alice's secret numbers.

Diffie-Hellman Drawbacks

The biggest problem with Diffie-Hellman key exchange is that there is no way for Bob to be sure that the person who claims to be Alice actually is Alice. Because the original large prime P and the integer N (upon which all key exchanges are based) are transmitted over a public medium—or even published for use by members of a group—anyone with access to those values can initiate a key exchange.

In other words, someone claiming to be Alice could start a key exchange going with Bob and there is no foolproof, in-band (using the same communication medium being used to do the key exchange) mechanism for Bob to determine whether or not it actually is Alice contacting him. Using an out-of-band mechanism, Bob and Alice could eliminate this problem by arranging to meet face to face or by passing P and N to each other during a phone conversation.

Rivest-Shamir-Adleman Public Key Encryption

Ron Rivest, Adi Shamir, and Len Adleman discovered a method of encryption that went beyond key exchange over a public network and enabled two parties to actually encrypt information using a publicly known key while permitting only the desired recipient to decrypt the ciphertext. The RSA algorithm was first published in the late 1970s, and a patent for the process was granted in the United States in 1983. Since then, the algorithm has succeeded in winning a large share of the commercial security market through its elegance and simplicity—as well as its high degree of security.

Public and Private Keys

Although the details of the mathematics behind RSA are discussed at the end of this chapter, the mechanics can be explained very simply. The first step in RSA is to generate a key pair: one private key to be kept secret by the owner of the pair, the other public key to be published and used by anyone wishing to encrypt a message to the owner. To generate a key, you must come up with the following values:

p and q Two large prime numbers chosen at random

n The product of p and q

e A value relatively prime to $(p - 1)(q - 1)$

The public key is simply the values n and e; the private key is the values of n and the multiplicative inverse of e. (This is a fairly simple function explained in Appendix A.) That's all there is to it. Encrypting a plaintext with one key will produce ciphertext that can be decrypted only with the other key; attempting to decrypt with the same key used to encrypt a text will not produce plaintext.

Public Key Encryption and Decryption

Encrypting data with a public key is simple. You encrypt a block of data (turn it into a value c for ciphertext) by treating it as a numerical value, m (for message), and calculating the value of

$$c = m^e \bmod n$$

In other words, the plaintext block is raised to a very large power of itself and then a remainder is calculated for that value relative to another very large number. That is all there is to that.

Decrypting a public key ciphertext is equally simple. Determining the message data is done by calculating the value of

$$m = c^e \bmod n$$

Digital Signatures

It should be obvious by now that Bob can publish a public key, which anyone (including people who know Bob as well as complete strangers) can use to encrypt data that only Bob can decrypt. Keep in mind that the public key encryption algorithm uses a one-way function: Run data through the one-way function using the public key and you get encrypted data; run the encrypted data through the function with the private key and you get plaintext. This works the other way around as well: Run plaintext through the one-way function with the private key, and the result is ciphertext that can be decrypted simply by using the public key.

While public key encryption, like symmetric encryption, renders the contents of a message illegible to anyone but the holder of the proper key, digital signatures merely add data to the message but do not change the message itself. If you choose not to verify a digitally signed message, you can still read it; the fact that it appears to be digitally signed does not necessarily imply any additional validity to the message. Figure 2.9 shows that it can be impossible (or at least difficult) to determine which message's signature is valid. The only sure way to know that a digital signature is actually certifying the validity of a message is to use the appropriate software and run through the process of verifying the message with the sender's public key.

Two important standards for digital signatures currently in general use include one from RSADSI that uses the same public key encryption algorithm as is used for RSA public key encryption; the other is the Digital Signature Standard (DSS) developed by the NIST, and it uses its own algorithm, known as the Digital Signature Algorithm (DSA). Both are discussed next.

RSA Digital Signature

RSADSI developed the Public Key Cryptography Standard (PKCS) as a method of specifying how cryptographic data was formatted for smoother interoperation. PKCS represents a set of standards for

This message's signature is valid:

```
-----BEGIN PGP SIGNED MESSAGE-----
Hash: SHA1
```

This message is signed with a digital signature using the PGP for Personal Privacy product that I
write about in _Personal Encryption Clearly
Explained_.

regards,

- -

```
-----BEGIN PGP SIGNATURE-----
Version: PGP for Personal Privacy 5.0
Charset: noconv

iQA/AwUBNB3U1hY2EkJV+7lIEQJb5gCgtYEufEEAQ5m1B
hbCUAdqlaT8JMMAoL1E ooCmu1Zffreu3+5/bNplmI/k
=A/b2
-----END PGP SIGNATURE-----
```

This message's signature is *not* valid:

```
-----BEGIN PGP SIGNED MESSAGE-----
Hash: SHA1
```

This message is signed with a digital signature using the PGP for Personal Privacy product that I
write about in _Personal Encryption Clearly
Explained_.

regards,
-Homer J. Simpson
```
-----BEGIN PGP SIGNATURE-----
Version: PGP for Personal Privacy 5.0
Charset: noconv

iQA/AwUBNB3U1hY2EkJV+7lIEQJb5gCgtYEufEEAQa;dlkie
fUAdqlaT8JMMAoL1E ooCmu1Zffreu3+5/bNplmI/k =A/b2
-----END PGP SIGNATURE-----
```

Figure 2.9. Two messages that appear to have been digitally signed; one of the messages can be certified, but the other can not.

different functions and types of data, with one standard, for example, to standardize how public keys are exchanged while another standardizes how encrypted data is formatted.

The RSA digital signature standard is part of PKCS #1, which defines how encrypted data is to be represented. The algorithm used to digitally sign a piece of data is the same as that used to encrypt data; the digital signature itself is generated in the following way:

- ◆ The data to be signed is run through a cryptographic hash function.
- ◆ The result of the cryptographic hash function is encrypted with the RSA public key encryption algorithm.
- ◆ The result of the hash function and the type of cryptographic hash being used are placed in PKCS format and the result is the digital signature.

The type of hash used must be specified so that a user can choose among different hashes. This helps to keep the standard fresh in the event that a weakness is found in a hash function (for example, one of RSADSI's functions, MD4 or MD5), but you would like to continue using the standard with some other hash function.

DSS and DSA

The NIST released a proposal for the Digital Signature Algorithm to be used with the Digital Signature Standard (DSS) in 1991, which was followed almost immediately by some controversy about the security of the algorithm because it was developed with the cooperation of the NSA, an agency whose function is to be able to monitor communications (and whose function is threatened by the universal availability of strong cryptography). However, DSA is meant to be strictly a digital signature algorithm, which means that if there are weaknesses they would enable anyone who knows them to impersonate an entity by sending out messages under that entity's signature.

DSA does not have the elegant simplicity of the RSA algorithm, and it has some drawbacks. DSA requires careful selection of public keys; public keys are selected by using groups of values that meet certain specifications, and it is possible to create families of public keys. If the values common to public key families are not chosen well, there may be some weakness; also, if a public key is compromised, all the public keys in the same family will be compromised too. Finally, DSA calls for a significant amount of processing to be done by both the signer and the verifier, making the algorithm slower than RSA.

The DSA public key consists of four different values, three of which can be shared by other users; the fourth is a value that is calculated based on one private key value. The public key values include

- p, a prime no less than 512 bits long and no more than 1024 bits long.
- q, a 160-bit prime that is a factor of p-1.
- g, a value calculated from p and q such that $g^q=1 \bmod p$ (with the only limit on this value being that it cannot be equal to 1).
- n, a value calculated with the private key, K, to be $g^K \bmod p$. K is some number less than q.

In effect, n is a long-term public key (along with the other parts of the public key), while K is the long-term private key associated with it.

When signing a message, there is another public/private key pair to be generated, to be used one time only, with that message. The actual processes of signing and verifying are more complicated than those used by the RSA algorithm, and are beyond the scope of this book. For those interested in understanding how DSA works, it is described in several places including Schneier's *Applied Cryptography*.

Nonrepudiation

A very important feature of digital signatures is that they provide the recipient with a guarantee, as long as the sender has properly protected its private key and as long as the digital signature algorithm is reliable. *Nonrepudiation* is the term given to the quality of a signed message that its sender can not deny having sent it and signed it. In the absence of written receipts or signed personal checks, the nonrepudiation of digitally signed messages is the only thing that makes digital commerce commercially viable. The following illustrations should demonstrate why this is so.

Nonrepudiation Example 1

Bob orders 1000 shares of a particular stock (say, the WXYZ Corporation) from his stockbroker Alice at the market price on Monday morning, $400 a share. Bob digitally signs that message, which includes the company name, number of shares, time and date of the order, and Bob's account number, and sends it to Alice who proceeds to purchase the stock and put it in Bob's account. The next day, that company goes belly up, and Bob's stock is worthless. Had Bob ordered the stock over the telephone, he might be able to argue that he really meant for Alice to order him shares in the Double-U XYZ Corporation (if there is such an entity) or to simply deny that he ever called in the order, perhaps claiming that his evil twin Billy did it without his knowledge.

Unfortunately for Bob, however, he did sign his order. He cannot claim that anyone else generated the signed message since he is the only one with the private key; only he could have generated the message that can be certified with Bob's public key. Alice can prove that Bob made the order, and she should be able to collect.

Nonrepudiation Example 2

Bob orders 1000 shares in the Too Good to Be True Company (TGTBTC) on Thursday afternoon just before the market closes. Alice sends back a digitally signed message committing to buy Bob his shares at the market price of $3 a share; after all, she just bought 1000 shares for herself at that price. She is called away from her desk, and cannot get Bob's order in before the market closes, but thinks she is in good shape since she just bought the shares for herself. Unfortunately for Alice, TGTBTC announces their discovery of a dietary supplement that helps people lose weight while making them immune to cancer and heart disease, it tastes just like ice cream, and costs only pennies per dose. Friday morning the shares open at $500, and Alice will have to give up her own shares.

Since Alice signed her response committing to making the purchase for Bob at the stated price, Alice cannot repudiate the message.

Certificates and Certification Authorities

Public key pairs are great things. As long as you keep the private key private, you can sign any data and always be able to prove that no one else signed it; you will also always be able to decrypt any data sent to you encrypted with your public key and know that no one else will be able to decrypt that data.

There is a problem with public keys, however, and that is how to be sure who belongs to which key. In other words, I can stand before you and read out my public key to you, and you can be fairly certain that I own that particular public key. Likewise, I can publish my public key in this book, and you can again be fairly sure that public key belongs to no one but the entity presenting itself as the author, Pete Loshin (as long as you trust that to be true). However, things break down fairly rapidly, if not sooner, unless you have some mechanism to ensure that the entity claiming to own a particular public key is really who you think they are.

To illustrate the problem, the author's web site is http://www.loshin.com/; there is nothing stopping anyone from creating a counterfeit Pete Loshin web page somewhere else (though why they might want to do that is not clear). For example, someone could create a web site at http://www.somedomain.net/pete_loshin.html. That person could publish a public key there, and claim that it belongs to Pete Loshin. Now, if you needed to send the author of this book a sensitive message and used the key you got at the counterfeit web site, the message would be decipherable only to the owner of the counterfeit public key—not by me.

Another important set of certificate functions relate to certificate validity. For example, in the discussion of nonrepudiation, the signer has no recourse in denying a signed message—unless the signer claims that its private key was somehow compromised. While it is possible for a private key to be compromised without the knowledge of its owner, that would require that the owner did not use proper caution in protecting the public key. Particularly when used for financial transactions, the owner must be particuarly careful about the private key. In that way, the owner would be more likely to be aware immediately if the private key were compromised (e.g., if the private key were stored only on a diskette to be placed in a bank vault, but stolen as the owner is on the way to the bank). Certificates, particularly when they are maintained by trusted third parties, can be revoked in such a case, allowing the owner of a compromised key to immediately revoke that key and allowing any recipients of messages signed with the key to immediately be made aware that the message was signed with a revoked key and is therefore not valid.

The idea behind a certificate is that the public key is not enough. There must be some kind of certification that goes with a public key to verify (in some form, and to greater or lesser extent) who the entity is that is presenting the public key. Certificates are issued by certification authorities (CAs), who take responsibility for ensuring some level of trust in the certificate. This section explains what a certificate is, how it works, and how certification authorities work. Also discussed here is an alternative approach to certifying public keys used by Pretty Good Privacy's PGP applications, called the web of trust.

What Is a Certificate

Very simply, a certificate consists of a public key and identifying information for the entity being linked to the key, as well as information about the certificate that may include

- ◆ The name of the certification authority.
- ◆ A serial number for the certificate.
- ◆ An expiration date for the certificate.

The most important piece of the certificate is the CA's digital signature. The CA signs the certificate to signify that it stands behind the validity of the certificate.

You can have a public key without having a certificate; however, anyone who communicates with you will have to trust that the certificate is yours, and that you are who you say you are. However, even if you get a certificate that has been signed by a CA you trust, you need to check the degree to which the CA will stand behind the data certified. For example, many CAs will issue low-trust certificates to anyone who asks for one, doing little more than linking a name and e-mail address to a public key. The entity requesting such a certificate has probably paid nothing (or a token fee) for the certificate, and the CA does little or no fact checking on the information provided by the applicant. All the CA certifies is that some entity purported to be the entity identified in the certificate.

Individuals may find that these less credible certificates are sufficient for most purposes, for example, to support a pseudonym or for encryption and digital signature of casual e-mail.

Alternatively, CAs may issue more reliable certificates to entities willing to submit more complete documentation of identity, and which documentation the CA verifies independently through credit reporting services and other databases. These certificates can provide a higher degree of reliability and generally cost more. While individuals may find these certificates useful, particularly as more retailers require them from customers to do on-line transactions, they are more commonly used by organizations running secure web sites and by software vendors who use them to certify the authenticity of code distributed over the Internet.

Certificates could reasonably be stored in almost any logical format, but an open standard, the X.509 specification, is increasingly the standard format in which certificates are stored and distributed.

The X.509 Specification and Certificates

X.509 is the specification of a standard for distribution and storage of public keys defined by the International Telecommunications

Union (ITU, formerly the CCITT). Associated with the more generalized directory specification, X.500, the X.509 specification defines the type of data that is stored in the certificate and how that data is formatted. In order to comply with the X.509 standard, a certificate must include

- ◆ A version number referring to the version of the standard the certificate supports.
- ◆ A serial number assigned to the certificate itself by the CA.
- ◆ The CA's signature on the certificate.
- ◆ The name of the certificate issuer.
- ◆ A period of time in which the certificate is valid (a start date and time and an end date and time).
- ◆ The name of the entity being linked to the certificate.
- ◆ Information about the entity's public key, including the algorithm used and the public key itself.
- ◆ A unique identifier issued by the CA.
- ◆ A unique identifier issued by the entity linked with the public key.

Certification Authorities versus Web of Trust

The model of a centralized authority to support the distribution and certification of certificates implied by X.509 and other standards is the predominant model. However, an alternative exists, and has been used successfully since 1991 when Phil Zimmerman first released the Pretty Good Privacy (PGP) program. (See Chapter 7 for more about using PGP for secure e-mail. Chapter 8 says more about using PGP for securing data on your desktop. Chapter 10 looks at the PGP certification model.) Called a web of trust, the model used for certification was one of distributing trust from one entity to another. In practice, one's certificate becomes more trustworthy based on who else you are able to convince to sign your certificate. Distributed servers can maintain information about certificates, but the individual gets to decide whose certificate to trust based on who else trusts the certificate.

The web of trust works like this: Bob gets a PGP public key and starts using it. One day, Bob gets together with an associate, Alice, who also has a PGP key. The two of them sign each other's public keys. This signifies that each believes the other to be the person associated with that public key—this is done with public key fingerprints, generated through a cryptographic hash, which the two exchange. Now, when someone who does not know Bob checks Bob's public key, that person can see that Alice has signed it (thereby indicating that she believes that Bob is the person who he represents himself to be and that the public key she signed is the public key belonging to Bob).

What this ultimately means is that someone who knows and trusts Alice but does not know Bob at all can (to the extent that this person trusts Alice) trust also that Bob's public key can be believed to be Bob's.

The more people sign a key, the more likely it is that a stranger will find someone trustworthy who has signed your key, and thus will trust your key. For example, if Bob has a signature on his key from someone purporting to be the president of the United States, I may not necessarily trust that key (unless I have a way to verify that the signature does indeed come from the White House, and even then I may not trust it depending on who is in office). However, if Bob's public key has also been signed by my brother, I would be more likely to trust it.

3

Social and Political Cryptographic Issues

This chapter raises the issues involved with the use of cryptography that lie outside the technical realm. Largely, this means the issues related to governmental controls over cryptographic tools, including attempts to

- Control access to cryptographic tools.
- Control the import and export of cryptographic tools.
- Ensure government access to data that has been encrypted.

The purpose of this chapter is not to chronicle the twistings and turnings of the politics of encryption. That is best covered in books like Bruce Schneier and David Banisar's *The Electronic Privacy Papers: Documents on the Battle for Privacy in the Age Surveillance* (John Wiley & Sons, 1997) and in other on-line sources including those mentioned in Appendix B. My purpose here is, instead, to examine what it means when a politician champions strict controls over the export of strong cryptography, and what it means when a law enforcement official claims that the security of the country is gravely threatened unless all ciphertexts, produced by any citizen, can be decrypted by the government when and if the need might arise without the permission or even knowledge of the owner of the ciphertext.

The political tide seems to be constantly turning. Concern early in 1997 about the increasing dominance of crypto-control adherents in Congress seemed to wane during the summer, when export controls on cryptography seemed to be loosening, only to wax full again as senators fresh out of closed-door sessions with national security agencies began calling for more controls rather than less. If it seems I'm hedging a little, it is only because political attitudes toward encryption tend to shift depending on whether the politicians have just been lobbied by the high-tech industry pushing for fewer restrictions, which would improve prospects for sale of crypto-enabled products globally, or by the law enforcement community, who brief politicians behind closed doors, very possibly raising the specter of high-tech terrorists and drug lords using encryption to ravage the country while the FBI stands by helpless to do anything about it.

Rather than go into the details of these political maneuverings, this chapter simply outlines what are perceived by government officials as the threats of personal cryptography, and the value of personal cryptography for improving individual freedoms and benefits despite these threats. Also discussed are the general means by which governments are attempting to control cryptography and the reasons why most of these attempts are doomed to failure. Finally, a summary is included of a report released in the summer of 1997 by top cryptographers on the difficulties raised by government and third-party key escrow schemes.

The Threat of Personal Cryptography

Prior to the discovery of cryptographic algorithms that could be strongly implemented in software, only governments (and the richest organizations and individuals) could afford to create or purchase the devices necessary to strongly encrypt and decrypt data. Strong cryptography is crucial to a nation's defense. With it, military commanders can control their forces and gather information without concern about their movements and decisions being intercepted during transmission. Without strong cryptography, those same movements and decisions can be monitored by anyone capable of intercepting and deciphering the transmissions.

This is the root of government concern over strong cryptography. The reasoning goes: If strong cryptography is an essential tool for the waging of war in its function as a facilitator of secret communication, then it should be controlled in the same ways as other tools of war including things like jet fighters, armored tanks, nuclear devices, and automatic firearms.

The Loss of Government Control over Data

The key to loss of government control over cryptography is that, despite its power to be used as an armament, cryptography is just so doggone useful for so many other applications. It is almost as if the mechanism of a nuclear bomb turned out to be the same mechanism central to building a better internal combustion engine capable of powering a pollution-free automobile capable of running 100 miles on a glass of tap water.

Similarly, bladed instruments, like knives, scythes, and axes, have been used as weapons of aggression for thousands of years—yet these instruments of destruction are readily available to all because their peaceful uses are so plentiful and vital that governments are willing to risk the occasional ax murder in exchange for allowing citizens easy access to a tool for splitting firewood.

The U.S. government in particular has in the past taken a stance that would attempt to regulate all cryptography by treating it as an armament. Unlike nuclear missiles or automatic firearms, however, cryptography has a dual nature. Like any piece of software, while it may be a tool that can be used for some purpose (whether evil or good depends on the user), it also happens to be a set of ideas that can be expressed in words and printed on paper, and is thus capable of enjoying constitutional protection as personal expression.

The end result is that while customs agents can relatively easily monitor the movement of metal-based weaponry through airports, it becomes much more complicated to attempt to control the movement of software algorithms that have been printed out (and in fact, such implementations appear to have been declared constitutionally protected by the courts) or actual implementations of software stored on computer disks or in computer memory. Its portability is part of what makes encryption technology so threatening.

The Threats

There is nothing unusual in a government that fears unfettered and unlimited communications among its citizens. The more freely that people can interact with each other, the more likely it is that they can do things the government would prefer they did not. For example, U.S. travelers to more or less repressive regimes come back relating with wide-eyed amazement how they were never permitted to speak with locals unless a government or party representative was present.

The unusual degree to which free speech is guaranteed in the United States has made it necessary for the government to dig deep to come up with compelling reasons to abridge this right in respect of cryptography. The U.S. government cannot compellingly argue, as more repressive governments might, that wrong-thinking people who want to vote for their leaders rather than have them forced on them would use encryption to plot against the government. We already have the right to vote for our leaders, and we have the right to express ourselves in public so there is no need to encrypt political speech.

However, U.S. politicians and government employees argue that encryption technologies sufficiently strong to protect encrypted data even from large government agencies can and will be used by certain entities to do such profound harm to the national security that those technologies must not be permitted. Most arguments against freely available strong encryption are based on certain activities and missions that such technologies will make difficult or impossible, including the ability to do wiretaps and monitor other communications to or from those suspected of criminal activities. Revelations about the activities of certain government agencies over the past 30 years, particularly as they relate to the monitoring of "suspicious" individuals, tend to make many citizens wary of giving the government increased powers of surveillance—most are opposed to monitoring of individuals holding legal but unpopular political beliefs (including those relating to issues like racial equality and nuclear disarmament).

As a result, government employees and politicians have, in the past few years, started to parade a set of scenarios in which, they believe, the use of encryption poses a threat to the national security and the American way of life. Apparently, the government agencies championing the elimination of freely available strong encryption believe that the normal threats to the social order are insufficient to justify the elimination of access to strong encryption—it is only extraordinary threats that are sufficiently compelling to convince Americans that they should voluntarily give up their access to strong encryption. These threats usually include

- ◆ Espionage. Spying by foreign powers was once the most serious threat to our national security that could be imagined. Before the general availability of encryption through software applications, intelligence activities probably generated a large portion of all encrypted communications. The use of strong encryption by agents of any country makes their activities (so the argument goes) that much less detectable as their communications could be made virtually unreadable by any government agency.
- ◆ Terrorism. A far more compelling argument against encryption, many believe, is that freely available strong encryption will enable the terrorist representatives of groups and governments that have declared the United

States an enemy to carry on their activities with impunity anywhere in the world. If strong encryption is widely available, the argument goes, terrorist groups can use encryption to protect all their communications—which would be virtually unreadable by any government agency.

♦ Drug dealing. Just as the communications of a terrorist organization become unavailable to government agencies, so too do the communications among drug dealers become unavailable to law enforcement agencies. The ongoing "war on drugs" in the United States might be lost (or, more properly, lost even worse) if drug dealers were to use encryption to protect all their communications.

♦ Money laundering, tax evasion, and other financial crimes. Electronic commerce, particularly as it relates to digital cash, is seen as a bonanza for those criminals whose profits are difficult to hide (for example, drug dealers). The use of digital funds and fund transfers, as enabled by strong encryption, is seen by many as potentially drying up what was previously a fruitful approach to law enforcement—especially when the criminals are able to eliminate all the evidence of their crimes except for the fruits.

♦ Child pornography and pedophilia. These truly horrible crimes, like terrorism, occur with or without strong encryption. However, there is a belief in this country and elsewhere that there are huge networks of pedophiles and child pornographers who use the Internet and strong encryption to secretly go about the practice of their crimes, and that by outlawing strong encryption, law enforcement agencies will better be able to monitor and apprehend these criminals.

I have attempted to relate these perceived threats in neutral tones, particularly since there are many well-educated and righteous citizens, politicians, and government employees who truly believe that free access to strong encryption will so stymie law enforcement agencies that they will lose all their effectiveness. I believe this to be wrong. Although the threats they cite are disturbing, I do not believe that the use of encryption by criminals can be used as a justification for outlawing it any more than that the use of electricity by criminals is a valid reason to have the government monitoring the use of every outlet.

The next section examines how personal encryption can add value to the life of any citizen who wishes to use it. The subsequent section explains how governments attempt to control the use of strong encryption, and is followed by a discussion of why government controls just do not make sense.

The Value of Personal Encryption

While there are evil, criminal uses to which personal encryption can be put, it is in and of itself a neutral tool. While some may argue the utility of a firearm for any purpose other than harming another living thing, there is no question that the function performed by a program that encrypts data is basically benign. It turns plaintext into ciphertext. Just as an individual may choose to enclose personal correspondence inside an envelope before mailing it, an individual may also choose to encrypt data before transmitting it over a public network. And just as an individual may keep a file cabinet with a lock on it to restrict access to personal papers and records that are no one else's business, so too an individual may choose to store data on a personal computer that has been encrypted to keep it private.

This section discusses why personal encryption is a valuable and worthwhile tool for all to use in their daily life.

Protecting Personal Data

Almost any personal information is potentially information you would want to protect with encryption, depending on how private a person you are. Encrypted personal data may be transmitted over a network or simply stored on a computer somewhere. Examples of information you might not want to make public, and why, include

- Credit card or other payment information, for the same reason you try not to lose your wallet or purse.
- Personal contact and address information, because you wish to control who knows your telephone number and where you live. For example, a single woman living in a large city may prefer not to give out her telephone number and address to someone she does not know; individuals with unlisted telephone numbers should also be concerned about passing out contact information over a network.
- Scheduling and calendar information, because the more people know your movements, the more likely a criminal can schedule a burglary for the day after you leave for your vacation. Similarly, executives, celebrities, and other high-profile individuals can be targets for harassment.
- Medical information is considered by some to be a very personal matter, particularly if they have used mental health services.
- Employment information is considered by some to be a very personal matter, particularly information about salary and remuneration in general, as well as employment history, personnel file information, job functions, and details of current tasks.
- Social information, which can range from who your friends are (and their contact information), to what organizations you belong to, to details of your romantic life.

Note on Personal Safety

Some people need to know that they can keep their personal information private not just to avoid embarrassment or inconvenience, but to protect their personal safety. For example, individuals who have entered witness protection programs need to know that their location is a secret that cannot be compromised.

There are other innocent victims who may need to rely on encryption to maintain their personal safety. It is unfortunate that there are individuals who feel it is their right to abuse members of their families physically or emotionally. Our society provides some legal recourse to victims of spousal, parental, or child abuse; for example, a court may issue a restraining order against the abuser prohibiting that person from contact with the person or people being abused. However, there is little or nothing a victim can do to protect against an abuser who disregards the restraining order, and law enforcement agencies are not always able to allocate their limited resources to enforce the restraining orders. As a result, abuse victims often need to relocate and to keep their new location a secret. Personal encryption provides a means of keeping this information secret while still allowing the victim to stay in touch with friends, nonabusive family members, and social service providers.

Protecting Business Data

While many of U.S. need or want to use encryption technologies in our business lives, anyone who wants to transact any business over the Internet needs to have the security of knowing that our personal business transactions are protected by encryption. Doing business over the Internet may cause many to reconsider what information they provide to any vendor, on-line or off. However, it is vital to evaluate a vendor's request for information in terms of what information you feel should be sufficient to complete the transaction.

The kind of information that you will very likely be required to provide to a vendor in order to buy something on-line will include

- ◆ Payment information, usually a name, credit card account number, and expiration date.
- ◆ Shipping information, which may include a street address and telephone number if the vendor ships by delivery service. (This should not be necessary if you are purchasing a digital product for immediate on-line delivery.)

Vendors often ask for additional information, which you may be able to omit without affecting the transaction (however, some vendors may require some or all of this additional information):

- Additional contact information, including home and business addresses in addition to shipping addresses, and home and business fax or telephone numbers.
- Additional identification information, including things like your Social Security number, financial institution account information, and drivers license numbers. (Some of this information may be required by law, for example, if you are opening a bank or brokerage account.)
- Demographic information including your age, marital status, gender, income, and education level.
- Marketing information, including what magazines you read, how you heard about the vendor, and what products you are interested in buying in the future or what products you have recently purchased.

Whether and what you choose to disclose to vendors may very well be affected by your having the assurance that it will be transmitted securely across the Internet.

Adding Assurance to Digital Communications

The flip side of public key encryption, the digital signature, is a vitally important tool in making digital commerce a reality. The digital signature provides a tool to the individual as well as to the corporation that makes it impossible for the owner of a certificate to deny a piece of data signed with that certificate. This quality of nonrepudiation means that if a merchant signs and sends you a receipt indicating that you have paid a certain amount for some product on a particular date, the merchant cannot later deny having sent the receipt. Likewise, a consumer who has signed a request for a delivery of product cannot later deny having submitted such a request.

Nonrepudiation of digital transactions that have been signed by the participants has the potential of making digital commerce safer than commerce in so-called meat-space. Digital signatures require the exact same technology as public key encryption, but digital signature implementations tend not to be as highly regulated as other cryptographic functions—after all, governments would be happy if all criminals using digital forms of communication were to sign their messages digitally as it would make it that much simpler to attribute those messages.

Enabling Next Generation Internet Applications

As of 1998, almost all individual consumers still connect to the Internet across relatively slow (modem links no faster than 56Kbps) connections. The potential to do really interesting applications, like video conferencing, audio or video on demand, real-time software leasing, on-line software distribution, and other high-bandwidth applications must wait until consumers have access to the Internet over much higher capacity links.

However, all of these commercial applications also require the deployment of secure commerce mechanisms—almost all of which depend on the use of strong encryption. Furthermore, merchants whose product is being fed down a virtual pipeline that passes through the Internet will not want to expose themselves to the risk of having criminals intercept and steal their content—which means that vendors will need a dependable mechanism for encrpyting content, as well as a dependable mechanism for encrypting the transactions themselves.

Limiting access to strong encryption will have the effect of stopping, or at least slowing, development of this type of commercial service. Development of the Internet as a medium for immediate delivery of goods and services is just a starting point. The Internet has the potential of being a conduit for delivering social services reliably, inexpensively, and immediately to those who need them. Distance learning programs can help educate those who are unable to leave their homes, while distance medicine can help improve delivery of medical services while at the same time keeping costs down.

None of this will be possible, however, unless those who are using the Internet can be assured that the information they send and receive over it can be kept private.

Government Controls on Cryptography

Governments that attempt to control the use of cryptography do so through a variety of methods. Three common ones are

- Limiting the ownership of cryptographic tools. Governments have in the past limited ownership of many devices and technologies that they felt were threatening to the social order, including printing presses, typewriters, fax machines, and computers (among others). Criminalizing the ownership of encryption technologies essentially makes the statement that only those with something to hide would have any recourse to the use of encryption. Currently, the U.S. government allows individuals (citizens) to own and use cryptographic tools.
- Limiting the export of cryptographic tools. Governments that attempt to limit the export of encryption technologies make the statement that while the use of encryption may be an acceptable behavior to be tolerated by one's own citizens, citizens of foreign countries are not to be trusted to use encryption for peaceful purposes. It also tends to imply that the government exercising its control believes that its own encryption technologies are superior to anything available outside its own borders. Currently, the U.S. government limits the export of cryptographic tools, mostly by forbidding the export of strong tools, subject to exceptions. In general, exportable cryptographic tools are those using shorter key lengths, for example, key lengths up to 56 bits are now exportable. Some vendors have been able to receive permission to export stronger encryption if they can prove that the product cannot be used for general cryptography (e.g., it

can be used only to secure a transaction, not to encrypt a message of any length), or if the vendors agree to build in mechanisms that may make it easier to compromise their products.

♦ Mandating the use of key escrow-key recovery systems for all uses of encryption. Governments have at various times proposed the use of key escrow-key recovery systems that either require all encryption users to register their keys with a trusted third party (for example) that would give access to those keys on receipt of appropriate authorization from law enforcement agencies. Key recovery systems can also be characterized as backdoor or trapdoor cryptosystems, which provide security to users but which include some secret method by which authorized entities could easily decrypt all ciphertexts. Governments propose to use key escrow and key recovery systems to permit them continued access to all communications of suspected criminals, just as they currently are able to use court-ordered wiretaps to investigate crime. While key escrow-key recovery has not yet been mandated with legislation by the U.S. government, there have been very strong indications that there is considerable backing for such action.

The Trouble with Government Control

So far, initiatives to limit free access to strong encryption have been limited in large part by their lack of attention to the realities of the state of encryption software distribution and lack of understanding of the market. By and large, they rely on voluntary compliance by individuals and businesses, and on the voluntary cooperation of sovereign states throughout the world. Controls fall into three categories:

♦ Limiting the ownership of strong encryption technologies.
♦ Limiting the export of strong encryption technologies.

♦ Requiring that all users of strong encryption technologies deposit copies of all encryption keys with a key escrow agent to allow law enforcement agencies to decrypt the ciphertexts as needed to enforce the law.

At the moment, the current legislation controlling the distribution of strong encryption has mostly affected the software industry in fostering the growth of cryptography suppliers in countries with minimal controls over the ownership, use, and export of strong encryption. Strong encryption is available within the United States as well as outside the United States; U.S. criminals undoubtedly have access to strong encryption, and the principles of strong public key encryption are well known and well understood throughout the world. In any event, governments still attempt to control the ownership and distribution of strong encryption, and they will face increasing difficulties as they continue to do so.

The Trouble with Limiting Ownership of Cryptography

Without making any comment on the propriety of firearm control laws, consider how difficult they would be to enforce if

♦ Any firearm, of any strength or size, could be duplicated instantly and infinitely.
♦ Anyone who wanted to design and build a firearm could get blueprints and all the machinery necessary to do so at any bookstore.
♦ Any firearm could be transported undetected inside any type of digital storage medium (including a music CD, a tape recording, or a diskette).
♦ Tens of millions of people already have their own firearms, most of them unregistered in any meaningful way.

This is essentially the problem with attempting to control the ownership of strong encryption.

♦ Anyone with a copy of an encryption software package can copy it endlessly and pass it around to relatives and acquaintances.

 ◆ Anyone with programming skills who wants to create his or her own encryption software can go to the bookstore and buy any number of texts that provide algorithms and implementation strategies.
 ◆ Anyone with encryption software can share it by putting it on disk, or sending it over a telephone connection, or using any other transmission method imaginable.
 ◆ Vendors of encryption software have been making their products available through Internet downloads with minimal identity checking for North American residents, and many products are on sale in shrink-wrapped versions in computer stores throughout the continent.

The genie is out of the bottle, and there is nothing anyone can do to make it technologically impossible to use strong encryption. While governments can decide that ownership of strong encryption is against the law, they will have a hard time enforcing any such legislation.

The Trouble with Export Controls

Any attempt to control the export of strong encryption will be subject to all the problems associated with attempting to control the use and ownership of strong encryption software within a nation's borders. However, there are additional problems that spring from commercial and economic issues. International customers faced with the choice of either purchasing exportable U.S. encryption products (which use weak key lengths or incorporate key escrow that essentially open their data to U.S. law enforcement agencies) or purchasing strong encryption products from non-U.S. vendors are most likely to choose not to put their data at risk with the U.S. products.

Some encryption control proposals call for international cooperation among governments to impose U.S.-style controls to include key escrow requirements for all users around the world. The problem with this is that it would require everyone in the world to choose unsecure encryption products (in order to allow U.S. law enforcement agencies to have access to all encrypted data, at least within the United States) rather than allowing individuals and countries to choose safer tools to protect their data.

The Trouble with Key Escrow

Government-mandated key escrow systems are troubling to many, including the author, though not to everyone. Unlike court-ordered wiretaps which permit law enforcement agencies to monitor and record telephone transmissions from particular lines, key escrow systems (if implemented) make it possible to decipher any and all encrypted information at any time. Key escrow systems have many problems, however, and would tend to do nothing more than make the users of escrowed encryption more vulnerable rather than less. Issues include

- ◆ Key escrow systems require very large infrastructures in order to work at all. Every user of encryption needs to register every key, which means that there must be a very large database keeping track of all users and all keys—from now until the key escrow system is removed.
- ◆ Key escrow systems are riskier than non-escrowed cryptosystems because they create new weak points of attack. The escrow agencies are prime targets for hacking, given that they concentrate access to a huge volume of encrypted data.
- ◆ Key escrow systems are riskier than non-escrowed cryptosystems because they require encryption users to trust not just their intended recipient but also every single individual and entity involved in the key escrow system. Employees of the key escrow agency must be trusted not to improperly provide access to keys (for example, not to steal data for themselves, not to do "favors" for friends who want to steal data, and not to do favors for law enforcement agents who feel they need access to data but who have not received or been turned down for authorization). Law enforcement agents and agencies must be trusted not to abuse their powers and give authorization

to access data belonging to individuals based, for example, on their political leanings or support for unpopular causes. Politicians must be trusted not to abuse their powers and force the escrow agencies to divulge data on their political enemies.

♦ Key escrow systems put a burden on users by making encryption more difficult to use (because of the requirements of submitting keys to the escrow agencies) while making it less effective.

Summary of the Report on Key Escrow

In an effort to educate members of the governing classes as well as the governed in the United States about the role of cryptography both as a force for good and the role of government-mandated and -designed key recovery systems as a tool that is both unnecessary and ill-advised, 11 leading cryptographers and computer scientists released a report in May 1997 that discusses the risks of such systems. The authors of the report, titled "The Risks of Key Recovery, Key Escrow, and Trusted Third-Party Encryption," include some of the ablest cryptographers of all time:

♦ Hal Abelson, a professor at MIT and fellow of the IEEE, who was on leave from MIT at the time of the report to serve as a scientific advisor on the Internet for the Hewlett-Packard Corporation.

♦ Ross Anderson is affiliated with Cambridge University, teaching and directing research into computer security, cryptology, and software engineering.

♦ Steven M. Bellovin, co-author of the seminal work on firewalls, *Firewalls and Internet Security: Repelling the Wily Hacker* (Addison-Wesley Professional Computing, 1994), is a researcher with AT&T Laboratories and a member of the Internet Architecture Board (IAB).

♦ Josh Benaloh is a cryptographer who works in the research arm of Microsoft Corporation.

- Matt Blaze, another researcher with AT&T Laboratories, has made significant contributions to the field of cryptology and secure computing.
- Whitfield Diffie is the "Diffie" half of the Diffie-Hellman team who created public key cryptography in 1976. He is currently a Distinguished Engineer with Sun MicroSystems specializing in security.
- John Gilmore, a co-founder of the Electronic Frontier Foundation, has made significant contributions in many ways involving the Internet and personal security.
- Peter G. Neumann, a Principal Scientist in the Computer Science Lab at SRI, is a noted expert on computer-related risks and moderator of the Risks Forum newsgroup.
- Ronald L. Rivest, a professor at MIT in the Electrical Engineering and Computer Science department, is also the "R" in the RSA public key cryptosystem and a co-founder of RSA, Inc.
- Jeffrey I. Schiller, Network Manager at MIT, is author of the Kerberos Authentication System and Area Director of Security for the Internet Engineering Steering Group.
- Bruce Schneier, author of *Applied Cryptography* (John Wiley & Sons, 1995) and inventor of the Blowfish encryption algorithm.

The report was a response to increasing activity on the part of politicians and government administrators who feel threatened by the uncontrolled use of technologies that make it possible to communicate securely with no way for a government agency to monitor the communication. To many, the idea of the government restricting access to strong cryptography is obviously a violation of individual rights, equivalent to restricting access to other communication technologies like fax machines, typewriters, or computers (restrictions put in place by repressive communist or fascist regimes). However, representatives of government agencies like the FBI have managed to do a good job of convincing politicians that without the ability to monitor all data communications, they will not be able to protect the national interests against those who would spy, sell drugs, commit terrorism, spread pornography, perpetrate acts of pedophilia, or evade taxes. The fact that strong cryptography is already available outside the United States (as well as inside), the politicians and administrators seem to consider to be beside the point.

The report, in a word, explains that the proposal to mandate that any user of encryption provide to government agencies access to keys for all data encrypted (variously known as "key escrow," "trusted third party encryption," "key recovery," or "government access to keys") is impractical because

◆ Key recovery systems will have very high costs associated with their creation and operation. The cost of collecting, storing, and being able to retrieve keys for every piece of ciphertext is daunting, to say the least. Each secure transfer over the Internet represents a single key, which means there may be millions of keys to keep track of every day.

◆ Key recovery systems will tend to be ineffective, reducing the degree of security possible with the system and increasing the degree of risk associated with using the system for secure communication. Key recovery systems tend to create additional risks by presenting a very attractive target to hackers (access to a vast amount of encrypted data from all over) and by requiring all users to trust the key escrow agents not to divulge data to law enforcement agencies without proper authorization and to trust law enforcement agencies to request and use only the data that they are legally permitted. Overall trust in the security of encrypted data tends to be eroded as a result.

◆ Key recovery systems will make use of encryption much more difficult (and will tend to also be very difficult for government agencies to use). The cost and reduced security are offset by the requirement of reporting all keys (securely) as well as identification information to the key escrow agencies. This adds an additional level of complexity to the process of encrypting data.

Explaining in balanced tones, with no specific reference to any particular key escrow system proposal or commercial product, the authors present a clear, concise, and cogent refutation of the validity of every government argument in favor of deploying a key escrow system to make encrypted data available to law enforcement agencies. The report itself is recommended reading for anyone concerned with government control of encryption and cryptographic technologies, and is available on-line in several places, including http://www.info-sec.com/crypto/report.html-ssi and http://www.crypto.com/key_study/report.shtml.

4

Implementing Encryption

This chapter discusses what is involved with building secure systems that use encryption. It includes what is involved in deciding how to build encryption into a system, how to decide what to use encryption for, how to decide how encryption is to be integrated into the system, and how the encryption is ultimately implemented in the system. Also discussed is how encryption is used to build secure software, secure hardware, and secure networking products.

Building Systems with Encryption

It is relatively easy to build a system that incorporates encryption in some form; what is difficult is to ensure that the system is secure. Simply adding encryption does not always guarantee that the system automatically becomes secure. Any time you hear a vendor extolling the security of a product because it does encryption, you should question how that encryption is implemented and what purpose the encryption fulfills. This section discusses issues involved in building a secure system by including encryption. There are three basic challenges:

- Defining the security objectives that adding encryption will solve.
- Defining the way encryption must be implemented in the system in order to solve the security objective.
- Actually building the encryption into the product in a safe, secure, and usable form.

Adding encryption to a product that does not need it is likely to make the product less usable by making it more complicated. Likewise, encrypting data that is not at risk just for the sake of adding encryption to a product also adds complexity without adding value. Finally, encrypting data in a way that does not actually protect it does the most harm—users are lulled into a false sense of security because they believe their data is protected when in fact it is not.

Encryption Objectives

The objective of adding encryption to a product should always be to protect data, where protection means keeping the data from being accessible to anyone but its authorized users. Before it can be possible to even think about adding encryption to a product, the designer must understand where the data is at risk and from whom. Questions that must be answered include

- Who owns and creates the data?
- Who needs to use the data?
- How is the data delivered?
- What is done with the data?
- How is the data stored?
- How is the data communicated to other entities?
- How important is the data to its users?
- How valuable is the data to its users?

The following sections explain why each of these questions is important.

Who Owns and Creates the Data?

The entity that creates the data, often the same as the owner of the data, has a vested interest in how the data is stored—and how the data is protected. As stated elsewhere, the greater the degree of security needed, the higher the cost is in actual monetary costs as well as in costs of time and effort in using the more secure system. Whoever creates the data will undoubtedly be interested in how the data is protected. If the entity that creates the data believes it to be sufficiently important, the added complexity of encrypting it as it is created will be worthwhile; on the other hand, if the entity that creates the data is more concerned with the ease with which the data can be used or distributed and less concerned with maintaining secrecy, there may be little point in encrypting the data as it is created.

Who Needs to Use the Data?

This is a key issue, and one that determines not just whether application data is to be encrypted, but how it will be encrypted and what kind of encryption is used. For one thing, are the only entities with a need for the data those entities authorized to use it? In that case, it is entirely possible that there is no need for encryption at all. On the other hand, if there are unauthorized entities with a need for the data, the system designer may want to consider using stronger security, perhaps through encryption.

If the only entities needing the data are the same entities that have created it, then it may be preferable to encrypt with symmetric keys maintained by those entities. On the other hand, if the data is created by one entity and passed along to some other entity, then public key encryption may be preferred.

How is the Data Delivered?

The actual physical flow of the data is important. It determines where and how data may be put at risk of interception or other attack. Applications that run on a single computer with no connections to any other systems, devices, or data communications networks may have less need for encryption than applications that are distributed on systems connected to open networks.

Flow of data includes not just output information but also inputs, so even though a system may operate only on a system behind closed doors, if it accepts inputs over more open channels it can be compromised if somehow those inputs are intercepted or counterfeited.

What Is Done with the Data?

The actual flow of data will show what happens when it enters the system, and understanding what happens to the data will often highlight security problems. For example, consider a system that encrypts all data stored on the system, but accepts queries from open networks and fulfills those queries in plaintext. Clearly, the data itself as it is stored in the system may be secure, but it is highly vulnerable as it is moved from the system in response to a simple request.

Another example of protecting only one part of the flow of data may occur when a web server encrypts data being transmitted from a browser using the SSL protocol. The data is entered into the browser by an end-user, after which the browser encrypts it with the server's public key and it is transmitted over the Internet in ciphertext. Once it hits the server, however, the server decrypts the ciphertext and is left with the sensitive plaintext—if the server simply sticks it into some directory locally without encrypting it again, it may be vulnerable on the server.

How Is the Data Stored?

This question is related to the previous one, but not exactly the same. Does the data get written to a network disk, a local fixed disk, a tape drive, or a removable disk? Is it stored only in memory? It is important to follow the trail of the data and consider that if part of the application is to publish some information onto a public server, then it may not be appropriate to attempt to keep it secret through encryption.

How is the Data Communicated?

Again, this question goes back to understanding how the data flows through the application. Is it a networked application that must use open networks to distribute information, or does it use secured networks for transport? If the application uses an open channel, does that channel already provide some security through encryption, and, if so, is that enough to protect the data?

How Important Is the Data to Its Users?

You can measure how important the application data is in two dimensions. On one hand, is the data so important that there can be no risk of losing access to it as a result of a lost key? On the other hand, is it worth risking the loss of access through a lost key to keep the data out of the hands of unauthorized entities? The importance of the data is related to, but not identical to, the next issue.

How Valuable Is the Data to Its Users?

The value of the data, both to the entity that owns it and to entities that do not own it but would like to (and that are unauthorized to have access to it), is one of the most important issues to address when considering the use of encryption to protect an application. The reason is that it is possible to put a fairly definite price tag on doing a brute force attack against the data. If the data is worth pennies per kilobyte, it may be sufficient to use low-strength 40-bit key symmetric encryption—after all, if the cost of the electricity needed to power a computer to do a brute force attack is higher than the value of the information being attacked, then there is no reason to use stronger encryption. Most data that gets encrypted currently very likely falls in or near this category. If I were to encrypt my e-mail to my friends, the information I send them (perhaps an invitation to a dinner party or an announcement about my family) is not really worth that much to anyone—even me.

However, there is a significant amount of data that gets encrypted that has a much higher value, including financial transactions or information about trade secrets or contact information for CIA operatives overseas. This information, if accessed by the wrong entity, could be very costly to the owner of the information, causing losses of huge sums of money or worse. The type of encryption used, strength of the key, and how the encryption is deployed must all be considered very carefully to avoid producing a system that may be secure for the next year but may be increasingly vulnerable as the years go by and costs of brute force attacks drop.

Encryption Functions

Employing encryption is not as simple as, say, turning on a light. There are many different ways that you can use encryption in a system. The value of implementing encryption in a system will depend on what the encryption is being used for, and how the encryption is being done. Issues related to what types of function encryption is to be used for include

- ♦ Choosing a cryptographic function.
- ♦ Choosing an algorithm.
- ♦ Deciding on key length.
- ♦ Knowing what to secure, and how to do it.

These issues are discussed next.

Choosing a Cryptographic Function

If you plan on building encryption into a system, you must determine what kind of encryption to use. On a gross scale, you need to decide what exactly is the security feature needed. In some cases, authentication using a public key digital signature scheme will be sufficient; in other cases, nothing else will do but to encrypt the data; in some other cases, the use of a cryptographic hash will be sufficient. Further choices must still be made—for example, whether to use symmetric or public key encryption if encryption is determined to be the appropriate choice.

Ultimately, the designer needs to determine exactly what cryptographic qualities are needed before choosing a function. For example,

- ♦ If the function required is verification of knowledge of a secret without disclosing the secret (as in a passphrase application), then the data can be securely hashed and the result used for verification.
- ♦ If the function required is the ability to encrypt data in such a way that only one entity can decrypt it (as in sending confidential information from a health service provider to a patient), then public key cryptography is called for.
- ♦ If the function required is to verify receipt of a message in full and unchanged from the way it was sent (as in commercial trade applications to confirm receipts of orders), then a public key digital signature function would be appropriate, but not necessarily sufficient by itself if confidentiality is also required.

As the examples demonstrate, some applications may call for more than one cryptographic function, while others can make do with a single function.

Choosing an Algorithm

The choice of cryptographic algorithm cannot be made until the cryptographic function required has been selected. Choosing the algorithm (or algorithms) requires analysis of more than simply the function required. For example, the following issues can affect the choice of algorithm:

- ♦ Where must the application be available? Products that employ strong cryptography may be export-restricted and thus unavailable outside the country of origin.

♦ What is the budget for creating the application? Algorithms available only under license may add to the cost of development.
♦ What are the specifications for application performance? Different algorithms can result in different levels of performance when implemented.

Deciding on Key Length

Choosing key length will depend strongly on the algorithm selected. For example, if you choose single DES you have no choice on key length—single DES uses a 56-bit key. Other considerations relating to the choice of key length are similar to those for choosing an algorithm, but of the two most important, one is political and the other technical. The political issue relates to the required distribution of the application and the size of the key that will be permitted. The technical issue is to choose a key long enough to be secure but short enough to reduce the impact of the encryption process on system performance.

Knowing What to Secure, and How to Do It

If you want to be completely safe, you should secure everything that travels over an open channel. The reason is that if you have to start to choose what needs to be secured and what does not need to be, you may make errors of judgment. For example, you may feel that personal e-mail does not need to be encrypted, but applying that rule may cause problems if you ever use your personal e-mail for business purposes. Also, allowing any information to go out as plaintext can compromise security in one way or another.

What becomes more complicated is figuring out the best way to protect information. Should you use a strong shared key for symmetric encryption? Should public key encryption be used? If you are using strong public key encryption to protect a stream cipher key, the stream cipher should be strong as well.

Encryption may not always be the right choice for protecting data, either. Encrypting passphrases and then sending them as ciphertext would require that the system receiving the pass-phrase would have to decrypt it and compare it to a passphrase stored in plaintext locally. This exposes the passphrase to attack against the local system as well as to attack against the ciphertext passphrase. A more usual approach to protecting passphrases is to have the client software hash the passphrase after the user enters it on the remote host, encrypt it, and then send the result to the system doing the authentication.

Implementing Encryption in Systems

Once it has been determined what objectives are to be attained through the use of encryption, and what encryption functions are to be included in the application, all that remains is to implement the system. Of course, this is a little like saying that once you have equipped yourself to scale Everest and arrived at base camp, all that is left is to actually climb the mountain.

Implementing encryption can be difficult. Not only do you have to solve all the usual problems of implementing a system, like making sure that the system meets these requirements:

- ◆ System accurately does all functions required by the system specification. If the system is an e-mail program, this means that the system must be able to deliver and send e-mail, for example.
- ◆ System does not do anything unintended by the specification. If the system is an e-mail program, this means that the system should not randomly send out messages that were not explicitly sent by a user, does not send out copies of messages unless specified by the user, and does not add or delete any part of the message on its own initiative.
- ◆ System performs within the system specification. This will vary from system to system, but for interactive systems this means minimizing the amount of time the user must wait for a result.

When you add encryption to the system, you must also be sure that the system now meets even more stringent requirements—while remembering that performance specifications may be impacted by the way the encryption is implemented. Additional requirements for encryption-enabled systems include

- ♦ The system must not open security holes as a result of adding security. In other words, if the system is to be secure, the entire system must be scrutinized for the soundness of its security. For example, if public key encryption is used to encrypt a session key for a stream cipher, the session key must be generated in a secure manner (e.g., choosing session keys from a small set of options or from an easily guessed parameter like the system clock is not secure).
- ♦ System requirements should not be changed radically by the addition of encryption. In other words, if a primary feature of the system is to be easy to use, adding a layer of complication relating to encryption may adversely affect the ability to keep the system simple. Alternatively, simplifying an encryption feature in a way that keeps it easy to use but compromises security of a system is also unacceptable.
- ♦ Encrypted system functions should not leave behind any artifacts (like disk cache files) that could be used to break the encryption.

Ultimately, anyone developing a system that incorporates encryption as a security feature would be well served by hiring the best cryptologist available to do design reviews of the system to ensure that no glaring errors have been committed in the product. The cryptologist may also be able to detect more subtle errors in implementation, but because these may not be obvious at first, a lengthy testing period is also recommended.

Encryption Hardware

Implementing encryption in hardware has some advantages and benefits over doing it in software, but also some drawbacks. On the plus side, it is possible to make a hardware device tamper-proof. This can help make the task of any attacker that much harder. Any system that can be taken apart and examined (like a piece of software) can be that much more vulnerable to attack. When the encryption is implemented as a piece of hardware, it can be designed to make it inaccessible to this kind of reverse-engineering.

Another advantage is that custom-designed hardware for encryption tends to perform better than software. It stands to reason, since a hardware solution can hard-wire all the functionality into circuits developed specifically to do the things that must be done to get the encryption done. Hardware implementations can be significantly more efficient than software implementations of the same encryption algorithms.

One other attribute of hardware-based encryption, at least in the past, was that hardware devices traditionally were easier to obtain patents for than software. In fact, the concept of software patents generally is a rather new one. However, this is no longer the case, and many cryptographic algorithms that have received patent protection have received it for their software incarnations.

This section introduces three types of encryption hardware:

- ◆ Dedicated special-purpose encryption machines.
- ◆ Encryption add-in cards.
- ◆ Smart cards enabled for encryption.

Dedicated Encryption Machines

Individuals would normally not use, or even need, a dedicated encryption machine. These are normally built specifically for encrypting large volumes of data, very quickly. Examples of dedicated encryption machines include devices that are used to enable electronic commerce or secure networking. They encrypt all data that passes from within an organization to the outside, and decrypt all data that comes into the organization from the outside. These devices interface to other systems through local area network or other data communications links, usually accepting plaintext inputs from the local input, encrypting it, and transmitting cipher-text over the link to remote networks.

Encryption Cards

Encryption functions can be added to a regular computer system through the use of add-in cards. These may be full-blown add-in cards that must be installed by opening up the system and insert-ing them into the system board, or they may be PCMCIA (PC) cards that can be inserted into a standard interface most often found on laptops but increasingly available to other systems including desktop computers as well as personal digital assis-tants (PDAs).

There are different types of these devices:

- ◆ Dedicated encryption devices that can be used for bulk encryption by the system as needed.
- ◆ Special-purpose devices that incorporate encryption as part of their function—for example, special network cards or disk controller cards that incorporate encryption services as part of their more general purpose.
- ◆ Devices that provide some particular user application or service that requires the use of encryption—for example, user authentication devices, or modems or Java network computers on a PC card.

Again, most of these products are aimed at larger organizations, although it is possible that PC cards that incorporate a Java virtual machine as well as cryptographically secured user information (like a digital wallet, perhaps) could become popular with some end-users for use with PDAs or rentable kiosks.

Smart Cards

PC cards (PCMCIA cards) are small and can be relatively inexpensive, but the price tag is unlikely to dip far below the $100 mark. Smart cards (devices about the size, shape, and thickness of a credit card) can be built to include some relatively sophisticated circuitry for a few dollars per device. Potential uses for these devices include

- ◆ Digital wallets, containing personal keys and digital currencies.
- ◆ Smart IDs, containing personal identification information.
- ◆ Medical record repositories, containing personal health information.

While they do not necessarily have much computing power on their own, what they have is sufficient to incorporate digital signature and/or encryption to protect data from unauthorized access and to ensure that data on the card has not been tampered with.

Encryption Software

The immense power (and a source of much of the threat) of modern cryptography is that it can be implemented in software on virtually any computer. With software, it is possible to bootstrap a secure communications network with no physical contact among the communicators: Simply distribute the software to all. The fact that encryption can be implemented in software means that its use is no longer limited to those applications that can justify huge expenditures for specially designed custom hardware; the fact that it can be widely installed on relatively inexpensive personal computers opens the door for applications as mundane as encrypting invitations to a surprise party or as generally useful as encrypting commercial transactions like ordering flowers for Mother's Day.

This section discusses how encryption is implemented in software:

- ◆ Encryption can be implemented as a function of a software program.
- ◆ Encryption can be implemented as a feature of a software application.
- ◆ Encryption can be implemented as the primary purpose of a dedicated encryption program.

The distinctions may seem to be overly fine, but can be useful when evaluating products that claim security through encryption. Understanding the distinctions can help differentiate products and gauge usefulness of the different products.

Encryption as a Software Function

Many products incorporate an encryption function as an adjunct to the primary purpose of the application. To illustrate, the following applications can use encryption as an added function, but none of these applications inherently require any security at all:

- A word processor can incorporate an encryption option to save document files securely.
- A file management program can incorporate an encryption option to convert stored data from plaintext to ciphertext.
- A workgroup application can incorporate an option to encrypt messages to workgroup members.
- An e-mail client can incorporate an option to encrypt messages sent over the Internet.

All these applications use encryption, though the way they incorporate encryption is of varying value to users. For example, while e-mail sent over the Internet actually is exposed to a potentially hostile environment in which there is a definite likelihood that the data will be intercepted or sniffed, encrypting word processing data does not necessarily protect it any more than saving the file to disk and storing the disk securely in a bank vault, for instance—or even just keeping the system on which the file is stored behind a locked door. Furthermore, there are risks to encrypting a stored word processing file that do not exist for encrypted e-mail:

- The user may decide not to do a physical backup of encrypted data, because "it is already protected."
- If the user encrypts files that are not used often, the passphrase may be lost or forgotten.

♦ If the user encrypts all files, either many unique passphrases must be generated (and remembered) or a single
passphrase (or a small set of passphrases) will be recy-
cled insecurely.

What is most important is that when implementing encryption as a
function of some application software,

♦ Encryption should be used when it adds to security by
protecting data that is at risk and cannot be sufficiently
protected in any other way.
♦ The function should be self-sufficient and complete, without adding undue complexity to the application and
within a framework that handles key management and
data recovery functions acceptably to the user.

Encryption as a Software Feature

Increasingly common are software applications that incorporate
encryption as a feature in some form that is not under the direct control
of the user, or that requires some act of faith on the part of the user that
data is being protected. One example was the original Netscape Navigator web browser. It contained a feature that allowed the browser to
support encryption through the Secure Sockets Layer (SSL) protocol.
The user had little or no control over how the encryption was used,
and had to trust that when the security indicators—a blue bar along
the top of the window and a whole key in the lower left corner—were
active, all data was secured. The user could not modify any keys, manage directories, or enter any passphrases; nor was that necessary, since
the encryption was incorporated as a feature rather than as a user-
accessible function.

Other examples of software that incorporate encryption as a feature
include

♦ LAN messaging software that encrypts (or hashes) passphrases submitted across a network.

♦ Software directories (implemented as part of larger applications) that use encrypted stores for user ID and passphrase information.

Dedicated Encryption Software

Adding encryption as a feature or function of an existing application is one approach to security. However, for the user to rely on such an approach can be a mistake. It requires that the user choose application products both on their ability to meet the user's requirements for the application and on their ability to protect data through encryption. This can be as difficult as trying to find a good engineer who is also a good manager. There are many good engineers, and many good managers, but many of the attributes that make a good engineer detract from management ability.

While hiring an engineer and a manager to share engineering management functions does not usually work very well, buying a good application software product and a separate dedicated encryption product can work out quite well. The reason is that the user is freed from having to evaluate an application not only on how well it performs the application but also on how well it performs encryption. The dedicated encryption product should work with data generated by any and all applications, and it can be evaluated on its own merits.

Another reason to opt for dedicated encryption products is that securely implementing encryption is very difficult and requires a very special set of skills. Many general application vendors cannot afford to hire the expertise necessary to ensure that the encryption features and functions are correctly and securely implemented; vendors whose products are dedicated entirely to encryption (or whose products are largely dependent on the secure use of encryption) are more likely to hire the most capable cryptologists and computer scientists.

Networking Encryption

Encryption in a networking setting, particularly when the network in question is the Internet, is not as simple as encrypting data through a particular application. There are several different layers in which data is generated and manipulated, and encryption or other cryptographic functions can take place at more than one layer in any particular transmission.

The networking protocols that are the basis of all internetworking, particularly the Internet, rely on a layered model of communications. When you enter data into a client program and send it to a server at the other side of the Internet, the data is wrapped up with addressing and routing information at each different layer; when the data is finally received by the destination host, it is unwrapped and the information inside is passed along to the server application for processing. This process is called encapsulation (when the data is being wrapped) and de-encapsulation (when the data is being unwrapped).

The process is not unlike that used to move business communications physically across physical space. A business executive wishing to send a message to an associate may dictate a letter to an assistant. The assistant writes the letter, addresses an envelope, and routes the envelope to the mail room. Someone in the mail room takes the envelope and puts it inside a delivery mailer, and routes the package to the right delivery service. An employee of the delivery service takes the package and puts it into a truck for delivery to a sorting station; from there, the package may be put into an air cargo container and sent off to a national distribution hub. From there, the package may change planes, until it is ultimately delivered to the distribution center local to the recipient; there, it will be removed from the cargo container and loaded into a truck. The truck will deliver it to the recipient's office mail room, where it will be sorted and ultimately delivered to the recipient's assistant, who removes the message from the mailer and delivers it to the recipient.

Something very similar happens to data over the Internet. An application program accepts data from the user, formats it and addresses it to the server program running across the Internet. From the application layer, the data is addressed (to another program) and passed down to the transport layer. This is comparable to choosing a delivery service or the government postal service; at this level, the networking software targets processes running on the destination host. The next layer down is the internetwork layer, where the data is addressed to the logical address of the network interface connecting the host running the destination process. The lowest layer is the link layer, where the actual physical movement of data can occur. This refers to the actual network cabling, for example, over which data flows.

What happens with data transmitted over the Internet is that the application layer accepts data from the end-user and addresses it to a destination server. The data (which includes the actual data wrapped up inside) includes information about the destination and is passed down the network stack to be addressed to the correct process by the transport layer. At the transport layer, the information received from the application layer is submerged and transport layer addressing is added. The internetwork layer accepts this from the transport layer, but adds its own routing and addressing information as it wraps up the data from the upper layers. Finally, this data is wrapped up inside information about how to properly physically route the bits of the data to their next destination.

The link layer in the Internet is comparable to the physical movement of the wrapped package as it moves from a truck at the local distribution center to another truck, or from an airplane to national distribution hub to another airplane—in other words, the movement of bits from one computer to another connected to the same local area network.

Moving from the source mail room to the destination mail room, via distribution centers, is comparable to the kind of routing that occurs at the internetwork layer. How the package moves from mailroom to mailroom depends on which intermediate distribution centers are used, but how the package actually moves between each point is determined locally. This is comparable to moving data from one router to another across the Internet—the bits themselves may be moving across an Ethernet or an ATM backbone or some other network medium, but at this layer all that is of concern is that the data be moved from source to destination by appropriate routing across the internetwork.

At this point, the metaphor breaks down a bit, but the most important concept is that there are different levels of communication involved with each piece of data transmitted across the Internet.

- Data can be sent from application to application, with encryption functions incorporated between the applications; data is encrypted at the source, and not decrypted until it arrives at its destination.
- Data can be sent from one router to another, with encryption functions incorporated into each transmission from router to router: data is encrypted at each router, and decrypted at the next hop router.
- Data can be sent from one network interface to another, with encryption functions incorporated into each transmission on the network medium. Data is encrypted before being transmitted, and decrypted when received.

 For more about how Internet and internetworking protocols work, see my *TCP/IP Clearly Explained* (AP Professional, 1997); for more about how security and encryption figure into the Internet and extranets, see my *Extranet Design and Implementation* (SYBEX, 1997).

5

Getting Crypto-Enabled

This chapter discusses what kind of encryption products are now available, how to decide which products to get and use, and how to use those products. Also provided here are detailed hands-on instructions for actually getting a certificate and public key pair for use with the most popular Internet encryption software.

Encryption Product Categories

With the enormous success of the Internet, vendors whose products previously needed minimal security—because they were standalone products or worked through proprietary networking protocols—are adding encryption and authentication functions at a furious pace. As applications are being made "Internet-ready" and "web-enabled" they require some means of keeping application data private and secure. There is not room (or need) to discuss every single product that employs encryption; for one thing, many of them do not really need encryption or authentication functions, many others do not use them properly, and most of the products in both those categories will not receive any significant market acceptance in any case.

This chapter introduces categories of products that make productive use of encryption technologies, explains how they do so, and provides the information you need to acquire those products—often through free downloads over the Internet. These categories include

- ◆ Web browser clients.
- ◆ E-mail clients.
- ◆ Internet commerce products.
- ◆ Desktop data protection products.
- ◆ Network protection products.

Each of these product categories is discussed later in this chapter, along with tips for acquiring them safely. First, though, comes a discussion of how to select safe and secure encryption products and how to safely acquire them. The chapter ends with a detailed explanation of what a certficate is and how to get one.

Selecting Encryption Products

Selecting a product to do encryption and other cryptographic functions is mostly a matter of determining the right tool for the job at hand, and then making sure that the particular product you select

- ◆ Actually does encryption securely and safely.
- ◆ Can be delivered to you in a verifiably secure format.
- ◆ Is legally available to you.

This section discusses how to go about meeting these conditions.

Choosing the Proper Tools

There is no question about the amount of trouble that arises from the improper use of even high-quality but improper tools. Whether you try to drive a screw into a wall with a hammer or try to encrypt e-mail with the wrong desktop security program, in either case the result will be wasted effort and a job poorly done. Choosing the correct cryptographic software (or hardware) tool depends on several factors:

- ♦ Identifying the data that must be protected.
- ♦ Determining the degree of protection that data must be given.
- ♦ Evaluating algorithm, key length, implementation, cryptographic, and other standards in light of the application.
- ♦ Certifying that the tool being considered is available for your platform and your operating environment, including consideration of computer hardware and operating system, network, organizational, and operational limitations.
- ♦ Determining the actual level of support being offered for the product. Is there a vendor offering ongoing technical support? Does the vendor intend to continue supporting the product, improving it, and fixing any bugs found after release?

Identifying At-Risk Data

There is a whole world of data, much being important or valuable enough to someone or some organization to want to protect it through encryption. However, for the purposes of this book, we can safely limit our discussion to data generated by an individual (whether a private person or an employee of an organization), either to be used *in situ* on a personal computer (stored on some form of disk, tape, or other portable storage medium) or to be transmitted across a network.

One way to classify data is by its most vulnerable location. Take, for example, a stand-alone computer that is not connected to any network and that has been physically fixed in place (with all disk drives physically secured as well). Data stored on this system might be sufficiently secured by the use of a user authentication system; if the system is located in a secured room, it may be possible to entirely forgo any additional security.

Alternatively, consider data created on a mobile user's laptop computer, sent over the Internet as an e-mail message, and forwarded by various intermediate e-mail servers before being stored by the recipient's e-mail server. Such data is almost continuously vulnerable. Should the laptop be lost or stolen, the message can be read from the system's hard drive; e-mail messages sent in the clear over the Internet can be intercepted en route by network sniffers or improperly viewed by anyone with access to an intermediate e-mail server (or to the destination e-mail server). Finally, once the message has been received at the destination host, it can be attacked there.

Individuals using laptops for sensitive data may want to consider a combination of products, or a single product that provides a selection of encryption services. For example, the ability to store and use encrypted data locally off the laptop hard drive would be a great benefit here, as would the ability to encrypt data to be sent as e-mail. Finally, the use of a Virtual Private Network (VPN) product to secure a communication channel between the laptop and a remote network through the Internet could also be beneficial.

It is also important to determine what cryptographic tools must be included in the product. For example, products intended to facilitate the transfer of information should include digital signature functions; those intended simply to encrypt and decrypt data in place do not necessarily need those functions. Issues of algorithm and key length are discussed below.

How Safe Is Safe?

As discussed at length elsewhere in this book, in general, security increases as encryption key length increases. Thus, wherever possible one should avoid the "international" version of any personal encryption product—increasingly, this is becoming unnecessary as the U.S. government continues to relax export controls on products from vendors like Netscape and Microsoft. However, there are still some products being made available that use shorter keys for international versions of stronger, domestic products that have not yet been approved for export or that are made available on the Internet as freely downloadable software intended to serve as a trial product.

Here are some key points to keep in mind when considering the relative security of encryption software:

- During 1997, a group of volunteers demonstrated that single DES really is vulnerable to credible attacks; it should be avoided for highly sensitive data that will remain sensitive for any length of time or when DES is the only block encryption algorithm offered by a product.
- Insist on products that offer standard algorithms; those offering a selection of more than one standard algorithm, with user-settable key lengths, are to be preferred. Products offering only a proprietary encryption algorithm, particularly when the vendor makes no further information about the algorithm available, should be avoided.
- Products with proprietary data interfaces (e.g., that require both encrypting and decrypting users to use the same software product) may be considered less safe than those using a standard data interface because accessibility to the data depends on all participants always having access to just that software. Should one party's copy of the software be lost or damaged, access to the data will depend on that person being able to get another copy of the software—data encrypted to a standard interface will be accessible through any program that conforms with that interface.
- While market acceptance in no way guarantees security, products with greater market penetration will generally receive much closer scrutiny in terms of verifying security

of the product. Likewise, products (and algorithms) that have been available for a longer time tend to have been exposed to more attacks—presumably successfully withstanding those attacks—than products and algorithms relatively new to the market. While ultimately, new algorithms like those employed by elliptic curve cryptography may prove to be more secure than those used by public key cryptography, at the moment it is probably still safer to use public key cryptography because it has withstood far greater scrutiny over a much longer period of time.

Determining the safety of an encryption product is largely a matter of determining to what degree you should trust that product. If you are merely interested in keeping information secure only from casual and unsophisticated attackers, almost any product will do— on the other hand, if you need to protect your information from determined, sophisticated attackers, you may want to use a much higher standard and consider more rigorous methods. One approach would be to hire the best cryptographers you can afford to subject the product to intensive study and testing to determine whether or not it appears likely to be secure against a determined attacker.

Another way to judge encryption products is by reputation—not of the vendor, but of the entities that use the product. Identifying users of a particular product and determining how they use the product (and how far they trust the product) can be useful. Although this approach is not necessarily open to everyone, you should certainly check around with colleagues and acquaintances whose opinion you respect about what products they feel are adequate to their needs.

Evaluating the Solution Implementations

Beyond the specific functions offered, like encryption-decryption and digital signature service, the cryptographic technologies underlying any product will dictate to some extent how the product is most effectively used. The single most important factor will be the type of standards used. Products that use open standards will be far more useful for communication applications than products that do not use open standards. Also critical to product selection is the type of data to be encrypted. Products tend to fall into one of these categories:

- ◆ Products for explicitly encrypting data files stored on a computer.
- ◆ Products for encrypting and digitally signing data communications (including e-mail messages and file attachments).
- ◆ Products that combine these tasks for desktop and communication encryption and digital signatures.
- ◆ Products that embed encryption and/or digital signature functions within other applications and functions (for example, as part of a database or workgroup application).

E-mail encryption implementations tend to fall into three categories:

- ◆ Products that implement proprietary encryption schemes other than PGP.
- ◆ Products that implement PGP-based encryption.
- ◆ Products that implement PKCS-based (Public-Key Cryptographic Standards) encryption. (This includes S/MIME-based products.)

Proprietary products may be effective for individuals wishing to protect data that does not go anywhere, particularly if the product does a very good job of easily and intuitively encrypting and decrypting data files as and when the user wants them encrypted and decrypted. However, such products tend to suffer from several drawbacks:

- ◆ Lack of support. Proprietary products may not have a sufficiently large user population to generate the demand for books, consultants, and services; vendors selling products that do not do well in the market may also not survive long (or may not continue to support products that have been discontinued).

♦ Lack of security. Proprietary products may not have had as much product testing, by as many different people, as more open products.

♦ Lack of interoperability. This is key if you ever need to encrypt a message to be read by someone else. If your product is proprietary, you can only exchange data securely with others who own the same product.

PGP-based products include the freeware versions of PGP, and the commercial PGP, Inc., products. To a certain extent, while PGP can be considered a "proprietary" product, its widespread distribution and documentation differentiate it from almost all other proprietary encryption products. Mid-1997 marketing estimates from competitors indicated that as many as two million people were already using PGP for their personal encryption needs. The PGP web of trust approach is not an official standard, and, while it may be a drawback in the long run, it is accepted by a large enough body of users to make it preferable to other proprietary approaches—however, it may suffer in the long run as open standards certification authorities become more prevalent both for public use and within organizations.

Environmental Concerns

Anyone considering using it should have concerns about how encryption software impacts their desktop computing environment. The degree of impact will depend in part on what the product is meant to do. Products that claim to encrypt all or part of your workspace have the potential to make that entire workspace inaccessible if something goes wrong with the installation, if you should forget your passphrase, or if you should lose any associated emergency recovery disks.

If your keys are not backed up, and your encryption software installation is damaged or destroyed, you will not have access to any data you encrypted with those keys. If your keys are backed up, and your encryption software is damaged or destroyed, your data should be accessible as soon as you are able to re-install the damaged software or software compatible with it. The compatibility issue is key, and this problem tends to make standards-based encryption software more attractive.

Avoiding Snake Oil

Cryptographic snake oil may be said to be anything that is too good to be true, much like the nostrums hawked before the days of food and drug regulations. In both cases, the seller often truly believes in the efficacy of the remedy being sold, but in both cases there are methods of differentiating between products that may be truly useful and those that may be harmful. But unless you are a skilled cryptographer yourself, it can be extremely difficult to determine the real worth of any given system.

There are a number of things the encryption consumer can check when considering an encryption product that can point to whether there is a relative probability that the product in question is actually useful and safe. Questions to ask include

- ◆ Who created the encryption algorithm? There are handful of world-class cryptographers who are capable of creating their own cryptographic algorithms; these algorithms are usually available to be licensed, and tend to have undergone the greatest scrutiny to produce confidence in them. If the algorithm was created by the same person who wrote the e-mail client or newsreader or workgroup product, chances are that it is not secure.
- ◆ What are the details of the algorithm being used? Are they available for public scrutiny in any form? If the algorithm would be compromised by being public, chances are good that the algorithm itself is not terribly secure. This includes products that have been submitted for patent protection. For serious peer review, algorithms can be published in academic journals and still receive protection if a patent is applied for. However, it is important to remember that not all vendors are interested in receiving patent protection for their algorithm. Patents

expire, at which point the algorithm would become available to anyone to implement. Some encryption product vendors keep some of their algorithms private so they can receive trade secret protection. The thing to keep in mind, however, is that a vendor with no prior products and no reputation will have a much harder time convincing the market that its secret algorithm is as secure as an algorithm kept secret by a better established vendor.

♦ Does the product claim to do something that is too good to be true? Things that would fall into this category include "unbreakable" security with very short pass-phrases and "one-time pad" implementations that do not require both communicating parties to physically hold the same source for the one-time pad data. Snake oil peddlers often make other absurd claims, like offering to give away the company to anyone who can prove their cryptosystem is unsafe, or claiming that their product will make all other existing and accepted cryptosystems obsolete, or main-taining that they have implemented a truly random num-ber generator in software.

One should not rule out the possibility that some untutored person will someday create an unbreakable encryption algorithm. How-ever, one should also expect that when that occurs, the algorithm will be recognized by expert cryptographers. In the meantime, it is probably safer to rely on products and methods that have proven themselves.

Encryption Product Channels

Typically, encryption software products are delivered either as soft-ware downloads over the Internet or in shrink-wrapped packages available through retail outlets. Inasmuch as encryption products must adhere to a somewhat higher standard of security than most other applications, it is wise to try to make sure that any encryption products you acquire are exactly what they purport to be. For this reason, you may prefer to purchase shrink-wrapped products direct from vendors or from authorized retailers.

One other consideration when acquiring software, particularly when downloading software over the Internet, is the status of the code in question. Many downloadable products are made available over the Internet in slightly different form than they would be available as retail products. In particular, vendors increasingly are providing beta, or pre-release, versions of their products for free downloads. These versions tend to be more buggy than general-availability products, and they may not be feature-complete. Some of the features claimed for the shipping product may not have been implemented in earlier beta versions.

Likewise, many vendors make available trial versions of their product that are limited in one way or another. Some expire after some specific date, either an expected date of release of a full retail version or some set number of days after the initial installation. Other products are limited in their functionality—for example, allowing only relatively weak encryption (with shorter key lengths), permitting only a limited number of files to be encrypted, or limiting some other factor of the product's feature set.

Consumers should be aware of what, exactly, they are getting when they acquire any piece of software. This carries even more weight when acquiring encryption software because you do not want to discover that your encryption product has expired 30, 60, or 90 days after you installed it—or to discover that all your files and messages have been encrypted using weak, 40-bit keys.

Political Considerations

The U.S. government has been increasingly though still cautiously granting software vendors, led by Microsoft and Netscape, permission to export strong encryption products in one form or another. This perceived relaxation in export controls may continue as politicians increasingly come to grips with the fact that the genie is out of the bottle and that pretty much anyone who wants strong encryption can get it.

Attempting to hold back U.S. vendors from selling strong encryption products inside or outside the U.S. merely harms the vendors, and does little or nothing to prevent strong encryption from falling into the "wrong hands." At the same time, the fact remains that there are export controls on a large number of products that incorporate strong encryption. This means that U.S. residents and organizations that need to use strong encryption outside the U.S. must use weaker encryption if they want to adhere to all rules and regulations concerning cryptographic export controls. Similarly, users should respect the laws of any other country in which they do business. What those laws are, and how they are enforced, may vary over time, but users can probably protect themselves best by doing business directly with reputable software vendors and avoiding any black market products or products that appear to be pirated. Not only might you be breaking a law, you might also be acquiring software tainted with viruses or trojan horse attacks.

Secure Web Clients

It has been some time since there were any more than two real contenders in the web client, or browser, market. Microsoft's Internet Explorer and Netscape's Communicator/Navigator have effectively crowded out all other browser products from any meaningful portion of the market.

Cryptographic security, in one form or another, has long been a critical feature of web browsers. Netscape's market dominance is based on being the first to support encrypted communication channels between browser and server through the SSL (Secure Sockets Layer) protocol in 1994 with the first version of Navigator. Since then, SSL has become standard equipment on all browsers and servers; however, SSL does little beyond encrypting the stream of data that passes between the server and the browser: once the data arrives at its destination, it is simply decrypted.

By 1996, however, things were different. There were only two browser vendors that still mattered to the market: Netscape and Microsoft. By early 1997, Netscape was including support for the S/MIME (Secure MIME) secure e-mail proposed standard in its Communicator suite and Navigator client. This specification permitted users to generate their own public key pair, get a certificate for that pair from a certification authority (CA), and store the certificate in a browser (or any other client software, for that matter). The key could then be used both to digitally sign e-mail and to encrypt e-mail with public key encryption. (Actually, the specification uses a 40-bit key for symmetric encryption of the message, with that key encrypted using the recipient's public key.) Microsoft followed suit by September 1997 with S/MIME support of its own in its Internet Explorer 4.0 release and in its Outlook and Outlook Express e-mail clients.

 The S/MIME specification originally called for recipients and senders to support, at a minimum, the RC2 algorithm using 40-bit keys, with other algorithms and key lengths permitted. Now, triple DES support is required, making the specification far more acceptable to security-conscious users.

By the late 1990s, web browsing security issues had also burgeoned beyond merely creating a secure channel between client and server. Users had become concerned with a host of other problems, including verification of who was behind a particular web site, handling of cookies (bits of data stored on a browser by a server to preserve state information about a user, and often including information that a user might prefer to keep private), and concern about the safety of software downloaded through web sites—particularly ActiveX controls and Java applets.

This section outlines the security features available with the browser software from Netscape and Microsoft and provides pointers to acquiring the browsers. More complete information about how to use these browsers securely and safely is provided in Chapter 6.

Microsoft Internet Explorer

Going to great effort and expense to create and distribute a piece of software from which it receives no direct revenue, Microsoft's Internet Explorer is probably one of the best free software packages around. Microsoft is marketing it aggressively, bundling it with several products including its Windows packages, and provides it to various third parties for bundling with books and in other forms. It can also be downloaded from Microsoft's web site, *www.microsoft.com*, but this may take some time unless you have a relatively fast connection to the Internet—the Internet Explorer installation files are not small.

Internet Explorer integrates security features throughout, with security-related functions controlled in different parts of the user interface. Security functions include

- ◆ Optional security settings that control the degree of vigilance with which your browser interacts with data from different sources.
- ◆ Content protection options to keep browser users from accessing inappropriate materials, using Internet rating systems.
- ◆ Certificate management tools for keeping track of individual and site certificates and software publisher certificates.
- ◆ Advanced options for controlling how to deal with activities that may trigger security issues.
- ◆ Access to security information (including certificate information) of any web page being browsed.

Digital ID (certificate) management options are also available in the Outlook and Outlook Express e-mail clients. These options allow you to use X.509 S/MIME certificates to encrypt and/or digitally sign e-mail sent with the Outlook clients. More details about using the Internet Explorer browser functions are provided in Chapter 6; details about secure e-mail with Outlook are provided in Chapter 7.

Netscape Navigator (Communicator)

Late in the summer of 1997, Netscape made a somewhat surprising announcement. Its Navigator browser, originally available as a stand-alone product (which had for some time been available only as part of the Communicator Internet client suite) would again be made available as a stand-alone product. This would help alleviate the browser bloat that was turning the process of downloading the latest version of your favorite browser over a modem (whether from Microsoft or from Netscape) into an exercise in graybar gazing, as well as make Netscape's browser more accessible to more users.

With Microsoft giving away its Internet browser, in early 1998 Netscape made an astonishing announcement. Not only would Netscape's standard client now be available free, but the code would also be made freely available for developers to improve and add to. Netscape will still market the Communicator Professional edition (adding enterprise clients for calendaring, autoconfiguration, and terminal emulation) for $29 per client. Other options, including subscriptions to software updates, are also available. The free client software can be downloaded from Netscape's web site, *www.netscape.com*.

Security features are all managed through a single button on the main browser toolbar, and include

- ♦ Access to security information (including certificate information) of any web page being browsed.
- ♦ Control over passphrase protection for your browser certificates.
- ♦ Browser security settings, including options for specifying which browser actions should trigger a warning, for selecting which certificate should be used to identify the user to a web site, and options for configuring encryption and other settings for SSL channels.
- ♦ E-mail security settings, including options for choosing which messages to encrypt and/or sign, for choosing a

certificate to use for digital signatures, for sending a certificate to a publicly accessible directory, and for configuring S/MIME encryption options.

♦ Java/JavaScript applets can be excluded or included based on certificates included with the applets on download.

♦ Extensive certificate management functions are provided for dealing with your own certificates, other people's certificates, and certificates linked with particular web sites. You can also manage trust levels for CAs.

♦ Cryptographic modules in use by the browser can also be viewed and managed.

More details about using the Netscape Navigator browser functions are provided in Chapter 6; details about secure e-mail with Netscape's Messenger e-mail client are provided in Chapter 7.

Secure E-Mail Clients

Keeping e-mail secure requires that a client be able to handle the following tasks:

♦ Encrypt messages (including attachments).
♦ Digitally sign messages (including attachments).
♦ Decrypt encrypted messages with your own private key.
♦ Verify messages signed with the sender's public key.

In support of these functions, a secure e-mail client must be capable of managing the sender's public and private keys, as well as public keys belonging to e-mail recipients.

As of early 1998, there are several e-mail clients available with more on their way; however, three dominate the market:

♦ Netscape's Messenger, a full-featured SNMP and POP e-mail client bundled with the Communicator package that is capable of sending and receiving S/MIME secured e-mail.

♦ Microsoft's Outlook and Outlook Express SNMP and POP e-mail clients offer more (Outlook) or less (Outlook Express) features, but both can be used to send and receive S/MIME secured e-mail.

♦ Qualcomm's Eudora and Eudora Light e-mail clients now ship with a fully functional plug-in version of PGP for Personal Privacy v 5.0, which permits the user to send and receive PGP secured e-mail.

AT&T offers a secure e-mail product called Secret Agent, and there are quite a few other products that function either as add-ins to mainstream e-mail clients or that are stand-alone e-mail clients in their own right. Many of these products use proprietary encryption schemes, proprietary key and certificate architectures, or are aimed at enterprise users, and therefore are not discussed here because they do not meet the need of the individual for personal encryption.

Microsoft Outlook Clients

Microsoft offers a pair of Internet-capable e-mail clients, Outlook 97 and Outlook Express, which can be used to do secure S/MIME e-mail. Outlook Express is a fairly basic Internet e-mail and news client, though it provides a fairly comprehensive set of messaging features. It is bundled with the Internet Explorer from Microsoft, and Outlook Express is competitive with other world-class e-mail clients including those from Netscape (Messenger, bundled with Communicator) and Qualcomm's Eudora.

Alternatively, with a list price of $109, Outlook 97 is a part of the Microsoft Office family and it has the same look and feel, including the familiar (to Microsoft Office users) toolbars and menus. Outlook 97 offers a more complete set of networking client tools, in particular more advanced e-mail features, as well as functions appropriate to enterprise network users including scheduling, task management, and journaling features.

By early 1998, Outlook was available for Windows 95 and Windows NT. Microsoft plans Windows 3.x and Macintosh versions of the client for the next Outlook release.

Netscape Messenger (Communicator)

Netscape started bundling an e-mail client with its browser in the second major release, Navigator 2.0. Messenger, the name of the client bundled with Communicator, is another world-class, full-featured e-mail and news client. Communicator is a communications suite that includes e-mail, browser, news reader, and conferencing, with options for calendaring, legacy system terminal emulation, and other functionality. Communicator software pricing starts at under $50 for on-line download purchase, and is available for a variety of platforms including Windows 3.x, Windows 95, Windows NT, Macintosh, and a full range of Unix flavors including Linux, the freeware operating system.

Qualcomm Eudora

Long before Microsoft had a usable Internet e-mail client, before Mozilla, Mosaic, and the World Wide Web, the Eudora e-mail client came out of the University of Illinois, Urbana-Champaign. Back in 1990, Eudora (named for Eudora Welty, in particular remembrance of the short story "Why I Live at the PO"), pioneered as a client that supported the Post Office Protocol (POP) that continues to dominate Internet e-mail. Now sold by Qualcomm, Inc. (although a freeware version, Eudora Light, is available for download at *http://www.eudora.com/eudoralight/*), Eudora clients are available for several platforms, including

- Windows 95 and Windows NT.
- Windows 3.x.
- Macintosh OS.
- Macintosh Newton.

As of mid-1997, Qualcomm began bundling a PGP plug-in with Eudora Pro and Eudora Light for Windows 95 and NT 4.0. It is this plug-in support that we will focus on in Chapter 7, where we discuss secure e-mail.

Secure Internet Commerce Products

Since Netscape released its first set of web client and server supporting an encrypted channel using the Secure Sockets Layer (SSL), the concept of secure web commerce became a reality. However, using SSL alone to attempt to secure web transactions is insufficient at best, and foolhardy or worse in practice. SSL protects credit card payment information only as it is being sent between the client and the server. This means that while it will be protected (that is, encrypted) as it passes through the Internet, once it arrives at the server it is decrypted and stored in plaintext on the server's disk—where it can be at risk through a wide variety of attacks from many different sources before the data is sent to a credit card settlement system and the transaction can be completed.

These products typically use encryption and digital signatures, but these functions are usually submerged within the software and not accessible to the end user. Detailed discussion of these products, therefore, is beyond the scope of this book.

Digital Wallets

More properly, secure Internet commerce must rely on a more complete approach to the concept of security as well as to the concept of transaction. CyberCash, Inc., pioneered this field with its system for completing transactions through web sites. It also pioneered the concept of a digital wallet with its CyberCash Wallet application. The digital wallet is a program that securely stores payment information—credit card account numbers and expiration dates as well as other methods of electronic payment—on the user's system and makes that information available to payment systems through the user's browser.

Secure Electronic Transaction (SET)

In 1996, as the web became increasingly appealing as a medium for commerce and as more and more merchants started offering their products for sale on-line, credit card issuers became concerned that existing protocols were insufficient to protect transactions passing through the Internet. Their response was to begin work on a specification for doing secure electronic transactions. MasterCard International and Visa International started out working together on the specification, joined by various other interested parties including Microsoft, IBM, and Netscape; later on in the process they variously split and reconciled and were eventually joined by others including Discover and American Express.

The resulting specification, appropriately named the Secure Electronic Transaction, or SET, specification, started to gel into a sufficiently complete document that implementers were able to do actual transactions with it as early as the end of 1996. Commercial implementations followed in 1997, with SET support expected to be increasingly generalized by 1998.

The specification itself is hundreds of pages long, and it provides in detail a blueprint for implementing secure transactions, including protecting and signing the payment information as it passes from consumer to merchant, use of public key cryptography to sign and encrypt data sent from merchant to credit card transaction settlement companies, and use of transaction processing techniques to handle completion of transactions in a data transmission environment that is by its nature unreliable.

Some experts feel that the specification is overly complicated, which may cause it to ultimately be defeated by attackers who take advantage of some of that complexity. However, it has a very important set of backers in the retail and financial sectors, who have been moving it forward despite potential flaws.

For more details of the SET protocol as well as other security protocols used in Internet commerce, see my *Electronic Commerce: On-Line Ordering and Digital Money*, 2nd edition (Charles River Media, 1997).

Secure Desktop Products

Desktop security products have long been a hodgepodge of assorted boot passphrase protection utilities, file encryption programs of varying quality and suitability, and secure delete tools. The growing awareness of the savvy computer consumer about what makes a security tool actually secure is changing the marketplace, driving out the snake oil salespeople and helping purveyors of useful and usable security products to improve their offerings.

Unlike secure web or e-mail clients, desktop security products generally take aim at the problems of keeping information stored on a personal computer available only to the entity that owns it and any entities the owner wants to share it with. The following features are commonly found in this type of product:

- ◆ File encryption and decryption. This allows the user to select files to be encrypted or decrypted in place; this usually means that only the owner can view the files after entering a passphrase to decrypt the file. Authentication may be required at the time of booting the system, or it may be required every time an encrypted file is accessed.
- ◆ Directory encryption and decryption. Some desktop security products allow you to designate one or more directories that are to contain only encrypted data. Any file created in or moved to such a directory is encrypted and accessible only after the owner authenticates itself to the application.
- ◆ Boot protection. Desktop products may allow you to require a passphrase before the system will complete booting at all; however, it is more common to require a passphrase at boot time to allow access to encrypted files—access to other files and applications is still permitted.
- ◆ System lock. Some desktop products provide a method of locking the system when the owner is away; an option is usually provided of locking the keyboard and

blanking the monitor after the owner hits some hot-key combination, or of requiring a passphrase after the system goes unused for some period of time (usually settable by the owner).

◆ Secure delete. To the relief of millions, deleting a file or directory under the DOS/Windows operating systems does not mean deleting the data but rather simply deleting the directory entry for the file or directory. More than one software fortune has been based on programs that are able to identify deleted files and recreate them. However, there are many entities that would prefer to be able to eradicate the contents of particular data files. For example, anyone donating a computer to a school (or simply discarding the system) will very likely want to delete any personal or proprietary business data from the disk. Many desktop security products provide the function of deleting data files by not only removing their directory entries but also of setting the bits of each byte to either a random value or to all ones or zeroes.

◆ Public key cryptography and digital signatures are sometimes supported by desktop security products, but not always.

◆ Emergency access to data and organizational (or "master") access to data is sometimes provided by the security product. For example, some products allow you to specify some entity (along with a passphrase and ID) that will be able to decrypt any data encrypted by any user of the product on a particular system or set of systems. This is usually done by having the desktop product encrypt with the master entity's public key the key secret used to encrypt the data. (That key is also encrypted with the recipient's public key.) This is a useful feature for businesses that wish to protect their access to corporate data in the event that a keyholder is unavailable.

We look at two of the better representatives of this product category in Chapter 8; these are introduced here.

RSA SecurPC v 2.0

RSA Data Security, Inc., is the company that owns the intellectual property rights to some of the most important cryptographic algorithms in current use. RSA also currently owns the rights to the S/MIME name as well as to critical pieces of this protocol for secure e-mail although it has agreed to freely allow their use in exchange for having them made part of an Internet proposed standard for secure e-mail. (Chapter 7 says more about the issues related to standards and standards bodies on the S/MIME specification.) However, even though every vendor with an implementation of S/MIME licensed RSA technology, RSA itself does not currently offer its own S/MIME client. RSA does publish a personal desktop encryption product called SecurPC, currently in version 2.0.

SecurPC is almost exclusively a personal desktop encryption product; it uses public key cryptography only minimally to support some of its features, but it does not even provide an option to digitally sign a file. SecurPC does provide a full range of desktop encryption and security functions, including

- Secret key encryption of files and directories.
- Ability to encrypt a file with a shared passphrase as a self-extracting ciphertext. (The file is encrypted and turned into an executable file, which can only be opened by running the program and supplying the valid passphrase.)
- Autoencrypt directories.
- Bootup authentication.
- Hot-key system protection.
- Secure delete.
- Transparent file and directory encryption. (Files and directories can be accessed by application programs as if they were not encrypted, but can only be accessed by authorized users.)
- Emergency data access.
- Desktop-level integration with Windows 95.

More details about what SecurPC can and cannot do, as well as some tips about how to use it, are provided in Chapter 8.

Pretty Good Privacy PGP for Personal Privacy 5.0

PGP for Personal Privacy provides some desktop security functions, like in-place encryption, but lacks others including the ability to lock the system, use automatically encrypting directories or do secure deletes. In addition to file encryption and excellent support for personal e-mail security (including encryption-decryption and digital signature-verification functions), however, PGP for Personal Privacy adds a set of functions in an application called PGPtray. PGPtray lets the user perform cryptographic functions on data resident in the system clipboard, so that unencrypted data need not be written to disk at all, and so that data that has been encrypted and/or signed and then inserted into some larger file can be cut out and decrypted or verified in the clipboard.

PGP for Personal Privacy features include

- ♦ Ability to encrypt and/or digitally sign data, e-mail messages, and files.
- ♦ Ability to decrypt and/or verify encrypted or signed data, e-mail messages, and files.
- ♦ Desktop integration of cryptographic functions as well as access to key management and administration functions.
- ♦ Support for Windows as well as Macintosh OS users.

PGP for Personal Privacy is discussed in greater detail as it relates to desktop encryption functions in Chapter 8, while its secure e-mail functions are detailed in Chapter 7. The PGP web of trust model, and more information about administering and using PGP for Personal Privacy are examined in Chapter 10.

Symantec's Norton Your Eyes Only

Norton Your Eyes Only for Windows 95, from Symantec, is a neat personal desktop encryption product with aspirations of being more than that. An administrator add-on is available to allow you to assign and manage users and certificates, which means that you can use true public key encryption and digital signatures—as long as all participants use the Norton Your Eyes Only product.

Features of NortonYour Eyes Only for Windows 95 include

♦ Encryption (with optional digital signature) of files and directories.
♦ Automatic (and transparent to the user) encryption of files and directories.
♦ Secure delete option.
♦ Screenlock function.
♦ Bootlock function.
♦ Emergency unlock function for secure backup of keys.
♦ Choice of various strong encryption algorithms.

Getting a Digital ID

The actual process of acquiring a digital ID for use with S/MIME e-mail/browser combinations like Netscape's Communicator (Navigator/Messenger) and Microsoft's Internet Explorer/Outlook is quite straightforward. The most important choice you should make is which certification authority (CA) you use. During the process of getting a digital ID with either Microsoft's or Netscape's products, both vendors make available pointers to CAs known to interoperate with each vendor's software.

This section walks you through the process of acquiring a digital ID from Verisign, Inc., using both the Microsoft Internet Explorer browser and the Netscape Communicator browser suite. Also included in this section is an examination of the process of generating a public key pair using the PGP for Personal Privacy product.

 As you get your own digital ID, certificate, or public key pair, be careful to pay attention to the instructions provided by the software and service providers that you are using. All dialog boxes and interactive panels should be read and the instructions provided there followed, as they may differ slightly from the descriptions here due to changes made by the vendors after publication of this book.

Getting a VeriSign Certificate with Netscape Communicator 4.0

VeriSign, Inc., was the first company to offer digital IDs, and continues to do so for individuals as well as for businesses. Individual IDs can be used for browsers and e-mail clients and for publication of network software applications; organization IDs can be used for servers, for software publishing, and for EDI. (Electronic Data Interchange provides a standard specification for exchange of commercial transaction information between organizations wishing to do electronic commerce.)

At this writing, VeriSign was offering two classes of digital ID: Class 1 and Class 2. Class 1 IDs, which simply offer an unambiguous identifier to users and which can use aliases, are available on a free trial basis, valid for six months, or on paid basis. Class 2 IDs also offer an unambiguous identification, but in addition they represent that VeriSign has verified identity information based on information like Social Security number and individual address, telephone number, and employer information.

VeriSign's Digital ID Center provides support for seven different functions relating to certificates to its customers. You can

- ♦ Request a new ID.
- ♦ Pick up an issued ID.
- ♦ Terminate an existing ID.
- ♦ Reactivate an ID.
- ♦ Replace an existing ID.
- ♦ Search the database for a specific ID.
- ♦ Certify an ID.

When requesting an ID, you must specify the type of ID you want. For example, you can request an individual ID for your browser (Microsoft Internet Explorer, Netscape Navigator, and Frontier Technology's browsers only at this writing) or for your e-mail package (support for Microsoft, Netscape, Frontier Technology, Premail, Deming, ConnectSoft, OpenSoft, and Eudora at this writing). You can also request an ID to be used for publishing software through Microsoft's Authenticode or Netscape's Object Signing.

This section describes the process of applying for and retrieving a VeriSign Digital ID certificate using Netscape Communicator 4.0. As with all the descriptions of software and services included in this book, the exact screens and steps you experience may vary from those displayed here.

 Be aware that web sites change, service offerings are modified and augmented, and companies change their names, go out of business, and merge with other companies. Although the descriptions and screenshots provided here are accurate at the time of this writing, keep in mind that your experience may very likely be different.

Connect to the VeriSign Web Site

Clicking on the Security icon in the Communicator menubar brings up information about certificates. Figure 5.1 shows the main security panel for Communicator. You have access to all the Communicator security features through this panel. By default it displays the security information of the page currently being browsed. For more information about the other Communicator security features accessible through this panel, see Chapter 6.

Figure 5.2 shows the panel that results when you do that and then select "Certificates, Yours" from the menu on the left side of the panel. Clicking on the button labeled "Get a Certificate" will send you to a Netscape page (*https://certs.netscape.com*) that points to certificate authority service providers, including VeriSign and Thawte, as well as others providing such services outside the U.S. This is a secured web page, meaning it uses SSL to encrypt a channel between the user and the server.

You can also go directly to the VeriSign site at *http://www.VeriSign.com*. This page, as seen recently, is shown in Figure 5.3.

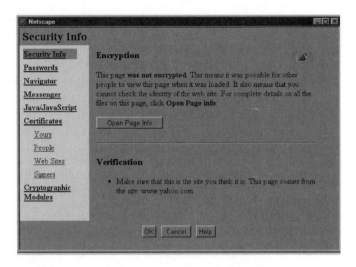

Figure 5.1. The main security panel on Netscape Communicator.

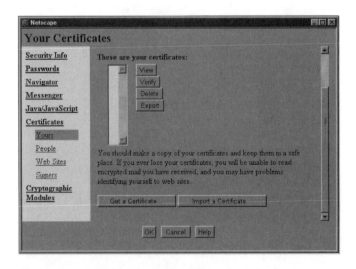

Figure 5.2. Choosing the "Certificates, Yours" option on the Netscape Communicator security panel displays your current certificate information.

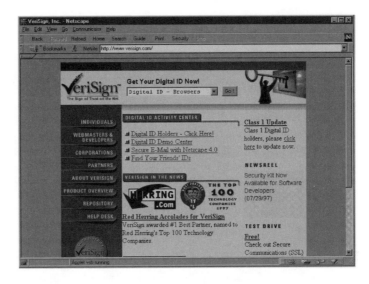

Figure 5.3. VeriSign, Inc.'s home page, where you can apply for VeriSign Digital IDs.

Requesting a VeriSign ID

Navigating at the VeriSign site, you will find there are several different ways to reach the appropriate page to apply for a VeriSign ID. Figure 5.4 shows the VeriSign Digital ID Center (*http://digitalid.VeriSign.com*), through which IDs can be requested. Individuals can select a Class 1 or 2 digital ID. As is clear in this illustration, you can use this page to request a new certificate as well as to retrieve, revoke, replace, or renew an existing ID for yourself, or to find or verify an ID that you have found or been given by someone else.

The process of requesting a Class 2 ID is similar, although much more information is required because the Class 2 ID provides a much higher degree of trust than the Class 1 ID. You must provide VeriSign with enough information to identify and confirm your

Figure 5.4. The VeriSign, Inc., Digital ID Center web page.

identity to a reasonable standard for business transactions. Information you must supply, beyond that required for the Class 1 ID, includes

- ◆ Date of birth.
- ◆ Social Security number.
- ◆ Driver's license number.
- ◆ Home telephone number.
- ◆ Spouse's first name.
- ◆ Your employer.
- ◆ A challenge phrase.
- ◆ Previous address information if you have moved in the past two years.

The Class 2 ID takes longer to generate, but otherwise the process is similar to that described here for the Class 1 ID.

Click on the Enroll button, and you will encounter the first page of the ID request process, as shown in Figure 5.5. You then should choose the appropriate type of certificate; in this case, you should select the Netscape browser option. Other options include other web browsers (particularly the Microsoft Internet Explorer), e-mail clients, and options for digital IDs for organizations.

The next page will be transmitted over an SSL link and is shown in Figure 5.6. The options available on this page are a

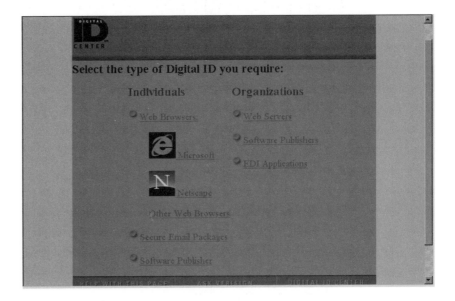

Figure 5.5. The first step in applying for a VeriSign, Inc., Digital ID is choosing the appropriate type of Digital ID.

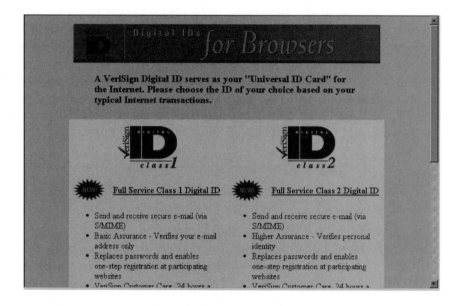

Figure 5.6. When choosing a Digital ID for a browser, you can opt for a Class 1 or Class 2 ID.

Class 1 ID, which verifies only that your e-mail address is correct, and a Class 2 ID, which verifies additional user information including name and address. Class 2 IDs were not available outside the U.S. and Canada as of early 1998, and use a mailback option along with appropriate identity checking done through a third-party information provider. Another option not shown in the figure is the trial Class 1 ID.

Selecting the Class 1 ID should suffice for most personal uses, though it is expected that Class 2 IDs may become useful for individuals wishing to interact with organizations (for example, by making purchases or doing other transactions on-line). Clicking on the "Enroll Me Now" button will load a secured application page.

Filling Out the VeriSign Enrollment Page

The first part of the VeriSign digital ID enrollment page is shown in Figure 5.7. You have the option of including your e-mail address in your digital ID, which you must do if you want to use the ID for S/MIME e-mail. You also have the option of using the digital ID for one-step web site registration. Limited access web sites that require a logon ID can use this information to enroll you in the web site automatically, rather than requiring you to re-enter the same information each time you set up a new web site access account.

The next two steps are shown in Figure 5.8. You need to choose a "challenge phrase" to protect your ID. This challenge phrase is the only way you have of identifying yourself to VeriSign in the event

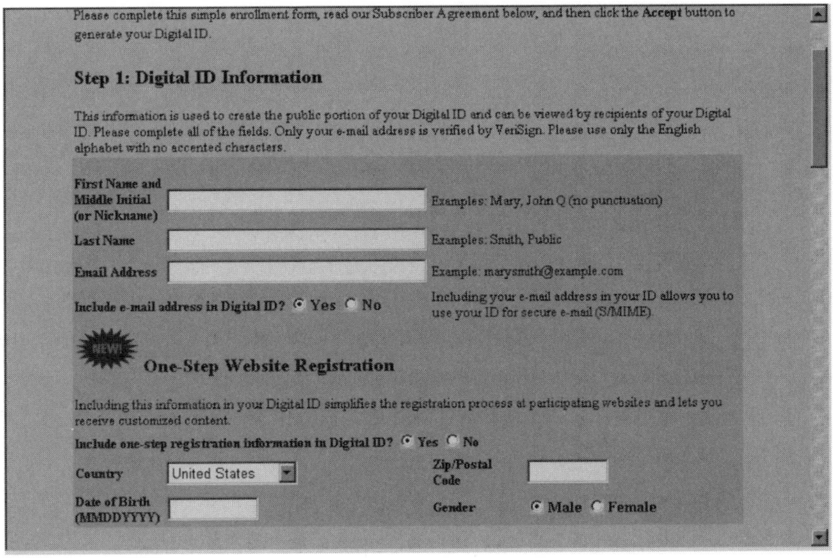
Please complete this simple enrollment form, read our Subscriber Agreement below, and then click the **Accept** button to generate your Digital ID.

Step 1: Digital ID Information

This information is used to create the public portion of your Digital ID and can be viewed by recipients of your Digital ID. Please complete all of the fields. Only your e-mail address is verified by VeriSign. Please use only the English alphabet with no accented characters.

First Name and Middle Initial (or Nickname) Examples: Mary, John Q (no punctuation)

Last Name Examples: Smith, Public

Email Address Example: marysmith@example.com

Include e-mail address in Digital ID? Yes No — Including your e-mail address in your ID allows you to use your ID for secure e-mail (S/MIME).

One-Step Website Registration

Including this information in your Digital ID simplifies the registration process at participating websites and lets you receive customized content.

Include one-step registration information in Digital ID? Yes No

Country United States **Zip/Postal Code**

Date of Birth (MMDDYYYY) **Gender** Male Female

Figure 5.7. Filling out the application form for a VeriSign Digital ID, first part.

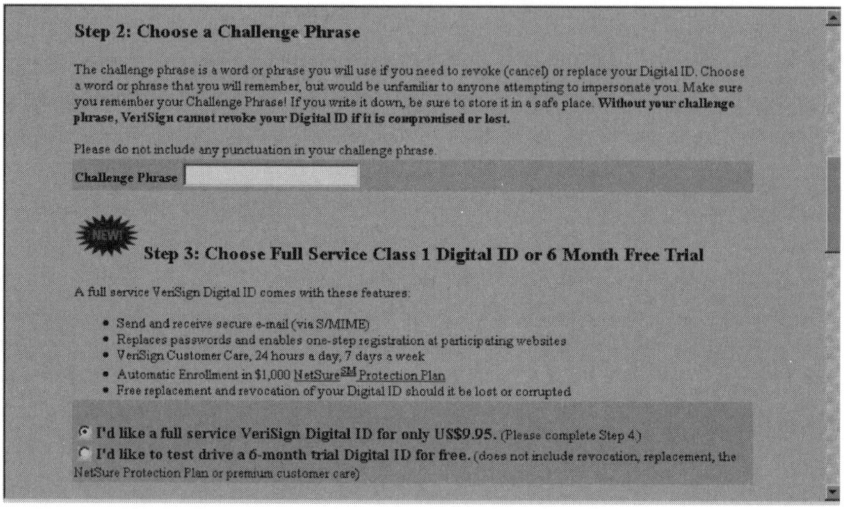

Step 2: Choose a Challenge Phrase

The challenge phrase is a word or phrase you will use if you need to revoke (cancel) or replace your Digital ID. Choose a word or phrase that you will remember, but would be unfamiliar to anyone attempting to impersonate you. Make sure you remember your Challenge Phrase! If you write it down, be sure to store it in a safe place. **Without your challenge phrase, VeriSign cannot revoke your Digital ID if it is compromised or lost.**

Please do not include any punctuation in your challenge phrase.

Challenge Phrase [   ]

Step 3: Choose Full Service Class 1 Digital ID or 6 Month Free Trial

A full service VeriSign Digital ID comes with these features:

- Send and receive secure e-mail (via S/MIME)
- Replaces passwords and enables one-step registration at participating websites
- VeriSign Customer Care, 24 hours a day, 7 days a week
- Automatic Enrollment in $1,000 NetSure™ Protection Plan
- Free replacement and revocation of your Digital ID should it be lost or corrupted

( ) **I'd like a full service VeriSign Digital ID for only US$9.95.** (Please complete Step 4)
( ) **I'd like to test drive a 6-month trial Digital ID for free.** (does not include revocation, replacement, the NetSure Protection Plan or premium customer care)

Figure 5.8. Filling out the application form for a VeriSign Digital ID, second part.

that you need to revoke or replace your VeriSign digital ID. The only time you would use this phrase is when dealing directly with VeriSign, during the process of revocation or replacement of this digital ID. As the instructions shown in the figure demonstrate, it is important to choose a phrase that only you would know (and that you will be able to remember when you want to replace your digital ID, or when you need to revoke a compromised digital ID).

The next step, also shown in Figure 5.8, is to choose a Class 1 digital ID version: either the trial version (which lasts six months) or the full-year, full-service version, which costs $9.95 for a full year. The next step, shown in Figure 5.9, is to fill in your payment information, which is only necessary if you have selected the full-year Class 1 digital ID.

Once all this information is completed, you can choose a key length (512, 784, or 1024 bits) from a pull-down at the bottom of the page;

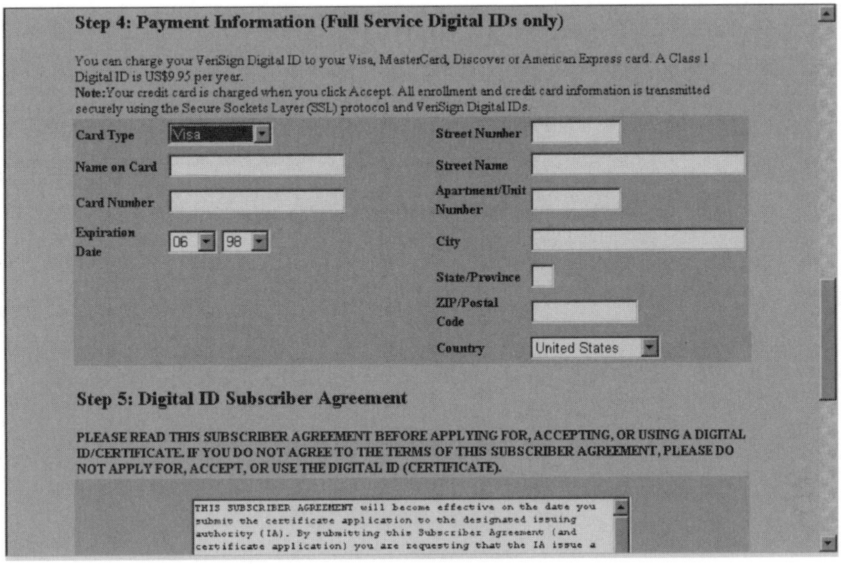

Figure 5.9. Filling out the application form for a VeriSign Digital ID, third part.

otherwise, clicking on the Accept button beneath the subscriber agreement, as shown in Figure 5.10, will submit your application to VeriSign.

Once the application is submitted, Communicator will display a panel, shown in Figure 5.11, indicating that it will generate a private key for the VeriSign ID certificate.

However, before it will generate a private key, Communicator offers you the opportunity to passphrase protect this private key with a separate passphrase, as shown in Figure 5.12.

At this point, the Communicator software attempts to generate a public key pair and submit the application information to VeriSign's systems. If there are any errors (or perceived errors), the

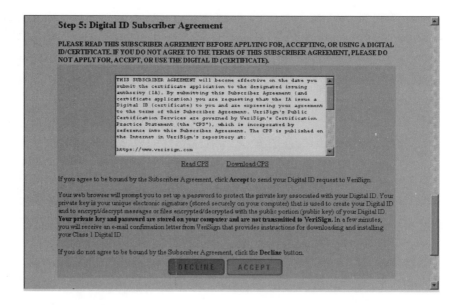

Figure 5.10. Submitting the application form for a VeriSign Digital ID.

application must be corrected and resubmitted. For example, credit card account numbers must be entered without any spaces between the digits, street number is a required field, and any use of punctuation that appears to be inappropriate (for example, in the street number field) will cause the system to bounce the application. Once the application is completed, submitted, and accepted by VeriSign, an enrollment completion page is displayed, as shown in Figure 5.13.

Getting Your VeriSign Digital ID

The next step is to wait for a little while—however long it takes for VeriSign to generate an e-mail message to you and for you to receive it. This message will include information about your account, as well as pointers to web pages with additional informa-

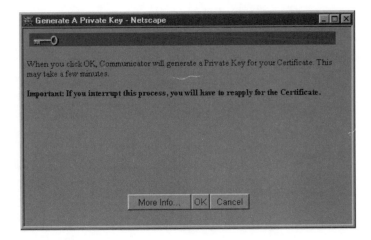

Figure 5.11. Netscape Communicator is aware of the application process and indicates when it begins to generate a new key.

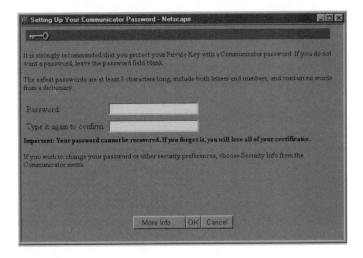

Figure 5.12. Storing your private key in Communicator, using a passphrase to protect access.

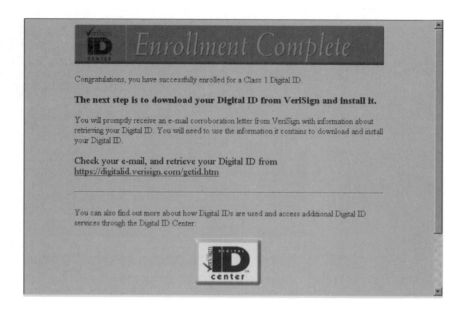

Figure 5.13. When the application is submitted and accepted by VeriSign, this page is shown.

tion about your account. Most important, though, it will include a pointer to the same web page referenced on your enrollment completion page—*https://digitalid.VeriSign.com/getid.html*—on which you enter the most important part of the message from VeriSign: a personal identification number (PIN) for retrieving your digital ID. This message also includes the name, e-mail address, and any other personal information that is included in the digital ID.

Going to that page, as shown in Figure 5.14, you must enter the digital ID PIN in the appropriate form, preferably by doing a cut-and-paste operation from the original e-mail message, and then clicking on the submit button. Communicator will then present a panel indicating that a new certificate has been received, as shown in Figure 5.15, and give you various options. First, you can modify the name

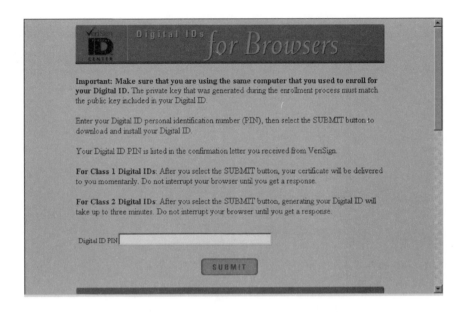

Figure 5.14. Entering a VeriSign PIN to retrieve a Digital ID.

assigned by Communicator to the certificate; you can also choose this certificate as the default certificate to be used for all encrypted and signed e-mail.

If you choose to have Communicator display the new certificate from this panel, as shown in Figure 5.16, you will see displayed the following information:

> ♦ To whom the certificate belongs. This includes the name associated with the certificate and any other personal information that was associated with the certificate, like e-mail address. Also included is information about the certificate, like the issuer and type of certificate.
>
> ♦ A serial number, in hexadecimal format.

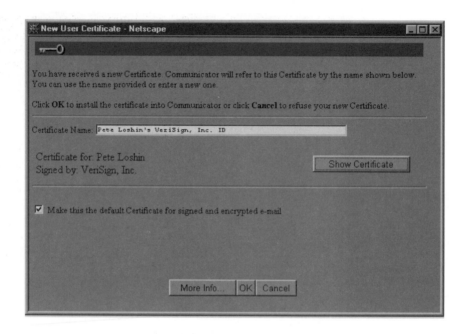

Figure 5.15. Loading the new Digital ID as a certificate into Communicator.

- ◆ Certificate validity dates. These include a date from which the certificate begins to be valid and a date after which the certificate is invalid.
- ◆ A certificate fingerprint, for authentication purposes.

Once you click on the OK button of the new certificate panel, indicating you have accepted it, you will be prompted to save the certificate. This is a very good idea, allowing you to store the certificate on a floppy diskette. In the event that your system or the installation of Communicator is damaged or destroyed, having the certificate stored on floppy means that you will still be able to access data encrypted with that certificate. Communicator will prompt you to

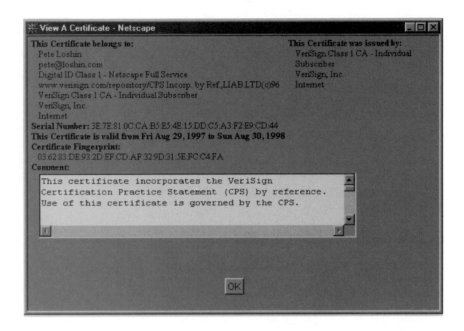

Figure 5.16. Communicator displays information about a certificate.

enter a passphrase (and re-enter it) to protect the certificate, then you can save the certificate in standard PKCS (Public-Key Cryptography Standards) format; this format should also work for systems that support X.509 certificates. You will then be able to use that certificate with other software that understands that format.

Getting a Digital ID with Microsoft Internet Explorer 4.0

The first part of the process, including contacting the certification authority and submitting personal information, is much the same as that for Netscape Communicator. However, once you finish the application for a Microsoft Internet Explorer 4.0 digital ID, you submit the application to Verisign, as shown in Figure 5.17.

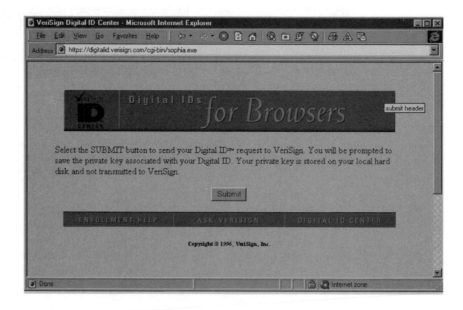

Figure 5.17. After filling in the Verisign Digital ID application, you submit the application to Verisign with Microsoft Internet Explorer 4.0.

Microsoft Internet Explorer 4.0 Credentials Enrollment Wizard

Completing the application form initiates the Microsoft Internet Explorer 4.0 Credentials Enrollment Wizard, as shown in Figure 5.18. This is a series of panels that help to walk you through the process of creating a key pair for Microsoft Internet Explorer, with explanatory material included.

The next panel lets you choose from the cryptographic services on your system; not all registered services will actually work with all certificate authority service providers. For example, Figure 5.19 shows two available services, of which only the Microsoft Base

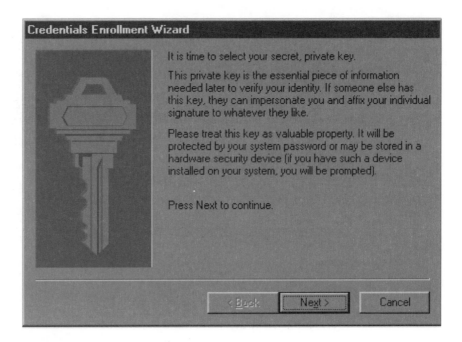

Figure 5.18. The Microsoft Internet Explorer 4.0 Credentials Enrollment Wizard opening panel.

Cryptographic Provider 1.0 would actually permit a key pair to be generated with Verisign at the time of this writing.

Once you have chosen a cryptographic provider, the last panel of the Credentials Enrollment Wizard permits you to name your private key for reference on your system, and allows you to complete the enrollment process, as shown in Figure 5.20.

At this point, the certificate is generated, and control is returned to the Verisign server, which will, if all information has been entered correctly and completely, return a page that indicates you should

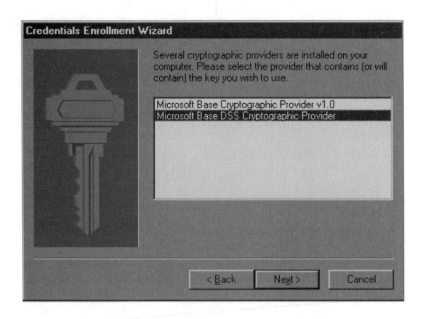

Figure 5.19. Choosing a cryptographic provider for Microsoft Internet Explorer 4.0 Digital ID generation.

check your e-mail for a PIN and return to a particular page to retrieve your Digital ID, as shown in Figure 5.21.

The retrieval web page, and the process of entering the PIN and registering the certificate with the browser, are much the same as with Netscape Communicator.

Getting a Certificate with Microsoft Outlook Express

Outlook Express supports both encryption and digital signatures. To set up to use a certificate that you have already received, you need first to select the Accounts option from the Tools pulldown menu. Select the desired account from those displayed, and click on

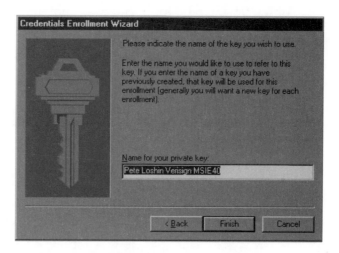

Figure 5.20. Completing the Microsoft Internet Explorer 4.0 Credentials Enrollment Wizard process.

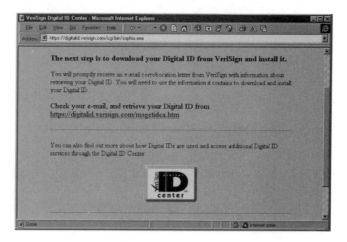

Figure 5.21. Once the application is submitted to and received by Verisign, and you have received a PIN by e-mail, you can go to the specified web page to retrieve the Digital ID.

the Properties button. A set of tabbed panels will be displayed; one of the tabs will be for Security as shown in Figure 5.22.

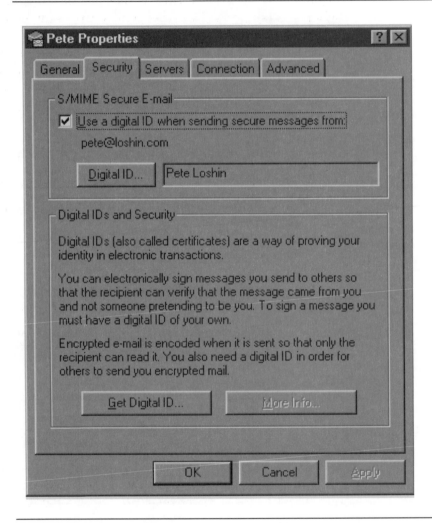

Figure 5.22. Microsoft Outlook Express e-mail client options for account security properties.

The details of this panel, and of using Outlook Express to send signed and/or encrypted e-mail, will be discussed at greater length in Chapter 7. However, the relevant item here is the button that reads "Get Digital ID . . ." Clicking on this button will open your browser on Microsoft's page that points to certificate authorities. A similar button can also be seen in Outlook Express when choosing the Tools menu from the main menubar and then the Options choice from the pull-down menu. A set of tabbed option panels, including a Security tab, will appear. Click on the Security tab, as shown in Figure 5.23, and you can also click on a "Get Digital ID . . ." button and be sent to the same Microsoft web page for certificate authorities.

Installing and Generating a Public Key Pair with PGP 5.0

Pretty Good Privacy, Inc.'s PGP 5.0 is the most recent commercial implementation of the PGP program that has been distributed globally (in one form or another) since 1991. Installation and key generation with PGP 5.0 for Windows 95 is described here; the program and its functions are described in greater detail in Chapters 7, 8, and 10.

 PGP 5.0 uses two key formats. One is backward compatible with previous versions of PGP, the other is not. If you receive messages signed with an older version, you will still be able to certify the signatures; if you must encrypt a message for a recipient who uses the older version, you will still be able to.

PGP 5.0 Installation

PGP 5.0 uses the standard InstallShield installation program. The process should be a simple matter of inserting the distribution CD and answering a series of prompts. These include

- A prompt to shut down all other programs.
- A license agreement acceptance panel.

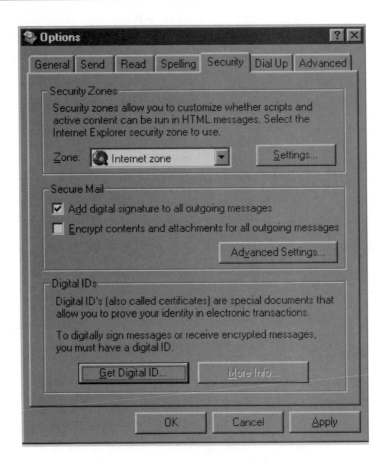

Figure 5.23. Another route to getting a digital certificate with Microsoft's Outlook Express e-mail client.

- ♦ A user registration panel to enter user name, company, and serial number.
- ♦ Install directory selection panel.
- ♦ A component selection panel for choosing which parts of the program to install, including the main program files, plugins for Eudora and Microsoft Outlook/Exchange clients, and the user manual.

After the install program copies the program files into the selected directory, the program will prompt you to indicate whether or not you have existing keyrings, giving you the option of pointing the new install at any existing keyrings, or of automatically starting up and generating a new keyring for you.

PGP 5.0 Key Generation

If you do not have a keyring already set up when you start the PGPkeys program, it will prompt you to begin the process. A panel will appear, as shown in Figure 5.24, briefly explaining what private and public keys are and what they are used for—and giving you the option to get more information by clicking on the Help button.

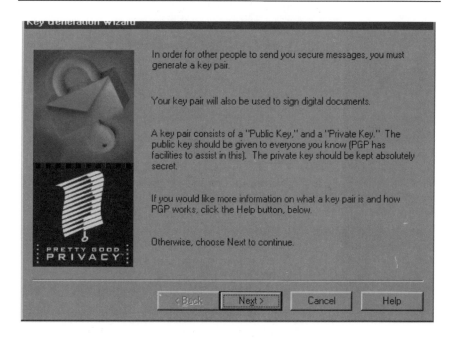

Figure 5.24. The opening panel in the process of creating a new set of keys.

The next step is to enter the name and e-mail address you wish to be associated with your key pair. Figure 5.25 shows the panel in which this information is entered; again, the panel provides a basic explanation of each step, with more details available by clicking on the Help button.

The next step is to select your key type. For reasons of backward compatibility with previous versions of PGP, the user has the option of choosing either the RSA key pair type or the DSS/Diffie-Hellman key pair type. Earlier versions of PGP used a key pair type based on RSA algorithms, but the newer versions can use the DSS, or Digital Signature Standard, combined with the Diffie-Hellman

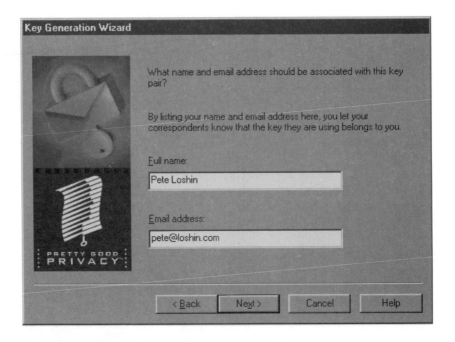

Figure 5.25. Entering your name and e-mail address when creating a PGP public key pair.

key exchange. Figure 5.26 shows the selection panel. The choice you make depends on who you are communicating with and how. If you need to be able to securely communicate with others who are using the old-style RSA keys, you should create your own key as an RSA key pair. If you need to communicate securely with other, newer users who are using the DSS key pair style, you should generate a DSS-style key pair. And, if you need to communicate with both groups, you will have to generate two pairs: one as an RSA pair, the other as a DSS pair.

The next panel allows you to select a length for your key pair. Standard lengths from 768 bits to 3072 bits are available, as is a custom

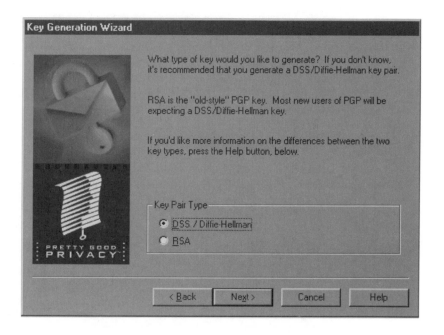

Figure 5.26. Choosing a key pair style when generating a new key pair with PGP.

size option allowing a choice of key length anywhere from 512 bits to 4096 bits. The panel, as shown in Figure 5.27, explains that larger key lengths are more secure but also slower, and that key lengths in the range of 1024 bits to 2048 bits should be sufficient for most users.

Once the key length is set, the next step is to set a key pair expiration date as shown in Figure 5.28. PGP recommends that you set an expiration date on key pairs only for special circumstances, and create your primary key pair with no expiration date. The idea is that when you create your key—and publish it as widely as possible within the PGP web of trust—you will not want to have to go

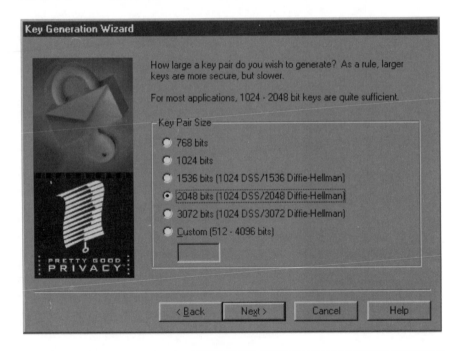

Figure 5.27. Choosing a key length when generating a new key pair with PGP.

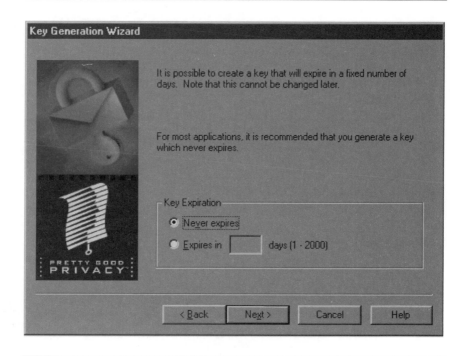

Figure 5.28. Setting an expiration date for your PGP key pair.

through that process again. Thus, setting no expiration date on that key pair makes sense. However, there may be times when you would prefer to have a more temporary key pair, in which case you can set an expiration date after which the keys will no longer be usable to do any encryption. In other words, you will be able to use the public key to verify signatures created while the key pair was valid but not to encrypt any new messages; the private key can be used to decrypt messages encrypted and sent during the time that the key pair was valid but not to sign any new messages.

The next panel prompts you for a passphrase and confirmation, as shown in Figure 5.29. This passphrase protects your private key.

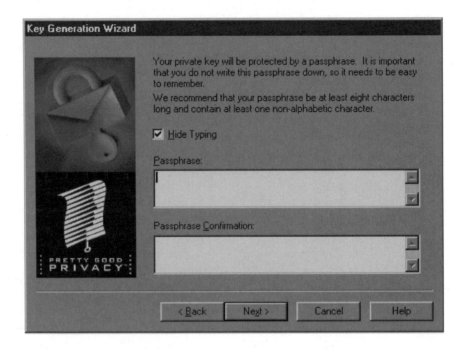

Figure 5.29. Entering a passphrase to protect your PGP private key.

PGP recommends that it should be at least eight characters long, with at least one nonalphabetic character. When filling in this panel, you can opt to display the characters you type, or to blank them out as you type them. While it is easier to leave the display on, particularly when retyping the passphrase, it is more secure to leave the display off, especially if you are using a monitor that can be viewed by others. Furthermore, leaving the display off will give you a better idea of how easily you will be able to remember your passphrase later.

Once the passphrase is entered, the program generates the key pair and displays an animation indicating that processing is continuing.

When the key pair is generated a completion panel is displayed as shown in Figure 5.30.

With the key pair generated, the next step, as shown in Figure 5.31, is to send the public key to a keyserver. Alternatively, if you are not connected to the Internet, you can opt to send the key to the keyserver at some later time.

Once the keyserver has been contacted and your public key uploaded to it, a completion dialog box will appear and you can continue, as shown in Figure 5.32. The default keyserver is

Figure 5.30. Once the PGP key pair is generated, the program displays this completion panel.

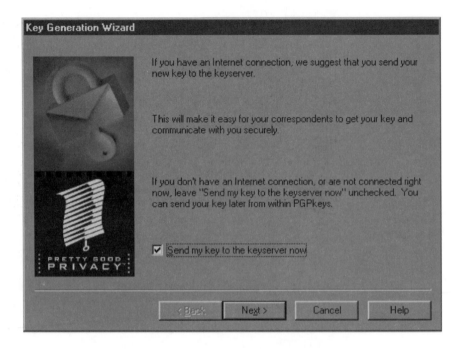

Figure 5.31. Choosing to send your public key to a keyserver.

pgpkeys.mit.edu, a host maintained at MIT. You may also later choose to use a different keyserver. The key pair generation process is completed after you upload your public key to the keyserver and choose the Finish button on the final panel of the key pair generation wizard.

Once complete, the PGPkeys application will start, displaying the public keys of some of the employees of PGP, Inc., along with your own (if you loaded it to the keyserver). Figure 5.33 shows the PGPkeys application. The details of this application will be discussed in Chapter 10.

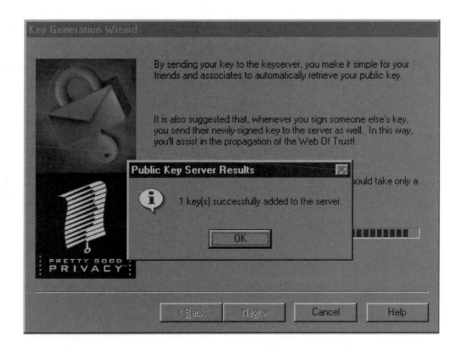

Figure 5.32. Once your public key has been uploaded to the keyserver, the key pair generation wizard is almost finished.

One last step remains in the process of generating your PGP public key pair: backing up your key pair to a diskette. When you exit PGPkeys after having generated a new public key pair, you will be prompted to save your key file, as shown in Figure 5.34. You will be prompted to enter a disk and filename for the backup of both your public and private keyrings.

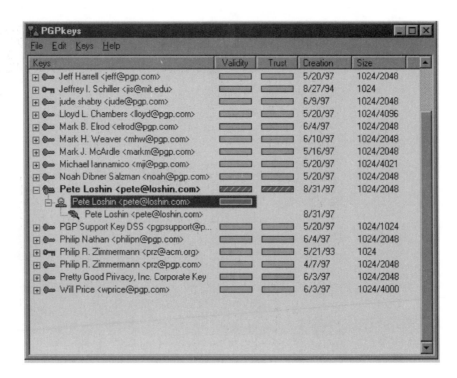

Figure 5.33. The PGPkeys application lets you manage your own keys, as well as include the keys of others in your own keyring.

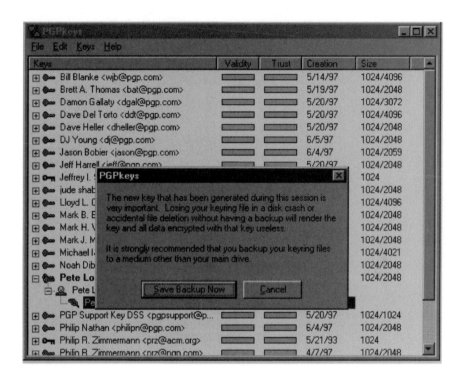

Figure 5.34. You cannot exit PGPkeys after creating a new key pair without being prompted to backup your new keys.

6

Secure Web Surfing

This chapter provides hands-on instructions for using cryptographic functions while surfing the World Wide Web. This includes security issues related to browsing the World Wide Web, the proper use of digital certificates while browsing, the correct interpretation of security information stored with Web pages, and how to use the most popular encryption-aware browsers now available from Microsoft and Netscape. Simply going from one web site to another can be a risky business—actually doing electronic commerce, as discussed in Chapter 9, poses a slightly different, though related, set of problems.

Web Browsing Security Issues

On the surface, web browsing seems to be a fairly innocuous activity. The web browser client software makes a request for a resource from a web server, and the web server responds to the request by sending the actual resource back to the client. The simplest transaction would be a request from a client for a file containing text; this interaction is illustrated in Figure 6.1.

In practice, things can be considerably more complicated—if they were not, web browsing would be considerably less interesting. Risks associated with web browsing are also mostly associated with web features that add to the richness of the web experience. Risks discussed in this chapter include

- ♦ Properly identifying web services. Not all web sites are what they seem, and there are ways to determine with whom you are dealing.
- ♦ Software security is increasingly important as the volume of static web content is displaced by the use of software downloads in the form of ActiveX components and Java applets. These are pieces of software that could be subverted.

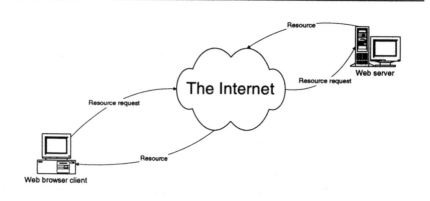

Figure 6.1. A web client requests a resource (for example, a file) from a web server—which responds by sending the resource to the client.

- ◆ Cookies are state-saving devices that can be used to gather and store information about you and your web browsing activities. Not everyone feels comfortable with them, but webmasters use them copiously to provide valuable interactive services.
- ◆ Loss of anonymity. There are no surveillance cameras at the library watching what books and magazines you read, but there are ways for webmasters to follow your browsing habits. There are also ways for you to maintain your anonymity.
- ◆ Nontechnological risks including any risk that is unrelated to technology but still poses a risk to web browsers—in a word, the things that could happen to you when you interact in any way with other individuals or organizations: fraud, theft, disclosure of personal information, and so on.

Each of these risks, and remedies for specific risks where they are available, is discussed in this chapter.

Know Who You Are Dealing With

Most people realize that you cannot believe everything you see on television or read in the newspaper, but having heard about something through these traditional media still confers a certain patina of truth, deserved or not. There is something compelling about seeing a story in print, particularly when the print comes from a prestigious newspaper or magazine; there is an extraordinary power to broadcast media that can reach tens of millions of information consumers in a moment.

A great deal of the power of the Internet has always been that it is not strictly necessary for an individual to have spent millions (or even thousands) to build the facilities to reach the masses with the same impact as a billion-dollar media corporation. For the same reasons that a single entrepreneur can use the World Wide Web to build a thriving business, other, less scrupulous individuals can use the World Wide Web to misrepresent themselves more actively in one way or another. Outright frauds will be discussed later in the chapter; this section discusses the issues of "knock-off" web sites (sites that may appear to be one thing, but in fact are something else) and hacked or hijacked web sites (sites that were genuine, but have been attacked and changed to something else). This part ends with a discussion of ways to check the integrity of a web site.

Knock-off Web Sites

Like the knock-off frauds sold on the streets of New York, there are those who would palm off their own version of reality by registering a domain name that comes close to being the one you would expect and then putting up a spoof of that site. The informed consumer needs to take the time to research a purchase and understand that there is a different between a Rolex and a Rollex (or Rolax or any number of other variations), so the web surfer needs to be aware that a URL name that sounds right is no guarantee that the URL is the one you think it is.

One source of confusion is the use of different top-level domains. Most commercial enterprises use the *.com* domain (for example, *loshin.com* is the author's domain), while network service providers often use the *.net* top-level domain (for example, The Internet Access Company, or TIAC, uses the *tiac.net* domain). Other top-level domains commonly used within the United States include the *.edu* domain for educational institutions and the *.org* domain for organizations that do not fall into the other categories.

It is vital to remember that the URL that would seem logically to be the one you want is not always the one you want. For example, the domain *acme.com* is currently owned by software developer and consultant Jef Poskanzer. This means that any other organization that uses the name *Acme* must use some other variation on its domain. Go to Poskanzer's web site and you can find a link to a list of other *Acmes* on the World Wide Web; according to Poskanzer's web site, at last count there were over 250, with many providing web sites on their own domains. The domains by necessity are variations, incorporating the word *acme* in a more complete description of the companies that registered their domains too late.

Finding the right web site is a matter of just being careful. If you are going to use the web site for business purposes (to collect information in support of making a buying decision, or for actually making a purchase on-line), you should always verify in some way through some trusted information resource that you are at the right place. This might be by using a web search site that verifies and describes its links, or by checking out the URL provided by your target in its own promotional material or advertising.

Hacked Web Sites

Even if you are at the right web page, it is possible that what you are viewing is not what was intended for you to be viewing. This occurs any time a web site is hacked. Criminals have been known to break into web servers and change the contents of web sites that do not belong to them. Some very high profile cases, including web sites offered by government agencies, have brought the issue of web site security to the fore. However, better security on web servers and supporting products will be necessary before it is possible to eliminate this problem.

As web sites increasingly interoperate with other sites and services (for example, web sites that support on-line transactions must interoperate with services that mediate the actual transactions among the consumer, merchant, and credit card issuers), the potential cost of hitting a hacked web site increases. For this reason it is important for consumers to verify certificates of web sites they plan to do business with, as will be discussed later in this chapter.

Web Spoofing with URL-Rewriting

Another very serious attack is one in which the attacker spoofs a web site to a victim and then uses a man-in-the-middle strategy to rewrite all the traffic between the victim and the spoofed (intended) web site. In this scenario, the victim sends requests (which may include commercial transactions) to the intended web site; the attacker receives all the requests from the victim and retransmits them to the intended site. The attacker could then simply steal the victim's credit card account information; the attacker could also actually intercept the victim's on-line order (change the delivery address for any goods to one accessible to the attacker). It is not clear whether it is possible to deter this type of attack.

Software Security

Surfing the web increasingly means downloading a piece of software in the form of an ActiveX control or Java applet. These things are actual programs, which in theory and potentially could just as easily contain harmful code as any other program that you download over the Internet. The ActiveX control is a program that runs within the Microsoft Windows framework, and it uses standards and specifications defined by Microsoft for distributed applications. Alternatively, in the Java/open standards corner, are Java applets which can run on any system that supports Java, originally defined by Sun MicroSystems.

Any software has the potential for harm, and both Microsoft and Sun have taken steps to keep the software distributed within their competing frameworks safe. These approaches are described next.

The Java Sandbox

When creating the Java programming language and environment, Sun engineers were concerned that applets might cause problems on the systems running them. These problems could just as easily be caused by bugs that were inadvertently included in the code as they could be by truly malevolent code, so the Java builders chose to use a concept called a sandbox—a virtual space in the system running the Java code, in which the Java code could play nicely, while not being permitted outside the sandbox. This means that Java code can manipulate data and resources that sit in the sandbox with it, but cannot get at other resources outside the sandbox— resources like disks or system memory that might cause the system to crash if harmed (on purpose or not).

The downside of this type of approach, of course, is that Java applets tend not to be capable of doing many of the useful things that people would like them to. Without access to system resources, Java applets cannot read or write data to the local host, or even print data out to a local printer.

Microsoft Authenticode

Rather than limit distributed applications to doing what might be considered the trivial tasks that Java applets are capable of, Microsoft chose a different approach to security for downloaded ActiveX controls. Authenticode is a framework within which software that is downloaded over the Internet is digitally signed by the publisher and by some other third party to certify that the code actually did come from the entity claiming to have published it.

The advantage of this approach is that it does not limit what an ActiveX control is able to do with system resources on the host downloading it. This leaves open some concerns about security. For one thing, the digital signature certifies only that the code you are downloading is the same code that was provided by the publisher to the certifying entity. There is no further guarantee about anything that the code might do—it could be full of bugs that cause it to crash your system or worse; it could be full of malevolent code (a problem if the certifying entity does not check the credentials of the software publisher); it could do functions that might not be considered malevolent but which you might prefer it not to (which amounts to the same thing).

Saving State and Using Cookies

HTTP (Hypertext Transport Protocol) was originally defined as a stateless protocol, meaning that interactions between clients and servers are all independent of each other. This makes for a more robust protocol because servers do not have to keep track of what happened before in order to respond to current requests from browsers. On the other hand, it makes it considerably more difficult to build any kind of web service that depends on interaction between the user and the service.

To simulate statefulness, web servers and browsers support a construct known as a cookie. This is a piece of data that the browser allows the server to write to disk on the browser's system.

The Purpose of a Cookie

The purpose of the cookie is to allow your session to take on some degree of statefulness, so that when you go from one page to another of a web site, the web site will be able to remember what happened in previous interactions with you. For example, one common use of cookies is to enable the use of virtual shopping carts. When you choose a product from an on-line merchant's catalog, a cookie (or cookies) can be set to indicate information about the item or items you want. That way, you are able to browse through many different pages and when you are ready to pay for your purchases, a checkout page will list all the items you have chosen. This is a use of cookies that benefits the user as well as the web site host.

Some web sites also collect information about what page you were at just prior to loading the current page, or what page you go to after the current page. This information may just be used as it applies to the pages of the current web site, or it may be used to track movement from one domain to another. You can get an idea of what kinds of cookies are being used by having your browser inform you whenever a cookie is requested, as discussed later in this chapter.

Defeating the Cookie Monsters

Merchants seem to be ever more hungry for information about their customers and about how they come in the door. There was a time when Radio Shack seemed to be the only store whose clerks would require you to give your name and zip code every time you made a purchase; now, merchants of all kinds want to know your last name, zip code, phone number, and more. This trend is even more true on the Internet, where it is possible to gather information about your surfing habits without having to ask your permission.

This may be threatening to some people; in fact, it may not be as menacing as it seems as long as you understand that it is happening and allow that part of the cost of doing business over the web is that you have to give up some privacy. Alternatively, there are some steps you can take to keep your web footprints private.

PGPcookie.cutter for Windows

Pretty Good Privacy, Inc., released a product called PGPcookie.cutter in 1997 but subsequently had to suspend distribution due to some problems with the software. PGPcookie.cutter is a plug-in program for both Netscape's Navigator and Microsoft's Internet Explorer browser that selectively blocks cookies. Important functions this software provided included

- The ability to selectively block cookies and the data they access. Users can choose which cookies can have access to password information while blocking more intrusive cookies.
- The ability for users to select privacy levels, blocking all cookies or permitting cookies based on domain.
- The ability for users to view contents of cookies, showing the value of the cookie as well as expiration date and privacy level.

Lucent Personalized Web Assistant

Another technology alternative for dealing with cookies is to use an anonymizer service. One demonstration of privacy technology was done in June 1997 by Lucent Technologies. Known as the Lucent Personalized Web Assistant (LPWA), the system provides users with a method of using aliases when registering with web sites, rather than using their own names and e-mail addresses.

LPWA is a proxy server running on a Lucent system. To use it, you have to point your browser to the LPWA proxy server, and access personalized web sites through it. Lucent announced it would continue to offer the service at least through September 30, 1997 (the service was still active early in 1998); for more details, try the LPWA web site

```
http://lpwa.com
```

The process of registering is fairly painless, and the result is that you can subscribe to any number of different personalized web pages—the kind that tend to use cookies for tracking your web browsing habits and linking them to your personal information—anonymously. The LPWA proxy server generates a unique and consistent set of ID for each site you want to subscribe to, and it logs onto them for you. Your LPWA logon information is not available to any of those subscription sites—in fact, that data isn't even stored on the LPWA proxy, so there is no way to associate your identity with any of the alias logons generated by LPWA.

Web Risks Unrelated to Technology

There is no way that technology can protect you against every threat. This is particularly true for web browsing. There are many criminals who would like to use the Internet and the World Wide Web to defraud. Just as criminals find willing victims in the real world, so too do they find them in the virtual world. By and large, the way to avoid being defrauded on-line is the same as it is in the real world: do not believe anything that sounds too good to be true, and do not believe everything you see on the Internet. Caveat emptor is as good a policy on-line as off-.

Securely Browsing with Netscape Navigator/ Communicator

Browsing securely with Netscape's Navigator as a stand-alone product or as part of Communicator, revolves around the proper use of the Security interface. In previous versions of Navigator, some or all security options could be set by choosing the Preferences option in the Edit pulldown menu; however, all security features are now accessible through the new security interface (excepting cookie management, as will be discussed). Figure 6.2 shows how to access the security interface from a typical web page.

Communicator's security interface provides access to several different functions, including

- ◆ Checking out the security information related to the page currently being browsed.
- ◆ Management of passwords to protect your Communicator certificates.

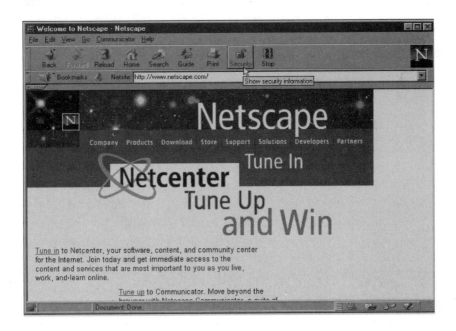

Figure 6.2. The Security button, which may also appear as a padlock, is the entry point for virtually all Navigator security functions.

- ◆ Controlling browser security settings.
- ◆ Controlling e-mail client security settings.
- ◆ Granting or forbidding access to your system by Java applets and JavaScripts depending on the applet signature.
- ◆ Managing certificates: your own, other individuals', web sites', and certification authorities'.
- ◆ Managing cryptographic modules being used by Communicator.

This section discusses how to use the Navigator security interface to perform all these functions. Using Navigator to actually get a personal S/MIME secure e-mail certificate was discussed in Chapter 5.

Checking Web Page Security Attributes

Practically the first thing that happens when you start browsing is that you start viewing pages. This section explains how to check out the security attributes of any page you browse using the Navigator security interface.

Figure 6.3 shows how this interface appears when you first click on the Security button. The interface opens up on a page showing security information about the page currently being browsed. Take a moment to look at the information provided in this panel. First, a depiction of an open padlock appears in the upper right corner of the panel, indicating that the page in question is not encrypted. This information is repeated in the text just below the icon, along with suggestions of the implications of the use or lack of encryption.

In the bottom third of the panel is a paragraph about verification. The name of the actual host from which the page was retrieved is displayed. Verifying the source of the host is important. Sometimes a web page may point you to other web servers without actually making it clear that you have left the web site.

Things become more interesting when you load a secure document. Now the security icon on the toolbar turns into a locked padlock (as does the figure in the lower left corner of the Navigator window).

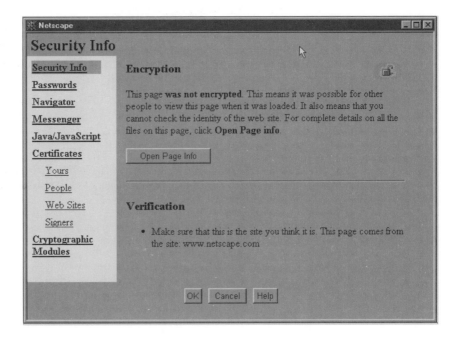

Figure 6.3. The Communicator/Navigator security interface applet provides access to all browser and client security features.

Figure 6.4 shows what happens when you click on the security icon. The panel explains that the page was encrypted, and you have the option of viewing the certificate associated with the page as well as of viewing a list of what else is on that page.

Figure 6.5 shows what happens when you choose to view the page's certificate by clicking on the View Certificate button. The window shows who the certificate was issued to in the upper left corner. On the top right side is displayed who issued the certificate, while underneath appears the serial number assigned to the certificate, the certificate's dates of validity, and the fingerprint of the certificate (the

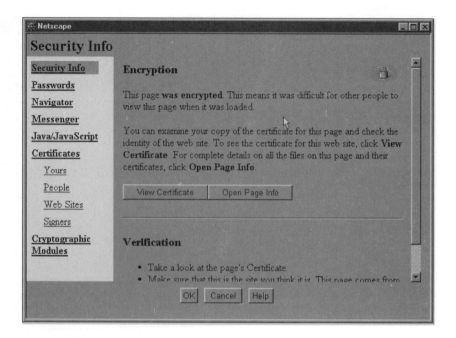

Figure 6.4. Checking security information for a web page that has been encrypted.

result of a secure hash function on the certificate that makes it more manageable to verify signatures).

Information about the web page itself can also be retrieved by clicking on the Open Page Info button. This button will always be available, whether the page you are currently browsing is secure or insecure.

As shown in Figure 6.6, it provides information about the page displayed in two separate windows. The top window shows the structure of the page, including pointers to each individual file that is displayed one page (for example, graphics files displayed as part of the page) as well as information about layer structures and pointers

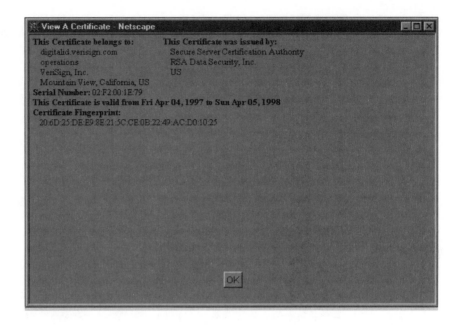

Figure 6.5. Viewing a web page's certificate through Netscape Navigator.

to background files (graphics used in the background of the page display). Each of the resources in this window is selectable, and more information about each is available in the lower part of the display.

The bottom window displays additional information about the resource selected in the upper window, including

- The complete URL of the resource, including the type of resource (e.g., HTTP for regular web resources, HTTPS for SSL web resources, FTP for File Transfer Protocol resources), the host name (e.g., *//www.loshin.com*), and the directory and file name of the resource (e.g., */home/ index.html*).

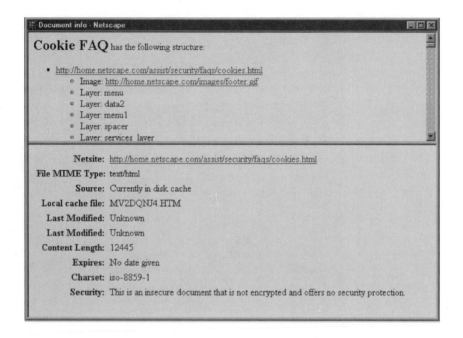

Figure 6.6. Viewing information about a web page with the Open Page Info button in Netscape Navigator's security interface.

♦ The page's file MIME type. This may specify some multimedia file type, or simply say that the resource is a text file.

♦ The source of the resource. This is where the resource was taken to load it into the browser, and it may often show up as having been taken from a cache file, or it may be from a memory cache.

♦ The local cache filename of the resource. This is the name the resource has been given by the local system to the cached resource.

♦ The time of the last modification of the resource—in both local time (to the browser) and in Greenwich Mean Time

(GMT). This will tell you when the file was last changed; this information is not always available.

♦ The content length of the resource. This is simply the number of bytes in the resource.

♦ Expiration date for the resource, if any.

♦ Charset, or character set, of the resource. Graphics and other multimedia files generally have no charset value, though text files will have one. This is what tells the browser which international character set to use, which is particularly useful for browsing in languages that use different character sets.

♦ Security information. This will usually indicate whether or not the resource is secured; if it is, it will indicate the type of security and encryption used to encrypt it.

♦ Certificate information. This will appear only for resources that have been secured; the same information available by clicking on the View Certificate button is shown here (viz., the entity to which the certificate was issued, the entity issuing the certificate, the serial number for the certificate, the validity dates for the certificate, and the fingerprint for the certificate).

This information can be useful when doing any secure interaction over the web, particularly for checking and verifying the origin of resources you download for viewing through your browser or for using on your system.

Managing Navigator Certificate Passwords

When you create your certificate for use with Communicator, you are prompted for a password to protect the certificate. This is to prevent unauthorized use of the certificate—for example, if you share your computer with other users, or if you leave your system connected to the Internet but unattended in a setting where others may be able to use the system. Beyond the normal caution you should use when selecting any password, you can also change some settings regarding your certificate password. Figure 6.7 shows the Password administration panel that is displayed when you select

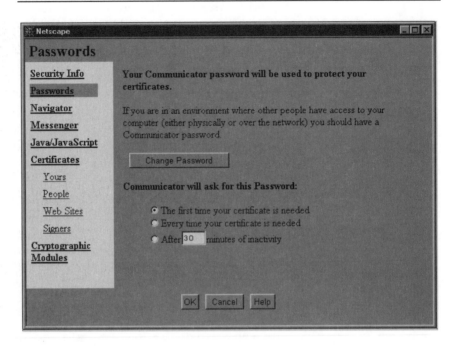

Figure 6.7. Certificate password management in the Communicator/Navigator security interface.

the Password option on the menu at the left of the Communicator/ Navigator security interface.

You can use this panel to change your password by clicking on the Change Password button (see Figure 6.8) or to change the frequency with which the browser prompts you for your certificate password. The default is to prompt you the first time every session that your certificate is required; for the next level of security you can choose either to be prompted every time your certificate is needed, or to be prompted for the password after 30 minutes of inactivity. Prompting for the password only when the certificate is needed is probably the best choice for security-conscious users.

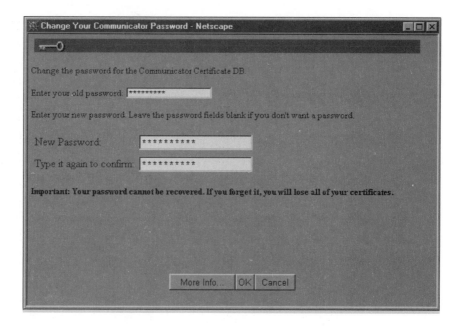

Figure 6.8. Changing your certificate password with the Communicator/Navigator security interface.

To change your password, click on the Change Password button. The resulting panel is shown in Figure 6.8. You must enter your old password correctly and enter a new password twice (both times the same way). Click on the OK button, and your password will be changed.

Controlling Navigator Browsing Security Settings

Browsing securely with Navigator depends on three groups of settings:

♦ Security warnings that may be displayed to alert the user to a change in security status or an action that is potentially dangerous.

♦ Determining how you should identify yourself to servers that request certificate information from you.
♦ Enabling and configuring SSL options for encryption and certification between the client software and servers.

Figure 6.9 shows the Navigator security panel, which appears when you click the Navigator option in the menu along the left side of the security interface.

Warning Settings

There are four actions that can trigger a warning dialog box from Navigator before any actual transmissions will proceed. These include

♦ Entering an encrypted site.
♦ Leaving an encrypted site.

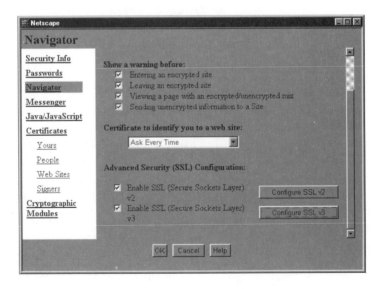

Figure 6.9. Setting Navigator security settings through the Communicator security interface.

♦ Viewing a page with an encrypted and unencrypted mix.
♦ Sending unencrypted information to a site.

These options can be checked on or off through the Navigator security panel shown in Figure 6.9 and are by default all set on when you first install Communicator.

Choosing Your Certificate Identification

There are times when a server requests a browser certificate—for example, in order to authenticate a user for entry into a controlled-access web site, or when the user is attempting to complete a commercial transaction. In these cases, you have some options, as shown in Figure 6.10. You can have the browser do one of the following:

♦ Prompt you each time you are queried for which certificate to provide to the requesting server.

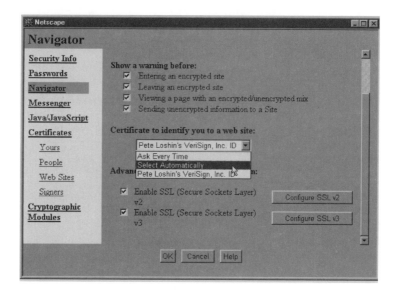

Figure 6.10. Choosing web site certificate identification through the Communicator security interface.

♦ Automatically respond with a certificate when a server requests one.
♦ Respond automatically with a particular certificate in all cases.

If you use more than one certificate, each of which you use for different web sites, you would select the first option. If you have only one certificate, you would choose the second option, while if you use only one certificate for all web interactions, you can select that certificate and have the browser treat it as your default certificate.

Configuring SSL

There are two versions of the Secure Sockets Layer (SSL) protocol: developed and implemented by Netscape and subsequently submitted to the IETF, SSL v. 2.0 was superseded by SSL v 3.0 to reflect a more open industry approach to the protocol. In either case, SSL's function is to allow a client and a server to initiate a secure, encrypted channel and communicate securely over that channel. Support for both versions is important so as to provide backward compatibility between newer clients communicating with versions of servers that support only the older protocol.

Should you desire, you can turn support for either SSL v. 2.0 or SSL v. 3.0 off, or you can select which cryptographic ciphers you would like your browser to support. Figure 6.11 shows the configuration options available for SSL v. 3.0. (This panel is similar to the configuration panel for SSL v. 2.0, except that the earlier version has fewer cryptographic options available.) Ciphers available for SSL v. 3.0 include

♦ RC4 encryption with a 128-bit key and an MD5 MAC.
♦ Triple DES encryption with a 168-bit key and an SHA-1 MAC.
♦ RC4 encryption with a 40-bit key and an MD5 MAC.
♦ RC2 encryption with a 40-bit key and an MD5 MAC.
♦ No encryption with an MD5 MAC.

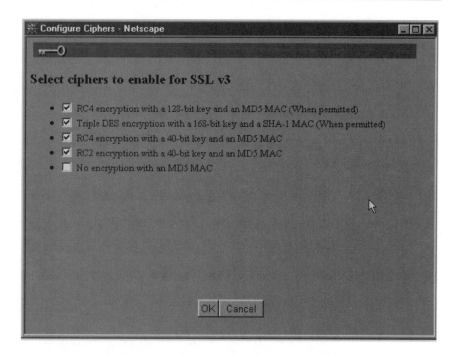

Figure 6.11. Choosing ciphers to be used with SSL through Communicator's security interface.

In general, you would tend to keep all of the options available; however, for higher security you might disable the less secure encryption options and leave only the strong ciphers (triple DES and RC4 with a 128-bit key) enabled.

Controlling Messenger Security Settings

Netscape took a sensible approach to security by centralizing all security functions into a single interface. That means that you can access e-mail security options to be used by the Messenger client through the same interface you would use to set Navigator security options. While Chapter 7 examines how to

use secure e-mail, we will look at how to set e-mail options for
Messenger here.

Figure 6.12 shows the Messenger option panel selected within the
Communicator security interface. The interface provides three different sets of options:

- Setting defaults for encrypting and signing messages.
- Selecting and managing a certificate to be used when
  signing messages.
- Setting preferences for S/MIME ciphers.

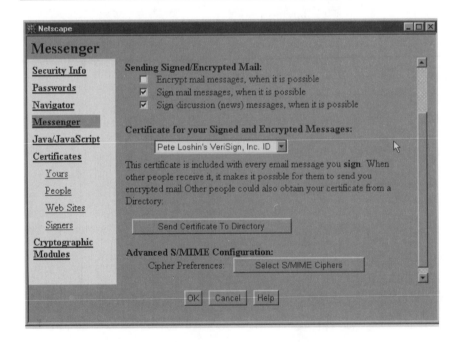

Figure 6.12. Setting Netscape Messenger secure e-mail options through the
Communicator security interface.

Setting Defaults for Encrypting and Signing Messages

You can choose to set as default any or all of the following options for Messenger secure e-mail:

♦ Encrypt all e-mail messages.
♦ Sign all e-mail messages.
♦ Sign all discussion (news) messages.

In each case, it should be noted that encryption and digital signatures will be used for all messages that it is possible to encrypt and/or sign. For example, you will only be able to encrypt e-mail messages for recipients whose certificates you already have.

Choosing and Disseminating a Certificate for Signing Messages

The next section, as was shown in Figure 6.12, is for choosing which certificate you would like to use for your own digital signatures. If you have only one certificate, this option is not that important; however, if you use more than one, you will need to specify which you would prefer to use for digital signatures.

Also in this section is a button labeled "Send Certificate to Directory" which, when clicked, will display something like what is shown in Figure 6.13. A number of network directories (supporting LDAP, the Lightweight Directory Access Protocol) will be displayed, and you can send your certificate to any or all of them (one at a time) by selecting a directory from the pulldown and clicking on the OK button. You will be prompted for the password that protects your certificate, after which you will see a progress box followed by notification that the directory has received your certificate.

S/MIME Cipher Preferences

Selecting S/MIME cipher preferences with the current version (4.02) of Communicator is a matter of either taking what there is (RC2 encryption in CBC mode with a 40-bit key) or leaving it, as

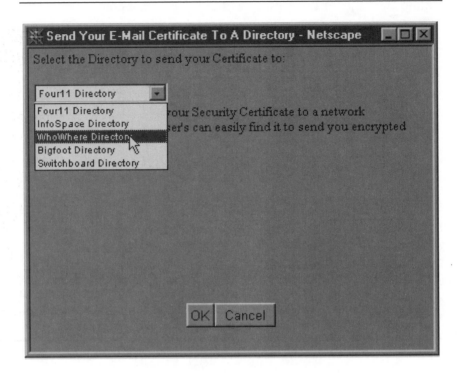

Figure 6.13. Sending your e-mail certificate to a public LDAP directory through the Communicator security interface.

shown in Figure 6.14; there was only one option to choose from when you click on the button labeled Select S/MIME Ciphers. Depending on the implementation, it is expected that there will be more options available for S/MIME e-mail encryption as the most recent standards drafts show that the Triple DES algorithm now must be supported.

Java/JavaScript Applet Security

To make your system more secure, it is possible to require all Java or JavaScript applets to submit their own certificates. However, while you can delete applet certificates or change privileges

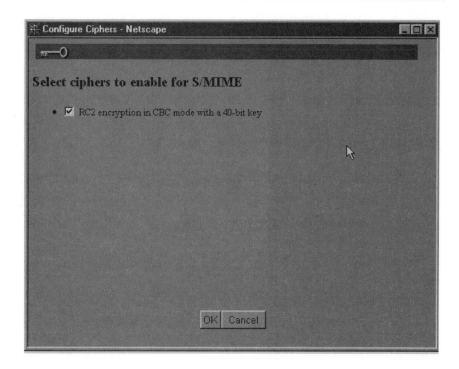

Figure 6.14. Selecting an S/MIME cipher for secure e-mail through the Communicator security interface.

manually through the panel shown in Figure 6.15, you cannot add certificates yourself. Applet certificates are automatically loaded when the applet itself is downloaded, or an organization may configure users' browsers to include certificates through a user database.

Communicator Certificate Management

This is one of the most important set of functions provided in Communicator's security interface. It is divided into four categories, which are explained in the panel that is displayed when you

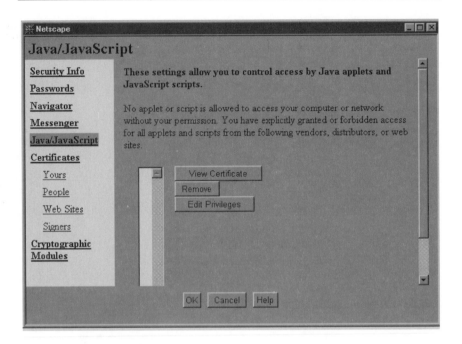

Figure 6.15. Managing Java/JavaScript applet certificates through this panel is similar to other certificate administration tasks.

click on the Certificates option in the menu on the left side of the security interface panel, as shown in Figure 6.16. The categories include

- ◆ Your certificates. This is where you manage the certificates that have been issued in your name, for you.
- ◆ People's certificates. This is where you manage certificates that belong to the people you communicate with.
- ◆ Web site certificates. This is where you manage the certificates that you get from web sites.

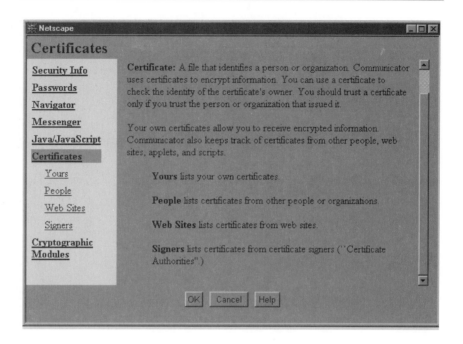

Figure 6.16. The Certificate option in Communicator's security interface provides an explanation of your certificate options.

♦ Signers' certificates. This is where you manage certificates that belong to CAs and other entities that can sign certificates.

Managing Your Certificates

Clicking on the "Yours" button under the Certificates heading in the left column on the Navigator security panel will bring up an interface through which you can manage your own certificates, as shown in Figure 6.17. Not shown in this illustration are buttons for getting a certificate and for importing a certificate. (See Figure 5.2 for a view of those buttons.)

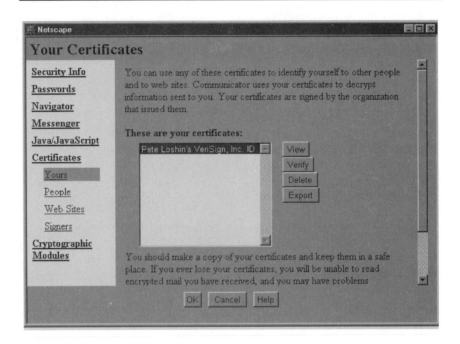

Figure 6.17. Managing your own certificates through Communicator's security interface.

PSEUDONYMS AND CERTIFICATES: The nature of the Internet allows for pseudonymous interaction through news groups, e-mail, and other public access applications. It is relatively easy to create a pseudonym—just pick your persona and start using it—it is less easy to protect your pseudonym from others who wish to use it. This is of particular importance to people who like to use their pseudonym to interact with others publicly over a period of time. It becomes easy for impersonators to simply start using the same pseudonym, with the same return address in their header.

Certificates help individuals protect their identities. By using a particular certificate to link a pseudonym to a public key, an individual can prove which messages originated from impersonators and which originated from the original holder of the pseudonym.

The functions available for managing your certificates include

- ◆ View the certificate. Choosing this option will cause the selected certificate to be displayed, as shown in Figure 6.18.
- ◆ Verify the certificate. For other certificate functions, this option will contact the certification authority to confirm that the certificate is one that it issued; when dealing with one of your own certificates, this option is of less use.
- ◆ Delete the certificate. You might do this if you wish to stop using a certificate, especially if the certificate has expired or has been canceled.

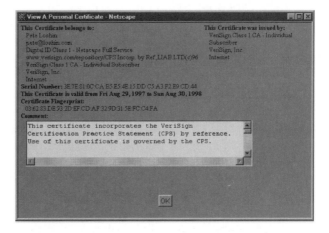

Figure 6.18. Viewing your own certificate through Communicator's security interface.

♦ Export the certificate. You use this option to create a file that contains your certificate, which you can use to load your certificate onto another computer (or into another piece of software that supports S/MIME). The certificate is exported into the PKCS (Public Key Cryptographic System) 12 format for certificates. This option will export the entire certificate along with your private key, so it should not be used casually. You can use a password to protect the data in exported form; in general, you should export the certificate to a diskette for secure storage in the event that something should happen to your system.

While many users will be satisfied with a single certificate, it will not be unusual for many people to use multiple certificates. (See the note on pseudonyms.) Likewise, individuals who use their browser and e-mail clients for personal as well as business purposes may have certificates for their personal correspondence as well as one or more certificates provided by their employer for use in their business correspondence.

Managing Other People's Certificates

The functions available to you for managing other people's certificates are similar to those for managing your own certificates. Figure 6.19 shows the panel that appears when you click on "People" under the Certificate heading on the left side of the security panel. The only difference is that you do not have the option of exporting other people's certificates.

Communicator automatically pulls out from e-mail messages the certificates of people you communicate with, as long as they are S/MIME-compliant. You can view, verify, or delete these certificates.

One other option, shown in Figure 6.20, is to search a directory for a person's certificate. You reach this panel by clicking on the "Search Directory" button. You may choose one of the directories listed and enter a person's e-mail address; if that e-mail address is listed in the directory selected, the results will be displayed.

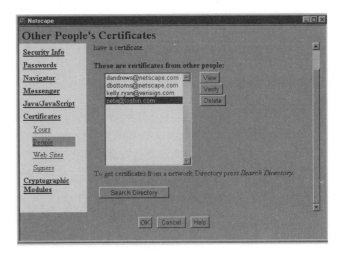

Figure 6.19. Managing other people's certificates through Communicator's security interface.

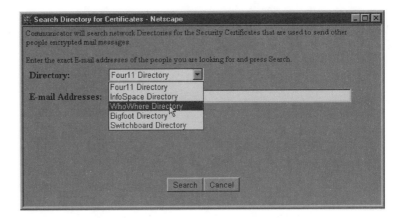

Figure 6.20. Searching for other people's certificates through Communicator's security interface.

Managing Web Site Certificates

As you connect to web sites offering encrypted web pages, the browser collects these certificates. These certificates can be managed through the Communicator security interface by clicking on the Web Sites option listed under the Certificates heading on the left side of the security interface panel. The resulting administrative panel provides functions similar to those provided in the panel for managing other people's certificates (as just mentioned), although there is no option for searching directories for web site certificates.

Managing Signers' Certificates

The last set of certificates that can be managed through the Communicator security interface, those of signers, are among the most important. These are the certificates that are used by the certification authorities to provide certification of other entity's own certificates. For example, when you acquire a personal certificate from an authority like Verisign, Inc., that certificate is signed by Verisign, and one of Verisign's certificates is appended to indicate what level of assurance should be associated with your own certificate.

There are three options for managing these certificates, as shown in Figure 6.21:

- ◆ Certificates can be edited to modify how to treat certificates that have been issued by these signers; this will be explained in more detail shortly.
- ◆ Certificates can be verified by confirming that the cryptographic hash of the data represented, run with the CA's own public key, matches the hash provided in the certificate.
- ◆ Certificates can be deleted from your list of approved signers.

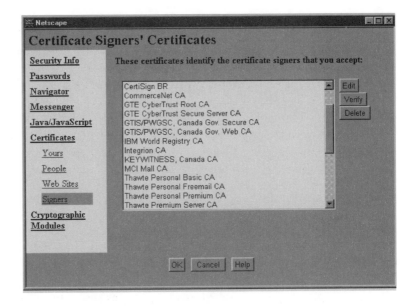

Figure 6.21. Managing signer's certificates—certification authorities' certificates—through Communicator's security interface.

If you choose a signer and click on the Edit button, a panel similar to that shown in Figure 6.22 will be displayed. Included in this display is information about the signer's certificate (the owner and issuer of the certificate, serial number, validity dates, and a fingerprint), and the statement that the certificate belongs to a certifying authority. Also shown are four check-box options relating to how you want your browser to deal with certificates that have been certified under the CA's authority:

- ♦ Accept this Certificate Authority for Certifying network sites.
- ♦ Accept this Certificate Authority for Certifying e-mail users.

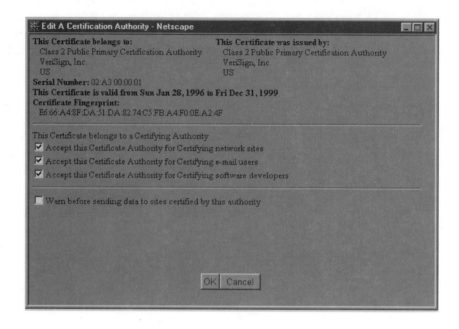

Figure 6.22. Editing a signer's (certification authority) certificate through Communicator's security interface.

- ◆ Accept this Certificate Authority for Certifying software developers.
- ◆ Warn before sending data to sites certified by this authority.

The first three choices allow you to choose how willing you are to accept certificates issued by the CA. Accepting the CA for network sites means that you will trust web site certificates issued by the CA; accepting it for e-mail users means that you will trust S/MIME messages using certificates issued by the CA. Accepting the CA for software developers means that you will permit applets signed with certificates issued by the CA to run on your system.

In general, you would be willing to accept e-mail from most CAs, even where the CA does not require significant proof of identity—as long as you are wary about opening files sent as attachments to e-mail messages. Likewise, you can be generous about accepting CAs who have issued network site certificates, as long as you are careful about what information you send to the sites. By the same token, you should be strictest about who you will trust to issue certificates to software developers.

The last option is particularly useful when dealing with popular CAs that issue certificates for web sites. There may be many sites that you are willing to trust to download information from, but you may be more concerned about limiting the sites you will send data to.

Administering Cryptographic Modules

Communicator supports the use of cryptographic modules, which are loadable pieces of software that provide some cryptographic service function. Examples of such modules may include

- Support for "smart card" functions.
- Special key distribution architectures.
- Support for hardware-accelerated encryption.
- New encryption ciphers or algorithms to be used in addition to the standard S/MIME implementation.

The basic interface is shown in Figure 6.23. The interface provides support for a number of functions, including view/edit, add, delete and logout/all. For most personal uses of the browser, additional cryptographic modules will not be used. However, you can view additional details of the standard PKCS #11 module that ships with Communicator by clicking on the view/edit button. The result is shown in Figure 6.24. The module itself consists of two parts. One is the cryptographic services module—the software that actually does the functions required to encrypt, decrypt, sign, and verify data. The other part is the browser's certificate database, which can actually be logged into or out of manually through this interface.

If you select a module that has a password associated with it—for example, the Communicator certificate database—the Change Password button becomes active and will, when clicked, bring up

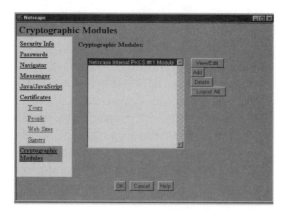

Figure 6.23. Administering cryptographic modules through Communicator's security interface.

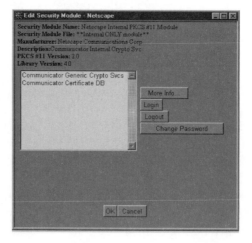

Figure 6.24. Viewing the Netscape PKCS #11 cryptographic module through Communicator's security interface.

the same password changing dialog box as just described above (and shown in Figure 6.8).

Choosing a module and clicking on the More Info button will display a dialog box showing pertinent information about the module. The information relating to the generic crypto services module included with Communicator is shown in Figure 6.25, and includes various product, vendor, and version information. Select the More Info option for the Communicator private key and certificate services database, and something like Figure 6.26 will be displayed, again showing vendor and version information, along with other identifying information about the module.

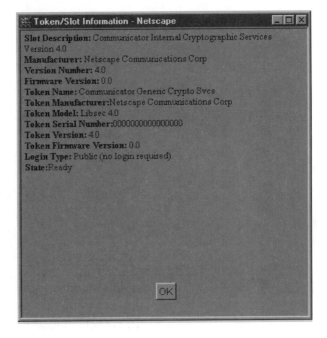

Figure 6.25. Viewing the Communicator Generic Crypto Services Module information window.

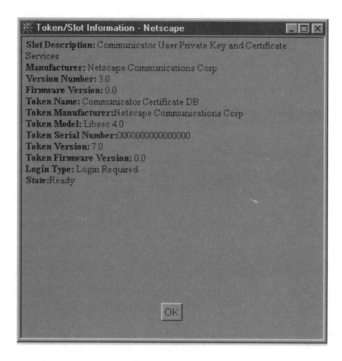

Figure 6.26. Viewing the Communicator User Private Key and Certificate Services information window.

Controlling Cookies with Navigator

Unlike other security issues, cookie-handling options are managed through the Preferences option within the Edit pulldown menu. Cookie handling responses can be set by going into the Advanced option category, by clicking on the word Advanced on the menu along the left side of the panel, as shown in Figure 6.27.

There are basically only three choices for what to do when when presented with a cookie:

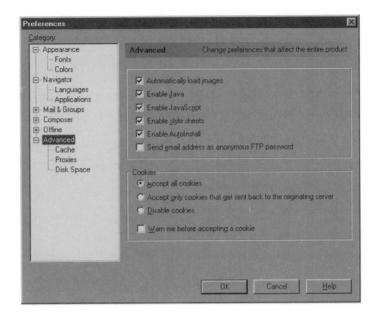

Figure 6.27. Cookie-handling behaviors of the Navigator browser are part of the advanced preferences.

♦ Accept all cookies.
♦ Accept only cookies that are sent back to the originating server.
♦ Disable cookies entirely.

You must choose one of these options; the default is to accept all cookies.

One other option is available no matter what you decide to do with cookies, and that is to be warned whenever a cookie is offered by a server. This option is turned off by default, very likely because cookies are used so ubiquitously. However, it is an educational experience to turn it on, if only temporarily, to see how many sites use cookies.

Securely Browsing with Microsoft Internet Explorer 4.0

Unlike the Netscape Internet clients, Microsoft's Internet Explorer 4.0 browser has a somewhat less comprehensive and fully integrated security interface. Security options are managed through separate areas of both the browser and the Microsoft e-mail clients. (Securely using Microsoft's Outlook Express client is discussed at greater length in Chapter 7.) However, many of the same functions are supported through Internet Explorer 4.0 as with Netscape's Navigator/Communicator client:

- Checking out the security information related to the page currently being browsed.
- Setting security "zones" and configuring security options.
- Controlling browser security settings (including cookies).
- Managing certificates, your own as well as certification authorities and software publishers.
- Configuring a personal profile and the Microsoft Wallet.

This section discusses how to use options within Internet Explorer 4.0 to perform all these functions.

Accessing Internet Explorer Security Features

Security and encryption features in the Internet Explorer are spread throughout the application, rather than being all grouped together through a single interface. This section summarizes the different entry points to security features in Internet Explorer.

Web Page Certificates

Information about security attributes relating to web pages is available through the Properties option under the File pulldown menu.

This is how you determine whether a page has a certificate and, if so, what are its contents.

Internet Options

The Internet Options option on the View pulldown menu provides an interface for doing most browser configuration tasks, including those relating to security. Internet Explorer has a notion of security "zones," a way of segmenting how the browser treats web interaction with various web sites depending on whether they are part of the Internet, an intranet, or some trusted site or domain. These zones function in conjunction with other security options relating to certificates for yourself, other people, web sites, and software publishers.

Unfortunately for usability, the tab labeled Security is where you configure your security zones, while the tab labeled Content is where you configure and administer certificates. Further complicating matters, advanced options for security configuration and security warnings are tucked in under the Advanced tab.

Web Page Security Attributes

Internet Explorer treats security attributes as a subset of the properties of the resource being browsed; this means that, as with any other Microsoft Windows-based product, you can select the File menu from the menubar, and choose the Properties option from the pulldown menu, and you will see all relevant information about the resource.

For web pages, the security attributes are incorporated into the general properties tab. To get information about any certificates associated with the resource, click on the Certificates button as shown in Figure 6.28. Nonsecured pages will turn up a dialog box indicating that there are no certificates associated with the resource. You may also be able to determine whether there is a certificate associated

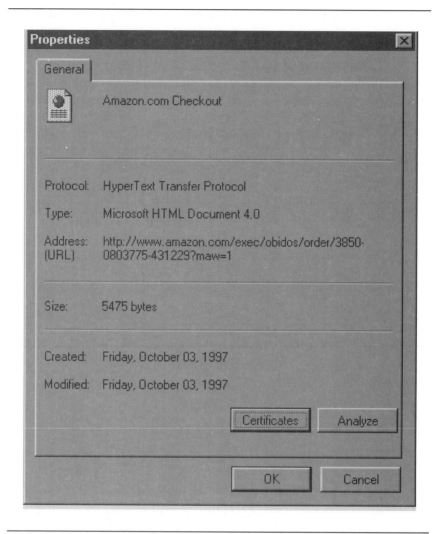

Figure 6.28. Viewing the security properties of a nonsecured web resource through Internet Explorer.

with the resource by checking out the protocol used. As shown in Figure 6.28, basic Hypertext Transfer Protocol (HTTP) pages will not have a certificate.

Figure 6.29 shows the properties for an on-line ordering page that uses SSL (Secure Socket Layer) for security; thus the protocol shown is HTTP with security. (This appears in the URL as "HTTPS" instead of "HTTP.") In this case, when you click on the Certificates

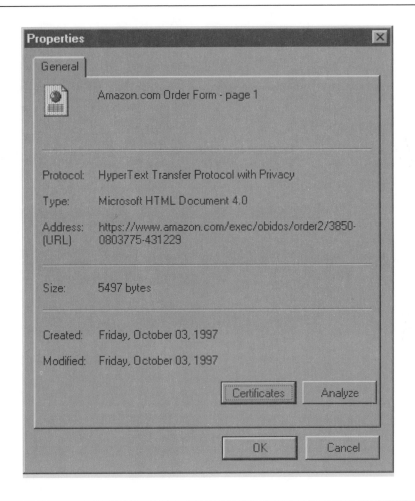

Figure 6.29. Viewing the properties of a secured web resource through Internet Explorer.

button, full information about the page's certificate will be displayed.

The certificate associated with this page is shown in Figure 6.30, and reflects the X.509 certificate fields in the way the information is displayed. On the left side of the panel, under the Field column, are different groupings of information, including

- The subject, which refers to the holder of the certificate, and which includes the holder's name and some location information.
- The issuer, which refers to the issuer of the certificate, and which includes the issuer's name and certification

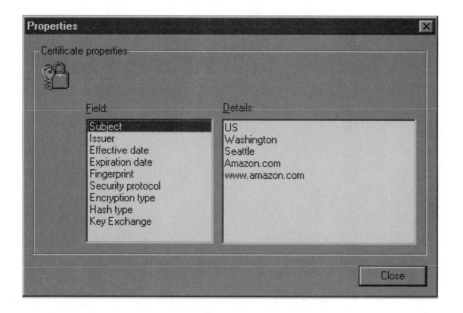

Figure 6.30. Viewing the certificate properties of a secured web resource through Internet Explorer.

authority. (Many CAs use different entities to issue different types of certificate.)

- ◆ The effective and expiration dates, which are simply the date on which the certificate was first effective and the date on which the certificate expires, respectively.
- ◆ The fingerprint, which is the cryptographic hash associated with the certificate.
- ◆ The security protocol, which refers to the protocol (and version number) that is using encryption—for example, SSL 2.0.
- ◆ The encryption type, which refers to the algorithm and key length—for example, RC4 with 40-bit keys.
- ◆ The hash type, which refers to the cryptographic digest algorithm—for example, MD5 with a 128-bit hash.
- ◆ The key exchange type, which refers to the public key exchange system being used—for example, RSA with 1024-bit keys.

Configuring Security Zones

Choosing Internet Options from the View pulldown menu produces an interface for configuring Internet Explorer. One of the unique features of Internet Explorer is that it has a notion of security zones: areas accessible by network connections that may be treated differently in terms of trust. Security zones are configured through the Security tab of the Internet Options dialog box, shown in Figure 6.31.

Internet Explorer provides a set of four different zones:

- ◆ The local intranet zone, which is defined by sites that originate on the same intranet to which the browser is connected. Exactly how those sites are defined is discussed shortly.
- ◆ The trusted sites zone, which is defined by manually adding Internet sites that the user is confident can be trusted.
- ◆ The Internet zone, which could also be called the "everything else" zone, includes all other sites that have not been otherwise categorized.

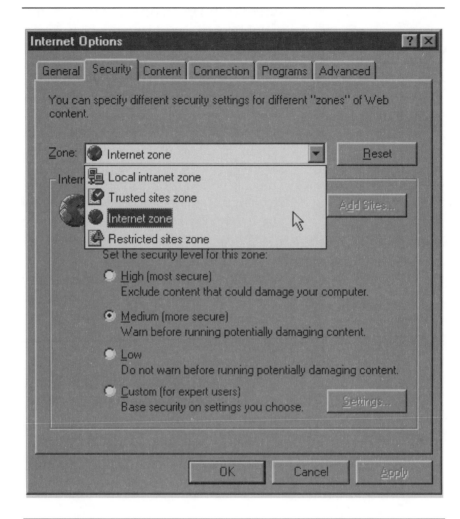

Figure 6.31. Configuring security zones with Internet Explorer.

♦ The restricted sites zone, which is defined by manually
adding Internet sites that the user believes contain data
that may be harmful.

You can select the security level for each zone based on the three preset options listed on the panel (high, medium, or low) or by defining your own custom response.

Security Levels

There are three default security configurations:

- ♦ High security provides the highest level of security, which excludes content that might be dangerous.
- ♦ Medium security provides warnings and prompts before loading content that might be dangerous.
- ♦ Low security enables almost all actions, without warning before loading content that might be dangerous.

It is possible to do a custom security configuration for any security zone, although the default is for the local intranet zone and the Internet zone to have medium security, the trusted sites zone to have low security, and the restricted sites zone to have high security. Security choices are available for six different categories:

- ♦ ActiveX Controls and plug-ins.
- ♦ Java.
- ♦ Scripting.
- ♦ Downloads.
- ♦ User authentication.
- ♦ Miscellaneous.

Table 6.1 shows the different options available for ActiveX controls and plug-ins. The choices are to enable or disable them, or prompt the user for a ruling when the browser tries to download a control.

The Java option is restricted to setting permissions for Java applets; there are five settings:

- ♦ Custom settings, which are normally to be set by system administrators.
- ♦ Low safety.

Action	Options
Script ActiveX controls marked safe for scripting	Enable/Prompt/Disable
Run ActiveX controls and plug-ins	Enable/Prompt/Disable
Download signed ActiveX controls	Enable/Prompt/Disable
Download unsigned ActiveX controls	Enable/Prompt/Disable
Initialize and script ActiveX controls not marked safe	Enable/Prompt/Disable

Table 6.1. ActiveX control security options under Internet Explorer security zones.

- ◆ Medium safety.
- ◆ High safety.
- ◆ Disable Java.

Java security options as implemented through Internet Explorer are beyond the scope of this book. However, the degree of safety is determined by what system resources the applet has, including things like user interface objects, network and file input and output, and system resources.

There are two scripting options, one each for Active scripting and for scripting of Java applets; the options for these are to enable, disable, or prompt the user for a decision when the action is taking place.

Download options include enabling or disabling file or font downloads. File downloads do not include a choice to prompt the user when the action takes place because the default for downloading files is to present the user with a dialog box that provides an option to decline the file download.

User authentication options are limited to choices for handling logons. These options include

- ◆ Automatic logon only for the Intranet zone.
- ◆ Anonymous logon (using the user name *anonymous*).

♦ Prompt for the user to enter a name and password.
♦ Automatically logon with the current user name and password.

Miscellaneous security settings are listed in Table 6.2.

Local Intranet Zone

The local intranet zone is intended to encompass all sites that are published through your organizational intranet. It would be an oversimplification to merely state that this zone would include any host originating on the same IP network, because there are many different ways of configuring systems to be connected to intranets—and because many users access their intranets from mobile systems.

To add sites to your local intranet zone, select it from the zone pulldown in the Internet Options/Security tab. The default security level is set to medium. Click on the Add Sites button to bring up a dialog box for adding web sites to the zone, as shown in Figure 6.32.

You can include sites based on three sets of rules:

♦ Include all local intranet sites not listed in other zones. In other words, select all sites that are on the same IP network.

Action	Options
Submit nonencrypted form data	Enable/Prompt/Disable
Launch applications and files in an IFRAME	Enable/Prompt/Disable
Install desktop items	Enable/Prompt/Disable
Drag and drop or copy and paste files	Enable/Prompt/Disable
Software channel permissions	Low/medium/high safety

Table 6.2. ActiveX control security options under Internet Explorer security zones.

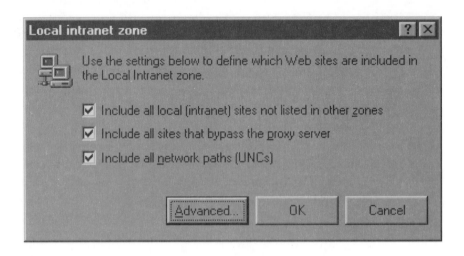

Figure 6.32. Adding to the local intranet security zone with Internet Explorer.

♦ Include all sites that bypass the proxy server. This allows access to any site that is considered local and does not need to be mediated through an organizational proxy server. This option will be similar to the first option, but available only to users in organizations using proxy servers.

♦ Include all network paths. This option may be preferable for users in organizations whose intranet is not directly connected to the Internet.

You may also add sites explicitly to the local intranet zone by clicking on the Advanced button. The resulting dialog box is shown in Figure 6.33.

You may want to add sites explicitly to the local intranet zone to limit it to only those network resources you wish to include in the

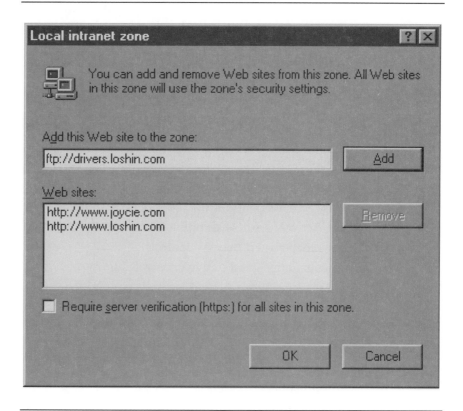

Figure 6.33. Adding sites explicitly to the local intranet security zone with Internet Explorer.

zone; some intranets may have many servers, only a few of which are relevant to (or secure for) a particular user.

Entering an Internet or intranet resource into this zone requires spelling out the entire URL, not just the host name and domain. Therefore, the URL *http://www.loshin.com* is acceptable, but *www.loshin.com* would generate an error dialog box.

The local intranet zone is granted a medium level of security by default. As of the initial release of Internet Explorer 4.0, the security settings associated with medium security are listed in Table 6.3.

Category-Action	Setting
ActiveX Controls and Plug-ins:	
Script ActiveX controls marked safe for scripting	Enable
Run ActiveX controls and plug-ins	Enable
Download signed ActiveX controls	Prompt
Download unsigned ActiveX controls	Disable
Initialize and script ActiveX controls not marked safe	Prompt
Java	
Set Java permissions	High safety
Scripting	
Active scripting	Enable
Scripting of Java applets	Enable
Downloads	
File downloads	Enable
Font downloads	Enable
User Authentication	
Logon	Anonymous logon
Miscellaneous	
Submit nonencrypted form data	Prompt
Launch applications and files in an IFRAME	Prompt
Install desktop items	Prompt
Drag and drop or copy and paste files	Enable
Software channel permissions	Medium safety

Table 6.3. Medium security settings under Internet Explorer security zones.

Trusted Sites Zone

The trusted sites zone uses a panel similar to that shown in Figure 6.32 to add resources that can be considered trustworthy. This zone is for those sites that you consider to be above suspicion, and about which you do not have any qualms concerning downloading data of any type. The default security setting for the trusted sites zone is low security; the default settings for various actions under low security are included in Table 6.4.

Internet Zone

The Internet zone is essentially a catchall zone for sites that have not been categorized elsewhere. The default security setting for the Internet zone is medium security; the default settings for various actions under medium security were included in Table 6.2.

Restricted Sites Zone

The restricted sites zone is where you put the known bad actors of the Internet, or at least those web sites that you may need to access for information but which you know or suspect may also contain harmful content. You can add sites to this zone with a dialog box very similar to that shown in Figure 6.32; one difference is that the option to require server verification for all sites in the zone is not available. This zone is for sites that you do not trust, whether they support server verification or not. Table 6.5 shows the security settings for high security, which is the default for the restricted sites zone. It should be noted that ActiveX controls that have been marked safe, as well as Active scripts, are still enabled under the high-security settings; almost everything else is disabled or set to prompt the user before taking an action.

Advanced Security Settings and Cookies

Internet Explorer's Internet Options dialog box has a tab for Advanced options; these include settings for many different aspects

Category-Action	Setting
ActiveX Controls and Plug-ins	
Script ActiveX controls marked safe for scripting	Enable
Run ActiveX controls and plug-ins	Enable
Download signed ActiveX controls	Enable
Download unsigned ActiveX controls	Prompt
Initialize and script ActiveX controls not marked safe	Prompt
Java	
Set Java permissions	Low safety
Scripting	
Active scripting	Enable
Scripting of Java applets	Enable
Downloads	
File downloads	Enable
Font downloads	Enable
User Authentication	
Logon	Automatic logon with current user ID and password
Miscellaneous	
Submit nonencrypted form data	Enable
Launch applications and files in an IFRAME	Enable
Install desktop items	Enable
Drag and drop or copy and paste files	Enable
Software channel permissions	Low safety

Table 6.4. Low-security settings under Internet Explorer security zones.

of using the browser including some advanced security settings. This is also where you can modify the browser's default universal acceptance of all cookies. The relevant section of this tab is shown in Figure 6.34.

Category-Action	Setting
ActiveX Controls and Plug-ins	
Script ActiveX controls marked safe for scripting	Enable
Run ActiveX controls and plug-ins	Disable
Download signed ActiveX controls	Disable
Download unsigned ActiveX controls	Disable
Initialize and script ActiveX controls not marked safe	Disable
Java	
Set Java permissions	High safety
Scripting	
Active scripting	Enable
Scripting of Java applets	Disable
Downloads	
File downloads	Disable
Font downloads	Prompt
User Authentication	
Logon	Prompt for user ID and password
Miscellaneous	
Submit nonencrypted form data	Prompt
Launch applications and files in an IFRAME	Disable
Install desktop items	Disable
Drag and drop or copy and paste files	Prompt
Software channel permissions	High safety

Table 6.5. High-security settings under Internet Explorer security zones.

Advanced Security Settings

As is shown in Figure 6.34, the following items can be turned on or off by clicking the check box next to them as listed in the Internet Options advanced settings:

♦ Enabling the Profile Assistant allows you to use a standard profile for all web sites that request personal information. (This chapter gives more details later.)

♦ PCT 1.0 is the Private Communications Technology protocol developed by Microsoft for secure channel trans-

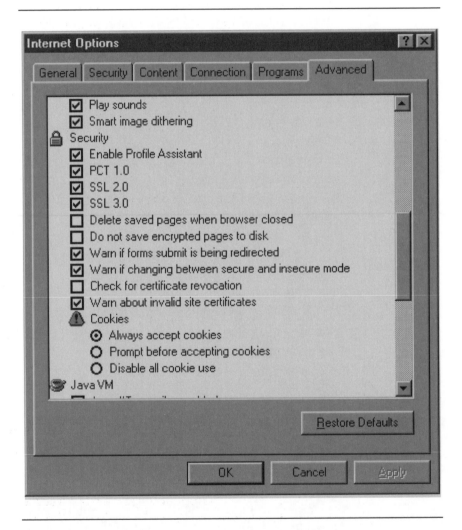

Figure 6.34. Additional security settings for Internet Explorer, including cookie management, are available through the advanced Internet Options tab.

missions. Checking this box means you want to allow the browser to use this protocol when communicating with servers that support it.

♦ SSL 2.0/3.0 are the Secure Sockets Layer protocol, versions 2.0 and 3.0. Enabling them means that you want to allow the browser to use the selected protocols when communicating with servers that support it.

♦ Choosing to delete saved pages when the browser is closed allows you to be sure that the content you download during a web surfing session will not be available in a stored cache for off-line browsing.

♦ Unless this option is checked, encrypted pages will be written to disk; checking this option causes all encrypted pages to be stored only in memory so that when the session is over, the pages cannot be accessed from the disk cache.

♦ Enabling a warning if a forms submission is being redirected notifies the user if a form being submitted to a web page is actually being re-sent to another web server.

♦ A warning can be enabled when switching between secure and insecure mode, producing a dialog box that announces the change.

♦ There is an option to check for certificate revocation when browsing a site that offers a certificate.

♦ There is an option to warn about invalid site certificates that would produce a dialog box announcing the fact to the user.

Cookie Handling

In the same advanced options tab of the Internet Options dialog box are three choices for handling cookies. (See Figure 6.34.) The only options for cookie handling are

♦ To always accept any cookie from a server.
♦ To prompt the user to decide whether or not to accept a cookie.
♦ To disable all cookie use.

Internet Options, Content

Selecting View/Internet Options and going to the Content tab reveals three tools that may be considered to relate to security:

- ◆ Content Advisor is a built-in Internet censor, or content filter, that can be used to deny access to rated sites that include material that may be offensive based on the presence of certain types of language, nudity, sex, and violence.
- ◆ The Certificates tool allows administration of your own certificates as well as those belonging to certification authorities and software publishers.
- ◆ The personal information tools include a Profile Assistant which provides personal information to web sites that request it to create an account, and the Microsoft Wallet which stores credit card payment information for on-line shopping.

Figure 6.35 shows the Content tab of the Internet Options dialog. While these options may relate to security as far as attempting to keep offensive material away from children, and managing data (credit card account numbers) that is encrypted, they are not strictly security functions and are therefore outside the scope of this book.

Managing Certificates

Managing certificates in Internet Explorer means being able to add, delete, view, import, and export them. Not all types of certificates can be manually added, imported, or exported (although there are tools available from Microsoft to allow organizations to add their certificates or certification authorities to Internet Explorer).

Personal Certificates

Clicking on the Personal button in the center of the Content tab of the Internet Options dialog box brings up a list of all personal certificates currently resident in the Internet Explorer certificate database, as shown in Figure 6.36.

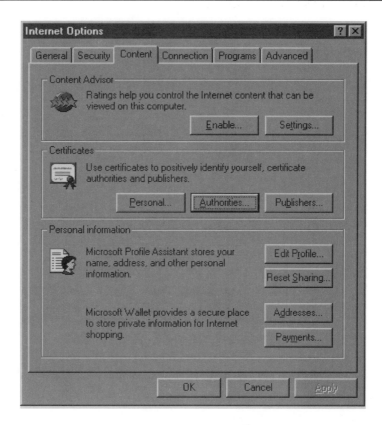

Figure 6.35. The Content Advisor, certificate management, Microsoft Profile Assistant, and Microsoft Wallet are handled through the Content tab of the Internet Options dialog.

There are three options available to the individual when dealing with your personal certificates:

♦ Import a certificate from a standard certificate file. This allows you to import a certificate that may have

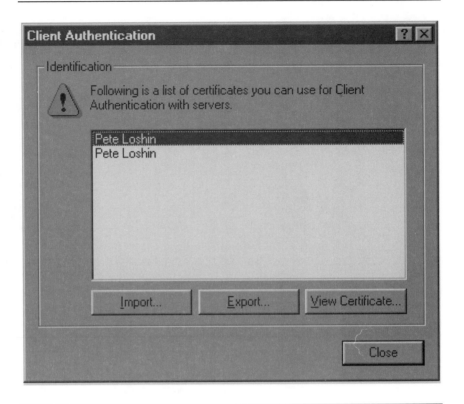

Figure 6.36. Viewing personal certificates with Internet Explorer.

been created with and issued to you through a different browser.

♦ Export a certificate to a standard certificate file. This allows you to use with a different browser a certificate generated with and issued to you through Internet Explorer.

♦ View a certificate. This allows you to see all the data associated with a certificate.

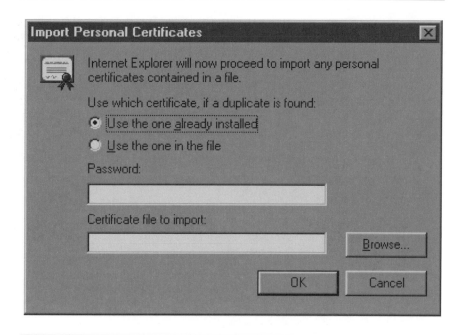

Figure 6.37. Importing a personal certificate with Internet Explorer.

Click on the Import button to import a certificate; a dialog box like that shown in Figure 6.37 will appear. If you are importing a certificate that duplicates one already installed, you can choose to add the new one by clicking on the option to use the certificate in the file; if you do not want to duplicate a certificate, leave the other option checked to use the certificate that has already been installed. If the certificate file has been encrypted, you will have to enter a password and, of course, the file name of the certificate file.

Exporting a file is a matter of clicking on the Export button and entering a password to use to encrypt the certificate file and a filename for the file.

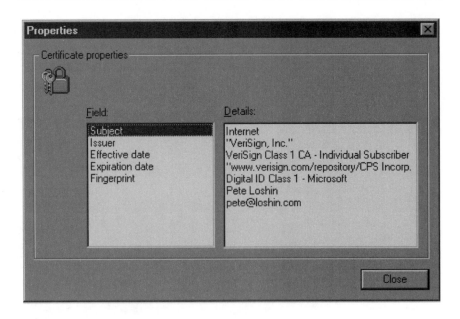

Figure 6.38. Viewing a personal certificate with Internet Explorer.

To view a certificate, click on the View Certificate button. The certificate will be displayed in a dialog box like that shown in Figure 6.38. Fields displayed from the certificate include

- The subject, which may include the type, issuer, and identification information of the holder of the certificate.
- The issuer, which includes the name of the issuer and the type of certificate that has been issued.
- Effective and expiration dates—the dates on which the certificate was first valid and will expire, respectively.
- Fingerprint, the cryptographic hash associated with the certificate.

There is no simple way to remove a certificate once it has been installed, but certificate can be associated with your e-mail address through the Profile Assistant.

Certifying Authorities Certificates

Internet Explorer stores the certificates of a number of national and international certification authorities, and sorts them out based on what type of issuer they are, including

♦ Network server authentication.
♦ Network client authentication.
♦ Secure e-mail.
♦ Software publishing.

You can change the selections of which CAs are listed as trusted for each type of issuer by checking (or unchecking) the box next to the issuer's name, as shown in Figure 6.39. You can also view

Figure 6.39. Viewing standard certification authorities with Internet Explorer.

the issuer's certificate by selecting one and clicking the View Certificate button; this displays the same certificate information as is shown with personal certificates. Finally, you can remove a CA entirely from the list by selecting it and clicking the Delete button.

Publisher's Certificates

This option allows you to control from whom you accept Authenticode signed software. Figure 6.40 shows the dialog box for managing publisher's certificates. It lists all software publishers that you have already downloaded programs from; your only option is to remove a publisher from this list.

When an Authenticode program is about to be downloaded from an unknown software publisher (who uses Authenticode), a dialog box like the one shown in Figure 6.41 is displayed. You have the option of choosing or declining to install the software by clicking either the Yes or No buttons. You also can choose to always trust the publisher for future Authenticode software downloads by checking the "Always trust software from . . ." checkbox. Finally, you can find out if the certificate checks out, as well as a more detailed explanation of what is happening, by clicking on the More Info button.

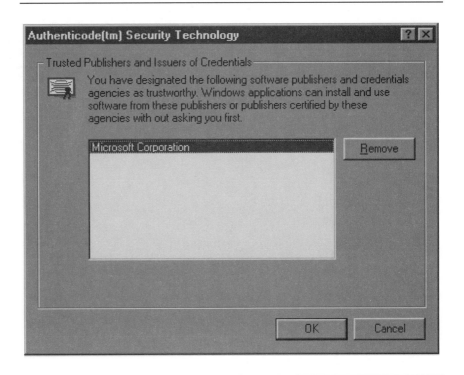

Figure 6.40. Viewing trusted publishers of Authenticode programs with Internet Explorer.

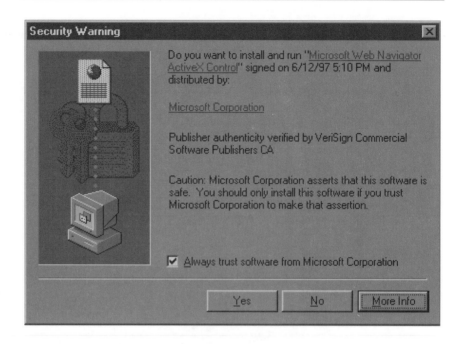

Figure 6.41. Being prompted to trust an Authenticode software publisher before downloading software through Internet Explorer.

7

Secure E-mail

This chapter details how to use three of the best-known Internet e-mail clients to encrypt, decrypt, digitally sign and digitally verify signed documents. Included are

- ◆ Qualcomm's Eudora e-mail client bundled with Pretty Good Privacy, Inc.'s PGP for Personal Privacy v. 5.0 plug-in.
- ◆ Microsoft's Outlook Express e-mail client.
- ◆ Netscape's Messenger e-mail client.

The chapter starts with a discussion of how you can use e-mail to securely communicate over the Internet.

Secure Communication with E-Mail

This section explains about the different things you can do to secure your e-mail. These include:

- ◆ Using a desktop encryption program to encrypt a file and send it to someone else who uses the same encryption program as an e-mail file attachment.
- ◆ Using a desktop encryption program to encrpyt a file as a self-extracting encrypted archive, sending it to someone else as an e-mail file attachment, and giving that person the passphrase to the file through some secure channel.
- ◆ Using a secure e-mail client that supports a proprietary encryption-digital signature implementation to send encrypted and/or digitally signed e-mail and/or enclosures to someone who uses the same proprietary secure e-mail client.
- ◆ Using an S/MIME-compliant secure e-mail client to encrypt and/or digitally sign a message and/or a file using the S/MIME protocol, and sending it to someone who uses an S/MIME-compliant secure e-mail client.

Each of these approaches has benefits and drawbacks, and each is discussed (with examples) in this chapter.

Desktop Encryption Enclosures

There are many products that can encrypt a file, with either symmetric encryption or public key encryption. It would be technically correct to claim that such a program enables secure e-mail, but only inasmuch as the resulting encrypted files can be attached to an insecure e-mail message and forwarded as an enclosure. In fact, many of these products claim e-mail encryption as one of their features.

However, using such a program for securing e-mail can have several disadvantages:

♦ Only the attached file is encrypted and/or signed, while the message itself is not protected at all. For example, a criminal who knows that you are sending a resume of a job candidate as an encrypted file could modify the text of your message to the opposite of what you intended. ("Hire this person" could be changed to "Don't hire this person."

♦ Unless the desktop encryption product supports public keys, you will have to find a secure channel to use for sending the key to the file. In other words, to get the passphrase to the recipient you may have to make a telephone call over a secured line or use a trusted courier or some other secure method.

♦ Your correspondent must have the same encryption software that you do to make it possible to successfully attach the encrypted/signed file.

Self-Extracting Desktop Encryption Enclosures

Some desktop encryption products include an option to encrypt and/or sign a file in such a way as to produce an executable file. This file, when run, will prompt for a passphrase and will decrypt to the original plaintext file when the valid passphrase is supplied. This function makes sending encrypted files as e-mail enclosures easier, but still suffers from some of the same problems as other desktop encryption products:

♦ Only the attached file is encrypted and/or signed, while the message itself is not protected at all. For example, a criminal who knows that you are sending a resume of a job candidate as an encrypted file could modify the text of your message to the opposite of what you intended. ("Hire this person" could be changed to "Don't hire this person.")

♦ Unless the desktop encryption product supports public keys, you will have to find a secure channel to use for sending the key to the file. In other words, to get the passphrase to the recipient you may have to make a telephone call over a secured line or use a trusted courier or some other secure method.

Proprietary E-Mail Client Security

Another alternative is to use an e-mail client that uses a proprietary set of architectures and protocols. There are many such clients, but perhaps the most popular is the Pretty Good Privacy, Inc., PGP program. The PGP program is not, strictly speaking, an e-mail client but rather a comprehensive data security tool that includes plug-ins that allow it to work with other e-mail clients including Qualcomm's Eudora and Microsoft's Outlook e-mail clients. However, it does use its own architecture for handling certificates and for encrypting, decrypting, signing and verifying data.

A PGP client can only interoperate with another PGP client, which is why I say it is proprietary. However, the installed base of PGP users is in the millions, and the product is implemented in free and paid versions on many different computer hardware and software platforms, including Windows, Macintosh OS, and Unix. Most other proprietary secure e-mail products have negligible installed bases, and can interoperate only in the most limited way with users of the same product.

 Lotus Notes provides cryptographic messaging functions; its installed user base is significant. But as it is not usually considered a product that individuals would purchase for their own personal use, it is not discussed in this book.

The secure e-mail client, in whatever form, secures the actual message, solving the problem of an insecure message having an encrypted attachment. The message itself can be encrypted and/or digitally signed, so it is not possible for a criminal to intercept and modify a signed message or to read an encrypted message—or any attached files. Other problems remain:

♦ Your correspondent must have the same secure e-mail client software that you do to make it possible to successfully exchange encrypted/signed e-mail. This is more or less of a problem depending on how popular the secure e-mail client is.

◆ If the secure e-mail client does not support public keys you must find a secure channel to use in order to share the secret key with your correspondent.

The secure e-mail client, however, may solve the problem of using strong encryption to protect messages that other solutions may fail to solve. In particular, PGP offers the user the option of using strong encryption algorithms with sufficiently long key lengths to keep data secure against any currently feasible brute force attacks—something that the next option, S/MIME e-mail security, cannot promise.

S/MIME E-Mail Client Security

Following Netscape's lead, Microsoft began incorporating S/MIME e-mail support in its Internet web and e-mail clients (Internet Explorer, Outlook, and Outlook Express) by the fall of 1997. With support from these two massively dominant vendors in the browser market, S/MIME stands a very good chance of becoming a de facto standard for casual e-mail security no matter what security standard the IETF ultimately selects for secure e-mail. (See the note.)

As implemented currently, S/MIME has a number of advantages over the other secure e-mail approaches discussed here:

◆ You do not need to be using the same e-mail client as your corespondent; as long as you both have S/MIME-compliant clients, you should be able to exchange encrypted and signed messages interoperably.
◆ It currently can be exported from the United States, so it can (at least in theory) be used to sign and encrypt messages both by U.S. users and by international users.
◆ S/MIME requires the use of triple DES, which is considered secure for most purposes.
◆ S/MIME-enabled clients are widely and freely available, and include the most popular Internet clients from Netscape and Microsoft.
◆ S/MIME clients can exchange both e-mail messages and e-mail attachments that have been digitally signed and/

or encrypted, eliminating concerns about the authentication or integrity of a message connected with an encrypted or signed enclosure.

♦ Certificates and public keys use standard formats, and most CA providers' certificates will be able to be used interchangeably under S/MIME; there is no requirement for clients to support any proprietary certificate file formats in order to interoperate.

However, S/MIME does have at least one critical drawback:

♦ S/MIME uses the same key for both encryption and digital signatures. This can be a drawback because it means that if you should want to change your encryption keys (due to an upgrade in key length, as a periodic precaution against key compromise, or in response to a known compromise of the key), you will have to also change the certificate you use for authentication purposes.

 S/MIME originally specified RSA's RC2 cipher using 40-bit keys as the only algorithm and key length required for all S/MIME implementations. While early implementations use this shorter key length, the specification was changed, and by the start of 1998 the triple DES algorithm was designated as a requirement for S/MIME implementations. This eliminated what was seen as one of S/MIME's most serious flaws. RC2 with 40-bit keys provides minimal protection against brute force attacks, which (depending on the computers being used) can produce a plaintext from a ciphertext fast enough to render the encryption largely worthless.

SECURE E-MAIL STANDARDS, PROPOSED STANDARDS, AND THE IETF: Late in the summer of 1997, quite a few tail-feathers were ruffled on both sides of the barnyard as the IETF, apparently, disqualified the RSA-led S/MIME secure e-mail effort from the running to be put on the Internet standards track. In what was later characterized as a misunderstanding, the S/MIME effort failed to meet certain prerequisites as of the August meeting in Munich (in particular, requirements that the RC2 cipher algorithm be released from trade secret status before it could be considered as part of an Internet standard, and that a formal proposal be submitted). After a flurry of articles in the trade press that characterized the S/MIME standard proposal as out of the running, PGP offered a new proposal based in part on its own architecture, called OpenPGP.

RSA responded by making it clear that RC2 implementations could be distributed without licensing fees. However, the eventual modification of the S/MIME specification making triple DES the default encryption method helped it gain wider acceptance.

Ultimately, IETF-standard secure Internet e-mail will probably look very much like S/MIME. As of 1998, S/MIME—implemented on market-leading browsers from Netscape and Microsoft—is probably already on tens of millions of desktops.

Secure E-Mail with Eudora and PGP

Eudora, the popular e-mail client from Qualcomm, is now packaged with a copy of PGP 5.0 from Pretty Good Privacy, Inc. Whether you purchase Eudora Pro or use a freeware version of Eudora, you can now also install PGP as a plug-in program. The Eudora Pro 3.0.3 installation program is shown in Figure 7.1. For more about setting up and using PGP, including how to generate and administer your own keys as well as managing correspondents' keys, see Chapter 10.

Once the plug-in version of PGP 5.0 is complete, a PGP pulldown menu is added to the Eudora menubar as shown in Figure 7.2.

This pulldown menu provide direct access to the PGPkeys key management tool, the PGP preferences interface, and PGP help topics. A

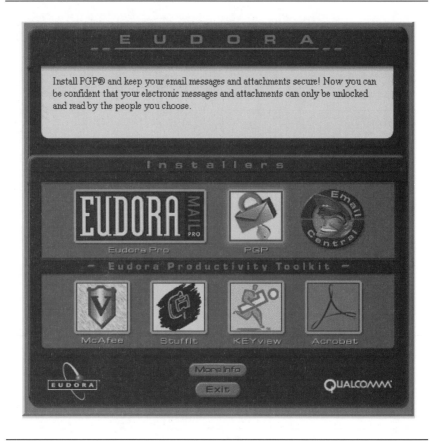

Install PGP® and keep your email messages and attachments secure! Now you can be confident that your electronic messages and attachments can only be unlocked and read by the people you choose.

Figure 7.1. When installing Eudora Pro 3.0.3, you can also install PGP 5.0 as a plug-in program.

set of special PGP buttons also appears in the upper right portion of message composition windows, as shown in Figure 7.3. These buttons, from left to right, perform the following functions (the Send button being at the far right of the figure):

- Provide direct access to the PGPkeys key management application.
- Toggle on the use of PGP/MIME for the current message.

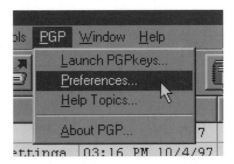

Figure 7.2. The PGP pulldown menu is added to Eudora's menubar when the PGP plug-in program is installed.

♦ Toggle on PGP encryption for the current message.
♦ Toggle on PGP digital signature for the current message.

The PGP plug-in also adds three icons to the view message toolbar (to the left of the Subject window). These are shown in Figure 7.4. These buttons, from left to right, perform the following functions:

♦ Decrypts the current PGP-encrypted message.
♦ Extracts a PGP key from the current message to add to your keyring.
♦ Opens the PGPkeys key management application.

Figure 7.3. Special PGP buttons added to the message composition window when the Eudora PGP plug-in program is installed.

Figure 7.4. Special PGP buttons added to the message view window when the Eudora PGP plug-in program is installed.

Getting Encryption-Enabled with Eudora PGP

The fastest way to get encryption enabled is to run the PGP Key Generation Wizard, which is described in greater detail in Chapter 10. To run the wizard, open the PGPkeys application, and select New Key from the Keys pulldown menu. This opens the Key Generation wizard, which will walk you through the process of generating a new key.

The process consists of the following steps:

♦ Enter the full name and e-mail address you want to associate with the public key you are generating.
♦ Choose to generate an RSA or DSS/Diffie-Hellman public key pair.

 PGP considers RSA key pairs to be "old style" keys and recommends using the DSS (Digital Signature Standard) key pair type. In fact, the PGP implementation shipped with Eudora Pro does not even allow the user to generate an RSA key pair. RSA keys are still displayed but using an old-fashioned style key icon to differentiate them from the more modern key icon used for DSS keys. RSA algorithms are not supported by this version of PGP, though an RSA upgrade for Eudora users who need to support RSA keys is available from PGP, Inc. (www.pgp.com).

- ◆ Choose a key pair size.
- ◆ Choose an expiration period. This is set as a number of days, from 1 to 2000, although PGP recommends not setting any expiration date for your key pair.
- ◆ Enter a passphrase to use to protect the private key you generate.
- ◆ The program will then commence to generate your private key pair.
- ◆ Once the key is generated, you can choose to send it to a keyserver (in other words, to publish it on an Internet server).
- ◆ Add the key pair to your keyring, and the process is complete.

 If you have already installed PGP 5.0 on your system when you set up Eudora, you can use the same PGP keys that you generated then.

Encrypting a Message with Eudora PGP

Encrypting a message with the Eudora PGP plug-in is very simple. Create the message as you would normally, then click on the PGP encryption button. This is the button in the center of Figure 7.3, which looks as if it were a cross between an envelope and a padlock.

If the recipient's e-mail address and public key are already in your PGP keyring, the message will automatically be encrypted with the recipient's PGP public key. Figure 7.5 shows a simple, short message that was encrypted and is ready to be sent.

If the recipient is not in your keyring, PGP brings up a window as shown in Figure 7.6. This window gives you the option of selecting

---

```
-----BEGIN PGP MESSAGE-----
Version: PGP for Personal Privacy 5.0
MessageID: 4Zn2pXFbBJAofbf0SnwQwZ8LfFJANVjY

qANQR1DBwU4D5ePoEeovDDEQB/9zd/xeKDcU6z8VOZrAXMNbh
VPzUCS05XTdgU4GEdp3C16LSlRCqcUA+gMSTQ/e+gcY9WBtYfz
Kj0R3jisjXs62WuxW6X0GPdPD/l73rnmrEMvopMHT2YvOailXo
IhQ09bYwwTRAxNQzWj2eBvesMGBAtjnVF8B0I2JFalOKaCPodfL
x3yViuCzSjm9W9FI0z3fV928LyFwZ+1Ik+VOqO9G3NW2ovGP4r/
qxPax+mNEJjtJPMoKb9clBYZyJ6iLSTtvkTJykrpMOy4EeLImw
UMTedYHLpk7TnC4m5Tk1WEJSU3EzzVng1gE3xKwWjkvlBejN3zd
2nCRmaV0k9wHQ5pbB/4raIF3XNcEwI7wQsX9Dp1fxSy+4ZtN3W
ZA16GonYVuSTvSegPRw0B8cFv1cvi8ZtPKuyVgczpUD7MqxGUY
7orPW6hSGa5PjZrPi2utAGGFM0sgqf0BKE2KnVEhM55ZuCv0h
Zz0NiwAYprXPkfuSgybhrFbueF0a7N6BKTGwWYIAREDS5MOa
wgxn/ak8yh/IvqjwN4xyIvltf9ApH9Vd//aSxo7IuumZoxbFVt
oRzK2G9RvDc5CQfufUyQalgSSe4ZBanm+YyyWUc7bzHTRofnV
9voViHO3oMq9YBLbcpUhYVBXFR5SD1QOsBJcMsiBhJTZn74HUc
VsemyeOWCOMK6yXBx87WSrT3Rv+PBNTDH0tBfReqrUxAE/sO
q40y1thGxiudQ29cUONQNBouOWouvo0tj09q0nrBDvmWiMQf4
1TBz5IvBqFiSBbIRAHfCMHteXzMDkZcCRGnv9cwaOcupE1a
AEJNVyHwgm4klv7ww2+ry
=tYhG

-----END PGP MESSAGE-----
```

Figure 7.5. A short message that has been encrypted with PGP for transmission with Eudora Pro.

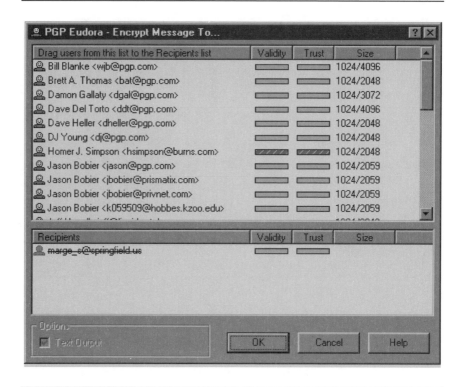

Figure 7.6. Choosing a recipient for an encrypted message.

the key of a different entity (from the recipient of the message) to encrypt the message to.

Decrypting a Message with Eudora PGP

When you receive a message with Eudora that has been encrypted with PGP, it will appear something like the message shown in Figure 7.5 (although it is likely to be longer, as that message contains only a single line). To decrypt it, you must click on the PGP open encrypted message icon—this is the icon shown in Figure 7.4 that shows a small piece of paper flying out of an envelope.

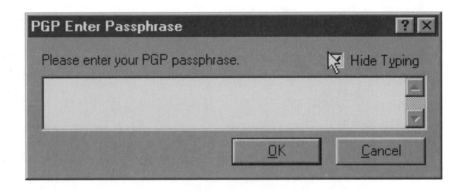

Figure 7.7. Entering the PGP passphrase to decrypt an encrypted message received with Eudora Pro.

You will be prompted to enter your PGP passphrase, as shown in Figure 7.7. Once the passphrase is successfully entered, PGP will decrypt the message with your private key and display the decrypted message in the standard Eudora message window.

At this point, however, it should be noted that the plaintext of the message has not been written to disk. This means that when you close the message window, you will be prompted by Eudora to make a decision about saving the changes that have been made to the message.

 If you wish to keep the contents of the message secure, you should not save the changes—the message will be stored in ciphertext (as it was received) and if you want to read it again, you will have to re-enter your passphrase to decrypt it again. If you choose to save the changes made to the message, the plaintext of the message will be stored on your system. This means that the message is no longer secure if an attacker can gain access to your system.

Digitally Signing a Message with Eudora PGP

Signing a message with PGP is also simple. Before the message is sent, click on the PGP signature icon next to the Send button. (See Figure 7.3.) This icon appears as a quill. When the message is sent, before it is put in the outbound queue, PGP generates a digital signature for the message and adds the signature to the message.

Before the message can be signed, you must enter your passphrase as shown in Figure 7.8. Note that if you have more than one PGP public key pair (for example, if you use one for your business and one for personal purposes), you will have to select the key you wish to sign with before entering a passphrase.

Figure 7.9 shows a very short message that has been digitally signed. Note that the message includes delimiters that indicate where the signed message begins and ends, and where the signature itself begins and ends.

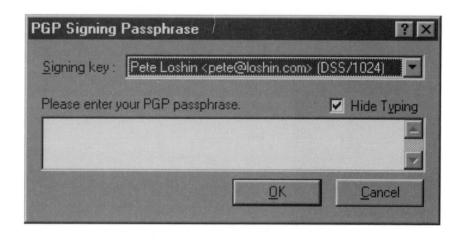

Figure 7.8. Choosing a public key to sign with and entering a passphrase before signing a message with PGP in Eudora Pro.

```
-----BEGIN PGP SIGNED MESSAGE-----

Hash: SHA1

This message should be signed digitally.

See ya!

- -pl

-----BEGIN PGP SIGNATURE-----

Version: PGP for Personal Privacy 5.0

Charset: noconv

iQA/AwUBNDgRc/duena/FdsDEQLp8ACgo4aRJ3dqdTb9piUN
yvronr2P3TEAoNY91W/DnOjnLlC2+u7T8oN5GgxE
=x1Gp

-----END PGP SIGNATURE-----
```

Figure 7.9. A very brief message that has been digitally signed with PGP in Eudora Pro.

 As the messages in Figures 7.5 and 7.9 show, PGP encrypted and signed messages use message part delimiters to set apart the different parts of the message. It is important to keep in mind that only the data inside the PGP message delimiters (that read "BEGIN PGP MESSAGE" and "END PGP MESSAGE") are encrypted. The same goes for digitally signed messages: only the data enclosed within the "BEGIN PGP SIGNED MESSAGE" and "END PGP SIGNED MESSAGE" delimiters has been signed. Any other data delivered as part of the message has not been signed.

Certifying a Signed Message with Eudora PGP

When you receive a message that has been signed with PGP, it looks like the message shown in Figure 7.9. The signature appears to be about 100 apparently random characters—a valid signature and a faked signature look very much alike. To certify a PGP-signed message with Eudora, you have to click on the same icon you use to decrypt a message—there is no separate certify icon. When a message is certified as having been signed authentically, a dialog box like that shown in Figure 7.10 appears. Included in the dialog are the name and e-mail address of the owner of the signing key, with the date and time the message was signed.

If the message signature does not certify, a dialog box will appear stating that the PGP text has been corrupted. The message does not provide any additional information because the signature would not certify if it was a pure fabrication or if the message was corrupted inadvertently at some point during its transmission, so there is no way to differentiate an accident from a fraud.

PGP Preferences

There are four tabs available in the PGP preferences dialog, as shown in Figure 7.11. These include

- ♦ General preferences, relating to how encryption is done, how passphrases are cached, and how keys are generated.
- ♦ Key file preferences, which simply point to your default public and private keyrings.

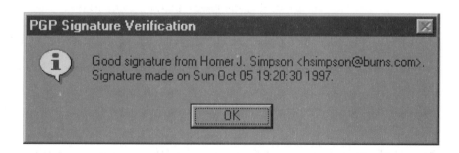

Figure 7.10. Certification that a digitally signed message has been authenticated with PGP in Eudora Pro.

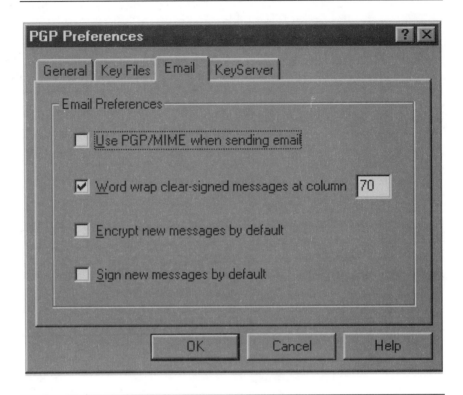

Figure 7.11. PGP e-mail preferences are set in this dialog box accessible through the PGP pulldown menu from Eudora.

- ♦ E-mail preferences, which are discussed shortly.
- ♦ Keyserver preferences, which identify the server and port used for PGP key service, and an option to retrieve unknown keys automatically.

There are four options listed under PGP e-mail preferences. These four options are set by clicking in the check boxes to either enable or disable them:

- ♦ Using PGP/MIME when sending e-mail ensures that messages are sent encrypted/signed using the MIME

(Multipurpose Internet Mail Extensions) format for mail attachments.

♦ Setting the word wrap length for signed messages ensures that signatures wrap from one line to the next without harming the integrity of the signature by adding an inadvertent carriage return or line feed.

♦ Encrypting new messages by default automatically causes each new message to be encrypted, as long as there is a key associated with the recipient.

♦ Signing new messages by default automatically causes each new message to be encrypted with the sender's public key.

For a complete discussion of PGP preferences, see Chapter 10.

 In general, it is a good idea to digitally sign all your messages by default. This gets your certificate out to all recipients of your messages over time, gets your correspondents used to the idea of your messages being signed, and ensures that any message that has any importance can be authenticated and certified. The downside of digitally signing all messages is the very slight performance hit you take and the very small amount of additional data that gets appended to your messages. Clients that do a passphrase challenge prior to allowing you access to any cryptographic function (like Netscape and PGP's products) also add a slight burden to the user in the form of frequent passphrase prompts.

PGP Plug-ins for Outlook and Other Clients

At this writing, PGP plug-in modules were available not only for Eudora e-mail clients but also for Microsoft's Outlook e-mail clients (Outlook 97 and Outlook Express). Plug-ins for other e-mail clients, including Netscape's Messenger client (bundled with the Communicator product) would be available soon. For more information, check Qualcomm's web page for Eudora at *www.eudora.com*.

Secure E-Mail with Microsoft Outlook Express

Microsoft includes a basic e-mail client with the Internet Explorer 4.0 distribution, called Outlook Express. This client software will probably be more than sufficient for most individuals' needs relating to e-mail as well as for Internet newsgroups, access to on-line directories, and support for personal address management. Also incorporated into the Outlook Express client is support for S/MIME e-mail security through message encryption and decryption as well as digital signature signing and certifying.

Getting Encryption-Enabled

The first step in using Outlook Express for securing your e-mail is to get a certificate, as described in Chapter 5. If you have an existing certificate generated through some other client, you will probably be able to use it with Outlook Express (as well as with Internet Explorer) by exporting it from the original client and importing it into Internet Explorer, as described in Chapter 6. Once the certificate is installed, you can configure Outlook Express for secure e-mail.

Once a certificate is installed, you must configure Outlook Express to associate the certificate with the e-mail account you select. To do this, select the Accounts option from the Tools pulldown menu, as shown in Figure 7.12.

By default, the mail accounts will be displayed; this panel will display all e-mail accounts that have been configured for use with Outlook Express. The next step is to select an account (if there is only one, be sure that it is highlighted) and click on the Properties button. The next dialog box that appears includes all properties associated with the account, including general information (like name and e-mail address), server configuration, network connection to be used to access e-mail, security (to be discussed shortly), and advanced settings (including server connection configuration).

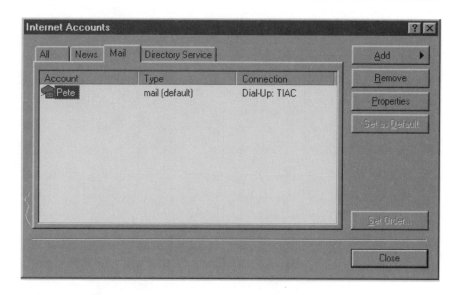

Figure 7.12. Configuring your e-mail account to use certificates within Microsoft Outlook Express.

The security tab of the account properties dialog, shown in Figure 7.13, provides two basic functions:

- ◆ Enabling (or disabling) use of the digital ID when sending secured messages from the account in question, and choosing which digital ID to use.
- ◆ Getting a digital ID or finding out more about how digital IDs work, through the Get Digital ID button and the More Info button.

The second functions have already been discussed at length in Chapter 5.

Enabling the use of a digital ID, by putting a check in the checkbox shown in Figure 7.13, is simple if there is only one digital ID available.

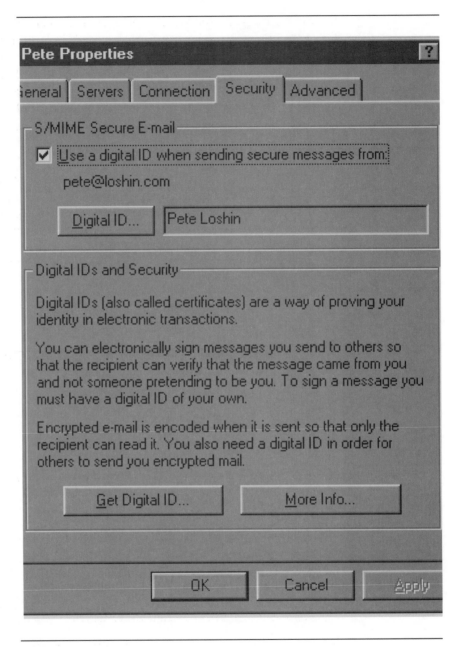

Figure 7.13. Configuring an e-mail account's security properties with Microsoft Outlook Express.

However, if there are more than one digital ID available, you will need to click on the Digital ID . . . button to select the appropriate one. Figure 7.14 shows a choice of two different digital IDs, both issued by Verisign, but one issued for use with Microsoft's Internet Explorer and the other issued for use with Netscape's Navigator. The only way to differentiate between the two is to explore the properties by choosing one and clicking on the Properties button and examining all the fields. (See Chapter 6 for more on certificate properties.)

Once a certificate is selected, click on the OK button, and you will return to the account properties panel; click on the Apply button (see Figure 7.13—the Apply button is grayed-out until a change has been made) and the new certificate will be enabled. Back out of the account configuration by clicking on the Close button (as shown in Figure 7.12) and you can now sign or encrypt messages automatically.

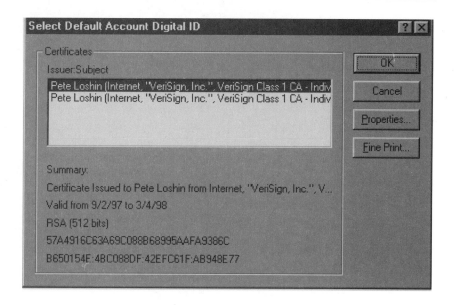

Figure 7.14. Choosing a digital ID to associate with an e-mail account using Outlook Express.

It is possible to set Outlook Express to automatically encrypt or digitally sign all outgoing messages by modifying the program's options. Select Options from the Tools menubar pulldown, and you get a dialog box with seven tabs relating to different sets of options that can be set for Outlook Express. Click on the Security tab to display the dialog shown in Figure 7.15. In the middle of the box is a section concerning secure mail, where you can enable the program to digitally sign all messages or encrypt the contents and attachments for all outgoing messages by clicking on one or both of the check boxes there.

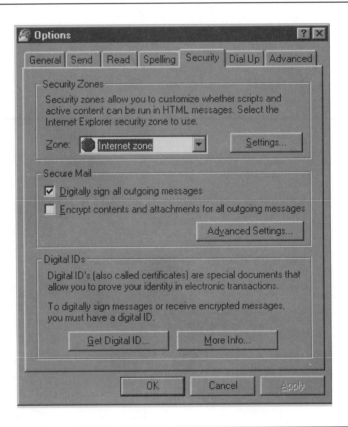

Figure 7.15. Setting Outlook Express encryption and digital signature options.

There are also some advanced settings, accessible by clicking on the Advanced Settings button, and shown in Figure 7.16. These settings allow you to enable the program to always include the sender when encrypting outgoing mail, and choosing the encryption algorithm (40-bit RC2 encryption is available in all versions, while nonexport versions currently support additional algorithms including 128-bit RC2, DES and triple DES).

Advanced options for digital signatures include two options that can be enabled: to include the sender's digital signature when sending signed messages, which allows the recipient to certify the message as well as to

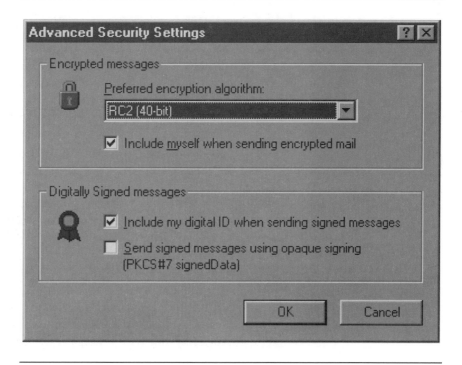

Figure 7.16. Setting Outlook Express advanced settings for encryption and digital signatures.

encrypt replies to the sender; or to send signed messages using the PKCS #7 standard for formatting the signature and related data.

 In general, it is a good idea to digitally sign all your messages by default. This gets your certificate out to all recipients of your messages over time, gets your correspondents used to the idea of your messages being signed, and ensures that any message that has any importance can be authenticated and certified. The downside of digitally signing all messages is the very slight performance hit you take and the very small amount of additional data that gets appended to your messages. Clients that do a passphrase challenge prior to allowing you access to any cryptographic function (like Netscape and PGP's products) also add a slight burden to the user in the form of frequent passphrase prompts.

Sending a Signed or Encrypted Message

Once a certificate has been associated with your e-mail account, encrypting or digitally signing e-mail is a simple matter. The simplest method of making sure that all messages are encrypted and/ or signed is to set the default for outgoing e-mail, as discussed in the previous section. However, this is not always practical; for now, in most cases it is simplest to digitally sign all messages but to not encrypt messages by default, since many recipients do not yet have digital IDs.

Figure 7.17 shows the Outlook Express window for creating a new e-mail message. The two icons at the right of the toolbar along the top of the window indicate whether the message will be signed or encrypted. When one of those icons is selected (active), the action will take place for that message. The digital signature icon is the second from the right and has a red ribbon superimposed over an envelope. The encryption icon is at the far right and has a blue padlock superimposed over an envelope. When you click on either one, the related symbol appears in the lower right corner of the message header window (under the Internet Explorer "e" symbol) as shown in Figure 7.17.

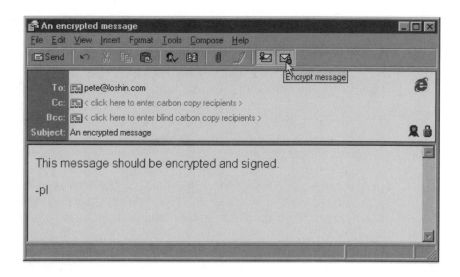

Figure 7.17. Encrypting and digitally signing a message using Outlook Express Toolbar icons.

You can also activate encryption and digital signature for a message by going to the Tools pulldown menu and selecting either Encrypt or Digitally Sign; when these are active, they are checked as shown in Figure 7.18; to turn them off, simply select them again (which disables the check next to them in the pulldown menu).

Once you have completed the message, simply send it. Outlook Express does not require a passphrase to sign or encrypt a message.

If you are attempting to encrypt a message and you do not have a digital ID on file for one or more of your message's recipients, you will get a warning message telling you that you must associate a digital ID with any recipient you want to encrypt a message to.

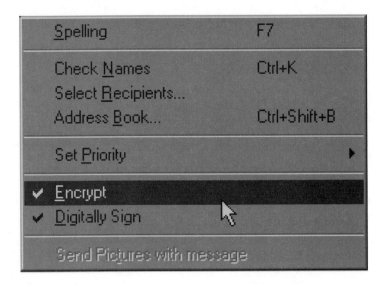

Figure 7.18. Encrypting and digitally signing a message using Outlook Express's Tools pulldown menu.

Decrypting and Certifying a Message

When you receive a message that has been signed, encrypted, or both, you will initially see a message like that shown in Figure 7.19 explaining what additional security has been added to the e-mail message. There is a check box that you can select to turn off this help screen when receiving similarly secured messages in the future.

To read the message, simply click on the Continue button at the bottom of the help message. The encrypted or signed message will then be displayed. The header information is shown in white text on a dark blue background as displayed in Figure 7.20, rather than the more usual black on gray for headers of nonsecured messages.

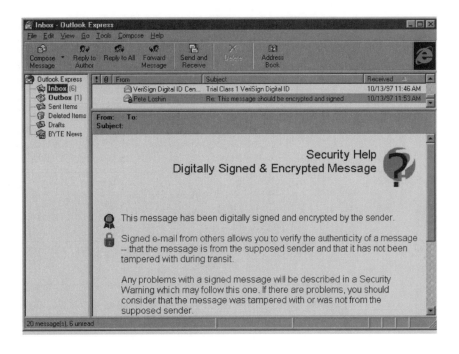

Figure 7.19. When first receiving signed or encrypted (or both) messages through Outlook Express, this help screen or one like it will be displayed.

This indicates that the header is selected; when it is deselected, the header will turn back to black on gray.

Note the ribbon and padlock shown to the far right of the header section; mousing over either of these will activate them. The ribbon turns red and the padlock turns blue; clicking on either of them will bring up a pulldown menu offering options for viewing information about the signature or message encryption, as shown in Figure 7.21, where the menu for the message signature is shown in the upper right.

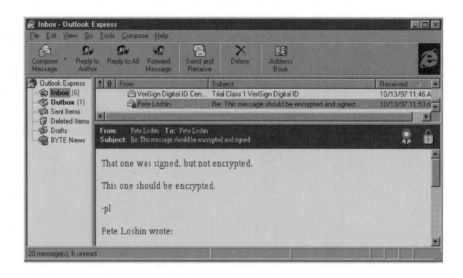

Figure 7.20. Reading an encrypted, digitally signed message with Outlook Express.

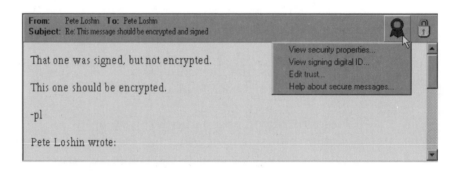

Figure 7.21. Pulldown menu for handling a message's digital signature in Outlook Express.

The options available to the user include

♦ View security properties. This option allows the user to certify the digital ID, making sure it is valid, as well as view the details of the digital ID used for signing or encrypting the message. Also accessible through this option is a button for adding the digital ID to your address book, so it can be used to encrypt messages in reply to the sender.

♦ View signing or encrypting digital ID. This option allows the user to view complete details of the certificate, including the general and detailed contents of the certificate, and allows the user to set trust levels for the certificate.

♦ Help about secure messages providing direct access to the on-line help function, specifically opening up help at the relevant page.

The first two of these options are discussed at greater length next.

Security Properties in Outlook Express

Choosing View Security Properties from the digital signature or encryption icons' pulldown menu brings up a dialog box similar to that shown in Figure 7.22. There are three tabs in this dialog, but the Security tab contains the most important information and functions. Included here are

♦ A section on the digital signature, including whether or not the message was signed, whether or not the contents appear to have arrived unchanged (the dialog says whether or not the contents were "altered after item was signed"), and whether or not the signature is trusted (based on trust levels for the CA as well as the signer's digital ID itself). Also in this section is a button that can be used to certify the signature and digital ID.

♦ A section on the sender's digital ID, indicating whether or not a digital ID is included in the message,

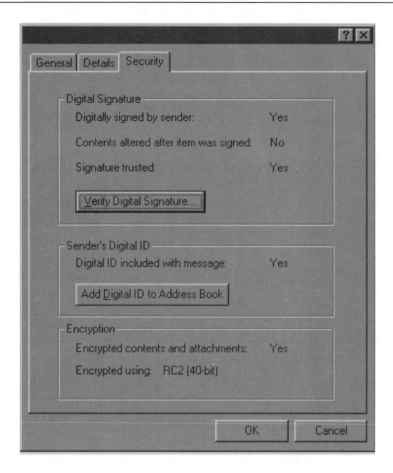

Figure 7.22. Examining and handling security attributes of an encrypted or digitally signed message in Outlook Express.

and a button that can be used to add the digital ID to the user's address book.

♦ A section on encryption, indicating whether or not the contents of the message have been encrypted and what algorithm has been used to encrypt the message.

The most important feature here is the button that can be used to add a digital ID to your address book. Clicking on this button will bring up a new entry for your address book or an existing one if the sender is already listed in your address book. You can add information to the entry or modify it, as long as you are certain to click the OK button to exit so that the digital ID is properly entered into the address book.

Viewing Digital IDs with Outlook Express

Figure 7.23 shows the dialog box that appears when you choose to view the digital ID of the signer or encrypter of a message. The general tab of this box simply indicates whether or not the certificate is acceptable, who owns it, and who issued it; there is also some explanatory text about certificates in general. The Details and Advanced tabs provide even more detailed information about the certificate itself.

The Trust tab, shown in Figure 7.24, is useful for managing how and who you trust. It allows you three options for generating trust based on the certificate and its issuer for the type of function specified in the top part of the dialog box (in this case, e-mail encryption and authentication):

♦ You can allow trust to flow from the issuer, usually the certification authority that issued the digital ID in question. This means that you will trust other digital IDs that are issued by the same CA.
♦ You can explicitly trust the certificate, which means that you trust the certificate to identify correctly the holder but it does not make any reference to the issuer.
♦ You can explicitly not trust the certificate, which means that you assume the certificate to not correctly or reliably represent the certificate holder.

Using PGP with Outlook Express

Pretty Good Privacy, Inc., produces plug-in versions of its PGP for Personal Privacy software that can be used with both Outlook

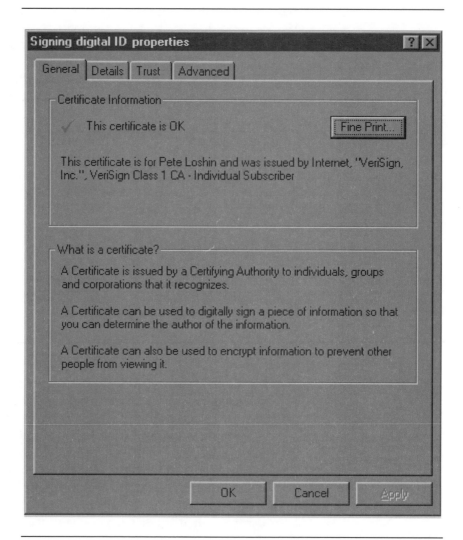

Figure 7.23. Examining the properties of a signer's digital ID with Outlook Express.

Express and the full Outlook e-mail client. The same functions already described in the section on using the Eudora client with PGP for Personal Privacy are available, and they function in much

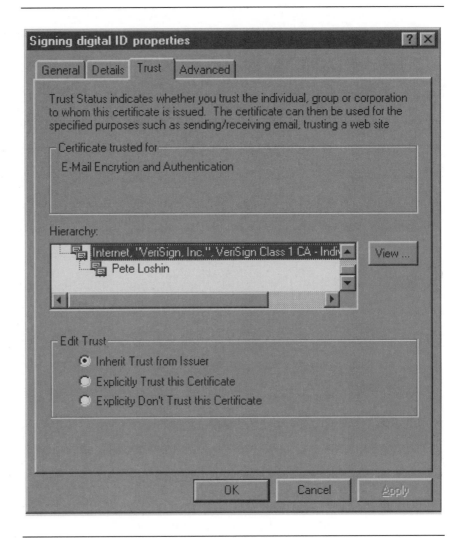

Figure 7.24. Setting trust levels from a digital certificate received through Outlook Express.

the same way. Icons are added to the client as is a pulldown menu accessible through the application's main menubar. For more on the specifics of using PGP as a plugin program, see the preceding section on using PGP with Eudora; for more on using PGP in general, see Chapter 10.

Security Zones and Outlook Express

Outlook Express uses the same notion of security zones as Internet Explorer, as described in Chapter 6. This means that you can choose to restrict the type of content and downloaded programs that can be run from within HTML-based messages. Figure 7.25 shows that you can set your tolerance for potentially harmful content only either to the same level as you do for the Internet zone (basically, everywhere but those sites you explicitly trust, and those sites you explicitly do not trust), or to the same level as you do for sites that you explicitly do not trust.

Changing the security level (from low to high, or custom) for a zone within Outlook Express will also change how that security zone is treated from other client software that uses Microsoft's security zone system—particularly, Internet Explorer. You can modify the level of security, and add or remove sites to each security zone as described in Chapter 6.

Secure E-Mail with Netscape Messenger

Netscape started bundling an e-mail client with its web browser quite early, adding news reading capability as well for good measure. With the latest release of Communicator and Navigator 4.0, secure e-mail becomes even easier than it was in earlier releases. While some users may find Microsoft's implementation of secure e-mail to be somewhat easier to deal with, most will find Netscape's implementation to be superior in terms of actual security.

Added features like the use of a passphrase challenge before doing anything relating to security—from signing or encrypting a message to decrypting a message—and a more generally accessible and usable interface make the Netscape client software more attractive to discerning users.

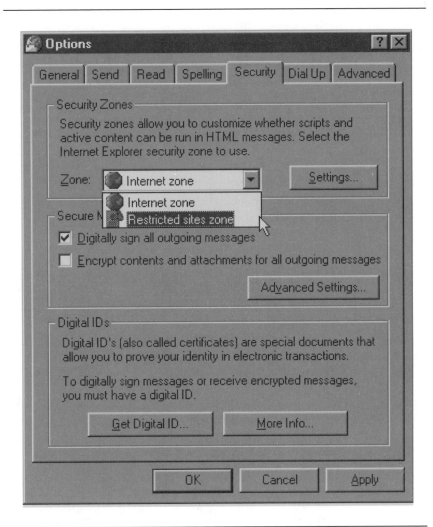

Figure 7.25. Microsoft Outlook Express uses the same notion of security zones as Internet Explorer.

Getting Encryption-Enabled

Once you have gotten your digital ID as described in Chapter 5, you are ready to roll with secure e-mail. You should click on the security icon (the padlock icon shown in the top toolbar) to bring up the Netscape security interface, then click on the Messenger option in the list on the left side of the window. The Messenger security interface, shown again in Figure 7.26, allows you to configure the following options:

+ Whether or not to encrypt e-mail messages when it is possible (in other words, when you have a certificate for the recipient).

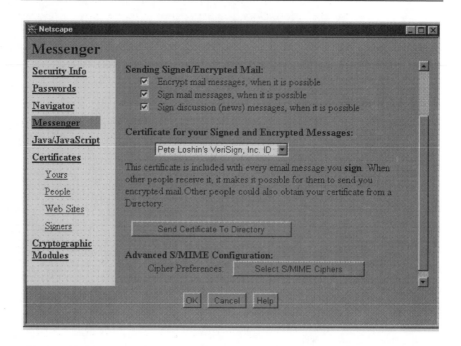

Figure 7.26. Setting basic secure e-mail defaults with Netscape's Messenger e-mail client.

◆ Whether or not to digitally sign your own e-mail messages, when it is possible (in other words, when you have a certificate for yourself).
◆ Whether or not to digitally sign your messages posted to news or discussion groups, when possible.

These options are set by clicking on the appropriate check boxes in the security interface.

 In general, it is a good idea to digitally sign all your messages by default. This gets your certificate out to all recipients of your messages over time, gets your correspondents used to the idea of your messages being signed, and ensures that any message that has any importance can be authenticated and certified. The downside of digitally signing all messages is the very slight performance hit you take and the very small amount of additional data that gets appended to your messages. Clients that do a passphrase challenge prior to allowing you access to any cryptographic function (like Netscape and PGP's products) also add a slight burden to the user in the form of frequent passphrase prompts.

You can also choose which certificate to use (if you have more than one) simply by selecting the desired certificate from the list displayed in the pick list.

You can send your certificate to a directory (so people can find it by looking it up on the directory rather than by corresponding directly with you) by clicking on the Send Certificate to Directory button. Doing so brings up a dialog box with a pick list showing currently supported directories. Choosing one of those directories will cause your certificate to be sent; your certificate will be accessible to anyone looking for it.

The last option, choosing the S/MIME cipher, should allow selection of triple DES or the RC2 cipher with 40-bit keys. (The most recent version available to the author supported RC2 only.)

Encrypting and Signing a Message

Netscape's Messenger e-mail client provides simple access to all of the added functions that one would want when sending an e-mail message in a set of tabbed message property categories in the top part of the message compose window, as shown in Figure 7.27. By default, the tab showing on top is the addressing property showing who will receive the message.

Figure 7.28 shows the property tab for message encryption and signature as well as for other delivery options. The check boxes for encrypting and digitally signing the message will by default be checked or not depending on what options the user has chosen for Messenger through the Netscape security interface. If the default is

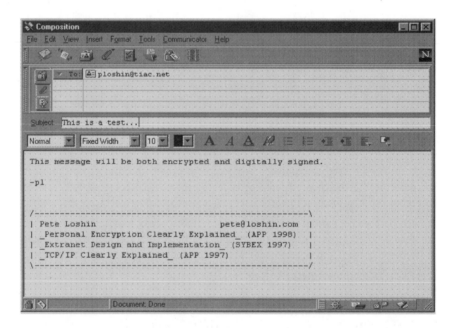

Figure 7.27. Netscape Messenger provides easy access to message properties through tabbed categories in the top part of the window.

Figure 7.28. The check box properties tab for a Netscape Messenger compose message window.

not to encrypt or sign a message, you can encrypt and/or sign any message by selecting the check box tab shown in Figure 7.28 and then checking either to encrypt or to sign the message (or both).

 When sending a signed or encrypted message with Netscape Messenger, you will be prompted for a passphrase. This is the passphrase you entered to protect your certificate, so it will be less likely that anyone but you can encrypt or sign a message using your certificate. Chapter 6 describes passphrase protection options for Netscape Communicator; if you choose to passphrase protect your certificate every time it is needed, you will have to enter the passphrase twice for the first time you need it to sign a message during a session.

You can also encrypt or sign a message by clicking on the security icon in the toolbar at the top of the compose message window. This brings up the standard Netscape security interface, but displays the security information for the current message as shown in Figure 7.29. The panel describes what message encryption and digital signature mean, and provides check boxes to turn on either encryption, digital signature, or both for the message.

Certifying a Digitally Signed Message

When you receive a message that has been digitally signed, there will be an icon in the upper right corner of the message window

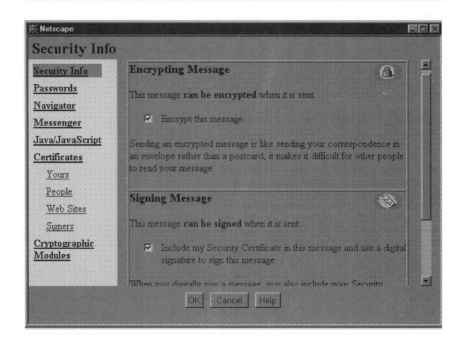

Figure 7.29. Using the Netscape Communicator security interface to sign or encrypt a message.

indicating that there is a signature associated with the message. This is shown in Figure 7.30.

To find out more about the digital signature, you can either single-click on the signature icon or click on the security icon in the Inbox toolbar; both actions will access the Netscape security interface and display the security properties of the message. In this case, they will indicate that the message was not encrypted but was digitally signed. Figure 7.31 shows that you can get more information by clicking on the View button.

Clicking on the View button will display a standard dialog box containing complete information derived from the digital ID included in the digital signature, as shown in Figure 7.32.

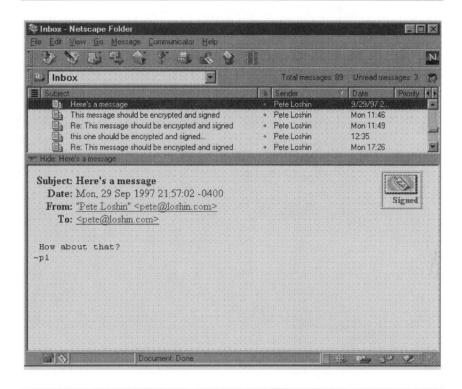

Figure 7.30. Receiving a signed message with Netscape Messenger.

 When you receive signed messages, Netscape Messenger automatically adds the sender's certificates to your database without you having to take any additional action. This makes replying with encrypted messages that much easier.

Decrypting an Encrypted Message

When you receive a message that has been encrypted, Netscape Messenger will not display the plaintext unless authorization has

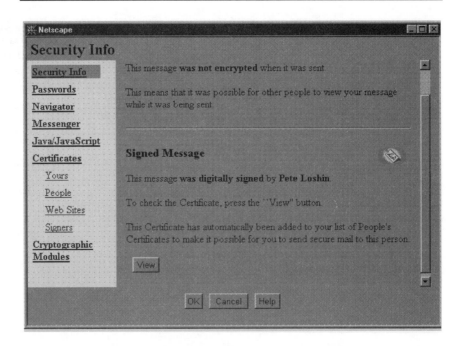

Figure 7.31. Reviewing security information about a signed message received with Netscape Messenger.

been given through a passphrase challenge. This means that if you have set your passphrase settings (see Chapter 6) to request passphrase entry every time the certificate is needed, you will be prompted to enter a passphrase every time you try to access an encrypted message. If you have chosen to be prompted only once per session, entering the passphrase for any reason (for example, to send a signed message) will allow you to access any encrypted message.

Attempting to open an encrypted message without prior authentication will produce a dialog box prompt to enter a passphrase for the Communicator Certificate database, as shown in Figure 7.33.

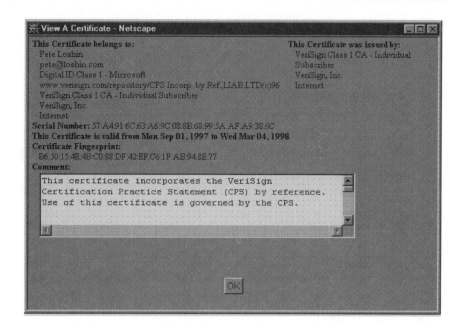

Figure 7.32. Viewing the certificate attached to a digitally signed message received with Netscape Messenger.

Enter the correct passphrase, and the message will be automatically decrypted and displayed, as shown in Figure 7.34. An icon in the upper right corner of the message window will indicate that the message was encrypted (or encrypted and signed, if that was the case).

Clicking on the icon in the message window—or clicking on the Netscape security icon in the toolbar—will produce a panel like that shown in Figure 7.35. In addition to finding out what kind of encryption was used and selected details from the signing entity's digital certificate, this panel provides some explanation of what signing and encryption are all about. The user can view complete details of the signer's certificate by clicking on the

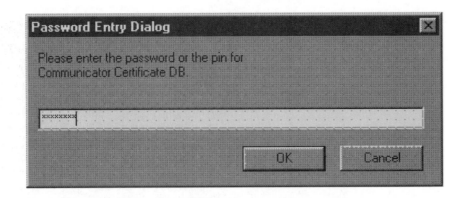

Figure 7.33. Passphrase challenge presented by Netscape Messenger before permitting access to an encrypted e-mail message.

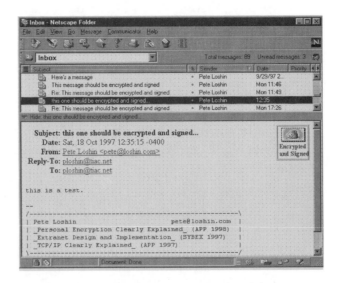

Figure 7.34. Viewing an encrypted message using Netscape Messenger.

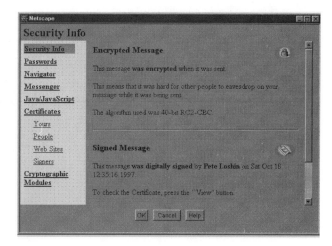

Figure 7.35. Viewing security properties of an encrypted message using Netscape Messenger.

View button. (The result will be similar to the panel shown in Figure 7.32.)

Failure to enter a valid passphrase means that the message header will still be displayed, but the rest of the message will not be visible, and an icon indicating that there is invalid encryption will be displayed in the upper right corner of the message window.

Figure 7.36 shows how an encrypted message is displayed when a passphrase for the recipient's certificate is not supplied. With such a message, clicking on either that icon or the security icon in the Messenger toolbar will display a security information window like that shown in Figure 7.37. The security interface will indicate only that the message was encrypted and that it could not be decrypted without access to the recipient's private keys; the fact that it was digitally signed is not available to the program without decrypting the message.

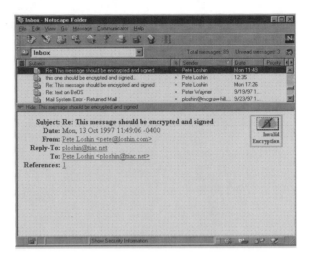

Figure 7.36. Attempting to view an encrypted message without entering a valid passphrase, using Netscape Messenger.

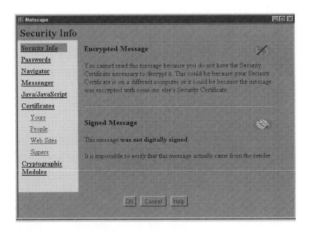

Figure 7.37. Viewing security information about an encrypted message, without the proper passphrase, in Netscape Messenger.

8

Securing the Desktop

Safeguarding data being transmitted as e-mail messages over an open network like the Internet is an important step to take to keep your data private. Protecting data on a personal computer presents a different set of issues in terms of how the data should be protected, how to control keys, and access to those keys. Perhaps the most important issue is how to select a data encryption product for your desktop.

This chapter examines how one should go about choosing a desktop encryption product, looking at which functions and features are useful and which are necessary. It also discusses what kind of products are currently available, and presents some of the most important criteria to use when making a decision about what product to use.

Also presented in this chapter is how to secure the desktop and all the files and programs running on the desktop using two of the best desktop security products:

- SecurPC from RSA Data Security, Inc. (a Security Dynamics company).
- Pretty Good Privacy, Inc.'s PGP for Personal Privacy.

Selecting a Desktop Encryption Product

Choosing a desktop encryption product is a matter of taking three steps:

- Examining your security needs, taking into consideration all the functions and features that you need to protect your programs and data to the degree necessary.
- Examining and understanding the products available for desktop encryption, how they work, and what they do to protect your data.
- Deciding on a set of criteria to judge the available products and then making a purchase decision based on those criteria.

The rest of this section provides information relevant to these steps to help the reader make a reasoned and reasonable choice for desktop data security.

Desktop Security Needs

Obviously and simply stated, the most basic data security needs are to encrypt files so they can only be accessed by an authorized user, and to make sure that only authorized users can access encrypted files. However, there are any number of additional considerations concerning how the files are to be encrypted, how they are to be decrypted, and how they are handled on the system that will determine what features are necessary to the user. These considerations include

- Is it more important that files be securely encrypted and inaccessible without proper authorization, or that files be readily accessible to authorized users even if that may sometimes put the data in peril?
- Is it important to be able to encrypt entire directories or directory hierarchies as well as individual files?
- Is it important to be able to select from a variety of encryption algorithms?
- Is it important to be able to use public key as well as private key encryption?
- Is it important to be able to digitally sign a file as well as encrypt it?
- Is it important to be able to digitally sign a file without encrypting it?
- Is it important to be able to create an encrypted file that can be transmitted to other users? What formats are acceptable? (In other words, how important is it that the product require encrypted file recipients to use the same product, to use the same operating system platform, or to use some standard format for encrypted data?)
- Is it important to have a mechanism by which an entity other than the user can decrypt data? (In other words, should a designated third party like an employer be able to access data in the absence of the owner of the data?)
- Is it important that the software have a "secure delete" feature? (In other words, should there be a mechanism by which data files are not just removed from the disk's directory listing but are actually zeroed out in the disk storage, to avoid undelete system functions from working?)
- Is it important that the software provide system and bootup access control? (In other words, should it provide a mechanism by which the system can be "locked up" to prohibit access without a passphrase?)
- Is it important that the software chosen be legally exportable for use outside the United States?

It is assumed that the primary consideration is that the product be capable of consistently, reliably, and securely encrypting data, and consistently, reliably, and accurately decrypting data. It goes without saying that this requires that, at a minimum, the software implements an algorithm (or set of algorithms) that are known to be strong, and that the vendor has sufficient resources and expertise to test and verify that its algorithms are in fact implemented securely.

Desktop Security Products

There are a lot of products currently available that claim to provide security for the individual. Some of the different types of products include

- ◆ Access control programs that prevent access to the system unless the user enters an authorized passphrase. This function, often offered in a package with other security and utility functions, does not necessarily protect data but simply puts a hurdle in place. For example, it may be possible to access data files on a system that has this type of protection in place simply by removing the drive in question and connecting it to another system or even as simply as booting from a floppy drive.
- ◆ Authentication programs that restrict access to system resources based on user ID and passphrase. This type of service is included as part of Windows, and other programs are available that implement more complicated, extensive, or sophisticated authentication schemes. Again, these programs or functions do not necessarily provide any encryption protection, but simply restrict access.
- ◆ Encryption programs that can be used to encrypt and decrypt data, and which may also provide certificate and digital signature services.

The last category is the one that is most relevant to this book and this chapter. Within this category, however, it should be noted that there are still many different products available. As has already been mentioned, most encryption products will fall into at least one of these categories:

♦ Programs that do cryptographic functions as their primary function and that implement well-known and strong encryption algorithms, whether they license the algorithms from patent holders or use algorithms that are available for public use through their inclusion in open standards or through their release into the public domain. Examples of such programs include RSA's SecurPC, Symantec's Norton For Your Eyes Only and PGP, Inc.'s PGP for Personal Privacy.

♦ Programs that do cryptographic functions as their primary function but implement algorithms of unknown origin or strength. Vendors who withhold their encryption algorithms' "brand names" (standard or well-known algorithm identifier—for example RSA, Diffie-Hellman, and MD5) or who claim that identifying the algorithms they use would compromise their product's security generally fall into this category. This type of product tends to have a relatively short lifetime, as few if any catch on with any significant market share.

♦ Programs that implement strong cryptographic functions securely as a support to their primary functions— for example, Lotus Notes, Netscape Communicator, and Microsoft Internet Explorer.

♦ Programs that implement cryptographic functions of unknown origin or strength as a support to their primary functions. Such products run the gamut from standard application software like databases and word processors to utility packages.

The programs in the first of these categories are the only ones that are of interest to us in this chapter, and while most have at least one or more unique feature or function, they tend to perform similarly.

Desktop Security Criteria

The two most important criteria, in order, when selecting a desktop security program are

- ◆ Does the product securely encrypt and reliably decrypt data?
- ◆ Does the product perform all the functions that you require?

In other words, if all you require is a mechanism that can render plaintext ASCII data unreadable to the casual viewer—simply obscuring data displayed on a monitor—you could probably use the simple substitution ROT-13 cipher. However, this type of cipher provides no real data security. If you expect to have any degree of protection for your data, you should get real encryption tools.

The issue is increasingly complicated by the degree to which algorithms that have been widely deployed and often deployed in situations that require real security are falling to brute force attacks. International-strength SSL, implemented in browsers using 40-bit keys for bulk encryption, is sufficient only for relatively trivial security applications as it is vulnerable to brute force attacks that can succeed with a relatively small pool of resources, relatively quickly. The announcement in October 1997 that a group had successfully completed a brute force attack against DES, using a pool of thousands of computers cooperating over the Internet over a period of months, indicates that 56-bit key DES should no longer be considered sufficient protection for data that must remain secure for any significant period of time (though it should be sufficient for data that must remain secret for a much shorter period).

Other criteria that are also of importance include

- ◆ Platform. Does the product run on your platform of choice: Windows NT, Windows 95, Windows 98, Macintosh, Unix?
- ◆ Usability. Is the product sufficiently easy to use?

- ◆ Recoverability. Does the product include any recovery features to protect you from loss of your passphrase or keys? This type of feature may be built in through the product's implementation, or it may incorporate the use of a recovery diskette that is meant to be stored securely itself.
- ◆ Interoperability. If you plan to encrypt data to be shared with others, do they have to purchase the exact same product? At present, most products require all correspondents to use the same program, but more interoperability may be available in software upgrades and new products in the next year or so as standards coalesce.
- ◆ Features. If you require some particular feature, your selection will be limited to the products that offer that feature.

One criterion that has not yet been mentioned is price. Consumers should have no trouble finding fairly high quality encryption software for under $100, and it is possible to find freeware implementations that can be trusted. However, if your data is worth millions to you and the only product you can find that meets all your requirements costs several hundred dollars or even more, common sense dictates that the extra money should not pose an obstacle to the purchase.

This chapter discusses two products that should meet the needs of most individual users (as well as many organizations and groups). RSA's SecurPC is available for Windows 95, NT, and 3.x as well as for the Macintosh OS; Pretty Good Privacy for Personal Encryption is also available for a variety of platforms including Windows 95 and NT, Macintosh OS, and various flavors of Unix. This chapter discusses using these products on the Windows 95 platform only because of its wide popularity; these products provide similar functionality and features on other the platforms they support.

Using RSA SecurPC

RSA's business is mostly oriented toward the sales of cryptographic programming toolkits and the licensing of their algorithms (including the RSA public key algorithm, the RC4 symmetric encryption algorithm, and the MD5 cryptographic hashing algorithm). SecurPC is one of the few products that RSA creates for use by actual consumers. Some of the more important features of the product include

- File and directory encryption using the RC4 cipher.
- Integration with Windows, adding menu options and file and directory options wherever appropriate.
- Boot protection to keep unauthorized users out of protected hard drives.
- SecurPC AutoCrypt allows authorized users to work with encrypted files transparently. When the user wants to open an encrypted file using an application (for example, a word processor), the file is opened, decrypted and re-encrypted without the need for the user to intervene manually.
- File and directory encryption means that individual files, groups of files or entire directories (and all files created within the encrypted directory) can be encrypted.
- Self-extracting, executable file encryption allows you to create an encrypted file that will open itself on Windows platforms and challenge the entity opening it for a passphrase. This lets you share encrypted data even with users who do not have a copy of SecurPC.
- Emergency access can be through a single passphrase (most applicable for individual use of the product) or can be split up to require two or more entities to be present and consenting to access the encrypted data.

While encryption with SecurPC uses symmetric algorithms, access to the emergency passphrase, a key part of setting up the administrator software, is protected through the use of RSA public key encryption. The end-user software can encrypt the individual's symmetric encryption key using the public key of the emergency administrator. In this way, when and if the end-user is absent and the data must be accessed, the emergency administrator can decrypt the keys using the emergency access private key to recover the user's symmetric encryption key. The setup process for this type of emergency access is described shortly.

SECURPC INSTALLATION ISSUES: SecurPC is far from an easy tool to install. While many products are relatively forgiving in terms of how closely you must follow directions, SecurPC installation requires that you not deviate. For example, if you have not made copies of the user setup disks before starting the administrative setup (which has to be done first), you will not be able to complete the installation.

Installing SecurPC on an individual computer is still relatively straightforward, and the reader is urged to follow all instructions included with the product and any directions provided during the installation process. Unlike many other products, the SecurPC administrator program must be initialized first before the user software can be installed; part of that process includes customizing the user software installation diskettes to reflect the administrative configuration chosen.

You should have five formatted diskettes available for use during the administrative installation process:

♦ Two must be used to make copies of the user setup diskettes before starting the process.
♦ One will be used for an administrative setup disk.
♦ One will be used for an emergency boot access disk.
♦ One will be used to back up your personal user preferences file.

Setting Up SecurPC

This section discusses the steps you need to take to install and set up SecurPC on an individual's computer. Getting ready means considering how you will administer your installation. This may require considerable thought if you are planning to use SecurPC as an organizational solution, though if you are planning to use it as a personal security tool you can run it all from a single computer. (See the note.)

USING SECURPC IN ORGANIZATIONS : The term *key escrow* has come to be associated with what some refer to as government access to keys. This is partially because proponents of government access to keys want to require that all encryption keys be stored with some kind of neutral and trusted third-party entity that will only dispense keys to those authorized to receive them. This type of key escrow for all encryption keys used for any purpose by any individual or organization, as discussed elsewhere, is not only repugnant to the sensibilities of any free people, but is also impractical.

However, key escrow has a definite place in the deployment of secure encryption systems within organizations. Imagine the difficulty that would ensue if all employees of a corporation used their own encryption keys and disclosed them to no one. Every time an employee's tenure is interrupted suddenly, whether through injury, illness, death, or voluntary or involuntary termination, all ciphertext data left behind would be inaccessible. Using a key escrow system, whereby some individual entity or group of entities can access encrypted data, helps eliminate this problem.

SecurPC implements an elegant solution that not only supports a single entity (in this case, a person holding a single diskette) to decrypt another user's data, but it can also be configured to distribute the emergency access key to two or more diskettes. In other words, you can set up your emergency access system so that three people would share the duty of emergency access to your encrypted information. For example, you could set it up so that only if your spouse, your business partner, and your attorney all agreed (by bringing together their diskettes) could anyone but you decrypt your data.

Even more useful is the option of sharing emergency duties among a number of entities and requiring agreement among some minimum number of them before emergency access could be granted. In other words, you might divide up emergency access among your spouse, a parent, two children, two business partners, your attorney, your accountant, and your personal trainer (a total of nine). However, since many of them may not be available at any given time, instead of requiring all nine to agree, you can specify that if any five of them agree, they can gain access to your data.

Administrator Setup

The first step in setting up SecurPC is to set up an administrator, by executing the SETUP program from the Administrator Setup diskette. After running through basic InstallShield installation dialog boxes, you will be shown a welcome box like that in Figure 8.1.

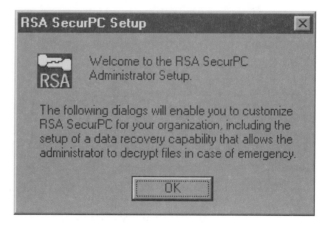

Figure 8.1. The first step in setting up SecurPC is to set up the administrator disk.

Attempting to install the SecurPC end-user programs without first running the administrator setup will get you an error message directing you to use a customized version of the application installation diskettes.

The next step is to begin filling in dialog boxes with the information requested. Figure 8.2 shows the next dialog box, requesting information about who will be administering the installation. This information is important because it will help users to know who to contact for help with their installations, as well as help to authenticate to users the software. (If they do not recognize the name and orga-

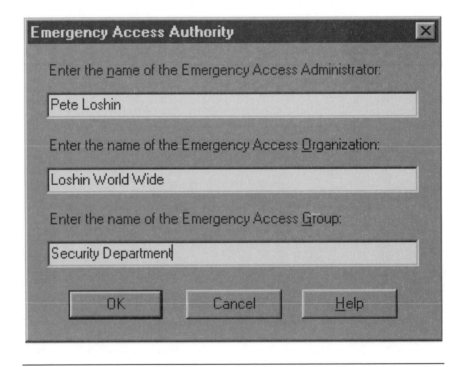

Figure 8.2. Entering information about the emergency access authority.

nization of the emergency access administrator, they can question the entire installation.) The next panel displays the data entered and gives the installer one last opportunity to modify the information before continuing.

The next step is to choose whether the emergency key will be protected with a single passphrase (which is most appropriate for an individual) or split among two or more trustees, as shown in Figure 8.3. Most individuals will want to choose the single-passphrase option.

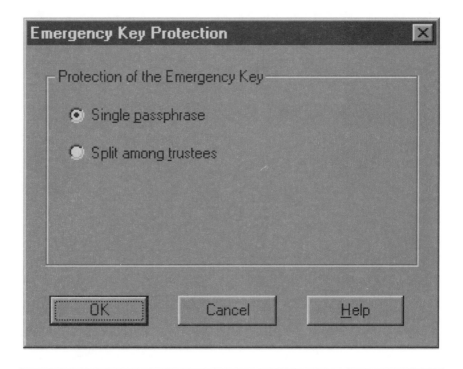

Figure 8.3. Choosing to assign emergency access to the holder of a single passphrase or to share it among trustees.

In the event that you decide to split access among two or more entities, you must indicate how many trustees there will be and how many of those trustees must agree before allowing any emergency access to encrypted data. Figure 8.4 shows what happens when you do this; attempting to specify a number of trustees higher than the total number of trustees will produce an error message. (The rest of this section deals with installing and using SecurPC with a single emergency access trustee as would be normal for an individual's installation.)

The next step is to generate some random data to be used to seed the generation of the encryption key. This is done by moving the

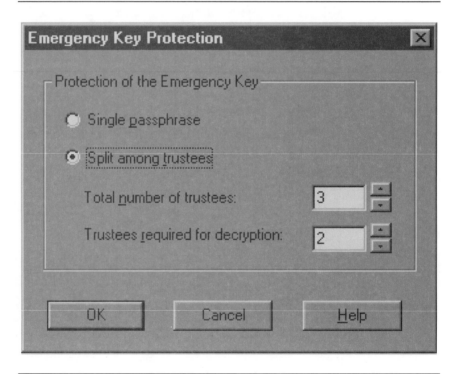

Figure 8.4. Specifying multiple trustees for emergency access with SecurPC.

mouse and/or by random typing, as shown in Figure 8.5. By banging on the keyboard and sliding the mouse around erratically, the user will throw off some entropy to generate a random number, which in turn is used to generate a secret key to encrypt data with.

After enough random data is collected, a dialog box will notify you, and when you continue you will be prompted for a passphrase to be used to protect the emergency key, as shown in Figure 8.6. You must enter the passphrase. Then re-enter it to confirm it.

The emergency key can be used to decrypt any data that has been encrypted with your SecurPC install diskettes. This means that if you use SecurPC within your organization, you must be sure that your emergency passphrase is a strong one because it effectively is the key to all your data.

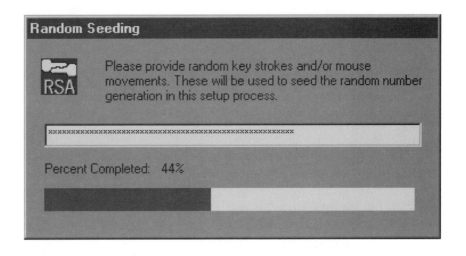

Figure 8.5. Generating a random encryption key through random keyboard and mouse input.

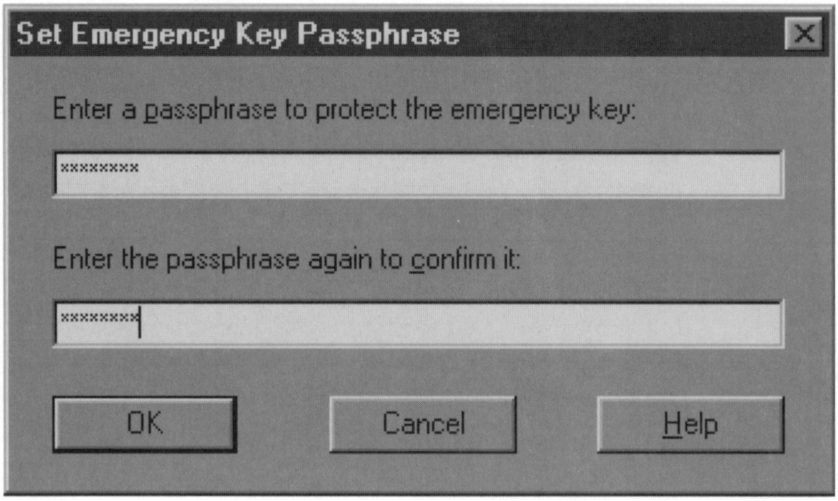

Figure 8.6. Entering a passphrase to protect the emergency key.

The next step is for SecurPC to generate the emergency key. A dialog box notifies the user that the process of generating an RSA public key pair for emergency access may take a few minutes. Click on OK and, when the process is complete, another dialog box will appear indicating that the key pair has been successfully generated.

User Software Installation Configuration

The next step in the administrative installation is to set up how the end-user is to use SecurPC. The panel in Figure 8.7 appears after successfully generating the emergency access key pair. This is where you can specify restrictions on passphrase composition and on passphrase-related actions. Passphrase options, shown on the left side of the panel, include

 ♦ Setting the minimum passphrase length. The default is 10 characters; the passphrase must be at least 8 characters and no more than 32 characters.

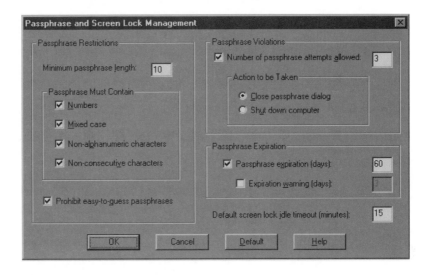

Figure 8.7. Setting up user parameters relating to pass phrases and screenlock function.

♦ Requiring the passphrase to include numbers. This means that simple words, names, or any combinations of letters only are prohibited. Adding numbers to pass-phrases complicates guessing by attackers.

♦ Requiring the passphrase to include mixed-case letters. This also adds complexity to the passphrase.

♦ Requiring the passphrase to contain non-alphanumeric characters, like punctuation marks (!@# and so on). This can make passphrases even more secure.

♦ Prohibiting consecutive characters from the passphrase. This eliminates relatively easy to guess combinations like "abcdefgh."

♦ Prohibiting easy-to-guess passphrases, which block use of the user ID as a passphrase, for example.

Also managed through this panel are options relating to passphrase violations: how many unsuccessful passphrase attempts are to be permitted and whether to simply close the passphrase dialog box or shut down the system. You can set the passphrase expiration (in days) and choose to warn users of impending expiration some number of days before the passphrase actually expires. Finally, you can set the default length of time (in minutes) before activating the screen lock option.

The next option for user functionality is to choose what options to set as the default for AutoCrypt folders. These are folders whose contents are automatically encrypted and which, if absent from a user's system, will be created for the user. Default AutoCrypt folders are optional for the administrator, and users can set up their own AutoCrypt folders as desired or needed. Setting up AutoCrypt folders on the desktop is discussed later in this chapter.

The next panel deals with options relating to setting up boot protection. Figure 8.8 shows that the options are simple:

♦ Automatically installing boot protection means that all installations will get boot protection; the user does not have the option of installing it or leaving it off the system.
♦ Not installing the boot protection means that it will not be installed automatically and also that the user cannot later decide to install it.
♦ Giving users the option means that boot protection will not be installed, but that the user can later decide to install it if desired.

If boot protection is offered automatically or as an option, the administrator has to enter a passphrase to protect access to the emergency access for boot protection. This is crucial for gaining access to a system that has been secured but whose owner or user is unavailable for any reason and on which important data or applications are stored. The administrator will be prompted to enter a passphrase and re-enter it to confirm it.

If boot protection is being set up, a prompt to enter a floppy diskette to be used as the emergency access disk will be shown after the passphrase is entered and confirmed. Figure 8.9 shows the dialog

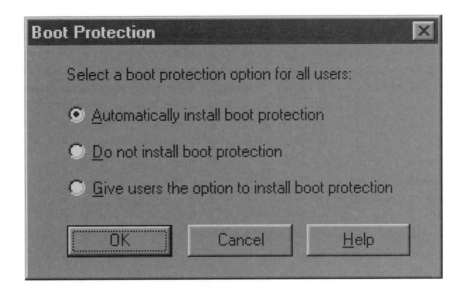

Figure 8.8. Setting up boot protection.

for setting up the emergency boot access diskette. After entering that disk, you will next be prompted to insert a disk to be used as the administrator preference disk, followed by a prompt to insert the second customized user install disk. These prompts are similar to that shown in Figure 8.9; once all three disks have been modified, the administrative installation is complete.

User Software Installation

Once the administrative installation and configuration is complete, you can install the end-user software by running the SETUP program from the first User Setup disk (the copy of the distribution diskette you made before starting). After walking through fairly standard installation dialogs, including one telling the install program in which directory to install the software, you will be shown a prompt welcoming you to the RSA SecurPC program, after which you will be prompted to enter mouse movements and/or keystrokes to generate a random seed to be used for generating your encryption key. This screen is the same as that shown in Figure 8.5.

After the seed number has been generated, you will be prompted to enter your name and a passphrase, repeating the passphrase for confirmation as shown in Figure 8.10. At this point, you will be prompted to insert the last blank diskette (with a dialog box similar to that shown in Figure 8.9) to be used for backing up the user preference file. After copying the file, the installation of the encryption software is complete, and any AutoCrypt folders specified in the administrative configuration data in those folders will be encrypted now.

If boot protection was turned off in the administrative setup (which we recently discussed), you are done now; if boot protection was turned on, you will now have to install it. If it was left to the discretion of the

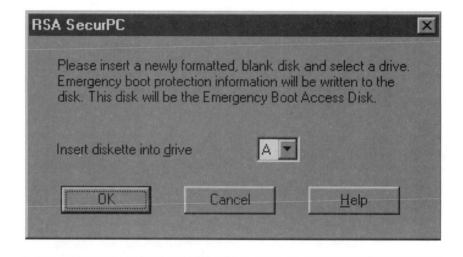

Figure 8.9. SecurPC prompts the user to enter a formatted floppy diskette to be used as the emergency boot access disk.

user, you can choose to install it now. In the last case, a dialog box will ask if you wish to install boot protection. If you choose to do so, you will be prompted to insert the Boot Protection installation diskette and press the Enter key. You will be notified that the installation is ready to start, followed by a prompt for your personal secret passphrase (not your administrative passphrase). If any programs are running, you

Figure 8.10. Entering your name and passphrase to protect your symmetric encryption key.

will be asked to turn them off before the installation can continue. Protection will be enabled, your system will reboot, and you will now be prompted for your passphrase every time you boot the system.

Using SecurPC

Once installed on Windows 95, SecurPC features are accessed through the Explorer File pulldown menu or by right-clicking on files that display RSA options in the file action menu. Figure 8.11 shows the menubar in Explorer that appears when SecurPC has been installed and a file is selected. (The RSA options disappear when no encryptable or decryptable file is selected.) Whether using the right-click method on a desktop icon or the File pulldown menu from Explorer, the available SecurPC options are the same.

A small icon that appears to be a cross between a padlock and a diskette appears to the left of each RSA option, and those options that are unavailable are grayed out. For example, a plaintext file cannot be decrypted (by definition). Important functions and features are discussed next.

For purposes of clarity and brevity, the rest of this section will simply speak of accessing SecurPC functions through the File menu rather than distinguishing direct access through Explorer or through right-clicking on a desktop icon.

Encrypting Files with SecurPC

Encrypting files on an individual basis is done by selecting the file or files to be encrypted. The File menu will now display SecurPC options; Figure 8.12 shows the SecurPC encryption options available:

- ♦ Encryption with the secret passphrase means the selected file or files will be encrypted using your own key and that the encrypted files are not intended to be shared with anyone.

Figure 8.11. The SecurPC additions to the Explorer File menu, which also show up when right-clicking on a file.

Figure 8.12. Encryption options available with SecurPC.

♦ Encryption with a shared passphrase means the selected file or files will be encrypted using a shared key and that the encrypted files are intended to be shared with one or more other users, with whom you are sharing the key.

Choose to encrypt the file or files with the secret passphrase, and a dialog like that shown in Figure 8.13 will appear; click on OK to encrypt. When encryption is complete, the file or files will still appear in the

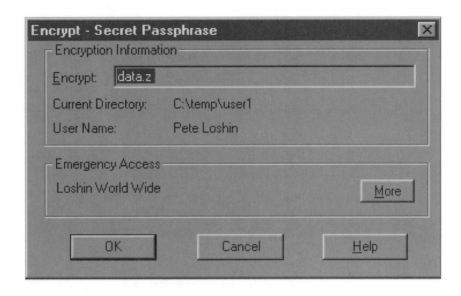

Figure 8.13. Encryption using the secret passphrase with SecurPC.

same directory, the only difference being that the file will appear just as it was except that the filename will have an added exclamation point within parentheses to indicate that it is an encrypted file.

Encrypting a file or files with a shared passphrase is slightly more complicated. Figure 8.14 shows the dialog box you must contend with to encrypt a file with a shared key. First, you must enter (and re-enter to confirm) a new passphrase. This passphrase must be communicated to authorized users in a secure way, which usually means not by e-mail (unless that can be sufficiently secured). In practice, it means sharing the passphrase in person, over the telephone, or by fax (all of which are more or less secure depending on the circumstances).

You must also choose whether or not to encrypt the file as a self-extracting Windows executable file. This option is an excellent choice

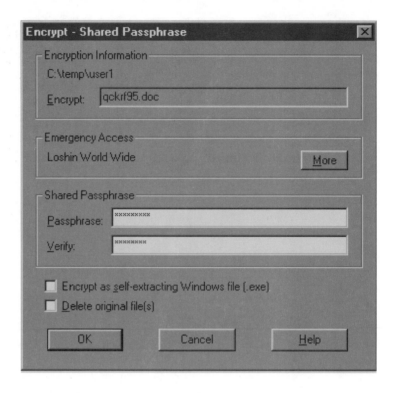

Figure 8.14. Encryption using a shared passphrase with SecurPC.

for sharing encrypted data with individuals who use Windows but who do not have SecurPC installed on their systems (and who do not wish to install it). The final option is whether or not to delete the original file (leaving only the encrypted file on the disk). This allows you to retain a file in plaintext on your system while having an encrypted version to share with others. In any case, clicking on OK will put the encrypted file in the same directory as the original.

When you encrypt a file to be used with a shared passphrase, a copy of the file, encrypted, will be placed into a self-extracting file. The icon for the file will appear as that shown in Figure 8.15; clicking on this icon will initiate the decryption process, which is described shortly.

Figure 8.15. The icon for a SecurPC file encrypted with a shared passphrase is on the left. The icon for a self-extracting encrypted file is on the right.

Decrypting Files with SecurPC

Files that have been encrypted on your desktop exist as encrypted files on disk, but when you work with them (as long as you have entered your SecurPC passphrase when starting up your system), they are automatically decrypted whenever you open them with a Windows application.

This means that the file cannot be used unless it is used by someone logging in as you, or by someone accessing your system after you have logged on. If you have not logged on through SecurPC, the file will not be accessible.

To decrypt a file (so that you can make a copy of it and pass it along to someone else as plaintext, for example), you can explicitly decrypt the file by choosing Decrypt from the File menu. This will return the file to plaintext, eliminating the exclamation point within parentheses from the filename.

Shared Passphrase File Decryption

A file that has been encrypted using a shared passphrase is displayed in Windows with a distinct icon (as shown in Figure 8.15), and its filename indicates the original file's extension in parentheses. These files can be copied and shared with others, but can only be decrypted by someone who has both the shared passphrase and a copy of SecurPC.

Decrypting such a file is simple. You can double-click on the encrypted file icon, and you will be prompted for the shared passphrase. Once entered correctly, the file will be opened with the appropriate application (if available).

Another way to decrypt such a file is to right-click on the icon, and select the RSA Decrypt option; the suboption to decrypt with a shared passphrase will be active and should be selected. The dialog box shown in Figure 8.16 will then be displayed; enter the shared passphrase and choose whether or not to delete the encrypted file.

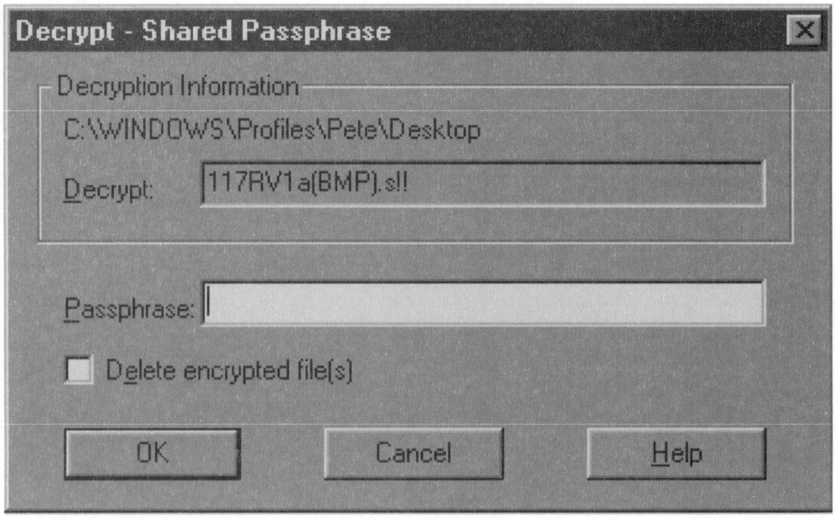

Figure 8.16. Decryption using a shared passphrase with SecurPC.

The file will be decrypted and, if desired, the encrypted version will be deleted while the plaintext version will be saved to disk.

Self-Extracting File Decryption

A self-extracting encrypted file can be executed as a program on any Windows system, eliminating the need for the recipient to be using SecurPC software. Simply double-click on the self-extracting file icon shown on the right of Figure 8.15. A dialog box like that shown in Figure 8.17 will appear, prompting the user for the shared passphrase. This dialog box also explains that the file was encrypted with RSA's SecurPC, and offers the user the option to

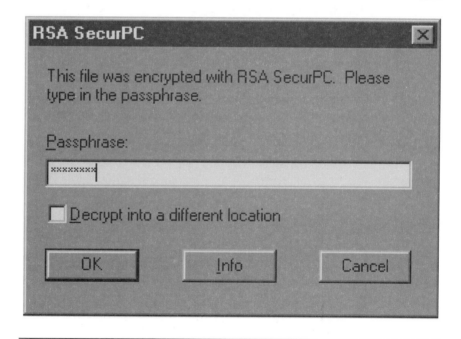

Figure 8.17. Decryption of a self-extracting file using a shared passphrase with SecurPC.

decrypt the file to a different location (drive or directory) than the one where the encrypted file is.

SecurPC AutoCrypt

SecurPC's AutoCrypt feature allows you to specify directories in which all files are to be automatically encrypted. Files in the AutoCrypt directories can be accessed by applications or directly written by applications; when they are stored on the disk, however, they are stored in encrypted form so that no one can copy or view them without your secret passphrase.

Figure 8.18 shows how the AutoCrypt list can be modified. Required AutoCrypt folders are shown in the bottom pane of this dialog; in this installation there are no required AutoCrypt folders. The middle pane shows folders that the user has selected as AutoCrypt folders; folders are selected in the top pane. By clicking on the Add button when a folder is selected, you can make that an AutoCrypt directory.

AutoCrypt directories can be accessed when the user has logged into SecurPC on booting up the system. This means that when the user steps away from the system, encrypted data can be accessed by anyone unless the user locks the system up with either SecurPC's access control or some other mechanism.

Access Control with SecurPC

SecurPC supports three different types of access control:

- ◆ Boot protection. This option modifies the boot sector of the hard drive (which may affect various utilities and may also be assumed to be viral by virus protection software) in such a way as to make it impossible for an ordinary boot floppy to be used to start up the system and to access the system hard drives. You will not be able to boot the system at all unless you have the correct pass-phrase.

♦ Restricted access to encrypted files, particularly those in AutoCrypt folders. Even if you have not installed boot protection, each time you start your system you will have to enter your SecurPC passphrase. While it is possible to boot the system without entering the passphrase, if you do not enter it (for example, if you forget it or if someone else is using your system) you will not have access to any encrypted data. This makes it possible to

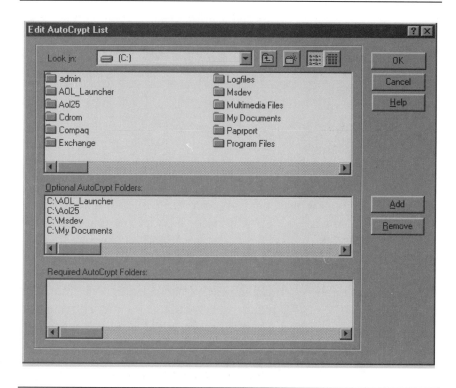

Figure 8.18. Editing the AutoCrypt folder list with SecurPC.

allow others to use your system without giving them access to your encrypted files.

♦ Screen locking. SecurPC includes an important feature, particularly for those whose computers are not physically secured at all times (for example, anyone who works in a cubicle). By pressing both shift keys at the same time, the user invokes the SecurPC screen lock function. This function can also be set to be invoked automatically when a certain amount of time has passed with no keyboard or mouse activity. When the screen is locked, the system will respond to keyboard activity only after a valid passphrase is entered.

Boot protection alters the system in a way that can disrupt or confuse the execution of other vital activities, like virus protection and various system utilities. As a result, it is probably most valuable for those who want the maximum protection not only for their encrypted data but also for the applications and nonencrypted data on their hard drives.

Emergency Access with SecurPC

A SecurPC user's secret keys are protected by a passphrase, but if this were the only way to access the encryption keys being used, the data would be unrecoverable in the absence of that passphrase. This can be a problem for a couple of reasons:

♦ The owner of the data may encrypt data and then forget the passphrase. This is probably more common than one might think, particularly if users install the software on a Friday and then fail to incorporate the passphrase in long-term memory, or if users install the software, use it to encrypt some data, and then do not use the software again for a while.

♦ The owner of the data may be unavailable physically. This can occur through absence—for example, when an employee leaves an organization (either voluntarily or not) and neglects to decrypt all encrypted data. Users may also die, in which case an employer would want to be able to retrieve data from the user's system.

All secret keys (protected by either a shared or a secret passphrase) are encrypted using a public key assigned to the administrator. When the administrator must gain access to the files, the administrator uses the secret key—which is stored on the emergency access disk—associated with the public key.

SecurPC allows for emergency access to data in several ways, including

♦ Access to encrypted files. Files that have been encrypted can be decrypted without the owner's passphrase, as long as the administrator or administrators feel that it is necessary and have their emergency access disks available. Files that have been encrypted either with the owner's secret passphrase or with a shared passphrase can be decrypted using the administrator's emergency access disk(s).

♦ Access to a boot-protected system. Again, access to systems requires an appropriately customized emergency access disk, which includes information that allows the user's system to authenticate the administrator through the emergency disk.

♦ Passphrase recovery. This is slightly different than access to encrypted files. By providing the administrator a mechanism for recovering passphrases, the user who forgets a passphrase can simply ask the administrator to help recover the passphrase rather than have to go through the trouble of decrypting all data and then having to re-encrypt it. This may also be useful for when the user is no longer available (through death or termination) and the employer wishes to turn over functional responsibility for the data to another user.

By using public key encryption for passphrases and symmetric keys, SecurPC is able to support these recovery options. Although

they are most useful for organizations that want to protect their
investment in data from loss due to loss of an employee, individuals who are protecting important information on their desktops can
be sure that the data can still be recovered by authorized agents (for
example, by agreement of a spouse, business partner, attorney,
accountant, or other trusted agents).

Using PGP for Personal Privacy

PGP for Personal Privacy is an unusual product in that it provides a reasonably open mechanism and infrastructure for
encrypting and digitally signing both e-mail messages and files,
for exchange with others as well as for personal protection.
Chapter 5 discussed how to create a new public key pair with
PGP for Personal Privacy, and Chapter 10 discusses at greater
length the PGP "web of trust" approach to certification, explaining how it works and how it differs from the certification authority approach. The rest of this chapter discusses how PGP works
to encrypt, decrypt, digitally sign, and certify files and data on
the desktop.

PGP Desktop Functions

Unlike many of the slicker encryption tools available commercially, PGP for Personal Privacy 5.0 does not support automatic
and transparent encryption and decryption of files on the desktop.
While this may be a useful feature for many, when encryption is
transparent, the user can easily lose track of what data is actually
encrypted and what data is not encrypted, with the result that it
can be very easy to confuse which data has been encrypted and
which has not been.

PGP does not provide this transparency, which some may consider
a positive feature (as the author does). When you encrypt a file, the
original file does not disappear, but an encrypted version of the file
appears. Decrypting the file does not cause the ciphertext version to
disapper, either.

PGP desktop functions include the following:

- ◆ PGP file options are the basic functions relating to personal cryptography, including encrypt, sign, and encrypt and sign a file. When the file is already encrypted and/or signed, the file option changes to decrypt/verify.
- ◆ The PGPkeys application is used to manage PGP keys and keyrings, and contains information about all the entities whose PGP keys you have or can use to encrypt data. This is where you add or delete keys from other entities, or modify the degree of trust you are willing to assign to any particular entity's public key (which is important for implementing the web of trust essential to the PGP certification model, as discussed in Chapter 10).
- ◆ The PGPtray application can be used to encrypt, decrypt, sign, or verify data held in the Windows clipboard, or to import a key from the clipboard into the PGPkeys database.
- ◆ PGP key management issues include the maintenance of trust levels in known keys, signing other people's keys, and revoking or disabling a key.

The reader is urged to refer to the most current guide to using PGP functions and features, the PGP documentation, available in electronic form and bundled with the product.

PGP File Options

File options, menu choices that are accessible either through the Windows Explorer or by right-clicking a file and choosing the PGP option from the file menu, depend on the context. When the file has not been encrypted with PGP already, the options include

- ◆ Encrypt.
- ◆ Sign.
- ◆ Encrypt and Sign.

When the file is a PGP file type, the only option available is

- ◆ Decrypt/Verify.

These options are discussed next.

PGP has two file types, .PGP and .ASC, both of which can be represented by a PGP icon on the Windows desktop. The .PGP file contains the cipher-text of the original file in binary form, while the .ASC file contains "ASCII Armored" data—the ciphertext data is converted to an ASCII-printable format so that data will not be lost in transmission across networks or between dissimilar computers that use different data representations.

Encrypt

Choosing to encrypt a file requires that you have the public key of the recipient available to you through the PGPkeys application. The dialog shown in Figure 8.19 is representative of what you will see when you choose to encrypt a file.

As long as you have the public key of an entity, you can encrypt a file for that entity. Simply double-click or drag and drop the name of the entity or entities you wish to encrypt the file for, and they will move from the frame at the top of the dialog to the frame at the bottom of the dialog. The only other option is what type of output to use; checking the Text Output option (at the lower left of the dialog) will product an ASCII Armored file that can be displayed in pure ASCII characters, making cross platform or network transfers more reliable. Leaving the box unchecked will generate a binary file rather than a printable file; such a file can be altered if it passes through any systems that do not handle binaries appropriately.

The resulting encrypted file will be represented by an icon like that shown in Figure 8.20; this is how PGP signed or encrypted files are displayed in Windows.

PGP does not prompt for any passphrases when you are encrypting a file. At least one organization rejected PGP as a security program because there was no apparent control over this process—this is not, in fact, a

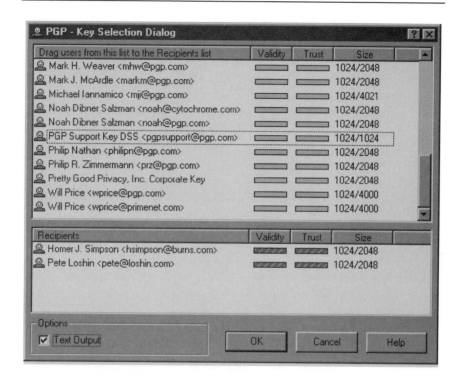

Figure 8.19. Encrypting a file with PGP means choosing a recipient, whose key will be used for the encryption.

security issue because encrypting data for a recipient using the recipient's public key does not reveal anything about the sender. It is only necessary to require a passphrase when a file is signed, because in that case the action actually represents an act that cannot be repudiated by the signer.

Sign

Signing a file with PGP is straightforward; Figure 8.21 shows the dialog box that prompts for the user's passphrase. It is possible to

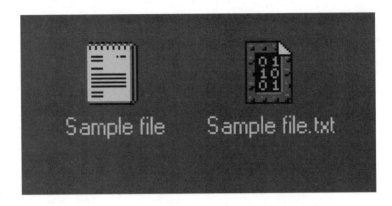

Figure 8.20. The PGP encrypted or signed file icon is on the right. On the left is
the original plaintext file it is based on.

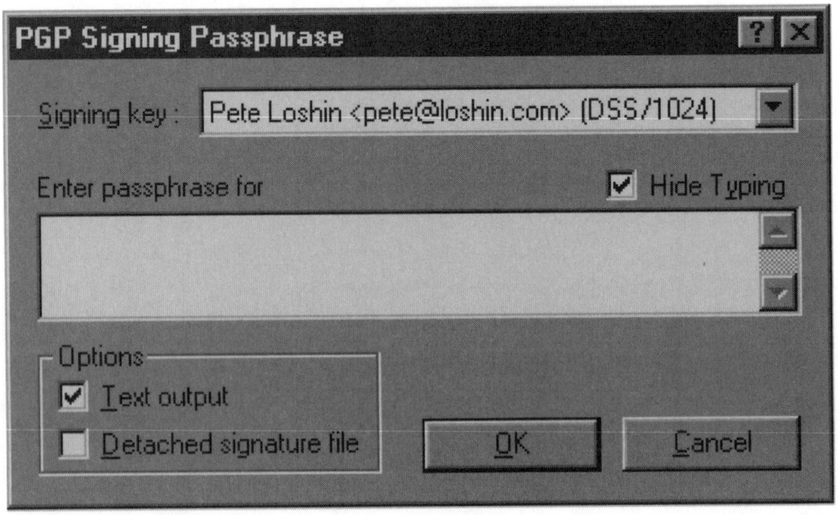

PGP Signing Passphrase

Signing key : Pete Loshin <pete@loshin.com> (DSS/1024)

Enter passphrase for   ☑ Hide Typing

Options
☑ Text output
☐ Detached signature file   OK   Cancel

Figure 8.21. Entering options and a passphrase to sign a file with PGP.

choose from more than one signing key, which is useful for individuals who prefer to use different keys for different functions (for example, one key for postings under a pseudonym, another for personal correspondence, and a third for business purposes). You can choose to hide the data being entered for the passphrase or display it on screen by checking or unchecking the Hide Typing option (on the right, above the passphrase entry field).

You can choose to output the signed file to a text file, which means that the output will be ASCII armored and can pass across platforms and networks without inadvertent modification. It also means that the resulting file will still be readable, but with additional content (the PGP signature); if you do not choose text output, even a text file will be modified to binary content by the signature.

The other option available for signing is to create a file separate from the original file for the signature. This allows you to sign a file without modifying the file itself. This allows you greater flexibility in authenticating data; for example, you can send a file to someone, and then sign an exact copy of that file and send the signature to the same person if that person has any questions about authenticity rather than signing the file and resending the larger resulting signed file.

Encrypt and Sign

The process of encrypting and signing a file is almost exactly the same as the two processes when performed separately, just combined. First, you are prompted for recipients, as shown in Figure 8.19. Choosing recipients is done by double-clicking or dragging and dropping them from the top frame to the bottom frame. At this point you can choose whether or not to generate an ASCII armored text file.

Next, you are prompted with a dialog very similar to that shown in Figure 8.21, but without the options of outputting the file to text (that option was offered in the encryption recipient dialog) or of outputting a separate file for the signature (the signature must be incorporated into the encrypted file). Enter the passphrase, and the encrypted and signed file is generated.

Decrypt/Verify

Because PGP-encrypted files use the same formats as PGP-signed files, there is only one option for either decrypting them or verifying their signatures. This means that for the three different types of files (encrypted, signed, encrypted and signed) you will choose the same option from the File menu, Decrpyt/Verify.

When the file has been encrypted, you are prompted for your PGP passphrase so that you can decrypt the file. The passphrase prompt is shown in Figure 8.22; there are no options other than to hide the characters as you type your passphrase. This occurs whenever the file is encrypted, whether or not it has been signed.

If the file has been signed as well, the signature will be automatically verified. If the file is from someone who is in your key database and the signature is verified, you will see a dialog like that shown in Figure 8.23.

Figure 8.22. Entering your passphrase before decrypting a PGP encrypted file.

Figure 8.23. This is the type of message shown when a signature is verified with PGP.

When decrypting a file, the program will bring up the standard save file dialog within Windows, allowing you to store the plaintext file wherever you prefer.

There may be times when you prefer not to store plaintext on your system at all, but would still like to know the contents of an encrypted message. The PGPtray application described next can be useful for those times.

PGPtray

Working with encrypted data strictly in memory has some advantages, in particular because it allows you to keep ciphertext files in ciphertext without exposing the plaintext to any of the vulnerability of stored files. If someone gains access to your system, that person can view any of your files (unless you are using some product like RSA's SecurPC, which can automatically encrypt data for you), and that person can even view files that have been deleted with some simple utilities (unless you have used a product that overwrites the physical disk areas where your file was stored).

PGPtray is an application accessible from an icon in the lower right corner of the Windows desktop; the icon looks like a cross between a padlock and an envelope. Figure 8.24 shows the PGPtray menu as it appears in the lower right corner of the Windows desktop. PGPtray allows you to do cryptographic functions on textual data; manipulating graphical or other binary data still must be done through the file system.

PGPtray options include

♦ Encrypt, sign, or encrypt and sign the clipboard. These three options are discussed together because they allow

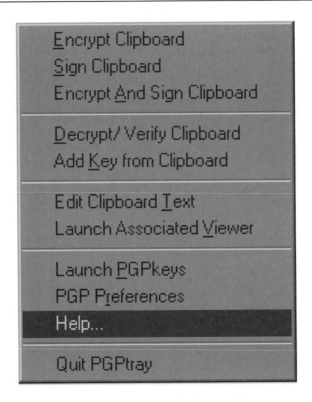

Figure 8.24. The PGPtray menu offers the option of manipulating PGP data saved in the clipboard.

you to cut text from a document or file and then encrypt and/or sign the data, which can then be pasted into some other document. This is useful, for example, for inserting certain data into an otherwise unsecured message or file and assuring the recipient or reader that the information specified was signed (or identifying it as having been encrypted with PGP). Figure 8.25 shows an example of some text that has been signed in this way and pasted

```
-----BEGIN PGP SIGNED MESSAGE-----

Hash: SHA1

This is the author's e-mail address:
pete@loshin.com
By digitally signing this bit of text, the reader
could re-enter the text and signature and verify
it and be sure that the address is correct. This
might be tricky without the original electronic
version, however, because the reader would have
to be sure to enter the exact same characters en-
tered here, including spaces, tabs and
carriage return/line feeds.

-----BEGIN PGP SIGNATURE-----

Version: PGP for Personal Privacy 5.0
Charset: noconv

iQA/AwUBNF/LGfduena/FdsDEQL93QCg3KSEeb8+SPWds99
fffcPrUioC18AnjzLuw7h3o2X156121TSIyz1Gmu2
=JppW

-----END PGP SIGNATURE-----
```

Figure 8.25. A digitally signed fragment that has been inserted into a word processing document.

into the word processor document used to write this book.

♦ Decrypt/verify the contents of the clipboard. This is a particularly useful feature if you receive encrypted data but you do not wish to store the plaintext on your system. It allows you to copy the encrypted data into the clipboard, decrypt it, and view the plaintext without writing the plaintext to the disk. When you are finished, the clipboard is cleared out so that no one else can view the plaintext without your passphrase.

♦ Adding a key from the clipboard. When you receive e-mail, read a news group posting, or receive a file that contains someone's PGP key, you can cut or copy the key into your clipboard and then add it to your PGP key database through PGPtray.

♦ Edit clipboard text. This opens a simple editor that allows you to modify, remove, or add data to the information stored in the clipboard. Sometimes this is useful, as when you modify some data that you have copied before you sign it; sometimes this is less than useful, as when you modify data after you have signed it. (In that case, attempting to verify the signature would fail.) The same would happen with encrypted data. You could encrypt data in the clipboard and then change the ciphertext, thus rendering the plaintext inaccessible.

♦ The launch associated viewer option. This launches an appropriate editor—for example, NotePad.

♦ Launch PGPkeys, another method of starting the PGP-keys application (described shortly).

♦ PGP preferences allowing you to set options that help determine how PGP works on your system. These are discussed shortly as well.

Encrypting, signing, decrypting, and verifying data in the clipboard is quite similar to doing those same functions with files, using the same prompts for passphrases and dialog boxes reporting results of certification. However, when doing decryption or certification, dialog boxes add the option of viewing the results with an external viewer or with the clipboard editor.

PGP Preferences and PGPkeys

The PGP Preferences interface, accessed through the PGPtray menubar, is used to manage program settings that affect the way PGP works for you, including

- General preferences regarding how passphrases are handled and how encryption is done.
- Identifying the files in which you are storing your public and private keyrings.
- Setting preferences for using PGP with e-mail messages.
- Choosing an Internet PGP keyserver and pointing the program to it.

PGP preferences are discussed at greater length in Chapter 10.

The PGPkeys application is simply the tool you use to manage your PGP keys. Shown in Figure 8.26, PGPkeys displays all the keys that

Figure 8.26. The PGPkeys application helps you manage key issues in PGP.

are important to you. This includes the keys you have generated for yourself and for any pseudonyms that you use, a set of keys for entities within the Pretty Good Privacy, Inc., organization, and any keys that you have picked up during your use of PGP.

PGPkeys gives you the ability to do several important functions:

- Create new key pairs for yourself.
- Import and export keys.
- Examine a key's properties, which can include key type, when the key was created, for how long it is valid, and more.
- Assign levels of trust to other entity's keys (both for the purpose of determining how much you trust that the key is actually owned by the entity that purports to own it and for the purpose of assigning how much you will trust keys of unknown entities that have been signed with that key).
- Set your default key.
- Certify someone's key.
- Sign someone else's key.
- Enable or disable your own key.

Details of PGP key management, as well as the PGP web of trust model for certification, are discussed in Chapter 10.

9

Digital Commerce

This chapter provides a brief overview on the ways in which cryptographic functions are used to help build the mechanisms by which digital commerce can take place over the global Internet. Instead of focusing on specific protocols or products that enable or implement commercial transactions, this chapter presents a high-level overview of how encryption, digital signatures, and cryptographic hashes make it possible for customers and vendors to complete commercial transactions over the Internet.

Anatomy of a Transaction

This section discusses what is involved in the typical commercial consumer transaction, whether it occurs over the Internet or in meatspace. The concept of the "card not present" credit card purchase, probably the most common method of making a consumer purchase over the Internet (as well as by telephone and mail order) is explained, and the steps necessary for a sale to be transacted are also discussed. There is a brief discussion of what are the risks involved in on-line transactions, where they occur, and who bears the brunt of the actual risk.

The concepts of on-line commerce are discussed in general, rather than as they are implemented in any particular commercial transaction protocol or specification. Of particular interest are how encryption and digital signatures are used to turn the Internet into a safe and reliable medium for transacting business.

This chapter addresses how digital commerce systems and protocols use digital signatures and encryption to make secure digital commerce possible. These approaches almost always automate the bulk of the transaction, particularly as it relates to the use of cryptographic functions. Thus, while there is a considerable amount of data to be signed and encrypted, the customer does not need to explicitly encrypt or sign anything—these functions are almost always performed automatically by digital wallet products that are often incorporated into web browsers.

The Typical Consumer Transaction

This section outlines the typical consumer transaction, walking through the process of making a purchase from start to finish. It is more complex, with more steps, than you might think. Many of the steps are taken for granted because they have significantly less relevance in human-mediated transactions—in other words, it is much more complicated to attempt to map transactions to unattended, automatic computerized systems than it is when you have a human available to supervise the transaction.

Before you can actually buy anything, you must be able to browse or find out in some other way what a merchant has to offer for sale. And before you can even browse or find out what the merchant has to offer, you must enter the store. Authentication of the merchant is not usually a problem in the real world. If you go to a shopping mall and enter the local branch of a national department store, for example, you can be reasonably certain of a number of things:

- The items on display in the store are being offered for sale by the merchant.
- The items on display in the store will be displayed with price and product information, and that information will be correct and complete.
- The merchant will have employed individuals able to help answer questions about the products on display (for example, pricing or features of products whose labeling is missing or incomplete), who will be able to determine whether or not the product is in stock, and who will be authorized to complete a transaction for you by accepting your payment and giving you with a receipt and the product.

Most consumers take these things for granted when they go shopping in commercial shopping centers in developed countries. However, the level of assurance that a storefront is what it seems to be drops as the consumer leaves the national retail chain stores in shopping malls and enters a store that is not in a mall, is not a chain outlet, and does not have a historic retail presence. Merchants of this type can still build trust with their customers by staying in the same community over the years and building personal ties with their customers, so the consumer can still hold a degree of trust that the merchant will be offering goods for sale and can be trusted to complete a sale.

The merchant also must build trust of the consumer, which may be simpler in person. The manner, dress, and demeanor of the shopper can help to clue the merchant into whether or not the consumer is actually a prospective customer. Once the customer decides to purchase, the merchant must also decide whether the payment tendered will be accepted (for example, by requiring identification to accept a check, or verifying the customer's signature against the customer's payment card signature).

What this means is that shopping on-line requires a constant nego-tiation of trust between merchant and consumer, with each needing some mechanisms to base their decisions of whether and what to buy, as well as whether or what to sell.

The rest of this section takes the typical consumer transaction and breaks it down into several parts (as shown in Figure 9.1), including

- Shopping, browsing, and pricing products in prepara-tion for the sale.
- Selecting a specific product for purchase and getting complete pricing information.
- Tendering payment.
- Getting a receipt.

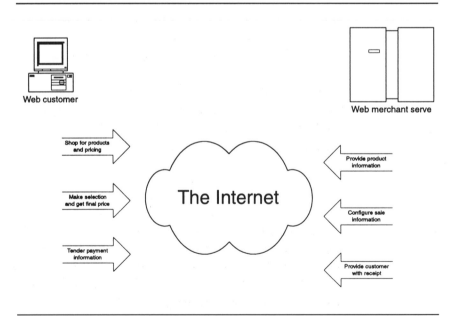

Figure 9.1. Information flows across the Internet between consumer and mer-chant to enable an on-line transaction.

Shopping On-line

When you enter the department store at the local mall that displays a sign reading *Sears*, you can be reasonably certain that you are dealing with the world-famous Sears, Roebuck and Co. retail organization. Sears protects its name and would not permit another organization to put up a department store using the Sears name. Consumers looking for products sold by Sears would not permit a counterfeit Sears to operate for long. Anyone building a counterfeit Sears store could hardly deny that the store existed or that it was using the name without permission.

The situation in the on-line world is not quite as clear-cut. Internet domain names generally go on a first-come, first-served basis. This means that it is entirely possible that someone other than the national or international brand-name holder may have registered the domain name that you would have expected. For example, it often happens that when there are more than one company with the same name, but in different industries, the first to register the domain name is not always the one you would expect. In our example, it would be as if the Sears Cookie Company registered the domain sears.com before Sears, Roebuck and Co.

Sears, Roebuck and Co.'s web site is at *www.sears.com*; the examples cited here in the text are purely hypothetical.

One solution is to use a trusted third party to get referred to merchant sites, in the same way that Yellow Pages directories do. Web directory services can provide a first-level cut at pointing you to the right place. By searching for department stores, for example, you would probably be directed to sites that include Sears as well as other department stores. Depending on the policies of the directory service, you could be more or less assured that the sites you are directed to are the sites they purport to be.

Another mechanism is to use the web server's digital certificate as a means of identifying the site. In general, this certificate does not come into play until you access a secured page. (See Chapter 6.) Once you do hit a secured page, for example, when you are ready to consummate a purchase by entering payment and billing information, you have the option of viewing the server certificate. At that point, you can see who issued the certificate, to whom it was issued, and what kind of certificate it is. This information is important, and can help you decide whether or not to do business with the merchant. For example, if the certificate is a commercial-class certificate issued by a reputable certificate authority (CA), you can be reasonably sure that the CA had sufficient documentation from the merchant to feel comfortable in issuing certification that the entity applying for the certificate was, in fact, that entity.

If the certificate does not include enough information about the level of certification, the user can also go directly to the CA to find out more about its policies for issuing certificates; certification of the certificate with the issuer may also be accomplished through the browser security interface.

Purchase Selection and Final Pricing

It is in the interests of both the merchant and the consumer that the prices and products offered for sale be verifiable and that neither can repudiate the terms of an offer. In other words, the consumer wants to know that the price listed in the merchant's web site is the price the consumer will pay—the merchant has to stick by the price, and the consumer has to have some mechanism by which the merchant can be held to the price quoted.

This is usually achieved in the real world through the mechanism of the printed receipt and the price tag. If a product is advertised at a particular price, either in some print medium or by an attached price tag, the consumer can hold the merchant to that price by going into the store and buying the product at that price. When the consumer tenders payment, the merchant issues a receipt indicating that the transaction has been satisfactorily completed: The consumer has released payment (by cash, check, payment card, or some other mechanism) for the stated product or service, and the merchant's receipt indicates that the sum received is satisfactory for the product or service indicated on the receipt.

In on-line commerce, it could be theoretically possible for the consumer to agree to make a purchase and provide payment information, but for the merchant to cause a different amount to be charged. However, to avoid this problem, consumer software that implements digital wallets, and the corresponding server software that implements the merchant's payment system use digital signatures to add nonrepudiation to the transaction. The consumer can decide to make a purchase and click on the appropriate buttons on the merchant's web site; the merchant sends a digitally signed message that details the transaction: the date and time, the product to be purchased, the price of the product, and the total cost to the consumer (among other information).

Digitally signing means that the merchant has made an offer to sell the stated product for the stated price, at the time and date specified. The only entity that could have signed that offering is the merchant, so the consumer can be confident that later the merchant will not make some change in the price or product—the consumer could go to its card issuer and show the merchant's original offer, which the merchant could not repudiate.

These offers may be encrypted as well as digitally signed; however, if the data is not encrypted and is intercepted and modified, the digital signature would not be certifiable by the consumer. Encrypting this information is a good idea, since the merchant would prefer to keep individual transactions private, as would the consumer.

Tendering Payment

Once the consumer has the offer from the merchant, the consumer can decide to make the purchase or to decline it. If the consumer decides to buy, the digital wallet software can reply to the merchant's offer by sending back the same information included in the offer (product, price, quantity, total charge) along with the consumer's payment information (usually a credit card number) as well as other supporting information (billing address and cardholder name, for example). This is also digitally signed, so that the consumer cannot later repudiate the purchase.

The consumer's software will digitally sign this data and will also encrypt it. Depending on the protocol, the encryption may be with the merchant's public key, or it may be with a card issuer's public key or even with the public key of the entity that will process the transaction. Digitally signing the request to purchase helps to protect the merchant and other interested parties (like the card issuer) by assuring them that the holder of the card in fact is the entity using the card. Depending on whose public key is used to encrypt the transaction, the consumer may have more or less assurance that the information (including payment card account) in that message will be protected.

Encrypting the transaction information with the merchant's public key means that the merchant's software will decrypt the data and then re-encrypt it when it sends the transaction data on to be processed by a payment clearing house. This method leaves the sensitive (payment) information vulnerable to attackers at the merchant's server.

A better method, at least for the consumer's peace of mind, is to bypass the merchant and encrypt the transaction data with the public key of the entity that processes the transaction. This reduces the exposure of the payment information, and actually can be considered a potential win for the merchant—who cannot be accused of stealing or misusing a payment card account if the merchant never had plaintext access to the account number.

Completing the Transaction

The transaction is not complete until the merchant has submitted payment card information to a clearing house, which charges the cardholder's account and credits the sum to the merchant's account. This financial transaction occurs (or should occur) between the merchant and the transaction processor only after the customer has submitted complete payment information and before the merchant delivers or ships the product being purchased.

Transactional processing, particularly of financial transactions, requires a higher level of reliability than other types of computing. Traditionally, this has meant that transactions are completed through a mechanism called the two-phase commit.

To understand the two-phase commit mechanism, it is useful to understand the alternative. A standard request-reply model would have the merchant submit a request to the payment clearing house, which would do what it needed to do to process the transaction and would then send back a reply to the merchant indicating that the payment would be made. The merchant could then deliver the goods.

With data communications networks being what they are, there is always the chance that a message may not be received. In that case, the recipient could request a retransmission. However, the Internet is a particularly unreliable transport medium, and it is common for messages to be received a (relatively) long time after they were sent—sometimes after a retransmission has been requested. In that case, two copies of the message may be received. In other cases, a request may be submitted and processed, but the connection may be severed before the requesting party can receive confirmation of the processed transaction. In that case, the requesting party might submit the transaction again.

Using the two-phase commit mechanism helps limit problems related to communications errors. A request is submitted and is processed, but the system does not commit the actual change until it has notified the requesting entity of the transaction completion and getting a positive acknowledgment from the requesting entity. At that point, the processor will commit the change to the database, but not before. If confirmation of the change is not received from the requesting entity, the processor will back out of the change. The requesting entity assumes that the request has not been processed and will resubmit the request, also rolling back any database modifications that have been made to correspond with the transaction.

The benefit of the two-phase commit process is that transactions are completed once and only once. The transaction cannot be conducted more than once, because neither side commits until both sides agree to commit to the transaction.

Once the transaction is approved by the clearing house and the merchant is satisfied that the purchase is a good one, a receipt, digitally signed by the merchant and encrypted with the consumer's public key, can be generated and sent to the consumer. The product or service being purchased usually follows.

Card Not Present Transactions

The meaty part of the consumer market is aimed at the credit card holder. These individuals have proven credit records, backed by the power of the credit card issuers to insure that products purchased are paid for. For what are known as card not present transactions— telephone, mail order, and, increasingly, on-line sales—the credit card is the payment mechanism of choice. Checks and currency do not travel too well through the phone or over the Internet (though there are check payment systems that work digitally), digital currency has yet to achieve any significant Internet market penetration, and currency works only for live interaction.

Unfortunately for merchants, mail order and telephone transactions are also the most likely to be fraudulent, so they cost more to process. It is not yet clear whether or not Internet transactions will have similar rates of fraud, but by using modern cryptographic mechanisms including digital signatures, it is quite possible that Internet fraud can be reduced dramatically.

Digital Commerce Protocols

There are a number of Internet protocols designed to support commerce in one form or another. These can be divided into two groups:

- ◆ Protocols devised to provide generally secure (that is, encrypted and/or digitally signed) data transmission between a client and a server. These protocols were not specifically designed to support transactional commerce, but were designed to simply allow any type of transmission be encrypted or digitally signed. These protocols are often said to support secure channels between client and server.

♦ Protocols that were devised specifically to support commercial transactions and that may be carried out over other secure protocols, like those used to secure channels.

Secure Channel Protocols

Two of the more important secure channel protocols are the Secure Sockets Layer (SSL) and the Secure Hypertext Transport Protocol (S-HTTP). These protocols defined how data could be encrypted and/or digitally signed and then transmitted between a client and a server across the Internet. Each is discussed briefly next.

Secure Sockets Layer (SSL)

The SSL protocol was originally devised by Netscape as a method of encrypting data being sent between a client and a server. The protocol itself is application-independent, meaning that it can be used to protect data being sent between a browser and a web server, between a terminal emulation client and server, between a file transport protocol client and server, or in any other Internet application.

Netscape incorporated support for the SSL protocol in its browsers, which it distributed widely and freely at first, as well as in its servers that it sold. By capturing a huge part of the web browser market initially, Netscape was able to sell its servers at a premium because they could support secure transmissions. Those secure circuits could be used to encrypt credit card numbers and make possible on-line commerce, albeit in a crude and embryonic form. By encrypting a data stream between client and server, a consumer can enter a credit card number and the server can upload it across the

Internet in ciphertext, decrypting it at the server and storing or processing it locally.

Shortly after introducing the protocol and its software that supported it, Netscape offered SSL to the Internet standards body, the Internet Engineering Task Force (IETF), to be used as the basis for an open standard.

Secure Hypertext Transport Protocol (S-HTTP)

At approximately the same time that Netscape was releasing its SSL-enabled browsers and servers, other vendors were concerned that they were losing market share by their lack of secure servers and browsers, and they wanted to create a new standard that would not favor any particular vendor. The result was a version of the Hypertext Transport Protocol (HTTP)—the underlying application transport protocol for the the World Wide Web—that included extensions for security in the form of encryption and digital signatures.

This protocol differed from SSL in that it would work only with HTTP and no other application protocols. What this means is that the security functions are performed by the network application software itself, rather than by the computer's networking software as is done with SSL.

The greatest difference, however, was in the way that the two protocols were deployed. SSL was widely available to users, and soon captured the lion's share of the browser market (a share only to be challenged by Microsoft's costly marketing of its free browser, Internet Explorer). Server sales followed for Netscape. The backers of S-HTTP, however, erred by trying to deploy S-HTTP on the server side. There were many servers available that supported S-HTTP, but very few browsers. In fact, well after S-HTTP support on the server was almost standard (with the exception of Netscape's offerings), it was still next to impossible to find a browser that could handle S-HTTP content.

As a result, the protocol withered and is now mostly important only as a footnote to the development of on-line commerce.

Secure Transaction Protocols

The problem with secure channel protocols is that they provide only a secure channel, but do nothing to protect the data being sent through them. In other words, while sensitive data may be protected from eavesdroppers and intercepters while it is traversing the Internet, once the data is received by a merchant's server it is decrypted and no longer secure. At that point, the customer must trust that the merchant knows how to handle sensitive customer information appropriately. In fact, it often happened that merchants did not know how to handle sensitive data securely. One of the best known examples was an on-line service provider from which an attacker stole tens of thousands of plaintext credit card numbers—stored on a system connected to the Internet.

The answer to this problem is to build a protocol that specifically addresses the problems involved in commercial transactions—one with support for things like two-phase commit transactions, rollbacks, and chargebacks. Unlike the secure channel protocols, which were relatively straightforward if not necessarily simple, creating a secure transaction protocol proved to be more complicated as a result of the need for these features.

There have been a number of different commerce protocols proposed and implemented over the past few years, but as of early 1998, only two are still worthy of mention. The first secure transaction protocol to be implemented and deployed for general commerce and to gain any significant market acceptance was the CyberCash protocol developed by CyberCash, Inc., of Reston, Virginia, and released in 1995.

By the start of 1996, however, a collection of most of the important players including charge and credit card issuers, software and hardware vendors, and other interested parties had settled on the Secure Electronic Transaction (SET) as a standard for secure and safe Internet transactions. The first SET transactions were occurring even before the specification was finalized.

CyberCash's early arrival on the scene meant that while it would have like its protocol to be used generally, it realized that it would have to align itself with whatever protocol or protocols were chosen by the industry through standards processes. When it became clear that the only solution agreeable to the majority of organizations involved, particularly the payment card issuers, would be SET, CyberCash announced that its software and services would also conform to the SET specification.

Both protocols are similar in that they address a full range of transactional issues, including the exchange of information about purchase information, payment information, and confirmation and receipt information. Both use digital signature and encryption mechanisms to protect the transaction information and to provide nonrepudiation to the parties of the transaction. The CyberCash protocol specification is longer and more complicated than the SSL or S-HTTP documents, but the SET specification is considerably more complex than that. The details of both are beyond the scope of this book, but the specifications themselves are available on the Internet.

DigiCash and Chaum's Blinding Protocol

An ingenious protocol devised by David Chaum has enabled him and his colleagues at DigiCash to create a mechanism by which it is possible to transfer currency values across open networks. Very simply, a bank that offers digicash™ actually signs a piece of data to indicate that it should be considered to represent some currency value. Anonymity is available through the use of blinding. The data being signed is chosen by the customer and then multiplied by another customer-chosen number before being submitted to the bank for its signature. The bank will sign the value (which is actually the real value times some other number), and the customer then factors out that extra number and the resulting value will still certify with the banks' signature. For more details on this protocol and the DigiCash service, see the DigiCash web site at:

www.digicash.com

Digital Commerce Products

At the dawn of time for Internet commerce (1995), consumers had to make choices in order to be able to make purchases on-line. For example, they might need to have Netscape's browser to buy from an SSL-enabled merchant, or they might need to sign up for an on-line commerce service like that offered by First Virtual Holdings, Inc. (which is in effect an aliasing service for credit card purchases of information and service products), or they might have had to download a digital wallet program like that offered by CyberCash so that they could make purchases from CyberCash-enabled merchants.

With a consolidation of Internet commerce software and services around the SET specification, the choice of software or services for the consumer is, thankfully, becoming less important. CyberCash consumer services will soon be available through the Microsoft Wallet, bundled in the Internet Explorer, and other vendors are expected to continue to simplify on-line commerce.

Consumers selecting software to be used for on-line commerce should be well informed about how that commerce is conducted, and should be wary of any of the following:

- Any service that requires an upfront charge or annual membership fee, particularly if that fee is more than a few dollars.
- Any service that limits you to purchasing from a small number of vendors.
- Any service that requires any deposit be made before making any purchase.
- Any service that does not provide clear instructions for how to reach its customer support or to reach the corporation sponsoring the service.
- Any service that does not provide detailed information about how its service works, how it maintains the security of your transactions, and how a merchant can support the service.

If you are in any doubt about whether or not you should sign up with some service, check with your card issuer for guidelines about how to use your payment card on-line. Most issuers maintain web sites with such information for their customers.

This chapter focused on digital commerce using credit, debit, and charge cards, but there are digital currency systems available that do not rely on the card payment infrastructure but that are cleared through banks or other issuers. For more details about these schemes as well as other relevant issues about Internet commerce, see Peter Wayner's *Digital Cash* (AP Professional, 1996) or this author's *Electronic Commerce: On-line Ordering and Digital Money,* 2nd edition (Charles River Media, 1997).

10

Understanding and Using PGP

The actual mechanics of using PGP for Personal Privacy, from Pretty Good Privacy, Inc., are discussed in Chapter 5 (getting set up with a public key pair), Chapter 7 (using it for e-mail), and Chapter 8 (using it to protect data on your desktop). However, unlike the more widely supported S/MIME approach, PGP does not use a concept of a centralized certification authority (CA) to issue certificates on public keys. Instead, it uses a decentralized model of trust that allows individuals to explicitly identify those entities they feel they can trust to sign someone's public key, with PGP servers distributed around the Internet to store and publish PGP keys.

This chapter examines how this model of trust works in the PGP application and also discusses how related key management and general PGP options are used in the application. For more complete discussion of the PGP trust model and other related topics, the reader is directed to the PGP documentation included with the program as well as to these books on PGP:

- ♦ *PGP: Pretty Good Privacy* (O'Reilly and Associates, 1995) by Simson Garfinkel.
- ♦ *The Official PGP User's Guide* (MIT Press, 1995) by Phillip K. Zimmerman.

The PGP Model of Trust

Part of the reason that Phil Zimmerman created the PGP program was to allow individuals a mechanism by which they could encrypt and digitally sign data while still retaining control over their own keys as well as control over whose keys they trusted. This model is built on the differences between the more traditional, centralized approach as well as on the possibilities inherent in driving trust through personal contacts and reputations.

This section introduces these topics as well as discussing how PGP implements this approach to distributing trust through the PGP program.

Centralized Trust versus Distributed Trust

With the certification authority (CA) model of trust, individuals generate their own public key pairs and have them signed by the centralized CA, which issues a certificate. This means that when you receive a certificate, it has been signed either by a CA that you trust or by a CA you do not trust. You may not trust it because you do not know about it, in which case you will need to check it out and make a decision about whether or not to trust. Or, you may have made a decision at some point to not trust certificates issued by some particular CA.

Two of the issues raised by the nature of the CA model are these:

♦ All trust is derived from the CA, making it imperative that the recipient trust the CA.

♦ Proliferation of CAs makes it difficult to determine how far to trust any given one.

Centrality of Trust

Central to the model of trust is that all trust flows through the CA. If the CA determines that an entity is entitled to a certificate, that entity will receive its certificate. Some CAs offer different levels of trust. For example, some will issue basic certificates that are sufficient for encryption and e-mail but that carry little or no user authentication or information beyond an e-mail address. Other types of certificates are available that are issued only on receipt of a variety of identifying information, which is confirmed through neutral channels by the certifying authority. However, it is necessary for the individual receiving such certificates to determine whether or not to trust the certificate, and how much to trust the certificate. (For example, is the certificate sufficiently trustworthy to allow the recipient to feel comfortable entering into a business relationship with the certificate holder?)

Ultimately, the most important security issue raised by the centrality of trust in CAs is that you must not only trust that the CA is issuing certificates that are trustworthy, but also that the CA itself is trustworthy. This means that the CA is managed and organized in such a way as to prevent it from being subverted in any of these ways:

♦ The CA should be securely managed, with reasonable assurance that no one can steal the keys with which it signs certificates.

♦ The CA should be accountable for checking any and all information it claims is required for issuing a certificate.

♦ The CA should be above any suspicion of knowingly issuing certificates falsely. (In other words, there should be no hint that someone within the organization hosting the CA can or will for any reason issue a certificate that person knows the applicant should not receive.)

It should be noted, too, that despite the fact that certificates derive their certification from a central authority, there is no Central Authority—there are already dozens of reasonably well known authorities dispensing certificates, with many more less well known and even more than that on their way. For comparison, consider the assortment of items in the typical person's wallet:

- Driver's license.
- Credit and charge cards.
- A bank ATM card.
- Library card.
- Health insurance ID card.

In addition to this set, consider all the other cards that different organizations issue, with these representing just a sampling:

- College or university ID.
- Employer's ID.
- Association and society membership cards.
- Organ donor card.

In meat-space, these cards all carry very different weights when presented for different purposes—your Audubon Society membership card or your public broadcasting donor card will usually not help much when you try to cash a check or are stopped for a traffic violation. However, at the moment there are far more certificate issuers, and there is not yet a general awareness of how much validity any of them should be accorded, or for what purposes that validity should be accorded.

Distributed Trust

The end result is that, in practice, encryption users must already be prepared to differentiate between different CAs. This means that, for example, if I am using S/MIME for digitally signing my e-mail messages, the validity of the signature can vary depending on which certificate I use. I may be using a trial certificate issued for no charge from one of the major CAs, with no verification of anything beyond my e-mail address. In that case, the signature means relatively little beyond proving that message is signed by the same entity that has in the past signed other messages with the same certificate.

On the other hand, I may be using a higher-level, higher-priced certificate. In this case, the CA will likely have required a relatively high payment as well as some documentation of my identity, which may have included things like a birth certificate, a passport, driver's license, and a taxpayer ID (Social Security number). The certificate may not have been issued until all the documentation was independently verified, resulting in a reasonably strong link between the certificate and the identity.

However, the ease with which certificates can be acquired means that verifying a certificate requires verifying the CA as well as scrutinizing the certificate itself to understand what it actually means.

Distributing Trust

Another approach to trust is to distribute it more explicitly. In other words, each certificate could be judged on its own merits in every case (which in practice is what should happen, but this is not as explicit an action when used with central CAs). This would mean that each certificate would carry around its own credentials that could represent why a recipient might want to trust it.

One way to ensure that you can connect a real human being with a particular certificate is to get the certificate directly from that person—in real life, rather than relying on an e-mail message, for example. Although this does not necessarily ensure that the person is who she says she is, it does ensure that the person you know in meat-space is the same person you communicate with by e-mail when you receive a message from her that has been signed using the same certificate she gave you in person or perhaps over the tele-phone.

Now, it is not reasonable to have a reasonable expectation of trust only by communicating securely with people (or entities) with which we have had some direct physical contact. This would severely limit our ability to communicate securely with people we have not yet met. This is a large part of the attraction of the central-ized CA model: Let someone else issue the certificates and vouch for them to whatever extent the CA is willing.

The alternative, however, is for people to take over part of the task themselves and create a sort of web of trust. In this approach, you would collect certificates from other entities and assign them each some level of trust. This trust level does not refer to the certificates themselves (or the bearers of the certificates). If you receive a certif-icate from someone, you have little choice but to accept it as authen-tic, and that implies that when you receive a message signed with it, you would be correct in accepting that the signature implies that it came from the person whose key it is.

However, you can assign each key a level of trust for introducing you to other people with whom you are unlikely to meet in person. This happens when people start signing each other's certificates with their own certificates. That way, when you receive my certifi-cate, it not only includes my certificate information but it also includes the certificate information about the person or people who have signed the certificate.

All of a sudden, you can emulate the function of a CA by trusting some particular entity as an introducer. In other words, you can decide that particular entity is sufficiently trustworthy and reli-able that you will accept any certificate it signs. The entity could be another person, or it could be an organization; if everyone signs other people's certificates, then a web of trust can be con-structed by examining the signatures on a certificate. If you know one or more of the entities signing the certificate of an unknown entity, you can assess how reasonable it is to trust that certificate.

PGP's web of trust uses the public key instead of a certificate. The key itself is inextricably linked to the private key, so while it does not carry any information about the entity that owns it, the key is very certainly a link to the entity that claims it. PGP uses a hash function to create a fingerprint of an entities' key so you can verify the full public key from a much shorter (and easier to handle) set of data. (A 128-bit fingerprint can be expressed as 32 hexadecimal digits.)

HEXADECIMAL REPRESENTATION: Hexadecimal digits are an easy way to represent binary data. Instead of the more usual decimal, or base-10, representation of numbers, hexadecimal is a base-16 representation. Each hexadecimal digit expresses a four-bit binary value of 0 to 15. The values from 0 to 9 are the same as in decimal format, with the values from 10 to 15 taking on the first six letters of the alphabet. Often, hex values are expressed with the characters 0x in front of them. Thus

0xA represents 10
0xB represents 11
0xC represents 12
0xD represents 13
0xE represents 14
0xF represents 15

Hex representations are useful because an eight-bit value can be easily represented as a two-character value ranging from 0x00 to 0xFF.

Scalability

Almost any system of certification, whether based on the certification authority (CA) or a web of trust, will work well with a limited number of entities. For dozens or hundreds or even thousands of users, almost any approach to certification would work acceptably and adequately. Limitations on scalability arise from two directions: the number of entities participating and the number of transactions that need to be certified. CAs, by their nature as central authorities, will tend to be bound by the limitations of any large database as the number of entities being certified increases. Certifying 10,000 or even 100,000 entities, as might be necessary to assign a certificate to each employee in the largest corporate organizations, is not really a problem. The problems of scalability start when attempting to assign certificates to millions or tens of millions of entities, as might be necessary for utility, cable television, or telephone companies that want to issue certificates to each of their customers, or for governments that want to issue certificates to each of their citizens.

The web of trust model may seem to have even more limited scalability. After all, a user will accept keys only from two categories of entities:

- ◆ Those other entities the user already trusts—for example, people the user has met in person and from whom the user has gotten a key.
- ◆ Those entities whose keys have been signed by entities the user has determined to be sufficiently reliable and trustworthy to introduce new key holders.

It would seem that the web of trust might not scale terribly well. It requires that you know, or know of, at least one of the same entities that any unknown entity knows as a signer. This means that when you have people sign your key, it is important to choose signers who are most likely to be trusted by the largest number of other entities.

While it might seem to make sense to have as many entities sign your key as possible, if you have everyone in your workgroup or class sign you key, you have a lot of signers but you may not have extended the level of trust of your key. Your key may now be accepted by others in your workgroup or class, but if none of your peers are well known and trusted outside the group, your key does not carry much additional weight.

Alternatively, consider what happens if you have the president of your company or dean of your college sign your key. Now (assuming the president or dean is well known and trusted) your key may be accepted by many more people both in and out of your company or school. The next logical step, especially if one wants to have a trust model that can be trusted across real-world-sized populations, is to start using something very much like a certification authority to sign entities' keys.

With the proliferation of certificates and public key pairs, the issue of scalability will continue to pose a challenge to implementers. Just as most individuals in developed countries have more than one physical certificate (things like driver's licenses, passports, birth certificates, credit cards, and so on), so will they have more than one public key pair as they increasingly transact their business on-line. Scalability issues are far from solved, and it remains to be seen how they will be solved.

Using the PGP Distributed Trust Model

The PGP distributed trust model relies on the concept of trusted introducers. Each entity can decide who it will trust to introduce other entities. A new entity may be introduced by some other, individual trusted entity, or the entity may require two or more trusted introducers to trust a new entity. Instead of using certificates, PGP uses the actual public key—this is, after all, the key piece of information for any of these transactions. The holder of the private key of a public key pair is the only entity capable of being usefully linked with the public key. The key's fingerprint (which will be discussed shortly) is a sort of abbreviation of the public key, the result of a hash function that can be used to certify that the public key in question is, in fact, the public key associated with an entity.

PGP public keys can have associated with them the signatures of other PGP key holders. This means that when you get someone's key, you can see who else has decided to sign the key (which is a way of investing some degree of trust in the key). The number of signers as well as the quality of the signers should be considered when deciding whether or not to trust the keyholder (as well as how far to trust the keyholder).

For example, the PGPkeys application distributed with PGP for Personal Privacy uses a public keyring that contains a set of keys from employees of the PGP organization. All keys are self-signed. This means that once you generate your own key, you can sign it yourself. This represents a very limited, but very important, item of trust: that the person who signed the public key is the person who holds the private key of the pair. The keys of PGP employees are also signed with the Pretty Good Privacy, Inc., corporate key (which is also included in the database).

To add keys to your public keyring, you can search and download keys from PGP keyservers or you can add a key that someone has sent you by e-mail or handed you on a floppy diskette. You can also sign someone's key and add your signature to that key, which can be propagated to the keyserver. This will mean that when other people go to the keyserver to check validity of the key, they will see your signature as well as all the other signatures that the keyholder has accumulated over time.

Signing someone's key—associating your name and key with their name and key—is not something you would do without permission. In practice, you may be asked to sign someone's PGP key, in which case there is no reason to hold back. However, if you have not been asked to sign a key, it is best not to do so.

PGP Key Management

There are two different types of keys that you can manage with PGP: your own keys and other entities' keys. In addition to viewing keys and key properties, key management requires the ability to do several other tasks:

- Generating a new public key pair for yourself.
- Checking a key's fingerprint to verify its validity.
- Signing someone's public key.

♦ Assigning a level of trust to someone's public key for the purpose of introducing new keys.

♦ Disabling or enabling a public key temporarily.

♦ Removing a public key or a signature from a public key.

♦ Changing the passphrase used to protect a key.

♦ Importing and exporting keys for distribution.

♦ Revoking a key, making it no longer valid.

The PGPkeys application is used for performing these functions as well as to set PGP preferences.

PGPkeys is started by choosing it from the Start Programs menu, from the PGP folder, or from the PGP icon at the far right of the Windows taskbar. The PGPkeys window will look something like that shown in Figure 10.1.

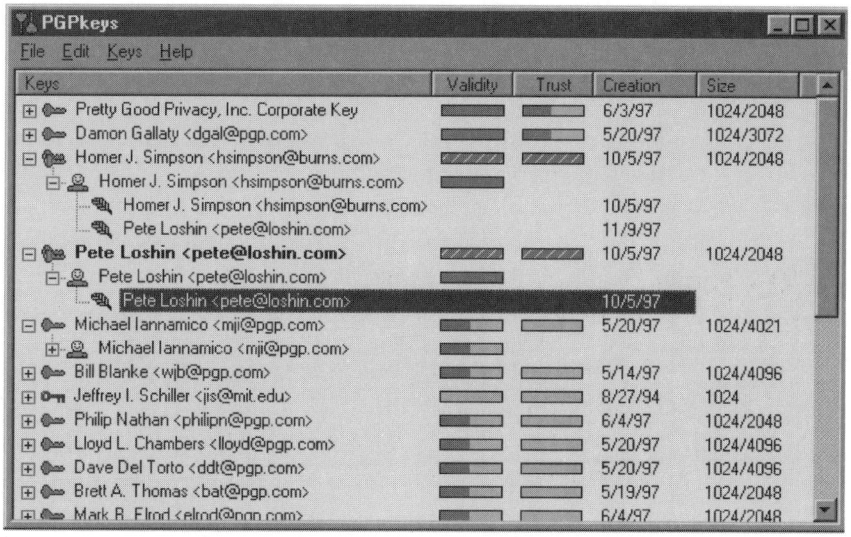

Figure 10.1. The PGPkeys application is used to manage all PGP keys.

Using PGPkeys

By default, your own keys and other entities' keys are stored in two files, called `secring.skr` (for your own secret keys) and `pubring.pkr` (for storing other entities' public keys). These files are associated with special icons showing three figures holding a large key (for the public keyring) and one figure holding a large key (for the secret keyring).

Keys on both rings are managed with PGPkeys, as discussed shortly. The application, as shown in Figure 10.1, displays all public keys in both the public and private keyrings. Every key is displayed with a key icon of one sort or another. The newer-style, yellow keys represent DSS/Diffie-Hellman standard keys (which are the newer style supported by PGP). Older-style keys, colored blue, represent the RSA-style public key standard. These are represented with the old-fashioned icon to remind the user that this type of key was used with earlier versions of PGP, but it is no longer recommended. (Some versions of PGP will not allow the user to generate a key of this type, though all versions will support encryption and digital signature verification with these keys.) All keys that you generate yourself are represented as double-keys.

Key Properties

Keys are displayed in a row-column format, with each key having the following attributes:

- ◆ Key name and e-mail address. This is the name and e-mail address of the entity claiming the key in question.
- ◆ A degree of validity. This is the level of confidence you have that the key actually belongs to the entity claiming it; highest validity is given to keys you have signed your-self, while lower validity may be attributed to keys that have been signed by introducers you trust less.
- ◆ Trust level. This is a level you can set yourself; there are four levels of trust available. You can assign a key implicit trust, which sets the trust level to ultimate (this is allowed only for keys you have generated yourself); you can also assign keys complete trust, marginal trust, and no trust (untrusted).

♦ Creation date of the key.

♦ Size of the key, in bits. DSS/Diffie-Hellman keys are represented in two parts, one for the DSS the other for the Diffie-Hellman portions, and the size shown in this column will also be displayed in two parts for these keys.

Validity and trust levels are indicated by the shading in the bars in those columns. Light-gray bars indicate that the validity of the key is none, and there is no trust of the user. Half-darkened bars indicate marginal validity or trust, while entirely dark gray bars are completely valid or completely trusted. Dark gray bars with stripes represent implicit validity and implicitly trusted keys; this option is available only for keys you have generated yourself.

You can see which entities have signed a key by clicking on the key's listing will expand the key, the names and addresses associated with the key, and its signers. Clicking on a key exposes one or more name-e-mail address pairs next to a head and shoulders icon. Click on one of these names, and the key or keys of the signing entities are displayed. Most keys have only one name-address, but you can use the same key with a different name-address pair—for example, if you want to use the same key to sign things with your business e-mail address as well as with your home e-mail address.

Each name-address is signed by at least one entity, its holder. Names-addresses can be signed by any number of other entities, which are listed beneath the keyholder's key when the entities' entry is fully expanded.

You can view and edit a key's properties by selecting a key and using the Key Properties option from the Keys pulldown menu. Figure 10.2 shows the key properties dialog for the author's key.

The properties box includes the key owner's name and e-mail address in the window banners, and includes the following items:

♦ Key ID. A unique identifier for each key, it allows several keys to be created with the same user name and e-mail address.

♦ Creation date.

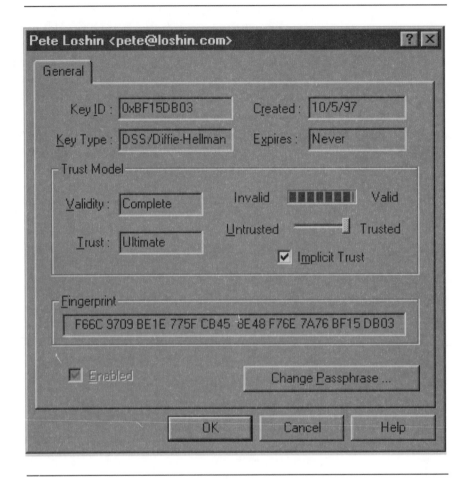

Figure 10.2. The key properties display for the author's own PGP key.

- ◆ Key type, either DSS/Diffie-Hellman or RSA.
- ◆ Expiration date. If the keys were not generated with an expiration date, this field will read "Never."
- ◆ The Trust Model section. This includes the validity and trust levels assigned to the key. If you have signed a key, or if the key has been signed by an entity or entities you

trust, the key will be validated—this is not something you can set explicitly through this dialog. The trust level, however, can be set through this dialog by moving the bar from Untrusted to Trusted. (You can set it in the middle for marginal trust.) The implicit trust checkbox is available only for your own keys, and by default all your own keys are accorded implicit trust.

♦ Fingerprint. This is a hash value of the public key, generated when the key is created and used to confirm that the key has been correctly transmitted. A 160-bit fingerprint is represented by 10 groups of four hexadecimal digits.

♦ The enabled check box. This indicates whether or not the key is currently available for doing PGP encryption or signatures. Your own keys (those assigned implicit trust) are always enabled, until you turn off the implicit trust checkbox.

♦ The passphrase change button. This is available only for your own keys and lets you modify the passphrase to the key. Figure 10.3 shows a properties box for a key not owned by the user; note that there is no option to set implicit trust for the key or to change the passphrase.

Setting the Default Key

If you have more than one key, you must specify which key is to be used as the default for signing your messages. Choosing a key as a default is a matter of selecting the Keys pulldown menu and choosing the option Set as Default Key. This option is normally grayed-out for keys you have not created yourself, but is available for any key you have created yourself.

Adding a Name or Address to Your Key

Another option available only for keys you have created and for which you are holding both the public and private key is to add a name and e-mail address to a key you are already using. This allows you to add a personal name and address to a key you are already using for your business communications. To do so, select

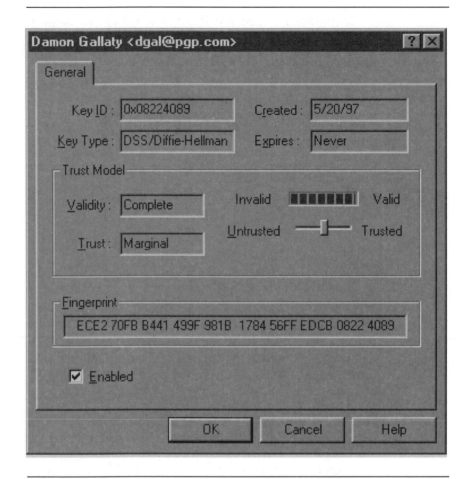

Figure 10.3. The properties box for a key not owned by the author.

the key you want to add a name to, then choose the Add Name option from the Keys pulldown menu. You will prompted for the new name and address; both are required even if you are using the same name or same address as before. Once entered, you will be prompted for the passphrase associated with the key, and the new name-address will be added. Figure 10.4 shows an instance where two names-addresses are being used under the same key.

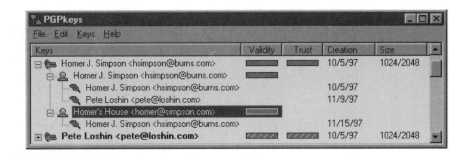

Figure 10.4. You are not restricted to one name and address for your PGP keys, and may add them at any time.

Generating a New Public Key Pair

Creating a new public key pair was described in Chapter 5.

Checking Fingerprints

A PGP key, like a digital certificate, can be cumbersome at the least. Figure 10.5 shows what one looks like. The DSS/Diffie-Hellman fingerprint, on the other hand, at 160 bits, can be expressed as a 40-digit hexadecimal number. When you have received the key (for example, downloaded it from a PGP keyserver or gotten it from someone on disk or by e-mail) and imported it into PGPkeys (see the following), you can verify that the key is correct by getting the fingerprint from the owner of the key. Usually, this is done in person (often PGP users include their fingerprint on their business cards) over the telephone. Open the key properties box with PGP-keys and compare the fingerprint you find there with that given to you by the key holder. If they match, you have the right public key.

Signing a Public Key

When you have a key in your public keyring, and it appears in the PGPkeys application window, you can sign it if you desire (and if

```
-----BEGIN PGP PUBLIC KEY BLOCK----Version: PGP for
Personal Privacy 5.0
```

```
mQGiBDQ4DVwRBAD0UfzLyc5cWHnukXLqor7YOFUGBCzDa33ZTP2
mGMb7Y0XYDnSts2ekLdofMDH2BYWBNQZmSOc8lugveBtD3Qs8oT
vNsydRTr3sP6ybYk8aGQotU13xacygPSahiVNO3M6T62+CXcXvX
D0b09b3nDeFyJ5dmvnCg8ewx7pHP6jawCg/6a8Uh+lYAmWVl0u
9J4H9/SZN6cEAK/wKwJwnsFDzNFA93/ECDNDuKL0lTVW0RmZZ2H
uNejiyg8VZd6qEV5nn2lyS+E2UQRihZxw8HlNNk3qtEGBJy+KUG
low79C8QBiFYuFPCNyE3rFOP11MpYVMzYTVkXFl3X28RFYqDfUZ
jxKosBdeqErliCEJDMQS06TQiCY0tBBACqjABtVsxH6PeJg8PZM
er3ru5rRsVVVutere4fm5bz0E3x6EepVOdIDytKBrfKpvN70Ld4
1fvdyCFW6FiMr7RFT5W9tGlPDGGwqGAQLiSViWnzjOvokHUEq9r
mHDfIfcPE26E5q1B74wCog3RqcMWY8s+vk6jctfn0NZQtNo7PkL
QdUGV0ZSBMb3NoaW4gPHBldGVAbG9zaGluLmNvbT6JAEsEEBECA
AsFAjQ4DVwECwMBAgAKCRD3bnp2vxXbA9tJAJ4yYQVgGDAIGQyT
npPGcOVaqh9wAgCfWbtzcDmofbN1bNp3hb04HC64zB25Ag0ENDg
NXBAIAPZCV7cIfwgXcqK61qlC8wXo+VMROU+28W65Szgg2gGnVq
MU6Y9AVfPQB8bLQ6mUrfdMZIZJ+AyDvWXpF9Sh01D49Vlf3HZST
z09jdvOmeFXklnN/biudE/F/Ha8g8VHMGHOfMlm/xX5u/2RXsc
BqtNbno2gpXI61Brwv0YAWCvl9Ij9WE5J280gtJ3kkQc2aNsOA
1FHQ98iLMcfFstjvbzySPAQ/ClWxiNjrtVjLhdONM0/XwXV0Oj
HRhs3jMhLLUq/zzhsSlAGBGNfISnCnLWhsQDGcgHKXrKlQzZlp
+r0QmwJG0wg9ZqRdQZ+cfL2JSyIZJrqrol7DVekyCzsAAgIIAJ
LwQZF3KQFzUo2JHyO/A7xoI5Dn6No7BsMdpJkblhwzIBntUS
aNRro/pv7C2BeBqRZs5lgh82waBqPfLAeIAilaK5dXgFNaVjeb
cTPblkkVtqaRdagPmesN+08IcC3C78wlFgCe1pZbl5NVMG7HZ
7w44bSsid+7G8IIl7JoJynuI2JjiOVhQqve43/t1CuylS7eNlo
9SUcPnu42jwSMNxZrF0vGElA6lEiOst9rBqRqBbg1liXaNvo
0tbjLSvC2L3Xwua7oyJaswKJ6ijVt9ky71/m7jEpVB7A6/uJi/
oqgfq2mOcoEsoP1fcpiafUQFuHW63vLbfmhAAAWMrlHs8aJA
D8DBRg0OA1c9256dr8V2wMRAmYOAJ42SdrSNE9sOqXT48HGslD
ayzZABwCgsHpCe eJ0CcJOhPg0qwnG6dqQ99c=
=8Su7
```

```
-----END PGP PUBLIC KEY BLOCK-----
```

Figure 10.5. A PGP public key.

you have been asked to do so). Select the key in question (it is important that you be certain you have the right key, so be sure to check the name as well as the fingerprint) and select the Sign option from the Keys pulldown menu. A dialog box explaining that you are about to sign someone's public key will appear, as shown in Figure 10.6.

As the dialog box explains, signing a key means that you are certifying that you have direct, first-hand knowledge that the person claiming to own the key actually is the person listed as owning the key. You would not sign a key from someone you had not met or spoken with, and you might not sign a key from someone you had not actually met in person.

To finish signing, decide whether or not to send the signature to the keyserver. Doing so will add your signature to the entities' key on the keyserver as well as on your own keyring. Click on the Yes button (or No, if you have decided not to sign) and you will prompted for the passphrase associated with your key, and you will have signed the key.

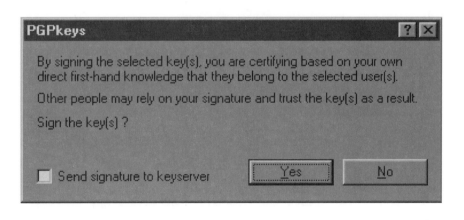

Figure 10.6. Signing a public key.

Trust and Validity

A key is not valid until it has been signed by a key that you trust. Ultimately, this means that you must start with your own key (which you trust implicitly, because it is *your* key) and you can build your own structure of trusted keys. For example, many users are willing to accept Phil Zimmerman's signature as trustworthy. It is distributed with PGP, and the fingerprint is readily available in print and on-line.

If you accept Phil's signature, then all the keys Phil has signed immediately take on validity—but they are not yet trusted by you. Validity simply means that you or someone you trust has certified the entity claiming the key. In other words, once you decide that my key and I are linked (by getting my fingerprint from my business card, for example), you can sign my key on your keyring—thus indicating that the key is valid.

Trust, however, is another issue. Once you have validated my key, you still can decide what degree of trust to assign it. Assigning me a high level of trust ("complete trust") means you believe that I will not sign any keys that are not actually valid (or at least that my standards for validity are at least as high as your own standards). This means that when you receive a key that I have signed, you will consider that key to be valid, just as I asserted by having signed the key.

If you assign a key marginal trust, it means that keys that have been signed by that key will have marginal validity—in other words, you believe that the key is probably valid, but would need more proof before trusting the key completely. When you receive a key that has been validated by the key of an entity that you trust marginally, you can accept the key with marginal validity, but you will be notified that the validity is not complete.

If you designate a key as untrusted, it means that you do not trust the keyholder to validate other keys, but it does not affect whether or not you will encrypt data to that keyholder or accept digital signatures from that keyholder.

A key that has not been signed by some entity you trust (whether it is you yourself or someone else) will be considered invalid; you cannot assign any level of trust to the key until it has been validated. A key that has not been validated can still be used to encrypt a message; it is assumed that the message will be accessible only to the holder of the private key associated with the public key in question—the issue still open with unvalidated keys is simply whether or not the entity is who it is represented itself as. A key that has been validated does not have this problem; the level of trust you assign it depends on whether or not you trust the holder of the key to validate other keys.

Handling Your Keys

As with any public key encryption mechanism, it is important to protect your private key with PGP. This should be done in at least three ways:

- ◆ You should use a passphrase to protect access to your private key. The passphrase is required for any function that requires the private key, which means that you will be prompted for it before signing any data and before decrypting any data.
- ◆ You should take steps to protect the private key from theft. This may require such extreme steps as keeping the key on a removable disk or diskette and storing it under lock and key at all times except those times it is being used. More practically, this means securing the system on which you store the key, both physically (for example, in a locked room) and digitally (protect access through passphrases and keeping permissions to a minimum).
- ◆ You should also protect the private key from loss. If you lose the private key, you will not have access to any encrypted data that has not been stored as plaintext, and you will no longer be able to digitally sign any data with that key. Protection from loss includes steps such as keeping a backup copy of the private key on a diskette stored

in a safe and secure location, preferably physically removed from the site at which it is normally used (to protect against flood, fire, or other devastation).

When creating your key, the wizard recommends protecting your keys with a passphrase and making backup copies, and it walks you through the process of doing so.

Key Revocation

Setting an expiration date for your keys means that in the event that the key is compromised (for example, by losing the key backup diskette or having it stolen), the length of time that the key can be exploited is limited. However, expiring your keys every year means that you must keep that many more keys on hand to handle old data, and those who have received your data over time must also keep track of old keys to verify your signatures.

On the other hand, creating keys with no expiration means that you can publish your key and fingerprint widely, in the full expectation that the key will be usable for the foreseeable future.

In either case, however, a mechanism for revoking a key is a requirement. Even if the exposure is limited, you would not want to go around for weeks, let alone months, aware that someone is (or might be) assuming your identity through your key.

Key revocation is done through PGP keyservers. When you create your key, you send a copy of the public key to a keyserver. (See the next section.) The servers act as a public repository of PGP public keys, and it includes not only the keys but also signatures on the keys. This allows individuals to use the keyservers to download current keys along with current certification information (signers).

When a key has been compromised, you can revoke it by choosing the Revoke option from the Keys pulldown menu. This brings up a dialog box like that shown in Figure 10.7, warning you of the consequences of revoking a key. You will no longer be able to use it to

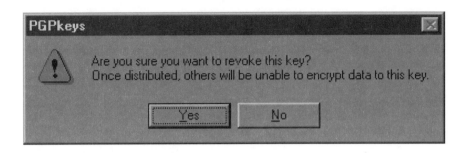

Figure 10.7. Revoking a PGP key.

sign messages, and others will no longer be able to use it to encrypt messages to you. You will still be able to use it to decrypt data that has already been encrypted with the public key before revocation, however. After answering yes to this prompt, you will be prompted to enter the passphrase for the key. The key will now appear in the PGPkeys window with a red bar through it to show it has been revoked. Send the key to the keyserver (see the next section), and the key will be officially revoked.

One situation in which it is advisable to revoke a key is when you have created the key and not used it in a long time—so long that you have forgotten the passphrase. In that case, you will not be able to revoke the key because you will not know the correct passphrase. The proper way to avoid this problem is to make a copy of the private key on a diskette and revoke the copy—then store the revoked key in a very safe place. Then, if and when you need to revoke the key, you can send the key (that has already been revoked) to the keyserver.

If you create a prerevoked copy of your key, be sure to store it very safely. If it should fall into the wrong hands, a criminal could revoke your key and create a new one in your name without your knowledge. Such a key should be stored at least as safely as your unrevoked private key; the private key backup is usable only if your passphrase is also compromised, but the revoked copy can be used without the passphrase. (You already entered it when revoking the key.)

PGP Keyservers

PGP keyservers propagate their information to all other PGP keyservers, and are used to retain information about keys like the name and e-mail address of the key holder, who has signed each key, and whether or not the key has been revoked by the holder.

Keyserver functions are accessible through the PGPkeys Keys pulldown menu by choosing the Keyserver option. There are three suboptions:

- ♦ Get selected key. This will cause the program to connect to the keyserver and look up the public key for the key currently highlighted in the PGPkeys application. Keys do not remain static. They are signed by other people, and they have additional e-mail addresses and names associated with them. Getting the key from the keyserver will update your public keyring with the most current information relating to that key.
- ♦ Send selected key. This option allows you to send updates to the keyserver, including the most current information about your own key.
- ♦ Find key. This option allows you to enter a key ID or e-mail address, and have the keyserver send back the key or keys that match.

A

Theory of Public Key Cryptography

 This section is purely optional. It is included as a service to those readers interested in having a deeper understanding of the theory behind public key cryptography. If you need to use public key cryptography, it is not necessary to understand or even to read this section—and reading this section will not necessarily provide any practical advantage in terms of being able to use software that uses public key cryptography.

Modular Arithmetic

Modular arithmetic is a very important topic in discrete mathematics, and concepts of modular arithmetic are basic not only to public key cryptography but also to computer science in general. The basic idea of modular arithmetic should be easy to understand if you already understand the basic simple offset substitution cipher—or if you are able to calculate calendar dates or clock times.

Clock and Calendar Calculation

To take a simple and easy example, consider this problem. Today is Monday, and you have 15 days to complete your taxes and mail them to the Internal Revenue Service. On what day must you get them to the post office in order to meet your deadline? If you had seven days from now, the answer would be Monday; the same goes for 14 or 21 or 28 (or for any number evenly divisible by 7). If you had only one day, you would have to get to the post office on a Tuesday; the same goes if you had 8, 15, 22, or any other number that, when divided by 7, results in a remainder of 1.

In other words, the solution to the problem can be generalized as shown in Figure A.1. The table maps the days of the week to numbers, with Monday (arbitrarily, in this case) chosen to correspond with numbers of days that leave a remainder of 0 (can be evenly divided by 7 with no remainder). The number of days to be used for the calculation is represented by n and can be any discrete number (a number with no fractional portion).

The relevant piece of information for this type of problem is not how far away the day falls. The stated problem is to determine what day of the week it will be in n days.

$n/7$ leaves a remainder of:	0	1	2	3	4	5	6
Day of the week:	Mon	Tues	Wed	Thur	Fri	Sat	Sun

Figure A.1   Calculating which day of the week it will be in n days.

Another way to express this solution is to say that with respect to calculating the days of the week, 8 is the same as 15 (which are both the same as 22). A more precise and mathematical way of saying this is

```
8 mod 7 = 1

15 mod 7 = 1

22 mod 7 = 1
```

The term mod represents the word *modulo*, which is the operation that we have been talking about: taking the remainder of a division.

Modular Arithmetic and Simple Encryption

Modular arithmetic comes into play often in temporal calculations like determining the day of the week, or calculating the 12-hour clock time as it changes by some number of hours. For example, if it is now 10:00 A.M., what time will it be in seven hours? Also, if it is now 10:45, what time will it be in 585 minutes?

Another example of modular arithmetic that the reader should be familiar with is that of the offset substitution cipher. In this case, if you were to assign numerical values to each letter, as in 1=A, 2=B, 3=C, and so on, you can calculate the ciphertext from plaintext with modular arithmetic. In the case of the Caesar cipher, the calculation would be

$$character_{plaintext} + 2 \bmod 26 = character_{ciphertext}$$

So to encrypt the plaintext character A, which is equal to 1, you would add 2 and calculate the result modulo 26 (which is the number of characters in the character set). The result is 3, or C. This does not get interesting until you reach the end of the alphabet, so for the letter Z, which is 26, you add 2 to get the result of 28. However, this result is larger than 26, so to calculate the result of 28 mod 26, you divide 26 into 28 and the remainder, 2, is the desired result. This is equivalent to the letter B in the Caesar cipher.

Modular Addition

In the operation called modular addition, you add numbers x and y, and divide the result by the modulus n. It is expressed as an equation in this form:

$(x + y) \mod n = z$

The value z is equal to the remainder when dividing the modulus, n, by the sum of x and y.

The addition modulo 10 table is shown in Figure 2.11. It should be immediately obvious that the function represented by modular arithmetic can be used for encryption, assuming that all characters can be represented by numbers. The function can take as its input a plaintext character (or, more exactly, the number that represents that character) and adds it to some predetermined number (this would be the key, or offset, of the cipher) modulo the total number of characters. As can be seen in Figure A.2, a 10-character alphabet can be encrypted with 10 different keys (however, one key, 0, will produce output that is the same as the input).

Modular arithmetic is a function that can be used to encrypt data, as can be demonstrated by considering data that can be represented by the digits from 0 to 9. To take an example, using the offset number 7 and the preceding modular addition table, the number 462 would be encrypted as 139:

$(4 + 7) \mod 10 = 1$

$(6 + 7) \mod 10 = 3$

$(2 + 7) \mod 10 = 9$

Modular Multiplication

Other modular arithmetic functions are possible, including multiplication. Figure A.3 shows a multiplication table for modulo 10; a

+	0	1	2	3	4	5	6	7	8	9
0	0	1	2	3	4	5	6	7	8	9
1	1	2	3	4	5	6	7	8	9	0
2	2	3	4	5	6	7	8	9	0	1
3	3	4	5	6	7	8	9	0	1	2
4	4	5	6	7	8	9	0	1	2	3
5	5	6	7	8	9	0	1	2	3	4
6	6	7	8	9	0	1	2	3	4	5
7	7	8	9	0	1	2	3	4	5	6
8	8	9	0	1	2	3	4	5	6	7
9	9	0	1	2	3	4	5	6	7	8

Figure A.2   A table showing the inputs and outputs for modulo 10 additions.

similar (but longer) table could be based on the alphabet. Modulo 10 sums demonstrate some of the characteristics that make modular multiplication useful for encryption.

Something interesting becomes apparent when you look at the mod 10 multiplication table: Certain of the rows (or columns) can be used for encryption purposes, because no number recurs in the row (or column). Doing modular multiplication with 1, 3, 7, or 9 means that given any input number to the function, the function will spit out a unique number that will always relate to the input number. Of course, in the case of doing modular multiplication with the number 1, the input and output will always be identical; in the other cases, however, the result will be a one-to-one substitution.

	0	1	2	3	4	5	6	7	8	9
0	0	0	0	0	0	0	0	0	0	0
1	0	1	2	3	4	5	6	7	8	9
2	0	2	4	6	8	0	2	4	6	8
3	0	3	6	9	2	5	8	1	4	7
4	0	4	8	2	6	0	4	8	2	6
5	0	5	0	5	0	5	0	5	0	5
6	0	6	2	8	4	0	6	2	8	4
7	0	7	4	1	8	5	2	9	6	3
8	0	8	6	4	2	0	8	6	4	2
9	0	9	8	7	6	5	4	3	2	1

Figure A.3   The multiplication table for mod 10 sums.

This means that taking a value x, and multiplying it by 1, 3, 7, or 9 modulo 10, will result in a value y that will be different from the input value and at the same time unique among the results of doing mod 10 multiplication on any other value. To illustrate, encrypting the value 462 using a modular multiplication by 7 (mod 10) results in the value 824, as shown here:

```
(4 * 7) mod 10 = 8

(6 * 7) mod 10 = 2

(2 * 7) mod 10 = 4
```

Characteristics of Modular Arithmetic

To actually work as an encryption function, there must also be a way to decrypt the ciphertext. Both modular addition and multiplication by some particular number, mod 10, will result in a function that can encrypt a ciphertext consisting of decimal numbers. As in the examples just provided, adding each of the digits of 462 with 7 mod 10 results in the value 139; multiplying each of them by 7 mod 10 results in the value 824. These values are both ciphertexts, but what function must you use to reverse the encryption and arrive back at the plaintext of 462?

The characteristics of modular arithmetic that make it interesting to cryptographers derive in large part from the fact that modular arithmetic behaves very much like regular arithmetic. It has the following properties:

- The commutative property, which is the property demonstrated by the fact that the expression

  $(A \bmod B) = (B \bmod A)$

  will always be true for any A and any B.

- The associative property, which is the property demonstrated by the fact that the expression

  $((A \bmod B) \bmod C) = (A \bmod (B \bmod C))$

  will always be true for any A, B, and C.

- The distributive property, which is the property demonstrated by the expression

  $A \bmod (B + C) = (A \bmod B) + (A \bmod C)$

  will always be true for any A, B, and C.

Arithmetic Inverses

First, we look at how to handle decrypting ciphertexts generated by using modular addition or multiplication. In regular arithmetic, there is a notion of an additive inverse—a number that, when added to some other number, produces a result of 0. Subtracting a value n from another value is the same as adding the additive inverse of n; in other words, the additive inverse of n is $-n$. The same goes for modular arithmetic: For each value x that you add modularly, there is another value that acts as an additive inverse that will take the ciphertext input and output the plaintext value.

The additive inverse for mod 10 addition will be the number that, when added to the original offset number, produce a 0—the remainder when dividing the sum by 10. So, for our example using 7 as the offset (the number to which plaintext is added mod 10), the additive inverse will be 3. Checking the preceding table, the ciphertext digits 139, when added to 3 mod 10, result in the plaintext 462:

```
(1 + 3) mod 10 = 4

(3 + 3) mod 10 = 6

(9 + 3) mod 10 = 2
```

You can logically prove this to yourself by considering that if you were to use an alphabetic offset of x, an additional offset of $(26-x)$ would put you back to where you started—with unencrypted plaintext.

Multiplicative Inverse

There is also a notion of a multiplicative inverse for regular multiplication: The value that produces 1 when multiplied by some other value x is the multiplicative inverse of x. If you were to take some number y and multiply it by x, multiplying it again by $1/x$ will return the original number y.

Likewise, there is a notion of a modular multiplicative inverse. If you were to multiply a value x by some value y mod n, you would get a result (let us call it z). The multiplicative inverse of x is the value by which you would have to multiply z by mod n to return the original value, x.

Not all number of modular multiplicative inverses, relative to some particular modulus. This should be moderately obvious from our previous example, using mod 10 multiplication. Numbers that can be used to create simple encrypting functions, like 1, 3, 7, and 9, produce a unique output value for each input value. These numbers have multiplicative inverses, because if there is a way to map input values uniquely to output values, there will be another way to map the output values uniquely to input values. For mod 10 multiplication, 7 and 3 are each other's multiplicative inverses; 1 and 9 serve as their own multiplicative inverses. To decrypt a ciphertext that was generated by multiplying by 7 mod 10 as in the preceding example, you would simply mutiply the ciphertext by 3 mod 10:

```
(8 * 3) mod 10 = 4

(2 * 3) mod 10 = 6

(4 * 3) mod 10 = 2
```

However, other numbers, like 2, 4, 5, 6, and 8, do not have multiplicative inverses mod 10. When you multiply any digit by 5, for example, the result will either be 0 or 5. Once that function has been performed, there is no way to reverse it—you cannot tell if the function took as its input 1, 3, 5, 7, or 9 to produce an output of 5. Some numbers will have multiplicative inverses and will produce usable encryption functions (though not necessarily very strong or good ones), because they are relatively prime to the modulus being used, as discussed next.

Relative Primeness

A prime number is a number that can be evenly divided only by itself or by 1. We will see more of primes later. However, a number can also be relatively prime to some other number. This means that the two numbers (neither of which is necessarily a prime number) do not share any factors in common other than 1. Continuing with our mod 10 arithmetic examples, the number 10 contains four factors: 1, 2, 5,

10. This means that these numbers can be used to "build" 10 through multiplication:

```
1 * 10 = 10

2 * 5 = 10
```

To figure out which of the numbers between 1 and 9 are relatively prime to 10, we can consider each individually:

- 1: Factors include only 1; does not share any other factors with 10.
- 2: Factors include 1 and 2; shares 2 with 10.
- 3: Factors include 1 and 3; does not share any other factors with 10.
- 4: Factors include 1, 2, and 4; shares 2 with 10.
- 5: Factors include 1 and 5; shares 5 with 10.
- 6: Factors include 1, 2, 3, and 6; shares 2 with 10.
- 7: Factors include 1 and 7; does not share any other factors with 10.
- 8: Factors include 1, 2, 4, and 8; shares 2 with 10.
- 9: Factors include 1, 3, and 9; does not share any other factors with 10.
- 0: Can include any integer as a factor, so thus shares 2 and 5 with 10.

It is interesting to cryptographers that if a number is relatively prime to the modulus, it can be used to create a cipher. If a number is not relatively prime to the modulus, it will not have a multiplicative inverse and as a result it cannot be used to create a cipher—it will not create a one-to-one mapping from the input characters to the output characters.

 Remember, just because a number with a multiplicative inverse relative to some modulus *can* generate a cipher does not mean that the cipher is actually any good—it just means that function behaves as an encrypting function.

By now it should be reasonably obvious that if you do multiplication modulo some number n, and you want to have lots of different options for creating a function that maps inputs to outputs uniquely, you should choose a modulus n that will be relatively prime to as many different numbers as possible. In other words, choosing a prime number—a number that is evenly divisible only by itself and 1—provides a modulus that will be relatively prime to every number between itself and 1.

Calculating Totients

It turns out that mathematicians and cryptographers have given a name to the quantity that expresses how many integers there are that are less than and at the same time relatively prime to some given number, n. (This value will turn out to have great relevance to public key encryption, but it will not be immediately apparent, so be patient.) The *totient*, or total quotient, function for a prime number n is equal to all the integers from 0 to $(n-1)$. In other words, the totient for a prime n is equal to $(n-1)$. You can prove this by creating a modular multiplication table for some small prime number—for example, 7 or 11. You will find that all the numbers from 1 to 6 (for 7) or from 1 to 10 (for 11) will have modular multiplicative inverses.

It is also interesting to determine how many of the numbers between 1 and n are relatively prime to n when n is not a prime. Consider a value n that is actually the product of two primes, p and q:

```
n = p * q
```

This is exactly the case for $n = 10$, with a $p = 2$ and a $q = 5$. The totient of 10, as we have determined from actually checking each integer from 0 to 9, is 4. (There are four numbers with multiplicative inverses, 1, 3, 7, and 9.) How would the totient of some larger value be determined?

The answer is to think about how many integers would be excluded, based on the fact that they share a common factor with the modulus n. Consider the case for $n = 10$ again.

```
n = 10

p = 2

q = 5

n = p * q

10 = 2 * 5
```

How many integers less than 10 are divisible by 2? There are five of
them: 0, 2, 4, 6, and 8. How many integers less than 10 are divisible
by 5? There are two of them: 0 and 5. That totals to 7, but that also
counts 0 two times. Calculating the number of integers less than 10
that share a factor with 10 can be represented by the following
equation:

```
2 + 5 - 1
```

For a modulus n that is the product of two primes, p and q, the equation to calculate the number of integers less than n that share factors
with n can be generalized to

```
p + q - 1
```

Since there are a total of n integers that are less than n (0, 1, 2 … n-1), and
since n is equal to the product of p and q, you can calculate the totient of
n by subtracting the number of integers that share factors with n from
the total number of integers less than n (which is equal to $p*q$):

```
totient(n) = (p * q) - (p + q - 1)
```

Factor this equation to get a simpler result:

```
totient(n) = (p - 1) * (q - 1)
```

Understand that the totient function is simply a count of the number of integers that have multiplicative inverses when multiplied
modulo n. It becomes very useful to know how to determine the

totient of a particular number because of the way this function relates to modular exponentiation, and the way they both can be used to create a one-way function.

Modular Exponentiation

Exponentiation is the arithmetic function of raising a value to a power; for example, 10 raised to the power of 2 (10^2) is equal to 10 multiplied by itself twice, or 100. Likewise, 2 raised to the power of 10 (2^{10}) is 2 multiplied by itself 10 times, or 1,024. Modular exponentiation is much like any other modular function. You perform the arithmetic function, in this case exponentiation, and then divide the result by the modulus. This means that 10^2 mod 2 is equal to 0 (there is no remainder when dividing 2 into 100), while 2^{10} mod 10 is equal to 4 (10 divided into 1,024 leaves a remainder of 4).

Figure A.4 shows what happens when you do modular exponentiation on values from 0 to 9. The values down the left side of the table represent x, the numbers across the top represent y, and the values in the table represent xy mod 10. Just as with our other modular arithmetic tables, it appears that some values will produce a valid cipher and some will not. For example, raising values to the power of 1 and then finding their value mod 10 produces a 1 to 1 mapping, but the values of the "cipher" are identical to the plaintext. On the other hand, raising values to the power of 7 and then taking their value mod 10 does produce a valid cipher.

This type of cipher appears to have more value for encryption because there does not seem to be a quickly intuitive way to come up with an inverse for this modular exponentiation. However, there is an inverse that we can use to reverse the function. It turns out that the totient function (which did not seem all that relevant before) will help here, because raising a value x to a power y, and then taking the result modulo n (x^y mod n) will produce the same result as raising the same value x to value of y modulo the totient of n, modulo n ($x^{y \bmod (\text{totient}(n))}$ mod n).

The totient function has another interesting feature. The totient of 10 is 4; the values of the modular exponentiation table cycle repeti-

X/Y	0	1	2	3	4	5	6	7	8	9
0		0	0	0	0	0	0	0	0	0
1	1	1	1	1	1	1	1	1	1	1
2	1	2	4	6	8	6	2	8	6	2
3	1	3	9	7	1	3	9	7	1	3
4	1	4	6	4	6	4	6	4	6	4
5	1	5	5	5	5	5	5	5	5	5
6	1	6	6	6	6	6	6	6	6	6
7	1	7	9	3	1	7	9	3	1	7
8	1	8	4	2	6	8	4	2	6	8
9	1	9	1	9	1	9	1	9	1	9

Figure A.4   The exponentiation table for mod 10.

tively. The values for exponentiation mod 1 are the same as for exponentiation mod 5; the values for exponentiation mod 3 are the same as for exponentiation mod 7; and so on. It turns out to be a value of the totient function that it defines the length of the cycle of such permutations. If the totient is equal to 4, skipping ahead four columns in the modular exponentiation table will show a repeat of the current column.

To illustrate, take $x = 3$, $y = 7$, $n = 10$.

$x^y \bmod n$

$3^7 \bmod 10$

```
2187 mod 10 = 7
```

Now, consider the value calculated from the totient; given that there are 4 values less than 10 that are relatively prime to it (the value of totient(10) is equal to 4):

$$x^{(y \bmod (\texttt{totient}(n)))} \bmod n$$

$$3^{7 \bmod (\texttt{totient}(10))} \bmod 10$$

$$37^{\bmod 4} \bmod 10$$

$$3^3 \bmod 10$$

$$27 \bmod 10 = 7$$

Finally, consider what happens when we happen to choose a y and an n such that y leaves a remainder of 1 when divided into the totient of n; in other words:

```
y = 1 mod totient(n)
```

The implication here, based on what we discovered about the value of $x^y \bmod n$ being the same as $x^{y \bmod (\text{totient}(n))} \bmod n$, is that when $y \bmod (\text{totient}(n)$ is equal to 1, then x^y becomes equal to x, and $x^y \bmod n$ is simply equal to $x \bmod n$.

What this means is that now we have a simple tool for quickly calculating $x^y \bmod n$ when we know that y leaves a remainder of 1 when divided by the totient of n.

Applying It All to Public Key Encryption

Now, it becomes clearer why we chose the values for public and private keys that we did. To review, generating a key requires the choice of the following values:

```
p and q   Two large prime numbers chosen at random
```

```
n          The product of p and q

e          A value relatively prime to (p − 1)(q − 1)

d          The multiplicative inverse of e
```

The public key is simply the values n and e; the private key is the values of n and d. The product of e and d (ed) becomes the equivalent of the value we were talking about above, y. In particular, by choosing e (and d) to be relatively prime to $(p − 1)(q − 1)$ you can guarantee that the product ed behaves like the value y discussed previously; in other words, we can get the value of x^{ed} mod n to be equal to x mod n.

This happens to be a very good thing, because now we can encrypt and decrypt using the RSA algorithm:

- The encrypting entity takes a piece of the message (m).
- The value m is raised to the public key value e.
- The encryptor calculates the result mod n.

In other words,

```
cyphertext = m^e mod n
```

Now, the recipient of the encrypted text, knows d—which is the value to which m has to be raised now—can decrypt the cyphertext:

- The recipient takes the cyphertext and raises it to the power of d.
- Take that value (m^{ed}) mod n.

The result will equal the original plaintext.

B

Guide to Internet Encryption Resources

The Internet is probably the best resource for up-to-the-second information about many topics, including encryption and cryptography. If you are looking for some information about a particular topic, your best bet is to do a search on your favorite on-line search engine. Use this appendix for more pointers to sites that offer general information, for pointers to other resources, and for pointers to standards bodies related to encryption. These URLs represent a selection of some web sites that you can use as stepping-off points for your Internet explorations. There are many other good sources of information, but these will help you get started.

Encryption Web Sites

Trusted Information Systems Worldwide Survey of Cryptography Products	*http://www.tis.com/research/crypto/crypt_surv.html*
Electronic Privacy Information Center (EPIC)	*http://epic.org/*
National Computer Security Association (NSCA)	*http://www.ncsa.com/*
RSA Data Security Inc.	*http://www.rsa.com*
Pretty Good Privacy, Inc.	*http://www.pgp.com*
Internet Security Systems, Inc. (signup for security mailing lists)	*http://www.iss.net/vd/maillist.html*
Microsoft Corporation	*http://www.microsoft.com*
Netscape Communications Corporation	*http://home.netscape.com*

Usenet Newsgroups

sci.crypt	Discussion of data encryption and decryption
sci.crypt.research	Moderated discussion of topics in cryptography, cryptanalysis, and related issues
talk.politics.crypto	Discussion of politics and cryptography

C

Selected RFCs on Internet Security

The Internet is *the* open network written about throughout this book. Understanding Internet standards and how other types of standards fit into the Internet is an important part of understanding how to securely communicate across the Internet, intranets, or extranets. This appendix includes a selection of four RFCs (Requests for Comment), the official documentation of most Internet standards. While an RFC does not necessarily document a standard, all standards are documented in RFCs. These four documents should aid the reader in understanding how Internet architects, engineers, and computer scientists working with the Internet Engineering Task Force (IETF) are approaching the issues of Internet security. These RFCs include

RFC 1636: *Report of IAB Workshop on Security in the Internet Architecture February 8-10, 1994.* This is an informational report on a meeting where Internet security was discussed.

RFC 1704: *On Internet Authentication.* This is an informational report discussing issues and strategies relating to authentication of entities over the Internet.

RFC 1825: *Security Architecture for the Internet Protocol.* This is a standards-track report that explains the different mechanisms for security as implemented in the Internet Protocol, both version 4 and version 6.

RFC 1984: *IAB and IESG Statement on Cryptographic Technology and the Internet.* This informational report, issued by the Internet Architecture Board (IAB) and the Internet Engineering Steering Group (IESG), outlines concerns about access to cryptographic technologies and the effect of political limitations to that access.

If you have any interest at all in technical matters pertaining to the Internet, you are strongly urged to go to these source documents, which contain much of interest technically as well as historically. All RFCs (and other IETF workgroup documents) can be retrieved from the InterNIC site:

```
http://ds.internic.net/
```

The RFC style and format, as demonstrated in the documents included here, provide a reasonably straightforward platform for the explanation of sometimes very complicated material. Of even more importance, the reader should note that all modern RFCs include a section titled "Security Considerations," which should give some indication of how important security considerations are to the Internet designers.

Network Working Group   R. Braden
Request for Comments: 1636   ISI
Category: Informational   D. Clark
                           MIT Laboratory for Computer Science
                                      S. Crocker
                         Trusted Information Systems, Inc.
                                      C. Huitema
                                INRIA, IAB Chair
                                     June 1994

                     Report of IAB Workshop on

                 Security in the Internet Architecture

                       February 8-10, 1994

Status of this Memo

Abstract

   This document is a report on an Internet architecture workshop,
   initiated by the IAB and held at USC Information Sciences Institute
   on February 8-10, 1994. This workshop generally focused on security
   issues in the Internet architecture.

   This document should be regarded as a set of working notes containing
   ideas about security that were developed by Internet experts in a
   broad spectrum of areas, including routing, mobility, realtime
   service, and provider requirements, as well as security. It contains
   some significant diversity of opinions on some important issues.
   This memo is offered as one input in the process of developing viable
   security mechanisms and procedures for the Internet.

Table of Contents

1. INTRODUCTION

The Internet Architecture Board (IAB) holds occasional workshops designed to consider long-term issues and strategies for the Internet, and to suggest future directions for the Internet architecture. This long-term planning function of the IAB is complementary to the ongoing engineering efforts performed by working groups of the Internet Engineering Task Force (IETF), under the leadership of the Internet Engineering Steering Group (IESG) and area directorates.

An IAB-initiated workshop on the role of security in the Internet Architecture was held on February 8-10, 1994 at the Information Sciences Institute of the University of Southern California, in

Marina del Rey, California. This RFC reports the results of the
workshop.

In addition to the IAB members, attendees at this meeting included
the IESG Area Directors for the relevant areas (Internet, Transport,
Security, and IPng) and a group of 15 other experts in the following
areas: IPng, routing, mobility, realtime service, and security (see
Appendix for a list of attendees). The IAB explicitly tried to
balance the number of attendees from each area of expertise.
Logistics limited the attendance to about 30, which unfortunately
meant that many highly qualified experts were omitted from the
invitation list.

In summary, the objectives of this workshop were (1) to explore the
interconnections between security and the rest of the Internet
architecture, and (2) to develop recommendations for the Internet
community on future directions with respect to security. These
objectives arose from a conviction in the IAB that the two most
important problem areas for the Internet architecture are scaling and
security. While the scaling problems have led to a flood of
activities on IPng, there has been less effort devoted to security.

Although some came to the workshop eager to discuss short-term
security issues in the Internet, the workshop program was designed to
focus more on long-term issues and broad principles. Thus, the
meeting began with the following ground rule: valid topics of
discussion should involve both security and at least one from the
list: (a) routing (unicast and multicast), (b) mobility, and (c)
realtime service. As a basis for initial discussion, the invitees
met via email to generate a set of scenarios (see Appendix)
satisfying this ground rule.

The 30 attendees were divided into three "breakout" groups, with each
group including experts in all the areas. The meeting was then
structured as plenary meetings alternating with parallel breakout
group sessions (see the agenda in Appendix). On the third day, the
groups produced text summarizing the results of their discussions.
This memo is composed of that text, somewhat rearranged and edited
into a single document.

The meeting process determined the character of this document. It
should be regarded as a set of working notes produced by mostly-
autonomous groups, containing some diversity of opinions as well as
duplication of ideas. It is not the output of the "security
community", but instead represents ideas about security developed by
a broad spectrum of Internet experts. It is offered as a step in a
process of developing viable security mechanisms and procedures for
the Internet.

2. OVERVIEW

2.1 Strategic and Political Issues

Despite the workshop emphasis on architectural issues, there was considerable discussion of the real-politik of security.

For a number of years, the IETF, with IAB backing, has worked on developing PEM, which provides email security with a great deal of functionality. A question was repeatedly raised at the workshop: why has user acceptance of PEM been slow? A number of answers to this question were suggested.

(a) High-quality implementations have been slow in coming.

(b) The use of a patented technology, the RSA algorithm, violates social conventions of the Internet.

(c) Export restrictions dampen vendor enthusiasm.

(d) PEM currently depends upon a certificate hierarchy for its names, and certificates form a new and complex name space. There is no organizational infrastructure in place for creating and managing this name space.

(e) There is no directory infrastructure available for looking up certificates.

     The decision to use X.500 has been a complete failure, due to the slow deployment of X.500 in the Internet. Because of UDP packet size restrictions, it is not currently feasible to store certificates in the DNS, even if the DNS were expanded to hold records for individual email users.

It seems probable that more than one, and possibly all, of these reasons are at work to discourage PEM adoption.

The baleful comment about eating: "Everything I enjoy is either immoral, illegal, or fattening" seems to apply to the cryptography technology that is required for Internet security.

2.2 Security Issues

Almost everyone agrees that the Internet needs more and better security. However, that may mean different things to different people. Four top-level requirements for Internet security were identified: end-to-end security, end-system security, secure QOS, and secure network infrastructure.

A.   End-to-End Security

One requirement is to support confidentiality, authentication
and integrity for end-to-end communications. These security
services are best provided on an end-to-end basis, in order
to minimize the number of network components that users must
trust. Here the "end" may be the end system itself, or a
proxy (e.g., a firewall) acting on behalf of an end system.

For point-to-point applications, the workshop felt that
existing security techniques are well suited to support
confidentiality, authentication and integrity services
efficiently. These existing techniques include symmetric
encryption applied on an end-to-end basis, message digest
functions, and key management algorithms. Current work in
these areas in the IETF include the PEM and Common
Authentication Technologies working groups.

The group favored a strategic direction for coping with
export restrictions: separate authentication from privacy
(i.e., confidentiality). This will allow work to proceed on
authentication for the Internet, despite government
restrictions on export of privacy technology. Conversely, it
will allow easy deployment of privacy without authentication,
where this is appropriate.

The workshop explored the implications of multicasting for
end-to-end security. Some of the unicast security techniques
can be applied directly to multicast applications, while
others must be modified. Section 6.2 contains the results of
these discussions; in summary, the conclusions were:

a)   Existing technology is adequate to support
      confidentiality, authentication, and integrity at the
      level of an entire multicast group. Supporting
      authentication and integrity at the level of an
      individual multicast source is performance-limited and
      will require technology advances.

b)   End-to-end controls should be based on end system or
      user identifiers, not low level identifiers or locator
      information. This requirement should spawn engineering
      work which consists of applying known key distribution

and cryptographic techniques.

B.   End-System Security

Every host has its own security defenses, but the strength of
these defenses depends upon the care that is taken in
administering them. Careful host security administration
means plugging security holes in the kernel and applications
as well as enforcing discipline on users to set good (hard to
crack) passwords.

Good security administration is labor-intensive, and
therefore organizations often find it difficult to maintain
the security of a large number of internal machines. To
protect their machines from outside subversion, organizations
often erect an outer security wall or "perimeter". Machines
inside the perimeter communicate with the rest of the
Internet only through a small set of carefully managed
machines called "firewalls". Firewalls may operate at the
application layer, in which case they are application relays,
or at the IP layer, in which case they are firewall routers.

The workshop spent considerable time on the architecture of
firewall routers. The results are contained in Section 3.

C.   Secure QOS

The Internet is being extended to provide quality-of-service
capabilities; this is the topic called "realtime service" in
the workshop. These extensions raise a new set of security
issues for the architecture, to assure that users are not
allowed to attach to resources they are not authorized to
use, both to prevent theft of resources and to prevent denial
of service due to unauthorized traffic. The resources to be
protected include link shares, service classes or queues,
multicast trees, and so on. These resources are used as
virtual channels within the network, where each virtual
channel is intended to be used by a particular subset or
"class" of packets.

Secure QOS, i.e., protection against improper virtual channel
usage, is a form of access control mechanism. In general it
will be based on some form of state establishment (setup)
that defines authorized "classes". This setup may be done
via management configuration (typically in advance and for
aggregates of users), or it may be done dynamically via
control information in packets or special messages (typically
at the time of use by the source or receiver(s) of the

flow/data). In addition to state establishment, some form of authentication will be needed to assure that successive packets belong to the established class. The general case to be solved is the multicast group, since in general the multicast problem includes the two-party case as a subset. The workshop developed an approach to the secure QOS problem, which appears in Section 4 below.

D.   Secure Network Infrastructure

Network operation depends upon the management and control protocols used to configure and operate the network infrastructure, including routers and DNS servers. An attack on the network infrastructure may cause denial-of-service from the user viewpoint, but from the network operators' viewpoint, security from attack requires authentication and integrity for network control and management messages.

Securing the routing protocols seems to be a straightforward engineering task. The workshop concluded the following.

a)   All routing information exchanges should be authenticated between neighboring routers.

b)   The sources of all route information should be authenticated.

c)   Although authenticating the authority of an injector of route information is feasible, authentication of operations on that routing information (e.g., aggregation) requires further consideration.

Securing router management protocols (e.g., SNMP, Telnet, TFTP) is urgent, because of the currently active threats. Fortunately, the design task should be a straightforward application of existing authentication mechanisms.

Securing DNS is an important issue, but it did not receive much attention at the workshop.

2.3   DNS Names for Certificates

As noted in Section 2.1, work on PEM has assumed the use of X.509 distinguished names as the basis for issuing certificates, with public-key encryption. The most controversial discussion at the workshop concerned the possibility of using DNS (i.e., domain) names instead of X.509 distinguished names as (at least) an interim basis for Internet security.

The argument in favor of DNS names is that they are simple and
well understood in the Internet world. It is easy for a computer
operating in the Internet to be identified this way, and users who
receive email on such machines already have DNS mailbox names. In
contrast, introducing X.509 distinguished names for security will
add a new layer of names. Most importantly, there is an existing
administrative model for assigning DNS names. There is no
administrative infrastructure for assigning X.509 distinguished
names, and generating them may be too complex for early
acceptance. The advocates of DNS names for certificates hope that
using DNS names would encourage the widespread use of security in
the Internet. It is expected that DNS names can be replaced later
by a more capable naming mechanism such as X.509-based
certificates.

The basic argument against DNS names as a basis for security is
that they are too "weak". Their use may lead to confusion in many
instances, and this confusion can only grow as more organizations
and individuals attach to the Internet. Some commercial email
systems employ numeric mailbox names, and in many organizations
there are uncertainties such as whether "bumber@foo.edu" belongs
to Bill Umber or Tom Bumber. While it is feasible to make DNS
names more descriptive, there is a concern that the existing
infrastructure, with millions of short, non-descriptive names,
will be an impediment to adoption of more descriptive names.

It was noted that the question of what name space to use for
certificates is independent of the problem of building an
infrastructure for retrieving those names. Because of UDP packet
size restrictions, it would not be feasible to store certificates
in the DNS without significant changes, even if the DNS were
expanded to hold records for individual email users.

The group was unable to reach a consensus on the issue of using
DNS names for security; further discussion in the Internet
community is needed.

3. FIREWALL ARCHITECTURE

   3.1 Introduction

      A firewall may be used to isolate a specific connected segment of
      Internet topology. When such a segment has multiple links to the
      rest of the Internet, coordinated firewall machines are required
      on all the links.

      Firewalls may be implemented at different layers in the protocol
      stack. They are most commonly implemented at the application
      layer by forwarding (application) gateways, or at the IP
      (Internet) layer by filtering routers. Section 3.2 discusses
      application gateways. Section 3.3 concerns Internet-layer
      firewalls, which filter IP datagrams entering or leaving a
      security perimeter.

      The general architectural model for a firewall should separate
      policy, i.e., determining whether or not the requester of a
      service should be granted access to that service, from control,
      i.e., limiting access to resources to those who have been granted
      access.

      3.1.1 The Use for Firewalls

         Firewalls are a very emotional topic in the Internet community.
         Some community members feel the firewall concept is very
         powerful because firewalls aggregate security functions in a
         single place, simplifying management, installation and
         configuration. Others feel that firewalls are damaging for the
         same reason: they provide "a hard, crunchy outside with a soft
         chewy center", i.e., firewalls foster a false sense of
         security, leading to lax security within the firewall
         perimeter. They observe that much of the "computer crime" in
         corporate environments is perpetrated by insiders, immune to
         the perimeter defense strategy. Firewall advocates counter
         that firewalls are important as an additional safeguard; they
         should not be regarded as a substitute for careful security
         management within the perimeter. Firewall detractors are also
         concerned about the difficulty of using firewalls, requiring
         multiple logins and other out-of-band mechanisms, and their
         interference with the usability and vitality of the Internet.

         However, firewalls are a fact of life in the Internet today.
         They have been constructed for pragmatic reasons by
         organizations interested in a higher level of security than may
         be possible without them. This section will try to outline
         some of the advantages and disadvantages of firewalls, and some

instances where they are useful.

Consider a large organization of thousands of hosts. If every host is allowed to communicate directly with the outside world, attackers will attempt to penetrate the organization by finding the weakest host in the organization, breaching its defenses, and then using the resources of that host to extend the penetration further within the organization. In some sense, firewalls are not so much a solution to a security problem as they are a reaction to a more basic software engineering/administration problem: configuring a large number of host systems for good security. If this more basic problem could be solved, firewalls would generally be unnecessary.

It is interesting to consider the effect that implementing a firewall has upon various individuals in the organization. Consider first the effect upon an organization's most secure host. This host basically receives little or no extra protection, because its own perimeter defenses are as strong or stronger than the firewall. In addition, the firewall will probably reduce the connectivity available to this host, as well as the reliability of the communications path to the outside world, resulting in inconvenience to the user(s) of this host. From this (most secure) user's point of view, the firewall is a loss.

On the other hand, a host with poor security can "hide" behind the firewall. In exchange for a more limited ability to communicate with the outside world, this host can benefit from the higher level of security provided by the firewall, which is assumed to be based upon the best security available in the entire organization. If this host only wants to communicate with other hosts inside the organization, the outside communications limitations imposed by the firewall may not even be noticed. From this host's viewpoint, better security has been gained at little or no cost.

Finally, consider the point of view of the organization as a whole. A firewall allows the extension of the best security in the organization across the whole organization. This is a benefit (except in the case where all host perimeter defenses in the organization are equal). Centralized access control also becomes possible, which may be either a benefit or a cost, depending upon the organization. The "secure" hosts within the organization may perceive a loss, while the "unsecure" hosts receive a benefit. The cost/benefit ratio to the organization as a whole thus depends upon the relative numbers of "secure" and "unsecure" hosts in the organization.

Consider some cases where firewalls do not make sense. An
individual can be thought of as an organization of one host.
The security of all the host(s) is thus (trivially) identical,
and by definition the best available to the organization. In
this case the choice of firewall is simple. Does this
individual wish to communicate with the outside or not? If
not, then the "perfect" firewall is implemented (by complete
disconnection). If yes, then the host perimeter will be the
same as the firewall perimeter, so a firewall becomes
unnecessary.

Another interesting case is an organization that consists of
individuals with few shared interests. This might be the case
of a service provider that sells public access to the network.
An unrelated community of subscribers should probably be
considered as individuals, rather than an organization.
Firewalls for the whole organization may make little sense in
this case.

To summarize, the benefit of a firewall depends upon the nature
of the organization it protects. A firewall can be used to
extend the best available protection within the organization
across the entire organization, and thus be of benefit to large
organizations with large numbers of poorly administered hosts.
A firewall may produce little or no perceived benefit, however,
to the individuals within an organization who have strong host
perimeters already.

3.2 Application-Layer Firewalls

An application-layer firewall can be represented by the following
diagram.

        C <---> F <---> S

Here the requesting client C opens its transport connection to the
firewall F rather than directly to the desired server S. One
mechanism for redirecting C's request to F's IP address rather
than S's could be based on the DNS. When C attempts to resolve
S's name, its DNS lookup would return a "service redirection"
record (analogous to an MX record) for S. The service redirection
record would return the IP address of F.

C enters some authentication conversation to identify itself to F,
and specifies its intention to request a specific service from S.
F then decides if C is authorized to invoke this service. If C is
authorized, F initiates a transport layer connection to S and
begins the operation, passing requests and responses between C and S.

A major advantage of this scenario over an IP-layer firewall is
that raw IP datagrams are never passed through the firewall.
Because the firewall operates at the application layer, it has the
opportunity to handle and verify all data passing through it, and
it may be more secure against illicit rendezvous attacks (see
below).

Application layer firewalls also have important disadvantages.
For full benefit, an application level firewall must be coded
specifically for each application. This severely limits the
deployment of new applications. The firewall also represents a
new point of failure; if it ceases to be reachable, the
application fails. Application layer firewalls also may affect
performance more than IP-layer firewalls, depending on specific
mechanisms in use.

3.3   IP-Layer Firewalls

Our model of an IP-layer firewall is a multi-ported IP router that
applies a set of rules to each incoming IP datagram, to decide
whether it will be forwarded. It is said to "filter" IP
datagrams, based on information available in the packet headers.

A firewall router generally has a set of filtering rules, each of
which specifies a "packet profile" and an "action". The packet
profile specifies values for particular header fields, e.g.,
source and destination IP address, protocol number, and other
suitable source and destination identifying information (for
instance, port numbers). The set of possible information that may
be used to match packets is called an "association". The exact
nature of an association is an open issue.

The high-speed datagram forwarding path in the firewall processes
every arriving packet against all the packet profiles of all
active rules, and when a profile matches, it applies the
corresponding action. Typical actions may include forwarding,
dropping, sending a failure response, or logging for exception
tracking. There may be a default rule for use when no other rule
matches, which would probably specify a drop action.

In addition to the packet profile, some firewalls may also use
some cryptographic information to authenticate the packet, as
described below in section 3.3.2.

3.3.1 Policy Control Level

This section presents a model for the control of a firewall
router, with some examples of specific mechanisms that might be
used.

1.   A client C attempts to access a service S. (Client here
      can mean either a person or a process - that also is an
      issue to be resolved.)

2.   The initiation of access to that service may result in an
      attempt to cross one or more boundaries of protection via
      firewall router(s).

3.   The policy control level sets filters in the firewall
      router(s), to permit or deny that attempt.

The policy control level consists of two distinct functions,
authentication and authorization. Authentication is the
function of verifying the claimed identity of a user. The
authentication function should be distributed across the
Internet, so that a user in one organization can be
authenticated to another organization. Once a user is
authenticated, it is then the job of the authorization service
local to the resource being requested to determine if that user
is authorized to access that resource. If authorization is
granted, the filter in the firewall can be updated to permit
that access.

As an aid to understanding the issues, we introduce a
particular detailed mechanism. We emphasize that this
mechanism is intended only as an illustrative example; actual
engineering of the mechanism will no doubt lead to many
changes. Our mechanism is illustrated by the following sketch.
Here a user wishes to connect from a computer C behind firewall
F1, to a server S behind firewall F2. A1 is a particular
authentication server and Z1 is a particular authorization
server.

C attempts to initiate its conversation by sending an initial
packet to S. C uses a normal DNS lookup to resolve S's name,
and uses normal IP routing mechanisms. C's packet reaches

firewall router F1, which rejects the packet because it does not match any acceptable packet profile. F1 returns an "Authentication Required" error indication to C, including a list of authentication/authorization servers that F1 trusts. This indication might be a new type of ICMP Destination Unreachable packet, or some other mechanism for communicating with C.

When C receives the error indication, authenticates itself with A1, one of the authentication servers listed in the error indication, after validating A1's identity. C then requests authorization from server Z1 (using a ticket provided by A1), informs Z1 of the application it wishes to perform, and provides a profile for the packets it wishes to pass through F1. Z1 then performs an authorization function to decide whether to allow C to penetrate F1. If C is to be allowed, Z1 then informs the firewall F1 to allow packets matching the packet profile to pass through the firewall F1.

After C's packets penetrate F1, they may again be rejected by a second firewall F2. C could perform the same procedures with authentication server A2 and authorization server Z2, which F2 trusts. This is illustrated by the following schematic diagram of the sequence of events.

```
 ----------+--------+--------+------------+------------+----
|    C     |   A1   |   Z1   |     F1     |     F2     | S
 ----------+--------+--------+------------+------------+----
| Sends pkt|        |        |            |            |
| to S  ----------------------->Intercept;|            |
|          |        |        | requires   |            |
|          |        |        |authenticat'n            |
|  <------------------------------         |            |
|Auth'cate |        |        |            |            |
| C to A1 ---->     |        |            |            |
|          |Provide |        |            |            |
|  <------- ticket| |        |            |            |
| Request  |        |        |            |            |
|authoriz'n|        |        |            |            |
|  ------------------> Is C|  |            |            |
|          |        |allowed?|            |            |
|          |        |  OK --------->      |            |
|Resend    |        |        | Set filter |            |
| first pkt|        |        |            |            |
| to S ------------------------->(OK)------>Intercept; |
|          |        |        |            | requires   |
|          |        |        |            |authenticat'n
|  <-------------------------------------------         |
| (Repeat  |        |        |            |            |
|procedure |        |        |            |            |
with A2,Z2)|        |        |            |            |
|  ...     |        |        |            |            |
|Resend    |        |        |            |            |
| first pkt|        |        |            |            |
|  ----------------------------->(OK)--------(OK)------>
|          |        |        |            |            |
 ----------+--------+--------+------------+------------+----
```

Again, we emphasize that this is only intended as a partial
sketch of one possible mechanism. It omits some significant
issues, including the possibility of asymmetric routes (see
3.3.3 below), and the possibility that the profiles may be
different in the two directions between C and S.

We could imagine generalizing this to an arbitrary sequence of
firewalls. However, security requires that each of the
firewalls be able to verify that data packets actually come
from C. This packet authentication problem, which is discussed
in the next section, could be extremely difficult if the data
must traverse more than one or possibly two firewalls in
sequence.

A firewall router may require re-authentication because:

*   it has been added to the path by a routing change, or

*   it has timed out the profile entry, or

*   it has been newly re-activated, perhaps after a crash that lost its list of acceptable profiles.

If C contacts authentication and authorization servers that S trusts, C may utilize tickets given it by these servers when initiating its use of S, and avoid re-authenticating itself to S.

Although the authentication server A1 and the authorization server Z1 are conceptually separate, they may run on the same computer or router or even be separate aspects of a single program. The protocol that C speaks to an An, the protocol that C speaks to a Zn, and the protocol that Zn speaks to Fn are not specified in these notes. The authentication mechanism used with An and the packet profile required by a firewall Fn are considered matters of policy.

3.3.2 Source Authentication

We next consider how to protect against spoofing the IP source address, i.e., injecting packets that are alleged from come from C but do not. There are three classes of mechanisms to prevent such spoofing of IP-level firewalls. The mechanisms outlined here are also discussed in Section 4.3 below.

o   Packet Profile Only

    The lowest level of security consists of allowing the IP-layer firewall to filter packets purely on the basis of the packet profile. This is essentially the approach used by filtering routers today, with the addition of (1) authentication and authorization servers to control the filtering profiles, and (2) the automatic "Authentication Required" notification mechanism. This approach provides almost no security; it does not prevent other computers from spoofing packets that appear to be transmitted by C, or from taking over C's transport level connection to S.

o   Sealed Packets

    In the second level of security, each packet is "sealed" with a secure hash algorithm. An authentication server Ai chooses a secret and shares it with the source host S and also with the authorization server Zi, which shares the secret with the firewall Fi. Every packet that C transmits contains a hash value that depends upon both the contents of the packet and the secret value. The firewall Fi can compute the same hash function and verify that the packet was originated by a computer that knew the shared secret.

This approach does raise issues of how much C trusts Zi and Fi. Since they know C's secret, Zi or Fi could spoof C. If C does not trust all Z's and F's in its path, a stronger mechanism (see below) is needed.

A more difficult problem arises in authenticating C's packets when more than one firewall lies in the path. Carrying a separate seal for each firewall that is penetrated would be costly in terms of packet size. On the other hand, in order to use a single seal, all the firewalls would have to cooperate, and this might require a much more complex mechanism than the one sketched in the previous section. Morever, it may require mutual trust among all of the authentication servers Ai and authorization servers Zi; any of these servers could undermine all the others. Another possibility to be investigated is to use hop-by-hop rather than end-to-end authentication of C's packets. That is, each firewall would substitute into the packet the hash needed by the next firewall.

Multi-firewall source authentication is a difficult problem that needs more investigation.

o   Packet Signatures

In the third level of security, each packet is "signed" using a public/private key algorithm. C shares its public key with Zn, which shares it with Fn. In this scenario, C can safely use one pair of keys for all authorization servers and firewalls. No authorization server or firewall can spoof C because they cannot sign packets correctly.

Although packet signing gives a much higher level of security, it requires public key algorithms that are patented and currently very expensive to compute; their time must be added to that for the hash algorithm. Also, signing the hash generally makes it larger.

3.3.3 Other Firewall Issues

o   Performance

      An Internet-layer firewall has the advantage of generality
      and flexibility. However, filtering introduces a
      potential performance problem. Performance may depend
      upon the number and position of the packet fields used for
      filtering, and upon the number of rules against which a
      packet has to be matched.

      Denial of service attacks require that the per-packet rule
      matching and the drop path be able to keep up with the
      interface speed.

o   Multicasting

      To allow multicast traffic to penetrate a firewall, the
      rule that is needed should be supplied by the receiver
      rather than the sender. However, this will not work with
      the challenge mechanism outlined in Section 3.3.1, since
      "Authentication Required" notifications would be sent to
      the sender, not to the receiver(s).

      Multicast conversations may use any of the three levels of
      security described in the previous section, but all
      firewalls will have to share the same secret with the
      originator of the data stream. That secret would have to
      be provided to the receivers through other channels and
      then passed to the firewalls at the receivers' initiative
      (in much the same way that resources are reserved at
      receiver's initiative in RSVP).

o   Asymmetric Routing

      Given a client computer C utilizing a service from another
      computer C through a firewall F: if the packets returning
      from S to C take a different route than packets from C to
      S, they may encounter another firewall F' which has not
      been authorized to pass packets from S to C (unlike F,
      which has been). F' will challenge S rather than C, but S
      may not have credentials to authenticate itself with a
      server trusted by F'.

      Fortunately, this asymmetric routing situation is not a
      problem for the common case of single homed administrative
      domains, where any asymmetric routes converge at the
      firewall.

o   Illicit Rendezvous

None of these mechanisms prevent two users on opposite
sides of a firewall from rendezvousing with a custom
application written over a protocol that may have been
authorized to run through a firewall.

For example, if an organization has a policy that certain
information is sensitive and must not be allowed outside
its premises, a firewall will not be enough to enforce
this policy if users are able to attach sensitive
information to mail and send it outside to arbitrary
parties. Similarly, a firewall will not prevent all
problems with incoming data. If users import programs and
execute them, the programs may have Trojan horses which
disclose sensitive information or modify or delete
important data. Executable code comes in many, many
forms, including PostScript files, scripts for various
interpreters, and even return addresses for sendmail. A
firewall can detect some of these and scan for some forms
of potentially hazardous code, but it cannot stop users
from transforming things that look like "data" into
programs.

We consider these problems to be somewhat outside the
scope of the firewall router mechanism. It is a matter of
the policies implemented by the organization owning the
firewalls to address these issues.

o   Transparency for Security Packets

For the mechanisms described above to operate, the
"Authentication Required" notification and the
authentication/authorization protocol that is used between
the client computer and the authentication and
authorization servers trusted by a firewall, must be
passed by all firewalls automatically. This might be on
the basis of the packet profiles involved in security.
Alternatively, firewall routers might serve as
application-layer firewalls for these types of
communications. They could then validate the data they
pass to avoid spoofing or illicit rendezvous.

3.3.4 Firewall-Friendly Applications

Firewall routers have problems with certain communication
patterns where requests are initiated by the server, including
callbacks and multiple connections (e.g., FTP). It was

suggested that it would be useful to have guidelines to application designers to help them to build 'firewall-friendly applications'. The following guidelines were suggested:

1)   no inbound calls (the xterm problem),

2)   fixed port numbers (no portmapper or tcpmux),

3)   integral redirection is good (application gateways),

4)   no redirection in the protocol,

5)   32 bit sequence numbers that are crypto-strong random #'s, and

6)   fixed length and number of header fields.

Type fields are good, but they may not be needed if there are fixed port numbers.

3.3.5 Conclusions

Compared to an application-layer firewall, an IP-layer firewall scheme could provide a number of benefits:

-    No extra authentication is required for end hosts.

-    A single authentication protocol can be used for all intended applications.

-    An IP-layer firewall causes less performance degradation.

-    An IP-layer firewall may be able to crash and recover state without disturbing open TCP connections.

-    Routes can shift without disturbing open TCP connections.

-    There is no single point of failure.

-    It is independent of application.

However, there are substantial difficult design issues to be solved, particularly in the areas of multiple firewalls, assymmetric routes, multicasting, and performance.

4. SECURE QOS FORWARDING

When the Internet supports special qualities-of-service (QOS) for particular packet flows, there will be a new set of security problems. There will be a need to authenticate and authorize users asking for those QOS values that are expensive in network resources, and it will be necessary to prevent theft of these resources and denial-of-service attacks by others. This section contains a conceptual model for these problems, which we may call secure QOS forwarding. The issues here differ from end-to-end security and firewalls, because QOS forwarding security may need to be enforced at every router along a path.

It was noted that this is not a new problem; it was stated and solved in a theoretical way in a thesis by Radia Perlman.

4.1 The Requirement for Setup

Setup is an essential part of any QOS mechanism. However, it may be argued that there are also good engineering reasons for setup in any Internet-layer security mechanism, even without QOS support. In the abstract, one could imagine a pure datagram model in which each IP packet separately carried the necessary authorizations for all the stages in the forwarding path. Realistically, this is not practical, since the security information may be both unacceptably large and computationally demanding for inclusion in every packet. This seems to imply the need for some form of state setup for security.

Thus, we presume a two stage process that moves somewhat away from the pure datagram model. In the first stage, the setup stage, some state is established in the routers (and other network elements) that describes how a subsequent stream of packets is to be treated. In the second stage, the classification stage, the arriving packets are matched with the correct state information and processed. The terminology in use today calls these different state descriptions "classes", and the process of sorting "classification".

Setup can take many forms. It could be dynamic, invoked across the network by an application as described above. The setup process could also be the manual configuration of a router by means of a protocol such as SNMP or remote login. For example, a network link, such as a link across the Atlantic, might be shared by a number of users who purchase it jointly. They might implement this sharing by configuring a router with specifications, or filters, which describe the sorts of packets that are permitted to use each share. Whether the setup is dynamic or manual, short-lived or semi-permanent, it has the same effect: it creates packet classes in the router and defines how packets are to be classified as they arrive.

Much of the current research on extensions to IP for QOS, such as realtime service, has assumed an explicit setup phase and a classification stage. The setup stage is accomplished using protocols such as RSVP or ST-II, which also specify how the subsequent classification is to be done. Security at the setup stage would thus simply be an extension to such a protocol. It should be noted that there are alternative proposals for realtime QOS, based on an implicit setup process.

4.2   Securing the Setup Process.

To secure the setup process, we require that a setup request be accompanied by user credentials that provide a trustworthy assurance that the requester is known and is authorized to make the request in question. We refer to the credentials used in the setup phase as the high-level identification (HLID).

A simple version of this authorization would be a password on the management interface to a router (the limitations of such a password scheme are well known and not the issue here). In the case of setup requests made by individual applications, some user-specific authorization must be assumed.

While there could be any number of ways to organize the HLIDs, the objective of scaling suggests that a global framework for user naming and authentication would be useful. The choice of naming framework is discussed further in Section 5. Note that this discussion, which concerns controlling access to network resources and security devices, is distinct from end-to-end authentication and access control; however, the same authentication infrastructure could be used for both.

In general, while significant engineering effort will be required to define a setup architecture for the Internet, there is no need to develop new security techniques. However, for the security aspects of the classification process, there are significant problems related to performance and cost. We thus focus on that aspect of the overall framework in more detail.

Above, we defined the high-level ID (HLID) as that set of information presented as part of a setup request. There may also be a "low-level ID" (LLID), sometimes called a "cookie", carried in each packet to drive classification. In current proposals for IP extensions for QOS, packets are classified based on existing

packet fields, e.g., source and destination addresses, ports, and
protocol type.

It is important to note that the LLID is distinct from the address
of the user, at least conceptually. By stressing this distinction
we make the point that the privileges of the user are not
determined by the address in use. If the user's address changes,
the privileges do not.

The LLID in a packet acts as a form of tag that is used by some or
all routers along a path to make decisions about the sort of QOS
that shall be granted to this packet. An LLID might refer to a
data stream between a single source-destination address pair, or
it might be more general and encompass a range of data streams.
There is no requirement that the LLID embody a syntax that permits
a router to discern the QOS parameters that it represents, but
there also is no prohibition against imposing such a structure.

We propose that an IP datagram contain one LLID, which can be used
at various stages of the network to map the packet to a class. We
reject the alternative that the packet should have a variable
number of LLIDs, each one for a different point in the net.
Again, this is not just a security comment, but it has security
implications.

The attributes of the LLID should be picked to match as broad a
range of requirements as possible.

*   Its duration (discussed below) must match both the needs of
        the security protocol, balancing robustness and efficiency,
        and the needs of the application, which will have to deal
        with renewal of the setup when the LLID expires. A useful
        end-node facility would be a service to renew setup requests
        automatically.

*   The degree of trust must be high enough to meet the most
        stringent requirement we can reasonably meet.

*   The granularity of the LLID structure must permit packet
        classification into classes fine-grained enough for any
        resource selection in the network. We should therefore
        expect that each separate stream of packets from an
        application will have a distinct LLID. There will be little
        opportunity for aggregating multiple streams under one LLID
        or one authenticator.

4.3 Validating an LLID

At a minimum, it is necessary to validate the use of an LLID in
context, i.e., to ensure that it is being asserted in an
authorized fashion. Unauthorized use of an LLID could result in
theft of service or denial-of-service attacks, where packets not
emitted by an authorized sender are accorded the QOS treatment
reserved for that sender (or for a group of which the sender is a
member). Thus, use of an LLID should be authenticated by routers
that make QOS decisions based on that LLID. (Note that not all
routers may "pay attention" to the LLID.)

In principle, the validity of an LLID assertion needs to be
checked on every packet, though not necessarily at every router;
it may be possible to restrict the checks to security perimeters.
At those routers that must validate LLIDs, there is an obvious
concern over the performance impact. Therefore, a router may
adopt a less rigorous approach to LLID validation. For example, a
router may elect to sample a data stream and validate some, but
not all, packets. It may also elect to forward packets first and
perform selective validation as a background activity. In the
least stringent approach, a router might log selected packets and
validate them as part of an audit activity much later.

There are several candidate techniques for validating the use of
LLIDs. We have identified three basic techniques, which differ in
terms of computational performance, bandwidth overhead, and
effectiveness (resistance to various forms of attack).

*   Digital Signatures

      The first technique entails the use of public key
      cryptography and digital signatures. The sender of each
      packet signs the packet (header and payload) by computing a
      one-way hash over the packet and transforming the hash value
      using a private key associated with the LLID. The resulting
      authenticator value is included in the packet header. The
      binding between the public key and the LLID is established
      through a connection setup procedure that might make use of
      public keys that enjoy a much longer lifetime. Using public
      key technology yields the advantage that any router can
      validate a packet, but no router is entrusted with data that
      would enable it to generate a packet with a valid
      authenticator (i.e., which would be viewed as valid by other
      routers.) This characteristic makes this technique ideal
      from the standpoint of the "principle of least privilege."

Public key cryptosystems such as RSA have the advantage that validation of a signature is much faster than signing, which reduces the router processing burden. Nonetheless, this approach is not likely to be feasible for anything other than selective checking by routers, given current public key algorithm performance.

*   Sealing

The next technique is based on the use of the same type of one-way hash function used for digital signatures, but it does not require signing the hash value. Here the sender computes a one-way hash with a secret quantity (essentially a "key") appended to the packet. This process is an example of what is sometimes referred to more generically as cryptographic "sealing." The inclusion of this key at the end of the hash computation results in a hash value that is not predictable by any entity not possessing the key. The resulting hash value is the authenticator and is included in the packet header. A router validates a packet by recomputing the hash value over the received packet with the same secret quantity appended. If the transmitted hash value matches the recomputed hash value, the packet is declared valid. Unlike the signature technique, sealing implies that all routers capable of verifying a seal are also capable of generating (forging) a seal. Thus, this technique requires that the sender trust the routers not to misuse the key.

This technique has been described in terms of a single secret key shared between the sender and all the routers that need to validate packets associated with an LLID. A related alternative strategy uses the same authenticator technique, but shares the secret key on a pairwise basis, e.g., between the sender and the first router, between the first router and the next, etc. This avoids the need to distribute the secret key among a large group of routers, but it requires that the setup mechanism enable Router A to convince his neighbor (Router B) that Router A is authorized to represent traffic on a specific LLID or set of LLIDs. This might best be done by encapsulating the packet inside a wrapper that both ends of the link can validate. Once this strategy is in place, it may even be most efficient for routers to aggregate traffic between them, providing authentication not on a per-LLID basis, since the router pairs are prepared to "trust" one another to accurately represent the data stream LLIDs.

For a unicast data stream, the use of pairwise keying between routers does not represent a real change in the trust required of the routers or of the setup mechanism, because of the symmetric sharing of the secret key. However, for a multicast connection, this pairwise keying approach is superior in that it prevents a router at one point in a multicast tree from being able to generate traffic that could be inserted at another point in the tree. At worst, a router can generate spurious, but authenticatable, traffic only for routers "below" it in the multicast tree.

Note that the use of network management fault isolation techniques, e.g., sampling router traffic statistics at different points along a data stream, should permit post hoc detection of packet forgery attacks mounted by rogue routers along a data stream path. Use of this technique could provide a deterrent to such activity by routers, further arguing for the pairwise keying approach.

The sealing technique is faster than the digital signature technique, because the incremental hash calculation (including the appended secret quantity) is much faster than the cryptographic transformation required to sign a hash. The processing burden is symmetric here, i.e., the sender and each router devote the same amount of processing power to seal a packet and to verify the seal. Also, a sealed hash may be smaller than a signed hash, even if the same function is used in both cases. (This is because the modulus size of the public key signature algorithm and any ancillary parameters tend to increase the size of the signed hash value.) Moreover, one could use a hash function with a "wide" value and truncate that value, if necessary to reduce overhead; this option is not available when the authenticator is a signed hash value.

As a variant on this technique, one could imagine a "clearinghouse" that would receive, from the sender, the secret key used to generate and validate authenticators. A router needing to validate a packet would send a copy of the packet to the clearinghouse, which would check the packet and indicate to the router whether it was a valid packet associated with the LLID in question. Obviously, this variant is viable only if the router is performing infrequent, selective packet validation. However, it does avoid the need to share the authenticator secret among all the routers that must validate packets.

For both of these techniques, there is a residual vulnerability to denial-of-service attacks based on replay of valid packets during the lifetime of a data stream. Unless

packets carry sequence numbers and routers track a sequence
number window for each data stream, an (external) attacker
can copy valid packets and replay them. It may be easiest to
protect against this form of attack by aggregating all
traffic between a pair of routers into a single flow and
providing replay protection for the flow as a whole, rather
than on a per data stream basis.

*   Temporary Passwords

The final technique explored in the workshop takes a very
different tack to packet validation. The preceding
techniques compute a function of the bits in a packet and
transform that value in a fashion that prevents an intruder
from generating packets with valid authenticators. The
ability to generate packets with valid authenticators for a
given LLID requires access to a secret value that is
available only to the sender, or to the sender and to routers
participating in a given data stream.

In contrast, this third technique calls for the authenticator
to be a short term, secret quantity that is carried in the
packet header, without benefit of further protection. In
essence, this technique incorporates a short term "password"
into each packet header. This approach, like its
predecessor, requires that all of the routers validating the
LLID be privy to this authenticator. Moreover, the
authenticator is visible to any other router or other
equipment along the path, and thus this technique is much
more vulnerable than the previous ones.

Here the same authenticator may be applied to all packets
with the same LLID, since the authenticator is not a function
of the packet it authenticates. In fact, this suggests that
it is feasible to use the LLID as the authenticator.
However, adopting this tack would not be consistent with the
two previous techniques, each of which requires an explicit,
separate authenticator, and so we recommend against this
optimization.

Nonetheless, the fact that the authenticator is independent
of the packet context makes it trivial to generate (forge)
apparently authentic packets if the authenticator is
intercepted from any legitimate packet. Also, if the
authenticator can be guessed, an attacker need not even
engage in passive wiretapping to defeat this scheme. This
latter observation suggests that the authenticator must be of
sufficient size to make guessing unlikely, and making the

LLID and the authenticator separate further supports this requirement.

The major advantage of this approach is one of performance. The authenticator can be validated very quickly through a simple comparison. Consistent with the need to protect against guessing attacks, the authenticator need not consume a significant amount of space in the packet header.

The use of a sequence number visible to the routers is an interesting technique to explore to make these somewhat vulnerable methods more robust. If each stream (each source of packets) numbers its packets, then an intruder attempting to use the network resource must delete the legitimate packets, which in many cases would be difficult. Otherwise, the router being attacked would notice duplicate sequence numbers and similar anomalies. The exact details of the numbering would have to be worked out, since for the legitimate stream packets might be lost, which would cause holes in the sequence space.

We do not consider here the issues of collusion, in which a user with a given LLID and authenticator deliberately shares this with another unauthorized user. This possibility should be explored, to see if there is a practical advantage to this act, and thus a real threat.

4.4 Dynamics of Setup

o   Duration of LLID's

A key question in the use of LLIDs is how long they remain valid. At one extreme, they last only a very short time, perhaps seconds. This limits the damage that can be done if the authenticator for the LLID is stolen. At the other extreme, LLIDs are semi-permanent, like credit card numbers. The techniques proposed above for securing the LLID traded strength for efficiency, under the assumption that the peril was limited by the limited validity of the LLID.

The counterbalancing advantage of long-term or semi-permanent LLIDs is that it becomes practical to use primitive setup techniques, such as manual configuration of routers to establish packet classes. This will be important in the short run, since deployment of security and dynamic resource allocation protocols may not exactly track in time.

We conclude that the correct short-term action is to design
LLIDs under the assumption that they are fairly short lived,
and to tolerate, in the short run, a longer period of
validity. This would imply that we will get an acceptable
long-term mechanism in place, which operationally will have a
lower level of security at first. As we get better tools for
automatic setup, we can shorten the duration of validity on a
individual basis, without replacing mechanism in the packet
forwarding path.

o   Setup Latency

The tradition of the Internet is not to impose any setup
latency in the communication path between end nodes. This
supports the classic datagram model for quick transactions,
etc., and it is a feature that should be preserved.

For setup that is done "in advance", either through a
management interface or by an end-node in the background, the
issue of latency does not arise. The latency issue occurs
for dynamic reservations made in response to a specific
application request.

We observe that while latency is a key issue, it is not
materially influenced by security concerns. The designers of
resource reservation protocols such as RSVP and ST-II are
debating the latency of these protocols today, absent
security. Adding an authenticator to the request message
will increase the processing needed to validate the request,
and might even imply a message exchange with an
authentication service, but should not substantially change
the real time of the setup stage, which might already take
time on the order of a round-trip delay. But the design of
the high level authentication and authorization methods for
the setup protocol should understand that this process, while
not demanding at the level of the per-packet processing, is
still somewhat time-critical.

One way of dealing with an expensive setup process is to set
up the request provisionally and perform the validation in
the background. This would limit the damage from one bad
setup request to a short period of time. Note, however, that
the system is still vulnerable to an attack that uses a
sequence of setup requests, each of which allows unauthorized
usage for at least a short period of time.

Note also that a denial-of-service attack can be mounted by
flooding the setup process with invalid setup requests, all

of which need to be processed and rejected. This could
prevent a valid user from setting up any state. However,
denial-of-service attacks based upon flooding leave very
large "finger prints"; they should not normally be an
important threat. If it is a problem, it may be possible to
incorporate a mechanism at the level of setup processing that
is equivalent to "fair queueing", to limits the damage from a
flooding attack at the packet level.

4.5   Receiver-Initiated Setup

Recent work on a QOS extension for the Internet, embodied in the
RSVP protocol, uses the model that the receiver will reserve
resources. This scheme is consistent with the current IP
multicast paradigm, which requires the receiver to join the
multicast group. The receiver reserves the resources to insure
that the multicast traffic reaches the receiver with the desired
QOS. In this case, it is the credentials (the HLIDs) of the
receivers that will be presented to the setup phase.

Note that receiver initiation requires an explicit setup phase.
Suppose setup were implicit, driven by pre-existing fields in the
packet. Then there would be no way to associate a packet with a
particular receiver, since in multicast, the address of the
receiver never appears in the packet.

Further, it is impossible in this case to perform a setup "in
advance", unless the sender and the receiver are very tightly co-
ordinated; otherwise, the receiver will not know in advance what
LLID will be in the packet. It is certainly impossible, in this
case, for the receiver to set up "semi-permanent" reservations for
multicast traffic coming to it. This, again, is not a security
issue; the problem exists without adding security concerns, but
the security architecture must take it into account.

4.6   Other Issues

4.6.1   Encrypting Firewalls and Bypass

Our view of security, both end node and network protection,
includes the use of firewalls, which partition the network into
regions of more or less trust. This idea has something in
common with the encrypting-firewall model used in the
military/intelligence community: red (trusted) networks
partitioned from black (untrusted) networks. The very
significant difference is that, in the military model, the
partition uses an encryption unit that encodes as much as
possible of the packet for its trip across the black network to

another red network. That is, the purpose of the encryption unit, among others, is to provide a very high degree of protection against disclosure for data housed within the red networks. In contrast, our version of a firewall is more to protect the trusted (red) region of the network from outside attacks. It is concerned both with what comes in and with what goes out. It does permit communication between a node on the trusted and nodes in the untrusted parts of the network.

We would like to be able to adapt our model of secure QOS to the case of military-style encrypting firewalls. However, this use of encryption raises a problem with our model of secure resource management, discussed above, which was based on a two-stage process of setup and classification. This model is problematic because it requires information to pass from the red region to the black region in the clear. This information includes both the setup packets themselves, if setup is done dynamically from the end node, and the classification fields (the LLIDs) in the data packets. Obviously, this information cannot be encrypted when leaving the red region of the network, since it would then be meaningless to the black net, so that the black network would be unable to make resource allocation decisions based on it.

To make this sort of control scheme work, it is necessary for the encryption device to be programmed to permit certain packets and fields in packets to pass through the encryptor in the clear. This bypass of the encryption is considered highly undesirable. In a high security situation, the process generating the bypassing information might be corrupted, with the result that information that should be controlled is removed from the secure network by hiding it in the bypassed fields of the packets.

We concluded, however, that this bypass problem is not insurmountable. The key idea, as in all cases of bypass, is to limit, rather than wholly outlaw, the information passing in the clear. To limit the information needed for bypass, one can either perform the setup as a management function totally within the black environment, or divide the process into two stages. The first stage, again totally in the black context, defines a limited number of setup situations. The second stage involves sending from the red net a very small message that selects one request to be instantiated from among the pre-defined set.

Perhaps the more difficult issue is the LLID in the packet header. If the LLID is an explicit field (as we have discussed

so far, but see below), it represents a new field in each
packet, with perhaps as many as 32 bits. Again, the solution
is to limit the way this field can be used. When the end-node
performs a setup, it will specify the value of the LLID to be
used. This fact can be observed by the red/black encryption
unit, which can then limit the components of this field to the
values currently in use. To further improve the situation, the
encryption unit might be able to aggregate a number of flows
onto one flow for the purpose of crossing the black net, which
would permit a further reduction in the number of distinct
LLIDs that must escape the red region.

The details of this proposal, including some important issues
such as the time duration of LLIDs in this case, must be
considered further. However, the initial conclusion that
bypass can be incorporated into a general resource control
framework is very encouraging, since it suggests that both
military and commercial forms of security can be built out of
the same building blocks.

4.6.2 The Principle of Consistent Privilege

A well understood principle of security is the principle of
least privilege, which states that a system is most robust when
it is structured to demand the least privilege from its
components.

A related rule we observe is the principle of consistent
privilege. This can be illustrated simply in the case of
denial of service, where it is particularly relevant. For a
particular route, no assumption of service can be justified
unless we trust the routers to deliver the packets. If a
router is corrupted and will not forward packets, the only
solution is to find another route not involving this router.
We do not concern ourselves here with protocols for finding new
routes in the presence of a corrupted router, since this topic
is properly part of another topic, securing the network
infrastructure. We only observe that either we will get
service from the router or we will not. If the router is
corrupted, it does not matter how it chooses to attack us.
Thus, as long as the router is part of a forwarding path (most
generally a multicast forwarding tree), we should not hesitate
to trust it in other ways, such as by giving it shared resource
keys or LLID verifiers.

This illustrates the principle of consistent privilege. This
principle is exploited in the scheme for hop-by-hop or pairwise
use of secrets to validate LLIDs in a multicast tree. If a

single key is issued for the whole tree, then the privilege is
not consistent. We only need to trust a router with respect to
the nodes "below" it in the tree. If it fails to forward
traffic, it can affect only those nodes. But if we give it the
group key, then it can generate bogus traffic and inject it
into the tree at any point, affecting traffic for other parts
of the tree. If, on the other hand, we use pairwise keys, then
a corrupt node can only generate bogus traffic with the key for
traffic it would directly receive, which is the part of the
tree it could damage anyway.

Another requirement we must place on the network concerns
routing. If a firewall is in place, we must trust the routing
architecture not to bypass that firewall. One way to
accomplish this is to eliminate any physical path between the
regions other than those that go through the firewall.
Operational experience will be required to see if this simple
physical limit is an acceptable constraint.

4.6.3 Implicit LLID's

We stress the importance of a strong conceptual distinction
between the addresses in a packet and the LLID which is used to
classify the packet. The conceptual distinction is important,
but under limited circumstances it may be possible to overload
some of the packet fields and create an LLID from the current
packet header. For example, current packet classifiers for
IPv4, which are not secure but which seem to work for
classifying the packets into service classes, use a number of
the packet fields together as a form of LLID: the source and
destination IP addresses and ports plus the protocol type.

This sort of "implicit" LLID must be short-lived, especially if
the host can change its IP address as it moves. But if the
LLID is established by some sort of dynamic setup protocol, it
should be possible reestablish the LLID as needed.

The current IPv4 header has no authenticator field to validate
the LLID. An authenticator field could be optionally carried
in an option; adding it gives robustness to network
reservations. Any of the schemes described above for creating
an authenticator could be used, except that if the simple
password-style authenticator is used, it must be an explicit
separate field, since the LLID cannot be picked randomly.

4.6.4 Security without Setup

As we describe this architecture, the setup phase is an
essential part of the sequence. This suggests that the current
Internet, which has no setup protocols, cannot be secured
against denial-of-service attacks. It is important to explore
the limits of this point. As we stressed above, setup can
occur in many ways. Routers today offer management options to
classify packets based on protocol types and other fields found
in the header, and to use this classification to create a few
fair queueing classes that can prevent one class from
overloading the net to the exclusion of the others.

There are two problem here. The first is that for a setup done
using a management interface, the secret that is shared among
the source and the routers to validate the LLID must remain
valid for a long time, and it must be manually configured. The
second problem is that the granularity of the categories may be
coarse. However, it has been proposed, in a thesis by Radia
Perlman, that a router might create a separate fair queueing
class implicitly for each source address. This approach, which
uses the addresses as an implicit LLID, must have some form of
authenticator for robustness. But if the LLID can be trusted,
this scheme provides classification of traffic based only on an
implicit setup operation. The granularity of classification is
not sufficient to provide any QOS distinction. The only
objective is to prevent the traffic from one source from
flooding the net to the exclusion of another.

4.6.5 Validating Addresses

We make a claim here that if the LLID and the addresses in the
packet are conceptually distinct, and if there is a suitable
means to validate the LLID, then there is no reason to validate
the addresses. For example, a packet constructed with a false
source address does not seem to represent any security problem,
if its LLID can be validated.

An exception to this might possibly lie in communication with
mobile hosts, but it will require a complete model of threats
and requirements in the mobile environment to be sure.
However, we make the claim, as a starting point for discussion,
that if LLIDs are distinguished from addresses, many of the
security concerns with mobility are mitigated and perhaps
removed. This point should be validated by more detailed
consideration of the mobility problem.

4.6 Conclusions

a) It is important to conceptually separate a LLID (Low-Level IDentifier) carried in a packet from addresses in the packet.

b) There will be a single LLID carried in each packet. Although this might imply some additional state in the routers than if multiple LLIDs were used, using only one LLID choice is more scalable.

c) Hop-by-hop LLID authentication mechanisms might provide a highly scalable approach that limits the distribution of secrets. However, the robustness limitations must be investigated thoroughly.

d) Statistical sampling or after-the-fact detection mechanisms may be employed by routers to address performance concerns.

5. AN AUTHENTICATION SERVICE

The purpose of an authentication service is simply to verify names, or more precisely to verify the origin of "messages". It differs from the authorization service, which determines what services are available to an authenticated name. We expect that authentication will be an Internet-wide service, while authorization will be specific to the resources to which access is being authorized.

This "identification" function can be used in several contexts, for example:

* One-time passwords: "it is really <huitema@inria.fr> that is responding to this challenge".

* Access to a firewall: "it is really <huitema@inria.fr> that is trying to send data to host-A at port-a".

There are many Internet objects that we may want to name, e.g.,:

             domain names: sophia.inria.fr

             machine names: jupiter.inria.fr

             service names: www.sophia.inria.fr
                              (in fact, a data base)

             users: huitema@sophia.inria.fr

```
processes:       p112.huitema@sophia.inria.fr
                 p112.sophia.inria.fr

universal resource locators:
                 http//www.sophia.inria.fr:222/tmp/foobar
```

One could be tempted to believe that the authentication service will only be concerned with naming humans, as only humans are "responsible"; a process obtains some access rights because it is acting on behalf of a person. However, this is too reductive and potentially misleading. We may have to authenticate "machines" or hardware components. For example:

*   When a machine boots it needs to access resources for configuring itself, but it is not yet "used" by a person; there is no user.

*   On a "distributed processor", component CPUs may need to authenticate each other.

Machines do differ from users; machines cannot keep their "secrets" in the same way that people do. However, there is a big value in having a simple and extensible name space.

5.1 Names and Credentials

We make the hypothesis that the authorization services will generally use "access control lists" (ACLs), i.e., some definition of a set of authorized users. A compact way to represent such a set would be to allow "wildcard" authorizations, e.g., "anybody at <Bellcore.com>", or "any machine at <INRIA.FR>". The authentication service should be designed to facilitate the realization of the authorization service and should support "wildcards".

However, wildcards are not general enough. Assuming that we have a hierarchical name space, a wildcarded entry is limited to the naming hierarchy. For example, a name like <huitema@sophia.inria.fr> could be matched by the wildcard <*@sophia.inria.fr> or <*.inria.fr> or <*.fr>. This is useful as long as one stays at INRIA, but does not solve the generic problem. Suppose that an IETF file server at CNRI is to be accessible by all IAB members: its ACL will explicitly list the members by name.

The classic approach to naming, as exemplified in the X.500 model, is to consider that people have "distinguished names". Once one has discovered such a name through some "white pages" service, can use it as an access key in a global directory service.

An individual may acquire authorizations from a variety of
sources. Using a pure, identity-based access control system, the
user would have to acquire multiple identities (i.e.,
distinguished names), corresponding to the roles in which she is
authorized to access different services. We discuss this approach
in the next section.

An alternative approach is for the user to have a very small
number of identities, and to have the grantors of authorizations
issue (signed) credentials granting permissions to the user,
linked to her ID. These additional signed credentials are known
as "capabilities". The user can then establish her identity
through a generic identity credential, e.g., an X.509 certificate,
and can establish authorization by presenting capabilities as
required. This is somewhat analogous to a person acquiring credit
cards linked to the name on a driver's license, and presenting the
appropriate credit card, plus the license for picture verification
of identity.

5.2 Identity-Based Authorization

Let's open the wallet of an average person: we find several
"credit cards" in it. We all have many "credit cards", e.g.,
company cards, credit cards, airline frequent flyers memberships,
driver licenses. Each of these cards is in fact a token asserting
the existence of a relation: the bank certifies that checks
presented by the bearer will be paid, the traffic authorities
certifies that the bearer has learned how to drive, etc. This is
an example of identity-based authorization, in which an individual
is given different names corresponding to different relations
entered into by that individual.

If we imagine that the name space is based upon DNS (domain)
names, then for example, the person mentioned above could be
authenticated with the names:

        customer@my-big-bank.com

        customer@frequent-flyer.airline.com

The model we used here is that "the name is an association". This
is consistent with name verification procedures, in which that one
builds a "chain of trust" between the user and the "resource
agent". By following a particular path in the trust graph, one
can both establish the trust and show that the user belongs to an
"authorized group".

The existence of "multiple names" for a person may or may not
imply the existence of an "equivalence" relation. It may be
useful to know that <huitema@sophia.inria.fr> and
<huitema@iab.isoc.org> are two names for the same person, but
there are many cases where the user does not want to make all his
tokens visible.

5.3 Choosing Credentials

Let's consider again the example of Christian Huitema accessing a
file at CNRI. He will have to interact with INRIA's outgoing
firewall and with CNRI's incoming controls. Regardless of whether
authorization depends upon capabilities or upon multiple
association names, a different credential may be needed in each
firewall on the path. For example, assuming multiple names are
used, he will use an INRIA name, <huitema@sophia.inria.fr>, to be
authorized by INRIA to use network resources, and he will use an
IAB name, <huitema@iab.isoc.org>, to access the file server. Thus
comes an obvious problem: how does he choose the credential
appropriate to a particular firewall? More precisely, how does
the computer program that manages the connection discover that it
should use one credential in response to INRIA's firewall
challenge and another in response to CNRI's request?

There are many possible answers. The program could simply pass
all the user's credentials and let the remote machine pick one.
This works, but poses some efficiency problems: passing all
possible names is bulky, looking through many names is long.
Advertising many names is also very undesirable for privacy and
security reasons: one does not want remote servers to collect
statistics on all the credentials that a particular user may have.

Another possibility is to let the agent that requests an
authorization pass the set of credentials that it is willing to
accept, e.g., "I am ready to serve CNRI employees and IAB
members". This poses the same privacy and security problems as
the previous solutions, although to a lesser degree. In fact, the
problem of choosing a name is the same as the generic "trust path"
model. The name to choose is merely a path in the authentication
graph, and network specialists are expected to know how to find
paths in graphs.

In the short term, it is probably possible to use a "default name"
or "principal name", at least for local transactions, and to count
on the user to "guess" the credential that is required by remote
services. To leave the local environment we need only the local
credentials; to contact a remote server we need only the
destination credentials. So we need one or maybe two credentials,

which may be derived from the destination. It will be very often
the case that the generic credential is enough; then wildcards;
then "FTP provided" tokens.

6. OTHER ISSUES

   6.1 Privacy and Authentication of Multicast Groups

   Multicast applications are becoming an increasingly important part
   of Internet communications. Packet voice, video and shared
   whiteboard can be powerful productivity tools for users. For
   these applications to have maximum value to their users, a variety
   of security services will be required.

   Existing techniques are directly applicable to providing privacy
   for a private teleconference. If each member of the conference
   shares a single key for a symmetric encryption algorithm (such as
   DES), existing point-to-point security techniques can be extended
   to protect communication within the group from outsiders.

   However, slight modifications to existing techniques are required
   to accommodate the multicast environment. Each packet will
   require independent cryptographic processing to ensure that
   packets from multiple sources can be independently decrypted by
   the numerous receivers, particularly in the presence of lost
   packets. N-party authentication and key management will be
   required to establish the shared key among the proper group
   members. This can be done by extending existing two-party key
   management techniques pairwise. For example, the conference
   manager may provide the key to each member following individual
   authentication; for example, this could be implemented trivially
   using PEM technology. The overhead experienced by each host
   computer in the conference will be similar to that of existing
   point-to-point encryption applications, This overhead is be low
   enough that, today, software encryption can offer adequate
   performance to secure whiteboard and voice traffic, while hardware
   encryption is adequate for video.

   The nature of multicast communication adds an additional
   requirement. Existing multicast conferences provide gradual
   degradation in quality as the packet loss rate increases. To be
   acceptable, authentication protocols must tolerate lost packets.
   Techniques to accomplish this efficiently need to be developed.
   One initial sketch is outlined below. Engineering work will be
   required to validate the practicality of this approach.

The use of symmetric encryption provides the members of the conference with effective protection from outsiders. However, because all members of the conference share a single key, it does not provide a means of authenticating individual conference members. In principle, existing techniques, based on one-way hash functions coupled with digital signatures based on asymmetric encryption algorithms, can provide individual authentication. One-way hash functions such as MD5 are comparable in cost to symmetric encryption. However, digital signatures are considerably more costly, both in computation and in communication size. The degree of overhead depends on the quality of authentication required.

In summary, realtime authentication at the granularity of group membership is easy and cheap, but individual authentication is costly in time and space. Over time, the costs of both communications and processing are expected to decline. It is possible that this will help make authentication at the level of individual conference participants. There are two conflicting trends: (1) increasing CPU speeds to provide symmetric encryption, and (2) increasing communication data rates. If both technologies increase proportionally, there will be no net gain, at least if the grain size is measured in terms of bits, rather than as a period in seconds.

The group felt that the correct approach to end-to-end controls is the use of encryption, as discussed above. The alternative is to control the ability of a user to join a multicast group as a listener, or as a speaker. However, we are not comfortable with the level of assurance that we can offer if we attempt to ensure end-to-end semantics using these means. Any passive penetration of the network, i.e., any wire-tap, can compromise the privacy of the transmitted information. We must acknowledge, however, that problems with deployment of encryption code and hardware, and especially problems of export controls, will create a pressure to use the tools described in Section 4 to implement a form of end-to-end control. Such a decision would raise no new issues in security technology. The shared key now used for encrypting the data could instead be used as the basis for authenticating a multicast group join request. This would require modification of the multicast packet format, but nothing more. Our concern is not the technical difficulty of this approach, but the level of assurance we can offer the user.

6.2 Secure Plug-and-Play a Must

Plug-and-play is the ability to plug a new device into a network
and have it obtain the information it needs to communicate with
other devices, without requiring any new configuration
information. Secure plug-and-play is an important Internet
requirement, and a central architectural issue is whether it can
be made to scale well.

For plug-and-play operation, a new machine that is "plugged" into
the network needs to:

(1) Obtain an locator so it can communicate with other devices

(2) Register or obtain a name to be identified by (e.g., machine
     name)

(3) Discover services available on the network (e.g., printers,
     routers, file servers, etc.)

(4) Discover other systems on the network so it can communicate
     with them.

In some environments, no security mechanisms are required because
physical security and local knowledge of the users are sufficient
protection. At the other end of the spectrum is a large network
with many groups of users, different types of outside connections,
and levels of administrative control. In such environments,
similar plug-and-play capabilities are needed, but the new device
must be "authenticated" before it can perform these functions. In
each step in the discovery process the new device must
authenticate itself prior to learning about services.

The steps might be:

-    Obtain a HLID from a smart card, smart disk, or similar
     device.

-    Authenticate itself with the first plug-and-play server using
     its HLID, to register a name and to find the location of
     other services.

-    Discover services available on the network (e.g., printers,
     routers, file servers, etc.) based on its HLID.

-    Discover other systems on the network so it can communicate
     with them.

The problem of taking a system out of the box and initially
configuring it is similar to the problem of a mobile or portable
machine that a human wants to connect to a local network
temporarily in order to receive services on that network. How can
the local network authenticate the human (and therefore the
human's machine) and know which services this visiting machine is
permitted to use?

The human must be endowed with a high level identifier (HLID)
which acts as his/her passport and can be verified by the local
network. This high level identifier must be globally unique and
registered/assigned by some recognized authority.

When the human plugs the machine onto a local net, the machine
identifies itself to the net with the human's high level
identifier. If local net has a policy of permitting anyone to
plug and play on its network, it will ignore the HLID and assign
an address (locator), permitting the visitor unrestricted access
and privileges. More likely, the local net will authenticate the
HLID prior to granting the visitor an address or any privileges.

At this point, the HLID has only authenticated the visitor to the
local network; the issue of which services or resources the
visitor is entitled to use has not been addressed. It is
desirable to develop a low-overhead approach to granting
authentications to new users. This will help in the case of
visitors to a site, as well as new users joining a facility.

6.3 A Short-Term Confidentiality Mechanism

Authentication has customarily been achieved using passwords. In
the absence of active attacks, the greatest threat to computer
system security may be the ease with which passwords can be
"snooped" by the promiscuous monitoring of shared-media networks.
There are known security techniques for achieving authentication
without exposing passwords to interception, for example the
techniques implemented in the well-known Kerberos system.
However, authentication systems such as Kerberos currently operate
only in isolation within organizational boundaries. Developing
and deploying a global authentication infrastructure is an
important objective, but it will take some years. Another useful
approach in the short term is the use of a challenge-response user
authentication scheme (e.g., S/Key).

One of the groups explored another interim approach to guarding
passwords: introducing a readily-used confidentiality mechanism
based on an encrypted TCP connection. This would operate at the
IP level to encrypt the IP payload, including the TCP header, to

allow the nature as well of the contents of the communication to
be kept private. It could be implemented to provide either
"strict" protection (the connection fails if the other side cannot
decrypt your data stream) or "loose" protection (falling back to
non-private TCP if decryption fails).

Loose protection would allow interoperability with older hosts in
a seamless (non-user-intrusive) manner.

One-time keys may be exchanged during the SYN handshake that
starts the TCP connection. Using one-time keys avoids a need for
infrastructure support and does not require trust between the
organizations on the two ends of the connection. Tieing the key
exchange to the SYN handshake will avoid the possibility of having
the connection fully open without knowing the state of encryption
on both ends of the connection. Although it may still be
theoretically possible to intercept the SYN exchange and subvert
the connection by an active "man-in-the-middle" attack, in
practice such attacks on TCP connections are quite difficult
unless the routing protocols have been subverted.

The keys could be exchanged using a new option that specifies the
key exchange protocol, the data encryption algorithm, and the key
to be used to decrypt the connection. It could be possible to
include multiple options in the same SYN segment, specifying
different encryption models; the far end would then need to
acknowledge the option that it is willing to use. In this case,
the lack of an acknowledgement would imply disinterest in
decrypting the datastream. If a loose privacy policy were in
force, the connection could continue even without an
acknowledgment. The policy, "strict" or "loose", would be set by
either the user or the default configuration for the machine.

One must however observe that a TCP option can carry only a
limited amount of data. Efficient protection against crypto-
analysis of the Diffie-Hellmann scheme may require the use of a
very long modulus, e.g., 1024 bits, which cannot be carried in the
40 bytes available for TCP options. One would thus have either to
define an "extended option" format or to implement encryption in a
separate protocol layered between TCP and IP, perhaps using a
version of "IP security". The detailed engineering of such a
solution would have to be studied by a working group.

A TCP connection encryption mechanism such as that just outlined
requires no application changes, although it does require kernel
changes. It has important drawbacks, including failure to provide
privacy for privacy for UDP, and the great likelihood of export
control restrictions. If Diffie-Hellman were used, there would

also be patent issues.

7. CONCLUSIONS

As a practical matter, security must be added to the Internet incrementally. For example, a scheme that requires, as a precondition for any improvement, changes to application code, the DNS, routers and firewalls all at once will be very hard to deploy. One of the reasons the workshop explored schemes that are local to the IP layer is that we surmise that they might be easier to deploy in practice.

There are two competing observations that must shape planning for Internet security. One is the well known expression: "the best is the enemy of the good." The other is the observation that the attacks are getting better.

Finally, it should noted that the principle of least privilege, which was mentioned above, may be in contradiction to the principle of least cost.

7.1 Suggested Short-Term Actions

The general recommendation for short-term Internet security policy was that the IETF should make a list of desirable short-term actions and then reach out to work with other organizations to carry them out. Other organizations include regionals, which may be in a good position to provide site security counseling services to their customers, vendors and other providers, and other societies. We should also give input to the US government to influence their posture on security in the direction desired by the community.

A suggested preliminary list of short-term actions was developed.

o   Perform external diagnostic security probes

Organizations should be encouraged to use CRACK and other tools to check the robustness of their own passwords. It would also be useful to run a variety of security probes from outside. Since this is a very sensitive issue, some care needs to be taken to get the proper auspices for such probing.

Useful probe tools include:

    ISS: Klaus (GA)
    SATAN: Farmer Venema
    ICEPICK: NRL

o   Determine Security-Risk Publication Channels

    What channels should be used for disseminating information of
    security risks?

o   Encourage use of one-time passwords.

    Available packages: S/Key, SecurID, Enigma, Digital Pathways.

o   Develop and publish guidelines for protocol developers, for
    security-friendliness and firewall-friendliness.

o   Control topology to isolate threats

o   Set privacy policy:

    *   Always

    *   As much as possible

o   Bring Site Security Handbook up to date

o   Support use of Kerberos

The subject of the "Clipper chip" came up several times, but there
was not sufficient discussion of this very complex issue for this
grouip to reach a recommendation. It has been observed that there
are a number of quite differing viewpoints about Clipper.

    o   Some people accept the government's Clipper proposal,
         including key escrow by the US government and the
         requirement that encryption be in hardware.

    o   Some people don't mind key escrow by the government in
         principle, but the object to the hardware requirement.

    o   Some people don't mind key escrow in principle, but
         don't want the government to hold the keys. They would
         be comfortable with having the organization which owns
         the data hold the keys.

    o   Some people don't want key escrow at all.

o   Some people don't mind the hardware or the key escrow,
     but they don't think this will be acceptable to other
     countries and thus will not work internationally.

This report takes no position on any of these viewpoints.

7.2 Suggested Medium-Term Actions

These actions require some protocol design or modification;
however, they use existing security technology and require no
research.

o   Authentication Protocol

      There is a problem of the choice of technology. Public key
      technology is generally deemed superior, but it is patented
      and can also induce relatively long computations. Symmetric
      key technology (Needham-Schroeder algorithm, as used in
      Kerberos) has some technical drawbacks but it is not
      patented. A system based on symmetric keys and used only for
      authentication would be freely exportable without being
      subject to patents.

o   Push Kerberos

      Engineering is needed on Kerberos to allow it to interoperate
      with mechanisms that use public key cryptography.

o   Push PEM/RIPEM/PGP...

o   Develop an authenticated DNS

o   Develop a key management mechanism

o   Set up a certificate server infrastructure

      Possible server mechanisms include the DNS, Finger, SNMP,
      Email, Web, and FTP.

o   Engineer authentication for the Web

7.3 Suggested Long-Term Actions

In this category, we have situations where a threat has been
identified and solutions are imaginable, but closure has not been
reached on the principles.

o   Executable Apps

o   Router sabotage counter-measures

o   Prevent Byzantine routing.

o   Proxy Computing

o   Decomposition of computers

o   Are there "good" viruses?

APPENDIX A -- Workshop Organization

The following list of attendees indicates also the breakout group to
which they were assigned.

Breakout Groups

Group I.1 Leader:
1 Christian Huitema, INRIA   (IAB)

1 Steve Bellovin, AT&T
1 Bob Braden, ISI   (IAB)
1 John Curran, NEARNET
1 Phill Gross, ANS   (IETF/IAB)
1 Stev Knowles, FTP Software   (Internet AD)
1 Barry Leiner, USRA   (IAB)
1 Paul Mockapetris, ISI
1 Yakov Rekhter, IBM   (IAB)
1 Dave Sincoskie, Bellcore   (IAB)

Group I.2 Leader:
2 Steve Crocker, TIS   (Security AD)

2 Jon Crowcroft
2 Steve Deering, PARC
2 Paul Francis, NTT
2 Van Jacobson, LBL
2 Phil Karn, Qualcomm
2 Allison Mankin, NRL   (Transport AD, IPng AD)
2 Radia Perlman, Novell
2 John Romkey, ELF   (IAB)
2 Mike StJohns, ARPA   (IAB)

Group I.3 Leader:
3 Dave Clark, MIT

3 Deborah Estrin, USC
3 Elise Gerich, Merit   (IAB)
3 Steve Kent, BBN   (IAB)
3 Tony Lauck, DEC   (IAB)
3 Tony Li, CISCO
3 Bob Hinden, Sun   (IESG->IAB liaison, Routing AD)
3 Jun Murai, WIDE   (IAB)
3 Scott Shenker, PARC
3 Abel Weinrib, Bellcore

The following were able to attend only the third day, due to a
conflicting ISOC Board of Trustees meeting:

```
    Scott Bradner, Harvard            (IPng AD)
    Jon Postel, ISI                   (IAB)

The workshop agenda was as follows.

    Tues Feb 8
        9:00 - 10:30  Plenary
            Discuss facilities, meeting goals, agenda, organization.
            Establish some minimal common understandings.  Assign
            scenarios to Breakout I groups.

        10:30 - 13:00  Breakout I meetings
            Each breakout group examine one or more scenarios and
            formulate a list of design questions.  Lunch available on
            11th floor.

        13:00 - 15:00  Plenary
            Report, discuss.  Collate and shorten list of design
            issues.  Organize Breakout II groups to work on these
            issues.

        15:00 - 17:30  Breakout IIa meetings
            Work on design issues.

    Wed Feb 9
         9:00 - 10:00   Plenary
            Report, discuss.

        10:00 - 13:30  Breakout IIb meetings
            More work on design questions, develop list of
            requirements.

        13:30 - 14:30  Plenary
            Report, discuss.

        15:30 - 17:30  Breakout III groups

    Thurs Feb 10
        9:00 - 9:30 Plenary

        9:30 - 11:00 Breakout Groups (wrapup)

        11:00 - 12:00 Plenary
            Discuss possible short-term security recommendations

        13:00 - 14:00  Plenary -- Discuss short-term security issues

        14:00 - 14:30  Plenary --  Presentation by Steve Bellovin
```

```
14:30 - 16:00  Plenary --  Long- and Medium-term
                            Recommendations
```

The following scenarios were used as a starting point for
discussions. It distinguished security-S (security as a service to
the end systems) from security-M, security as a mechanism to support
other services. The workshop was intended to be primarily concerned
with interactions among the following different *services*:

o   Security-S

o   Routing

o   Multi-destination delivery (mcast-S)

o   Realtime Packet scheduling (realtime)

o   Mobility

o   Accounting

     (and maybe large-scale?)

These categories were then applied to the following scenarios:

S1. Support a private teleconference among mobile hosts connected to
     the Internet. [Security-S, mcast-S, realtime, mobility]

S2. The group in S1 is 1/3 the Internet, i.e., there are VERY severe
     scaling problems. [Security-S, mcast-S, realtime, mobility,
     large-scale]

S3. Charge for communication to support a video teleconference.
     [Accounting, realtime, mcast-S]

S4. I am travelling with my laptop. I tune in to radio channel IP-
     RADIO, pick-up the beacon and start using it. Who gets the
     bill? Why do they believe this is me? Is "me" a piece of
     hardware (IP address) or a certified user (PEM certificate)?
     [Mobility, accounting (, realtime, mcast-S)]

S5. A Politically Important Person will mcast an Internet
     presentation, without danger of interruptions from the audience.

S6. The travel industry wants to use Internet to deliver tickets to
     customer premises directly in a secure way, but the customer has
     only dial-up capability. [Security-S, mobility]

S7. I am traveling with my laptop and this friendly host is running
     the autoconfiguration protocol. I immediately get an address as
     "mac1.friendly.host.com".   (What is the difference between my
     laptop and a bona fide autoconfigured local station?)
     [Security-S, mobility]

S8. Multiple people are connected to a subnetwork providing mobility
     (e.g., cellular, packet radio). The subnetwork is connected to
     multiple places in the "fixed" backbone. How can routing be done
     efficiently? [Routing, mobility]

The following scenarios that were suggested do not fit into the
primary thrust of the workshop, generally because they are single-
issue topics. Most of them are pure security topics and are
concerned with the security perimeter. The last two do not fit into
our classification system at all.

S9. XYZ corporation has two major branches on opposite ends of the
     world, and they want to communicate securely over the Internet,
     with each branch having IP-level connectivity to the other (not
     through application gateways).

S10. I am visiting XYZ corporation, with my laptop. I want to
     connect it to their LAN to read my email remotely over the
     Internet. Even though I am inside their corporate firewall,
     they want to be protect their machines from me.

S11. XYZ corporation is trying to use the Internet to support both
     private and public networking. It wants to provide full
     connectivity internally between all of its resources, and to
     provide public access to certain resources (analogous of
     anonymous ftp servers)

S12. The travel industry wants to use Internet to deliver tickets to
     customer premises directly in a secure way.

S13. Some hacker is deliberately subverting routing protocols,
     including mobile and multicast routing. Design counter
     measures.

S14. Part of the Internet is running IPv4 and part is running IPng
     (i.e. the Internet is in transition). How can we assure
     continued secure operation through such a transition?

S15. A corporation uses ATM to connect a number of its sites. It also
     uses Internet. It wants to make use of the ATM as its primary
     carrier, but also wants to utilize other networking technologies
     as appropriate (e.g., mobile radio). It wants to support all

media (data, voice, video).

Security Considerations

This memo is entirely concerned with security issues.

Authors' Addresses

Bob Braden [Editor]
USC Information Sciences Institute
4676 Admiralty Way
Marina del Rey, CA 90292-6695

Phone: (310) 822-1511
EMail: Braden@ISI.EDU

David Clark
MIT Laboratory for Computer Science
545 Technology Square
Cambridge, MA 02139-1986

Phone: 617-253-6003
EMail: ddc@lcs.mit.edu

Steve Crocker
Trusted Information Systems, Inc.
3060 Washington Road (Rte 97)
Glenwood, MD 21738

Phone: (301) 854-6889
EMail: crocker@tis.com

Christian Huitema
INRIA, Sophia-Antipolis
2004 Route des Lucioles
BP 109
F-06561 Valbonne Cedex
France

Phone: +33 93 65 77 15
EMail: Christian.Huitema@MIRSA.INRIA.FR

Network Working Group   N. Haller
Request for Comments: 1704   Bell Communications Research
Category: Informational   R. Atkinson
                                           Naval Research Laboratory
                                                       October 1994

On Internet Authentication

Status of this Memo

1. INTRODUCTION

   The authentication requirements of computing systems and network
   protocols vary greatly with their intended use, accessibility, and
   their network connectivity. This document describes a spectrum of
   authentication technologies and provides suggestions to protocol
   developers on what kinds of authentication might be suitable for some
   kinds of protocols and applications used in the Internet. It is
   hoped that this document will provide useful information to
   interested members of the Internet community.

   Passwords, which are vulnerable to passive attack, are not strong
   enough to be appropriate in the current Internet [CERT94]. Further,
   there is ample evidence that both passive and active attacks are not
   uncommon in the current Internet [Bellovin89, Bellovin92, Bellovin93,
   CB94, Stoll90]. The authors of this paper believe that many
   protocols used in the Internet should have stronger authentication
   mechanisms so that they are at least protected from passive attacks.
   Support for authentication mechanisms secure against active attack is
   clearly desirable in internetworking protocols.

   There are a number of dimensions to the internetwork authentication
   problem and, in the interest of brevity and readability, this
   document only describes some of them. However, factors that a
   protocol designer should consider include whether authentication is
   between machines or between a human and a machine, whether the
   authentication is local only or distributed across a network,
   strength of the authentication mechanism, and how keys are managed.

2. DEFINITION OF TERMS

This section briefly defines some of the terms used in this paper to aid the reader in understanding these suggestions. Other references on this subject might be using slightly different terms and definitions because the security community has not reached full consensus on all definitions. The definitions provided here are specifically focused on the matters discussed in this particular document.

Active Attack: An attempt to improperly modify data, gain authentication, or gain authorization by inserting false packets into the data stream or by modifying packets transiting the data stream. (See passive attacks and replay attacks.)

Asymmetric Cryptography: An encryption system that uses different keys, for encryption and decryption. The two keys have an intrinsic mathematical relationship to each other. Also called Public~Key~Cryptography. (See Symmetric Cryptography)

Authentication: The verification of the identity of the source of information.

Authorization: The granting of access rights based on an authenticated identity.

Confidentiality: The protection of information so that someone not authorized to access the information cannot read the information even though the unauthorized person might see the information's container (e.g., computer file or network packet).

Encryption: A mechanism often used to provide confidentiality.

Integrity: The protection of information from unauthorized modification.

Key Certificate: A data structure consisting of a public key, the identity of the person, system, or role associated with that key, and information authenticating both the key and the association between that identity and that public key. The keys used by PEM are one example of a key certificate [Kent93].

Passive Attack: An attack on an authentication system that inserts no data into the stream, but instead relies on being able to passively monitor information being sent between other

parties. This information could be used a later time in what
appears to be a valid session. (See active attack and replay
attack.)

Plain-text: Unencrypted text.

Replay Attack: An attack on an authentication system by recording
     and replaying previously sent valid messages (or parts of
     messages). Any constant authentication information, such as a
     password or electronically transmitted biometric data, can be
     recorded and used later to forge messages that appear to be
     authentic.

Symmetric Cryptography: An encryption system that uses the same key
     for encryption and decryption. Sometimes referred to as
     Secret~Key~Cryptography.

3. AUTHENTICATION TECHNOLOGIES

There are a number of different classes of authentication, ranging
from no authentication to very strong authentication. Different
authentication mechanisms are appropriate for addressing different
kinds of authentication problems, so this is not a strict
hierarchical ordering.

3.1 No Authentication

For completeness, the simplest authentication system is not to
have any. A non-networked PC in a private (secure) location is an
example of where no authentication is acceptable. Another case is
a stand-alone public workstation, such as "mail reading"
workstations provided at some conferences, on which the data is
not sensitive to disclosure or modification.

3.2 Authentication Mechanisms Vulnerable to Passive Attacks

The simple password check is by far the most common form of
authentication. Simple authentication checks come in many forms:
the key may be a password memorized by the user, it may be a
physical or electronic item possessed by the user, or it may be a
unique biological feature. Simple authentication systems are said
to be "disclosing" because if the key is transmitted over a
network it is disclosed to eavesdroppers. There have been
widespread reports of successful passive attacks in the current
Internet using already compromised machines to engage in passive
attacks against additional machines [CERT94]. Disclosing
authentication mechanisms are vulnerable to replay attacks.
Access keys may be stored on the target system, in which case a

single breach in system security may gain access to all passwords.
Alternatively, as on most systems, the data stored on the system
can be enough to verify passwords but not to generate them.

3.3 Authentication Mechanisms Vulnerable to Active Attacks

Non-disclosing password systems have been designed to prevent
replay attacks. Several systems have been invented to generate
non-disclosing passwords. For example, the SecurID Card from
Security Dynamics uses synchronized clocks for authentication
information. The card generates a visual display and thus must be
in the possession of the person seeking authentication. The S/Key
(TM) authentication system developed at Bellcore generates
multiple single use passwords from a single secret key [Haller94].
It does not use a physical token, so it is also suitable for
machine-machine authentication. In addition there are challenge-
response systems in which a device or computer program is used to
generate a verifiable response from a non-repeating challenge.
S/Key authentication does not require the storage of the user's
secret key, which is an advantage when dealing with current
untrustworthy computing systems. In its current form, the S/Key
system is vulnerable to a dictionary attack on the secret password
(pass phrase) which might have been poorly chosen. The Point-to-
Point Protocol's CHAP challenge-response system is non-disclosing
but only useful locally [LS92, Simpson93]. These systems vary in
the sensitivity of the information stored in the authenticating
host, and thus vary in the security requirements that must be
placed on that host.

3.4 Authentication Mechanisms Not Vulnerable to Active Attacks

The growing use of networked computing environments has led to the
need for stronger authentication. In open networks, many users
can gain access to any information flowing over the network, and
with additional effort, a user can send information that appears
to come from another user.

More powerful authentication systems make use of the computation
capability of the two authenticating parties. Authentication may
be unidirectional, for example authenticating users to a host
computer system, or it may be mutual in which case the entity
logging in is assured of the identity of the host. Some
authentication systems use cryptographic techniques and establish
(as a part of the authentication process) a shared secret (e.g.,
session key) that can be used for further exchanges. For example,
a user, after completion of the authentication process, might be
granted an authorization ticket that can be used to obtain other
services without further authentication. These authentication

systems might also provide confidentiality (using encryption) over insecure networks when required.

4. CRYPTOGRAPHY

Cryptographic mechanisms are widely used to provide authentication, either with or without confidentiality, in computer networks and internetworks. There are two basic kinds of cryptography and these are described in this section. A fundamental and recurring problem with cryptographic mechanisms is how to securely distribute keys to the communicating parties. Key distribution is addressed in Section 6 of this document.

4.1 Symmetric Cryptography

Symmetric Cryptography includes all systems that use the same key for encryption and decryption. Thus if anyone improperly obtains the key, they can both decrypt and read data encrypted using that key and also encrypt false data and make it appear to be valid. This means that knowledge of the key by an undesired third party fully compromises the confidentiality of the system. Therefore, the keys used need to be distributed securely, either by courier or perhaps by use of a key distribution protocol, of which the best known is perhaps that proposed by Needham and Schroeder [NS78, NS87]. The widely used Data Encryption Standard (DES) algorithm, that has been standardized for use to protect unclassified civilian US Government information, is perhaps the best known symmetric encryption algorithm [NBS77].

A well known system that addresses insecure open networks as a part of a computing environment is the Kerberos (TM) Authentication Service that was developed as part of Project Athena at MIT [SNS88, BM91, KN93]. Kerberos is based on Data Encryption Standard (DES) symmetric key encryption and uses a trusted (third party) host that knows the secret keys of all users and services, and thus can generate credentials that can be used by users and servers to prove their identities to other systems. As with any distributed authentication scheme, these credentials will be believed by any computer within the local administrative domain or realm. Hence, if a user's password is disclosed, an attacker would be able to masquerade as that user on any system which trusts Kerberos. As the Kerberos server knows all secret keys, it must be physically secure. Kerberos session keys can be used to provide confidentiality between any entities that trust the key server.

4.2 Asymmetric Cryptography

In the late 1970s, a major breakthrough in cryptology led to the availability of Asymmetric Cryptography. This is different from Symmetric Cryptography because different keys are used for encryption and decryption, which greatly simplifies the key distribution problem. The best known asymmetric system is based on work by Rivest, Shamir, and Adleman and is often referred to as "RSA" after the authors' initials [RSA78].

SPX is an experimental system that overcomes the limitations of the trusted key distribution center of Kerberos by using RSA Public Key Cryptography [TA91]. SPX assumes a global hierarchy of certifying authorities at least one of which is trusted by each party. It uses digital signatures that consist of a token encrypted in the private key of the signing entity and that are validated using the appropriate public key. The public keys are believed to be correct as they are obtained under the signature of the trusted certification authority. Critical parts of the authentication exchange are encrypted in the public keys of the receivers, thus preventing a replay attack.

4.3 Cryptographic Checksums

Cryptographic checksums are one of the most useful near term tools for protocol designers. A cryptographic checksum or message integrity checksum (MIC) provides data integrity and authentication but not non-repudiation. For example, Secure SNMP and SNMPv2 both calculate a MD5 cryptographic checksum over a shared secret item of data and the information to be authenticated [Rivest92, GM93]. This serves to authenticate the data origin and is believed to be very difficult to forge. It does not authenticate that the data being sent is itself valid, only that it was actually sent by the party that claims to have sent it. Crytographic checksums can be used to provide relatively strong authentication and are particularly useful in host-to-host communications. The main implementation difficulty with cryptographic checksums is key distribution.

4.4 Digital Signatures

A digital signature is a cryptographic mechanism which is the electronic equivalent of a written signature. It serves to authenticate a piece of data as to the sender. A digital signature using asymmetric cryptography (Public Key) can also be useful in proving that data originated with a party even if the party denies having sent it; this property is called non-repudiation. A digital signature provides authentication without confidentiality and without incurring some of the difficulties in full encryption. Digital signatures are being used with key certificates for Privacy Enhanced Mail [Linn93, Kent93, Balenson93, Kaliski93].

5. USER TO HOST AUTHENTICATION

There are a number of different approaches to authenticating users to remote or networked hosts. Two types of hazard are created by remote or networked access: First an intruder can eavesdrop on the network and obtain user ids and passwords for a later replay attack. Even the form of existing passwords provides a potential intruder with a head start in guessing new ones.

Currently, most systems use plain-text disclosing passwords sent over the network (typically using telnet or rlogin) from the user to the remote host [Anderson84, Kantor91]. This system does not provide adequate protection from replay attacks where an eavesdropper gains remote user ids and remote passwords.

5.1 Protection Against Passive Attack Is Necessary

Failure to use at least a non-disclosing password system means that unlimited access is unintentionally granted to anyone with physical access to the network. For example, anyone with physical access to the Ethernet cable can impersonate any user on that portion of the network. Thus, when one has plain-text disclosing passwords on an Ethernet, the primary security system is the guard at the door (if any exist). The same problem exists in other LAN technologies such as Token-Ring or FDDI. In some small internal Local Area Networks (LANs) it may be acceptable to take this risk, but it is an unacceptable risk in an Internet [CERT94].

The minimal defense against passive attacks, such as eavesdropping, is to use a non-disclosing password system. Such a system can be run from a dumb terminal or a simple communications program (e.g., Crosstalk or PROCOMM) that emulates a dumb terminal on a PC class computer. Using a stronger authentication system would certainly defend against passive attacks against remotely accessed systems, but at the cost of not being able to use simple terminals. It is reasonable to expect that the vendors of communications programs and non user-programmable terminals (such as X-Terminals) would build in non-disclosing password or stronger authentication systems if they were standardized or if a large market were offered. One of the advantages of Kerberos is that, if used properly, the user's password never leaves the user's workstation. Instead they are used to decrypt the user's Kerberos tickets, which are themselves encrypted information which are sent over the network to application servers.

5.2 Perimeter Defenses as Short Term Tool

Perimeter defenses are becoming more common. In these systems,
the user first authenticates to an entity on an externally
accessible portion of the network, possibly a "firewall" host on
the Internet, using a non-disclosing password system. The user
then uses a second system to authenticate to each host, or group
of hosts, from which service is desired. This decouples the
problem into two more easily handled situations.

There are several disadvantages to the perimeter defense, so it
should be thought of as a short term solution. The gateway is not
transparent at the IP level, so it must treat every service
independently. The use of double authentication is, in general,
difficult or impossible for computer-computer communication. End
to end protocols, which are common on the connectionless Internet,
could easily break. The perimeter defense must be tight and
complete, because if it is broken, the inner defenses tend to be
too weak to stop a potential intruder. For example, if disclosing
passwords are used internally, these passwords can be learned by
an external intruder (eavesdropping). If that intruder is able to
penetrate the perimeter, the internal system is completely
exposed. Finally, a perimeter defense may be open to compromise
by internal users looking for shortcuts.

A frequent form of perimeter defense is the application relay. As
these relays are protocol specific, the IP connectivity of the
hosts inside the perimeter with the outside world is broken and
part of the power of the Internet is lost.

An administrative advantage of the perimeter defense is that the
number of machines that are on the perimeter and thus vulnerable
to attack is small. These machines may be carefully checked for
security hazards, but it is difficult (or impossible) to guarantee
that the perimeter is leak-proof. The security of a perimeter
defense is complicated as the gateway machines must pass some
types of traffic such as electronic mail. Other network services
such as the Network Time Protocol (NTP) and the File Transfer
Protocol (FTP) may also be desirable [Mills92, PR85, Bishop].
Furthermore, the perimeter gateway system must be able to pass
without bottleneck the entire traffic load for its security
domain.

5.3 Protection Against Active Attacks Highly Desirable

In the foreseeable future, the use of stronger techniques will be required to protect against active attacks. Many corporate networks based on broadcast technology such as Ethernet probably need such techniques. To defend against an active attack, or to provide privacy, it is necessary to use a protocol with session encryption, for example Kerberos, or use an authentication mechanism that protects against replay attacks, perhaps using time stamps. In Kerberos, users obtain credentials from the Kerberos server and use them for authentication to obtain services from other computers on the network. The computing power of the local workstation can be used to decrypt credentials (using a key derived from the user-provided password) and store them until needed. If the security protocol relies on synchronized clocks, then NTPv3 might be useful because it distributes time amongst a large number of computers and is one of the few existing Internet protocols that includes authentication mechanisms [Bishop, Mills92].

Another approach to remotely accessible networks of computers is for all externally accessible machines to share a secret with the Kerberos KDC. In a sense, this makes these machines "servers" instead of general use workstations. This shared secret can then be used encrypt all communication between the two machines enabling the accessible workstation to relay authentication information to the KDC in a secure way.

Finally, workstations that are remotely accessible could use asymmetric cryptographic technology to encrypt communications. The workstation's public key would be published and well known to all clients. A user could use the public key to encrypt a simple password and the remote system can decrypt the password to authenticate the user without risking disclosure of the password while it is in transit. A limitation of this workstation-oriented security is that it does not authenticate individual users only individual workstations. In some environments for example, government multi-level secure or compartmented mode workstations, user to user authentication and confidentiality is also needed.

6. KEY DISTRIBUTION & MANAGEMENT

The discussion thus far has periodically mentioned keys, either for encryption or for authentication (e.g., as input to a digital signature function). Key management is perhaps the hardest problem faced when seeking to provide authentication in large internetworks. Hence this section provides a very brief overview of key management technology that might be used.

The Needham & Schroeder protocol, which is used by Kerberos, relies on a central key server. In a large internetwork, there would need to be significant numbers of these key servers, at least one key server per administrative domain. There would also need to be mechanisms for separately administered key servers to cooperate in generating a session key for parties in different administrative domains. These are not impossible problems, but this approach clearly involves significant infrastructure changes.

Most public-key encryption algorithms are computationally expensive and so are not ideal for encrypting packets in a network. However, the asymmetric property makes them very useful for setup and exchange of symmetric session keys. In practice, the commercial sector probably uses asymmetric algorithms primarily for digital signatures and key exchange, but not for bulk data encryption. Both RSA and the Diffie-Hellman techniques can be used for this [DH76]. One advantage of using asymmetric techniques is that the central key server can be eliminated. The difference in key management techniques is perhaps the primary difference between Kerberos and SPX. Privacy Enhanced Mail has trusted key authorities use digital signatures to sign and authenticate the public keys of users [Kent93]. The result of this operation is a key certificates which contains the public key of some party and authentication that the public key in fact belongs to that party. Key certificates can be distributed in many ways. One way to distribute key certificates might be to add them to existing directory services, for example by extending the existing Domain Name System to hold each host's the key certificate in a new record type.

For multicast sessions, key management is harder because the number of exchanges required by the widely used techniques is proportional to the number of participating parties. Thus there is a serious scaling problem with current published multicast key management techniques.

Finally, key management mechanisms described in the public literature have a long history of subtle flaws. There is ample evidence of this, even for well-known techniques such as the Needham & Schroeder protocol [NS78, NS87]. In some cases, subtle flaws have only become known after formal methods techniques were used in an attempt to verify the protocol. Hence, it is highly desirable that key management mechanisms be kept separate from authentication or encryption mechanisms as much as is possible. For example, it is probably better to have a key management protocol that is distinct from and does not depend upon another security protocol.

7. AUTHENTICATION OF NETWORK SERVICES

In addition to needing to authenticate users and hosts to each other, many network services need or could benefit from authentication. This section describes some approaches to authentication in protocols that are primarily host to host in orientation. As in the user to host authentication case, there are several techniques that might be considered.

The most common case at present is to not have any authentication support in the protocol. Bellovin and others have documented a number of cases where existing protocols can be used to attack a remote machine because there is no authentication in the protocols [Bellovin89].

Some protocols provide for disclosing passwords to be passed along with the protocol information. The original SNMP protocols used this method and a number of the routing protocols continue to use this method [Moy91, LR91, CFSD88]. This method is useful as a transitional aid to slightly increase security and might be appropriate when there is little risk in having a completely insecure protocol.

There are many protocols that need to support stronger authentication mechanisms. For example, there was widespread concern that SNMP needed stronger authentication than it originally had. This led to the publication of the Secure SNMP protocols which support optional authentication, using a digital signature mechanism, and optional confidentiality, using DES encryption. The digital signatures used in Secure SNMP are based on appending a cryptographic checksum to the SNMP information. The cryptographic checksum is computed using the MD5 algorithm and a secret shared between the communicating parties so is believed to be difficult to forge or invert.

Digital signature technology has evolved in recent years and should be considered for applications requiring authentication but not confidentiality. Digital signatures may use a single secret shared among two or more communicating parties or it might be based on asymmetric encryption technology. The former case would require the use of predetermined keys or the use of a secure key distribution protocol, such as that devised by Needham and Schroeder. In the latter case, the public keys would need to be distributed in an authenticated manner. If a general key distribution mechanism were available, support for optional digital signatures could be added to most protocols with little additional expense. Each protocol could address the key exchange and setup problem, but that might make adding support for digital signatures more complicated and effectively discourage protocol designers from adding digital signature support.

For cases where both authentication and confidentiality are required on a host-to-host basis, session encryption could be employed using symmetric cryptography, asymmetric cryptography, or a combination of both. Use of the asymmetric cryptography simplifies key management. Each host would encrypt the information while in transit between hosts and the existing operating system mechanisms would provide protection within each host.

In some cases, possibly including electronic mail, it might be desirable to provide the security properties within the application itself in a manner that was truly user-to-user rather than being host-to-host. The Privacy Enhanced Mail (PEM) work is employing this approach [Linn93, Kent93, Balenson93, Kaliski93]. The recent IETF work on Common Authentication Technology might make it easier to implement a secure distributed or networked application through use of standard security programming interfaces [Linn93a].

8. FUTURE DIRECTIONS

Systems are moving towards the cryptographically stronger authentication mechanisms described earlier. This move has two implications for future systems. We can expect to see the introduction of non-disclosing authentication systems in the near term and eventually see more widespread use of public key crypto-systems. Session authentication, integrity, and privacy issues are growing in importance. As computer-to-computer communication becomes more important, protocols that provide simple human interfaces will become less important. This is not to say that human interfaces are unimportant; they are very important. It means that these interfaces are the responsibility of the applications, not the underlying protocol. Human interface design is beyond the scope of this memo.

The use of public key crypto-systems for user-to-host authentication simplifies many security issues, but unlike simple passwords, a public key cannot be memorized. As of this writing, public key sizes of at least 500 bits are commonly used in the commercial world. It is likely that larger key sizes will be used in the future. Thus, users might have to carry their private keys in some electrically readable form. The use of read-only storage, such as a floppy disk or a magnetic stripe card provides such storage, but it might require the user to trust their private keys to the reading device. Use of a smart card, a portable device containing both storage and program might be preferable. These devices have the potential to perform the authenticating operations without divulging the private key they contain. They can also interact with the user requiring a simpler form of authentication to "unlock" the card.

The use of public key crypto-systems for host-to-host authentication appears not to have the same key memorization problem as the user-to-host case does. A multiuser host can store its key(s) in space protected from users and obviate that problem. Single user inherently insecure systems, such as PCs and Macintoshes, remain difficult to handle but the smart card approach should also work for them.

If one considers existing symmetric algorithms to be 1-key techniques, and existing asymmetric algorithms such as RSA to be 2-key techniques, one might wonder whether N-key techniques will be developed in the future (i.e., for values of N larger than 2). If such N-key technology existed, it might be useful in creating scalable multicast key distribution protocols. There is work currently underway examining the possible use of the Core Based Tree (CBT) multicast routing technology to provide scalable multicast key distribution [BFC93].

The implications of this taxonomy are clear. Strong cryptographic authentication is needed in the near future for many protocols. Public key technology should be used when it is practical and cost-effective. In the short term, authentication mechanisms vulnerable to passive attack should be phased out in favour of stronger authentication mechanisms. Additional research is needed to develop improved key management technology and scalable multicast security mechanisms.

SECURITY CONSIDERATIONS

This entire memo discusses Security Considerations in that it discusses authentication technologies and needs.

ACKNOWLEDGEMENTS

This memo has benefited from review by and suggestions from the IETF's Common Authentication Technology (CAT) working group, chaired by John Linn, and from Marcus J. Ranum.

REFERENCES

[Anderson84] Anderson, B., "TACACS User Identification Telnet Option", RFC 927, BBN, December 1984.

[Balenson93] Balenson, D., "Privacy Enhancement for Internet Electronic Mail: Part III: Algorithms, Modes, and Identifiers", RFC 1423, TIS, IAB IRTF PSRG, IETF PEM WG, February 1993.

[BFC93]   Ballardie, A., Francis, P., and J. Crowcroft, "Core Based Trees (CBT) An Architecture for Scalable Inter-Domain Multicast Routing", Proceedings of ACM SIGCOMM93, ACM, San Franciso, CA, September 1993, pp. 85-95.

[Bellovin89]   Bellovin, S., "Security Problems in the TCP/IP Protocol Suite", ACM Computer Communications Review, Vol. 19, No. 2, March 1989.

[Bellovin92]   Bellovin, S., "There Be Dragons", Proceedings of the 3rd Usenix UNIX Security Symposium, Baltimore, MD, September 1992.

[Bellovin93]   Bellovin, S., "Packets Found on an Internet", ACM Computer Communications Review, Vol. 23, No. 3, July 1993, pp. 26-31.

[BM91]   Bellovin S., and M. Merritt, "Limitations of the Kerberos Authentication System", ACM Computer Communications Review, October 1990.

[Bishop]   Bishop, M., "A Security Analysis of Version 2 of the Network Time Protocol NTP: A report to the Privacy & Security Research Group", Technical Report PCS-TR91-154, Department of Mathematics & Computer Science, Dartmouth College, Hanover, New Hampshire.

[CB94]   Cheswick W., and S. Bellovin, "Chapter 10: An Evening with Berferd", Firewalls & Internet Security, Addison-Wesley, Reading, Massachusetts, 1994.   ISBN 0-201-63357-4.

[CERT94]   Computer Emergency Response Team, "Ongoing Network Monitoring Attacks", CERT Advisory CA-94:01, available by anonymous ftp from cert.sei.cmu.edu, 3 February 1994.

[CFSD88]   Case, J., Fedor, M., Schoffstall, M., and J. Davin, "Simple Network Management Protocol", RFC 1067, University of Tennessee at Knoxville, NYSERNet, Inc., Rensselaer Polytechnic Institute, Proteon, Inc., August 1988.

[DH76]   Diffie W., and M. Hellman, "New Directions in Cryptography", IEEE Transactions on Information Theory, Volume IT-11, November 1976, pp. 644-654.

[GM93]   Galvin, J., and K. McCloghrie, "Security Protocols for Version 2 of the Simple Network Management Protocol (SNMPv2)", RFC 1446, Trusted Information Systems, Hughes LAN Systems, April 1993.

[Haller94] Haller, N., "The S/Key One-time Password System", Proceedings of the Symposium on Network & Distributed Systems Security, Internet Society, San Diego, CA, February 1994.

[Kaufman93] Kaufman, C., "Distributed Authentication Security Service (DASS)", RFC 1507, Digital Equipment Corporation, September 1993.

[Kaliski93] Kaliski, B., "Privacy Enhancement for Internet Electronic Mail: Part IV: Key Certification and Related Services", RFC 1424, RSA Laboratories, February 1993.

[Kantor91] Kantor, B., "BSD Rlogin", RFC 1258, Univ. of Calif San Diego, September 1991.

[Kent93] Kent, S., "Privacy Enhancement for Internet Electronic Mail: Part II: Certificate-Based Key Management", RFC 1422, BBN, IAB IRTF PSRG, IETF PEM, February 1993.

[KN93] Kohl, J., and C. Neuman, "The Kerberos Network Authentication Service (V5)", RFC 1510, Digital Equipment Corporation, USC/Information Sciences Institute, September 1993.

[Linn93] Linn, J., "Privacy Enhancement for Internet Electronic Mail: Part I: Message Encryption and Authentication Procedures", RFC 1421, IAB IRTF PSRG, IETF PEM WG, February 1993.

[Linn93a] Linn, J., "Common Authentication Technology Overview", RFC 1511, Geer Zolot Associate, September 1993.

[LS92] Lloyd B., and W. Simpson, "PPP Authentication Protocols", RFC 1334, L&A, Daydreamer, October 1992.

[LR91] Lougheed K., and Y. Rekhter, "A Border Gateway protocol 3 (BGP-3)", RFC 1267, cisco Systems, T.J. Watson Research Center, IBM Corp., October 1991.

[Mills92] Mills, D., "Network Time Protocol (Version 3) - Specification, Implementation, and Analysis", RFC 1305, UDEL, March 1992.

[NBS77] National Bureau of Standards, "Data Encryption Standard", Federal Information Processing Standards Publication 46, Government Printing Office, Washington, DC, 1977.

[NS78] Needham, R., and M. Schroeder, "Using Encryption for Authentication in Large Networks of Computers", Communications of the ACM, Vol. 21, No. 12, December 1978.

[NS87]   Needham, R., and M. Schroeder, "Authentication Revisited", ACM Operating Systems Review, Vol. 21, No. 1, 1987.

[PR85]   Postel J., and J. Reynolds, "File Transfer Protocol", STD 9, RFC 959, USC/Information Sciences Institute, October 1985.

[Moy91]   Moy, J., "OSPF Routing Protocol, Version 2", RFC 1247, Proteon, Inc., July 1991.

[RSA78]   Rivest, R., Shamir, A., and L. Adleman, "A Method for Obtaining Digital Signatures and Public Key Crypto-systems", Communications of the ACM, Vol. 21, No. 2, February 1978.

[Rivest92]   Rivest, R., "The MD5 Message-Digest Algorithm", RFC 1321, MIT Laboratory for Computer Science and RSA Data Security, Inc., April 1992.

[Simpson93]   Simpson, W., "The Point to Point Protocol", RFC 1548, Daydreamer, December 1993.

[SNS88]   Steiner, J., Neuman, C., and J. Schiller, "Kerberos: "An Authentication Service for Open Network Systems", USENIX Conference Proceedings, Dallas, Texas, February 1988.

[Stoll90]   Stoll, C., "The Cuckoo's Egg: Tracking a Spy Through the Maze of Computer Espionage", Pocket Books, New York, NY, 1990.

[TA91]   Tardo J., and K. Alagappan, "SPX: Global Authentication Using Public Key Certificates", Proceedings of the 1991 Symposium on Research in Security & Privacy, IEEE Computer Society, Los Amitos, California, 1991. pp.232-244.

AUTHORS' ADDRESSES

Neil Haller
Bell Communications Research
445 South Street   -- MRE 2Q-280
Morristown, NJ 07962-1910

Phone: (201) 829-4478
EMail: nmh@thumper.bellcore.com

Randall Atkinson
Information Technology Division
Naval Research Laboratory
Washington, DC 20375-5320

Phone: (DSN) 354-8590
EMail: atkinson@itd.nrl.navy.mil

Network Working Group   R. Atkinson
Request for Comments: 1825   Naval Research Laboratory
Category: Standards Track   August 1995

              Security Architecture for the Internet Protocol

Status of this Memo

    This document specifies an Internet standards track protocol for the
    Internet community, and requests discussion and suggestions for
    improvements. Please refer to the current edition of the "Internet
    Official Protocol Standards" (STD 1) for the standardization state
    and status of this protocol. Distribution of this memo is unlimited.

1. INTRODUCTION

    This memo describes the security mechanisms for IP version 4 (IPv4)
    and IP version 6 (IPv6) and the services that they provide. Each
    security mechanism is specified in a separate document. This
    document also describes key management requirements for systems
    implementing those security mechanisms. This document is not an
    overall Security Architecture for the Internet and is instead focused
    on IP-layer security.

1.1 Technical Definitions

    This section provides a few basic definitions that are applicable to
    this document. Other documents provide more definitions and
    background information [VK83, HA94].

    Authentication
            The property of knowing that the data received is the same as
            the data that was sent and that the claimed sender is in fact
            the actual sender.

    Integrity
            The property of ensuring that data is transmitted from source
            to destination without undetected alteration.

    Confidentiality
            The property of communicating such that the intended
            recipients know what was being sent but unintended
            parties cannot determine what was sent.

    Encryption
            A mechanism commonly used to provide confidentiality.

Non-repudiation
        The property of a receiver being able to prove that the sender
        of some data did in fact send the data even though the sender
        might later desire to deny ever having sent that data.

SPI
        Acronym for "Security Parameters Index". An unstructured
        opaque index which is used in conjunction with the
        Destination Address to identify a particular Security
        Association.

Security Association
        The set of security information relating to a given network
        connection or set of connections. This is described in
        detail below.

Traffic Analysis
        The analysis of network traffic flow for the purpose of
        deducing information that is useful to an adversary.
        Examples of such information are frequency of transmission,
        the identities of the conversing parties, sizes of packets,
        Flow Identifiers used, etc. [Sch94].

1.2 Requirements Terminology

In this document, the words that are used to define the significance
of each particular requirement are usually capitalised. These words
are:

- MUST

    This word or the adjective "REQUIRED" means that the item is an
    absolute requirement of the specification.

- SHOULD

    This word or the adjective "RECOMMENDED" means that there might
    exist valid reasons in particular circumstances to ignore this
    item, but the full implications should be understood and the case
    carefully weighed before taking a different course.

- MAY

    This word or the adjective "OPTIONAL" means that this item is
    truly optional. One vendor might choose to include the item
    because a particular marketplace requires it or because it
    enhances the product, for example; another vendor may omit the
    same item.

1.3 Typical Use

There are two specific headers that are used to provide security
services in IPv4 and IPv6. These headers are the "IP Authentication
Header (AH)" [Atk95a] and the "IP Encapsulating Security Payload
(ESP)" [Atk95b] header. There are a number of ways in which these IP
security mechanisms might be used. This section describes some of
the more likely uses. These descriptions are not complete or
exhaustive. Other uses can also be envisioned.

The IP Authentication Header is designed to provide integrity and
authentication without confidentiality to IP datagrams. The lack of
confidentiality ensures that implementations of the Authentication
Header will be widely available on the Internet, even in locations
where the export, import, or use of encryption to provide
confidentiality is regulated. The Authentication Header supports
security between two or more hosts implementing AH, between two or
more gateways implementing AH, and between a host or gateway
implementing AH and a set of hosts or gateways. A security gateway
is a system which acts as the communications gateway between external
untrusted systems and trusted hosts on their own subnetwork. It also
provides security services for the trusted hosts when they
communicate with the external untrusted systems. A trusted
subnetwork contains hosts and routers that trust each other not to
engage in active or passive attacks and trust that the underlying
communications channel (e.g., an Ethernet) isn't being attacked.

In the case where a security gateway is providing services on behalf
of one or more hosts on a trusted subnet, the security gateway is
responsible for establishing the security association on behalf of
its trusted host and for providing security services between the
security gateway and the external system(s). In this case, only the
gateway need implement AH, while all of the systems behind the
gateway on the trusted subnet may take advantage of AH services
between the gateway and external systems.

A security gateway which receives a datagram containing a recognised
sensitivity label, for example IPSO [Ken91], from a trusted host
should take that label's value into consideration when
creating/selecting an Security Association for use with AH between
the gateway and the external destination. In such an environment, a
gateway which receives a IP packet containing the IP Encapsulating
Security Payload (ESP) should add appropriate authentication,
including implicit (i.e., contained in the Security Association used)
or explicit label information (e.g., IPSO), for the decrypted packet
that it forwards to the trusted host that is the ultimate
destination. The IP Authentication Header should always be used on
packets containing explicit sensitivity labels to ensure end-to-end

label integrity. In environments using security gateways, those
gateways MUST perform address-based IP packet filtering on
unauthenticated packets purporting to be from a system known to be
using IP security.

The IP Encapsulating Security Payload (ESP) is designed to provide
integrity, authentication, and confidentiality to IP datagrams
[Atk95b]. The ESP supports security between two or more hosts
implementing ESP, between two or more gateways implementing ESP, and
between a host or gateway implementing ESP and a set of hosts and/or
gateways. A security gateway is a system which acts as the
communications gateway between external untrusted systems and trusted
hosts on their own subnetwork and provides security services for the
trusted hosts when they communicate with external untrusted systems.
A trusted subnetwork contains hosts and routers that trust each other
not to engage in active or passive attacks and trust that the
underlying communications channel (e.g., an Ethernet) isn't being
attacked. Trusted systems always should be trustworthy, but in
practice they often are not trustworthy.

Gateway-to-gateway encryption is most valuable for building private
virtual networks across an untrusted backbone such as the Internet.
It does this by excluding outsiders. As such, it is often not a
substitute for host-to-host encryption, and indeed the two can be and
often should be used together.

In the case where a security gateway is providing services on behalf
of one or more hosts on a trusted subnet, the security gateway is
responsible for establishing the security association on behalf of
its trusted host and for providing security services between the
security gateway and the external system(s). In this case, only the
gateway need implement ESP, while all of the systems behind the
gateway on the trusted subnet may take advantage of ESP services
between the gateway and external systems.

A gateway which receives a datagram containing a recognised
sensitivity label from a trusted host should take that label's value
into consideration when creating/selecting a Security Association for
use with ESP between the gateway and the external destination. In
such an environment, a gateway which receives a IP packet containing
the ESP should appropriately label the decrypted packet that it
forwards to the trusted host that is the ultimate destination. The
IP Authentication Header should always be used on packets containing
explicit sensitivity labels to ensure end-to-end label integrity.

If there are no security gateways present in the connection, then two
end systems that implement ESP may also use it to encrypt only the
user data (e.g., TCP or UDP) being carried between the two systems.
ESP is designed to provide maximum flexibility so that users may
select and use only the security that they desire and need.

Routing headers for which integrity has not been cryptographically
protected SHOULD be ignored by the receiver. If this rule is not
strictly adhered to, then the system will be vulnerable to various
kinds of attacks, including source routing attacks [Bel89] [CB94]
[CERT95].

While these documents do not specifically discuss IPv4 broadcast,
these IP security mechanisms MAY be used with such packets. Key
distribution and Security Association management are not trivial for
broadcast applications. Also, if symmetric key algorithms are used
the value of using cryptography with a broadcast packet is limited
because the receiver can only know that the received packet came from
one of many systems knowing the correct key to use.

1.4 Security Associations

The concept of a "Security Association" is fundamental to both the IP
Encapsulating Security Payload and the IP Authentication Header. The
combination of a given Security Parameter Index (SPI) and Destination
Address uniquely identifies a particular "Security Association". An
implementation of the Authentication Header or the Encapsulating
Security Payload MUST support this concept of a Security Association.
An implementation MAY also support other parameters as part of a
Security Association. A Security Association normally includes the
parameters listed below, but might include additional parameters as
well:

- Authentication algorithm and algorithm mode being used with
  the IP Authentication Header [REQUIRED for AH implementations].

- Key(s) used with the authentication algorithm in use with
  the Authentication Header [REQUIRED for AH implementations].

- Encryption algorithm, algorithm mode, and transform being
  used with the IP Encapsulating Security Payload [REQUIRED for
  ESP implementations].

- Key(s) used with the encryption algorithm in use with the
  Encapsulating Security Payload [REQUIRED for ESP implementations].

- Presence/absence and size of a cryptographic synchronisation or
  initialisation vector field for the encryption algorithm [REQUIRED
  for ESP implementations].

- Authentication algorithm and mode used with the ESP transform
  (if any is in use) [RECOMMENDED for ESP implementations].

- Authentication key(s) used with the authentication algorithm
  that is part of the ESP transform (if any) [RECOMMENDED for
  ESP implementations].

- Lifetime of the key or time when key change should occur
  [RECOMMENDED for all implementations].

- Lifetime of this Security Association [RECOMMENDED for all
  implementations].

- Source Address(es) of the Security Association, might be a
  wildcard address if more than one sending system shares the
  same Security Association with the destination [RECOMMENDED
  for all implementations].

- Sensitivity level (for example, Secret or Unclassified)
  of the protected data [REQUIRED for all systems claiming
  to provide multi-level security, RECOMMENDED for all other systems].

The sending host uses the sending userid and Destination Address to
select an appropriate Security Association (and hence SPI value).
The receiving host uses the combination of SPI value and Destination
Address to distinguish the correct association. Hence, an AH
implementation will always be able to use the SPI in combination with
the Destination Address to determine the security association and
related security configuration data for all valid incoming packets.
When a formerly valid Security Association becomes invalid, the
destination system(s) SHOULD NOT immediately reuse that SPI value and
instead SHOULD let that SPI value become stale before reusing it for
some other Security Association.

A security association is normally one-way. An authenticated
communications session between two hosts will normally have two
Security Parameter Indexes in use (one in each direction). The
combination of a particular Security Parameter Index and a particular
Destination Address uniquely identifies the Security Association.
The Destination Address may be a unicast address or a multicast group
address.

The receiver-orientation of the Security Association implies that, in the case of unicast traffic, the destination system will normally select the SPI value. By having the destination select the SPI value, there is no potential for manually configured Security Associations that conflict with automatically configured (e.g., via a key management protocol) Security Associations. For multicast traffic, there are multiple destination systems but a single destination multicast group, so some system or person will need to select SPIs on behalf of that multicast group and then communicate the information to all of the legitimate members of that multicast group via mechanisms not defined here.

Multiple senders to a multicast group MAY use a single Security Association (and hence Security Parameter Index) for all traffic to that group. In that case, the receiver only knows that the message came from a system knowing the security association data for that multicast group. A receiver cannot generally authenticate which system sent the multicast traffic when symmetric algorithms (e.g., DES, IDEA) are in use. Multicast traffic MAY also use a separate Security Association (and hence SPI) for each sender to the multicast group . If each sender has its own Security Association and asymmetric algorithms are used, then data origin authentication is also a provided service.

2. DESIGN OBJECTIVES

This section describes some of the design objectives of this security architecture and its component mechanisms. The primary objective of this work is to ensure that IPv4 and IPv6 will have solid cryptographic security mechanisms available to users who desire security.

These mechanisms are designed to avoid adverse impacts on Internet users who do not employ these security mechanisms for their traffic. These mechanisms are intended to be algorithm-independent so that the cryptographic algorithms can be altered without affecting the other parts of the implementation. These security mechanisms should be useful in enforcing a variety of security policies.

Standard default algorithms (keyed MD5, DES CBC) are specified to ensure interoperability in the global Internet. The selected default algorithms are the same as the standard default algorithms used in SNMPv2 [GM93].

3. IP-LAYER SECURITY MECHANISMS

There are two cryptographic security mechanisms for IP. The first is
the Authentication Header which provides integrity and authentication
without confidentiality [Atk95a]. The second is the Encapsulating
Security Payload which always provides confidentiality, and
(depending on algorithm and mode) might also provide integrity and
authentication [Atk95b]. The two IP security mechanisms may be used
together or separately.

These IP-layer mechanisms do not provide security against a number of
traffic analysis attacks. However, there are several techniques
outside the scope of this specification (e.g., bulk link encryption)
that might be used to provide protection against traffic analysis
[VK83].

3.1 AUTHENTICATION HEADER

The IP Authentication Header holds authentication information for its
IP datagram [Atk95a]. It does this by computing a cryptographic
authentication function over the IP datagram and using a secret
authentication key in the computation. The sender computes the
authentication data prior to sending the authenticated IP packet.
Fragmentation occurs after the Authentication Header processing for
outbound packets and prior to Authentication Header processing for
inbound packets. The receiver verifies the correctness of the
authentication data upon reception. Certain fields which must change
in transit, such as the "TTL" (IPv4) or "Hop Limit" (IPv6) field,
which is decremented on each hop, are omitted from the authentication
calculation. However the omission of the Hop Limit field does not
adversely impact the security provided. Non-repudiation might be
provided by some authentication algorithms (e.g., asymmetric
algorithms when both sender and receiver keys are used in the
authentication calculation) used with the Authentication Header, but
it is not necessarily provided by all authentication algorithms that
might be used with the Authentication Header. The default
authentication algorithm is keyed MD5, which, like all symmetric
algorithms, cannot provide non-repudiation by itself.
Confidentiality and traffic analysis protection are not provided by
the Authentication Header.

Use of the Authentication Header will increase the IP protocol
processing costs in participating systems and will also increase the
communications latency. The increased latency is primarily due to
the calculation of the authentication data by the sender and the
calculation and comparison of the authentication data by each
receiver for each IP datagram containing an Authentication Header
(AH).

The Authentication Header provides much stronger security than exists in most of the current Internet and should not affect exportability or significantly increase implementation cost. While the Authentication Header might be implemented by a security gateway on behalf of hosts on a trusted network behind that security gateway, this mode of operation is not encouraged. Instead, the Authentication Header should be used from origin to final destination.

All IPv6-capable hosts MUST implement the IP Authentication Header with at least the MD5 algorithm using a 128-bit key. IPv4-systems claiming to implement the Authentication Header MUST implement the IP Authentication Header with at least the MD5 algorithm using a 128-bit key [MS95]. An implementation MAY support other authentication algorithms in addition to keyed MD5.

3.2 ENCAPSULATING SECURITY PAYLOAD

The IP Encapsulating Security Payload (ESP) is designed to provide integrity, authentication, and confidentiality to IP datagrams [Atk95b]. It does this by encapsulating either an entire IP datagram or only the upper-layer protocol (e.g., TCP, UDP, ICMP) data inside the ESP, encrypting most of the ESP contents, and then appending a new cleartext IP header to the now encrypted Encapsulating Security Payload. This cleartext IP header is used to carry the protected data through the internetwork.

3.2.1 Description of the ESP Modes

There are two modes within ESP. The first mode, which is known as Tunnel-mode, encapsulates an entire IP datagram within the ESP header. The second mode, which is known as Transport-mode, encapsulates an upper-layer protocol (for example UDP or TCP) inside ESP and then prepends a cleartext IP header.

3.2.2 Usage of ESP

ESP works between hosts, between a host and a security gateway, or between security gateways. This support for security gateways permits trustworthy networks behind a security gateway to omit encryption and thereby avoid the performance and monetary costs of encryption, while still providing confidentiality for traffic transiting untrustworthy network segments. When both hosts directly implement ESP and there is no intervening security gateway, then they may use the Transport-mode (where only the upper layer protocol data (e.g., TCP or UDP) is encrypted and there is no encrypted IP header). This mode reduces both the bandwidth consumed and the protocol processing costs for users that don't need to keep the entire IP datagram confidential.

ESP works with both unicast and multicast traffic.

3.2.3 Performance Impacts of ESP

The encapsulating security approach used by ESP can noticeably impact
network performance in participating systems, but use of ESP should
not adversely impact routers or other intermediate systems that are
not participating in the particular ESP association. Protocol
processing in participating systems will be more complex when
encapsulating security is used, requiring both more time and more
processing power. Use of encryption will also increase the
communications latency. The increased latency is primarily due to
the encryption and decryption required for each IP datagram
containing an Encapsulating Security Payload. The precise cost of
ESP will vary with the specifics of the implementation, including the
encryption algorithm, key size, and other factors. Hardware
implementations of the encryption algorithm are recommended when high
throughput is desired.

For interoperability throughout the worldwide Internet, all
conforming implementations of the IP Encapsulating Security Payload
MUST support the use of the Data Encryption Standard (DES) in
Cipher-Block Chaining (CBC) Mode as detailed in the ESP
specification. Other confidentiality algorithms and modes may also
be implemented in addition to this mandatory algorithm and mode.
Export and use of encryption are regulated in some countries [OTA94].

3.3 COMBINING SECURITY MECHANISMS

In some cases the IP Authentication Header might be combined with the
IP Encapsulating Security Protocol to obtain the desired security
properties. The Authentication Header always provides integrity and
authentication and can provide non-repudiation if used with certain
authentication algorithms (e.g., RSA). The Encapsulating Security
Payload always provides integrity and confidentiality and can also
provide authentication if used with certain authenticating encryption
algorithms. Adding the Authentication Header to a IP datagram prior
to encapsulating that datagram using the Encapsulating Security
Protocol might be desirable for users wishing to have strong
integrity, authentication, confidentiality, and perhaps also for
users who require strong non-repudiation. When the two mechanisms
are combined, the placement of the IP Authentication Header makes
clear which part of the data is being authenticated. Details on
combining the two mechanisms are provided in the IP Encapsulating
Security Payload specification [At94b].

3.4 OTHER SECURITY MECHANISMS

Protection from traffic analysis is not provided by any of the
security mechanisms described above. It is unclear whether
meaningful protection from traffic analysis can be provided
economically at the Internet Layer and it appears that few Internet
users are concerned about traffic analysis. One traditional method
for protection against traffic analysis is the use of bulk link
encryption. Another technique is to send false traffic in order to
increase the noise in the data provided by traffic analysis.
Reference [VK83] discusses traffic analysis issues in more detail.

4. KEY MANAGEMENT

The Key Management protocol that will be used with IP layer security
is not specified in this document. However, because the key
management protocol is coupled to AH and ESP only via the Security
Parameters Index (SPI), we can meaningfully define AH and ESP without
having to fully specify how key management is performed. We envision
that several key management systems will be usable with these
specifications, including manual key configuration. Work is ongoing
within the IETF to specify an Internet Standard key management
protocol.

Support for key management methods where the key management data is
carried within the IP layer is not a design objective for these IP-
layer security mechanisms. Instead these IP-layer security
mechanisms will primarily use key management methods where the key
management data will be carried by an upper layer protocol, such as
UDP or TCP, on some specific port number or where the key management
data will be distributed manually.

This design permits clear decoupling of the key management mechanism
from the other security mechanisms, and thereby permits one to
substitute new and improved key management methods without having to
modify the implementations of the other security mechanisms. This
separation of mechanism is clearly wise given the long history of
subtle flaws in published key management protocols [NS78, NS81].
What follows in this section is a brief discussion of a few
alternative approaches to key management. Mutually consenting
systems may additionally use other key management approaches by
private prior agreement.

4.1 Manual Key Distribution

The simplest form of key management is manual key management, where a
person manually configures each system with its own key and also with
the keys of other communicating systems. This is quite practical in

small, static environments but does not scale. It is not a viable
medium-term or long-term approach, but might be appropriate and
useful in many environments in the near-term. For example, within a
small LAN it is entirely practical to manually configure keys for
each system. Within a single administrative domain it is practical
to configure keys for each router so that the routing data can be
protected and to reduce the risk of an intruder breaking into a
router. Another case is where an organisation has an encrypting
firewall between the internal network and the Internet at each of its
sites and it connects two or more sites via the Internet. In this
case, the encrypting firewall might selectively encrypt traffic for
other sites within the organisation using a manually configured key,
while not encrypting traffic for other destinations. It also might
be appropriate when only selected communications need to be secured.

4.2 Some Existing Key Management Techniques

There are a number of key management algorithms that have been
described in the public literature. Needham & Schroeder have
proposed a key management algorithm which relies on a centralised key
distribution system [NS78, NS81]. This algorithm is used in the
Kerberos Authentication System developed at MIT under Project Athena
[KB93]. Diffie and Hellman have devised an algorithm which does not
require a centralised key distribution system [DH76]. Unfortunately,
the original Diffie-Hellman technique is vulnerable to an active "man
in the middle" attack [Sch93, p. 43-44]. However, this vulnerability
can be mitigated by using signed keys to authentically bootstrap into
the Diffie-Hellman exchange [Sch93, p. 45].

4.3 Automated Key Distribution

Widespread deployment and use of IP security will require an
Internet-standard scalable key management protocol. Ideally such a
protocol would support a number of protocols in the Internet protocol
suite, not just IP security. There is work underway within the IETF
to add signed host keys to the Domain Name System [EK94] The DNS keys
enable the originating party to authenticate key management messages
with the other key management party using an asymmetric algorithm.
The two parties would then have an authenticatible communications
channel that could be used to create a shared session key using
Diffie-Hellman or other means [DH76] [Sch93].

4.4 Keying Approaches for IP

There are two keying approaches for IP. The first approach, called
host-oriented keying, has all users on host 1 share the same key for
use on traffic destined for all users on host 2. The second
approach, called user-oriented keying, lets user A on host 1 have one

or more unique session keys for its traffic destined for host 2; such
session keys are not shared with other users on host1. For example,
user A's ftp session might use a different key than user A's telnet
session. In systems claiming to provide multi-level security, user A
•will typically have at least one key per sensitivity level in use
(e.g., one key for UNCLASSIFIED traffic, a second key for SECRET
traffic, and a third key for TOP SECRET traffic). Similarly, with
user-oriented keying one might use separate keys for information sent
to a multicast group and control messages sent to the same multicast
group.

In many cases, a single computer system will have at least two
mutually suspicious users A and B that do not trust each other. When
host-oriented keying is used and mutually suspicious users exist, it
is sometimes possible for user A to determine the host-oriented key
via well known methods, such as a Chosen Plaintext attack. Once user
A has improperly obtained the key in use, user A can then either read
user B's encrypted traffic or forge traffic from user B. When user-
oriented keying is used, certain kinds of attack from one user onto
another user's traffic are not possible.

IP Security is intended to be able to provide Authentication,
Integrity, and Confidentiality for applications operating on
connected end systems when appropriate algorithms are in use.
Integrity and Confidentiality can be provided by host-oriented keying
when appropriate dynamic key management techniques and appropriate
algorithms are in use. However, authentication of principals using
applications on end-systems requires that processes running
applications be able to request and use their own Security
Associations. In this manner, applications can make use of key
distribution facilities that provide authentication.

Hence, support for user-oriented keying SHOULD be present in all IP
implementations, as is described in the "IP Key Management
Requirements" section below.

4.5 Multicast Key Distribution

Multicast key distribution is an active research area in the
published literature as of this writing. For multicast groups having
relatively few members, manual key distribution or multiple use of
existing unicast key distribution algorithms such as modified
Diffie-Hellman appears feasible. For very large groups, new scalable
techniques will be needed. The use of Core-Based Trees (CBT) to
provide session key management as well as multicast routing might be
an approach used in the future [BFC93].

4.6 IP Key Management Requirements

This section defines key management requirements for all IPv6 implementations and for those IPv4 implementations that implement the IP Authentication Header, the IP Encapsulating Security Payload, or both. It applies equally to the IP Authentication Header and the IP Encapsulating Security Payload.

All such implementations MUST support manual configuration of Security Associations.

All such implementations SHOULD support an Internet standard Security Association establishment protocol (e.g., IKMP, Photuris) once such a protocol is published as an Internet standards-track RFC.

Implementations MAY also support other methods of configuring Security Associations.

Given two endpoints, it MUST be possible to have more than one concurrent Security Association for communications between them. Implementations on multi-user hosts SHOULD support user granularity (i.e., "user-oriented") Security Associations.

All such implementations MUST permit the configuration of host-oriented keying.

A device that encrypts or authenticates IP packets originated other systems, for example a dedicated IP encryptor or an encrypting gateway, cannot generally provide user-oriented keying for traffic originating on other systems. Such systems MAY additionally implement support for user-oriented keying for traffic originating on other systems.

The method by which keys are configured on a particular system is implementation-defined. A flat file containing security association identifiers and the security parameters, including the key(s), is an example of one possible method for manual key distribution. An IP system MUST take reasonable steps to protect the keys and other security association information from unauthorised examination or modification because all of the security lies in the keys.

5. USAGE

This section describes the possible use of the security mechanisms provided by IP in several different environments and applications in order to give the implementer and user a better idea of how these mechanisms can be used to reduce security risks.

5.1 USE WITH FIREWALLS

Firewalls are not uncommon in the current Internet [CB94]. While many dislike their presence because they restrict connectivity, they are unlikely to disappear in the near future. Both of these IP mechanisms can be used to increase the security provided by firewalls.

Firewalls used with IP often need to be able to parse the headers and options to determine the transport protocol (e.g., UDP or TCP) in use and the port number for that protocol. Firewalls can be used with the Authentication Header regardless of whether that firewall is party to the appropriate Security Assocation, but a firewall that is not party to the applicable Security Association will not normally be able to decrypt an encrypted upper-layer protocol to view the protocol or port number needed to perform per-packet filtering OR to verify that the data (e.g., source, destination, transport protocol, port number) being used for access control decisions is correct and authentic. Hence, authentication might be performed not only within an organisation or campus but also end to end with remote systems across the Internet. This use of the Authentication Header with IP provides much more assurance that the data being used for access control decisions is authentic.

Organisations with two or more sites that are interconnected using commercial IP service might wish to use a selectively encrypting firewall. If an encrypting firewall were placed between each site of a company and the commercial IP service provider, the firewall could provide an encrypted IP tunnel among all the company's sites. It could also encrypt traffic between the company and its suppliers, customers, and other affiliates. Traffic with the Network Information Center, with public Internet archives, or some other organisations might not be encrypted because of the unavailability of a standard key management protocol or as a deliberate choice to facilitate better communications, improved network performance, and increased connectivity. Such a practice could easily protect the company's sensitive traffic from eavesdropping and modification.

Some organisations (e.g., governments) might wish to use a fully encrypting firewall to provide a protected virtual network over commercial IP service. The difference between that and a bulk IP encryption device is that a fully encrypting firewall would provide filtering of the decrypted traffic as well as providing encryption of IP packets.

5.2 USE WITH IP MULTICAST

In the past several years, the Multicast Backbone (MBONE) has grown rapidly. IETF meetings and other conferences are now regularly multicast with real-time audio, video, and whiteboards. Many people are now using teleconferencing applications based on IP Multicast in the Internet or in private internal networks. Others are using IP multicasting to support distributed simulation or other applications. Hence it is important that the security mechanisms in IP be suitable for use in an environment where multicast is the general case.

The Security Parameters Indexes (SPIs) used in the IP security mechanisms are receiver-oriented, making them well suited for use in IP multicast [Atk95a, Atk95b]. Unfortunately, most currently published multicast key distribution protocols do not scale well. However, there is active research in this area. As an interim step, a multicast group could repeatedly use a secure unicast key distribution protocol to distribute the key to all members or the group could pre-arrange keys using manual key distribution.

5.3 USE TO PROVIDE QOS PROTECTION

The recent IAB Security Workshop identified Quality of Service protection as an area of significant interest [BCCH]. The two IP security mechanisms are intended to provide good support for real-time services as well as multicasting. This section describes one possible approach to providing such protection.

The Authentication Header might be used, with appropriate key management, to provide authentication of packets. This authentication is potentially important in packet classification within routers. The IPv6 Flow Identifier might act as a Low-Level Identifier (LLID). Used together, packet classification within routers becomes straightforward if the router is provided with the appropriate keying material. For performance reasons the routers might authenticate only every Nth packet rather than every packet, but this is still a significant improvement over capabilities in the current Internet. Quality of service provisioning is likely to also use the Flow ID in conjunction with a resource reservation protocol, such as RSVP [ZDESZ93]. Thus, the authenticated packet classification can be used to help ensure that each packet receives appropriate handling inside routers.

5.4 USE IN COMPARTMENTED OR MULTI-LEVEL NETWORKS

A multi-level secure (MLS) network is one where a single network is used to communicate data at different sensitivity levels (e.g., Unclassified and Secret) [DoD85] [DoD87]. Many governments have

significant interest in MLS networking [DIA]. The IP security
mechanisms have been designed to support MLS networking. MLS
networking requires the use of strong Mandatory Access Controls
(MAC), which ordinary users are incapable of controlling or violating
[BL73]. This section pertains only to the use of these IP security
mechanisms in MLS environments.

The Authentication Header can be used to provide strong
authentication among hosts in a single-level network. The
Authentication Header can also be used to provide strong assurance
for both mandatory access control decisions in multi-level networks
and discretionary access control decisions in all kinds of networks.
If explicit IP sensitivity labels (e.g., IPSO) [Ken91] are used and
confidentiality is not considered necessary within the particular
operational environment, the Authentication Header is used to provide
authentication for the entire packet, including cryptographic binding
of the sensitivity level to the IP header and user data. This is a
significant improvement over labeled IPv4 networks where the label is
trusted even though it is not trustworthy because there is no
authentication or cryptographic binding of the label to the IP header
and user data. IPv6 will normally use implicit sensitivity labels
that are part of the Security Association but not transmitted with
each packet instead of using explicit sensitivity labels. All
explicit IP sensitivity labels MUST be authenticated using either
ESP, AH, or both.

The Encapsulating Security Payload can be combined with appropriate
key policies to provide full multi-level secure networking. In this
case each key must be used only at a single sensitivity level and
compartment. For example, Key "A" might be used only for sensitive
Unclassified packets, while Key "B" is used only for Secret/No-
compartments traffic, and Key "C" is used only for Secret/No-Foreign
traffic. The sensitivity level of the protected traffic MUST NOT
dominate the sensitivity level of the Security Association used with
that traffic. The sensitivity level of the Security Association MUST
NOT dominate the sensitivity level of the key that belongs to that
Security Association. The sensitivity level of the key SHOULD be the
same as the sensitivity level of the Security Association. The
Authentication Header can also have different keys for the same
reasons, with the choice of key depending in part on the sensitivity
level of the packet.

Encryption is very useful and desirable even when all of the hosts
are within a protected environment. The Internet-standard encryption
algorithm could be used, in conjunction with appropriate key
management, to provide strong Discretionary Access Controls (DAC) in
conjunction with either implicit sensitivity labels or explicit
sensitivity labels (such as IPSO provides for IPv4 [Ken91]). Some

environments might consider the Internet-standard encryption algorithm sufficiently strong to provide Mandatory Access Controls (MAC). Full encryption SHOULD be used for all communications between multi-level computers or compartmented mode workstations even when the computing environment is considered to be protected.

6. SECURITY CONSIDERATIONS

This entire memo discusses the Security Architecture for the Internet Protocol. It is not a general security architecture for the Internet, but is instead focused on the IP layer.

Cryptographic transforms for ESP which use a block-chaining algorithm and lack a strong integrity mechanism are vulnerable to a cut-and-paste attack described by Bellovin and should not be used unless the Authentication Header is always present with packets using that ESP transform [Bel95].

If more than one sender uses shares a Security Association with a destination, then the receiving system can only authenticate that the packet was sent from one of those systems and cannot authenticate which of those systems sent it. Similarly, if the receiving system does not check that the Security Association used for a packet is valid for the claimed Source Address of the packet, then the receiving system cannot authenticate whether the packet's claimed Source Address is valid. For example, if senders "A" and "B" each have their own unique Security Association with destination "D" and "B" uses its valid Security Association with D but forges a Source Address of "A", then "D" will be fooled into believing the packet came from "A" unless "D" verifies that the claimed Source Address is party to the Security Association that was used.

Users need to understand that the quality of the security provided by the mechanisms provided by these two IP security mechanisms depends completely on the strength of the implemented cryptographic algorithms, the strength of the key being used, the correct implementation of the cryptographic algorithms, the security of the key management protocol, and the correct implementation of IP and the several security mechanisms in all of the participating systems. The security of the implementation is in part related to the security of the operating system which embodies the security implementations. For example, if the operating system does not keep the private cryptologic keys (that is, all symmetric keys and the private asymmetric keys) confidential, then traffic using those keys will not be secure. If any of these is incorrect or insufficiently secure, little or no real security will be provided to the user. Because different users on the same system might not trust each other, each user or each session should usually be keyed separately. This will also tend to increase the work required to cryptanalyse the traffic since not all traffic will use the same key.

Certain security properties (e.g., traffic analysis protection) are not provided by any of these mechanisms. One possible approach to traffic analysis protection is appropriate use of link encryption [VK83]. Users must carefully consider which security properties they require and take active steps to ensure that their needs are met by these or other mechanisms.

Certain applications (e.g., electronic mail) probably need to have application-specific security mechanisms. Application-specific security mechanisms are out of the scope of this document. Users interested in electronic mail security should consult the RFCs describing the Internet's Privacy-Enhanced Mail system. Users concerned about other application-specific mechanisms should consult the online RFCs to see if suitable Internet Standard mechanisms exist.

ACKNOWLEDGEMENTS

Many of the concepts here are derived from or were influenced by the US Government's SDNS security protocol specifications, the ISO/IEC's NLSP specification, or from the proposed swIPe security protocol [SDNS, ISO, IB93, IBK93]. The work done for SNMP Security and SNMPv2 Security influenced the choice of default cryptological algorithms and modes [GM93]. Steve Bellovin, Steve Deering, Richard Hale, George Kamis, Phil Karn, Frank Kastenholz, Perry Metzger, Dave Mihelcic, Hilarie Orman and Bill Simpson provided careful critiques of early versions of this document.

REFERENCES

[Atk95a] Atkinson, R., "IP Authentication Header", RFC 1826, NRL, August 1995.

[Atk95b] Atkinson, R., "IP Encapsulating Security Payload", RFC 1827, NRL, August 1995.

[BCCH94] Braden, R., Clark, D., Crocker, S., and C. Huitema, "Report of IAB Workshop on Security in the Internet Architecture", RFC 1636, USC/Information Sciences Institute, MIT, Trusted Information Systems, INRIA, June 1994.

[Bel89] Steven M. Bellovin, "Security Problems in the TCP/IP Protocol Suite", ACM Computer Communications Review, Vol. 19, No. 2, March 1989.

[Bel95]   Steven M. Bellovin, Presentation at IP Security Working
           Group Meeting, Proceedings of the 32nd Internet Engineering
           Task Force, March 1995, Internet Engineering Task Force,
           Danvers, MA.

[BFC93]   A. Ballardie, P. Francis, & J. Crocroft, "Core Based Trees:
           An Architecture for Scalable Inter-Domain Multicast Routing",
           Proceedings of ACM SIGCOMM 93, ACM Computer Communications
           Review, Volume. 23, Number 4, October 1993, pp. 85-95.

[BL73]   Bell, D.E. & LaPadula, L.J., "Secure Computer Systems:
           Mathematical Foundations and Model", Technical Report
           M74-244, The MITRE Corporation, Bedford, MA, May 1973.

[CB94]   William R. Cheswick & Steven M. Bellovin, Firewalls &
           Internet Security, Addison-Wesley, Reading, MA, 1994.

[DIA]   US Defense Intelligence Agency, "Compartmented Mode
           Workstation Specification", Technical Report
           DDS-2600-6243-87.

[DoD85]   US National Computer Security Center, "Department of Defense
           Trusted Computer System Evaluation Criteria", DoD
           5200.28-STD, US Department of Defense, Ft. Meade, MD.,
           December 1985.

[DoD87]   US National Computer Security Center, "Trusted Network
           Interpretation of the Trusted Computer System Evaluation
           Criteria", NCSC-TG-005, Version 1, US Department of Defense,
           Ft. Meade, MD., 31 July 1987.

[DH76]   W. Diffie & M. Hellman, "New Directions in Cryptography",
           IEEE Transactions on Information Theory, Vol. IT-22, No. 6,
           November 1976, pp. 644-654.

[EK94]   D. Eastlake III & C. Kaufman, "Domain Name System Protocol
           Security Extensions", Work in Progress.

[GM93]   Galvin J., and K. McCloghrie, "Security Protocols for
           version 2 of the Simple Network Management Protocol
           (SNMPv2)", RFC 1446, Trusted Information Systems, Hughes LAN
           Systems, April 1993.

[HA94]   Haller, N., and R. Atkinson, "On Internet Authentication",
           RFC 1704, Bell Communications Research, NRL, October 1994.

[Hin94]   Bob Hinden (Editor), Internet Protocol version 6 (IPv6)
           Specification, Work in Progress, October 1994.

[ISO]   ISO/IEC JTC1/SC6, Network Layer Security Protocol, ISO-IEC
         DIS 11577, International Standards Organisation, Geneva,
         Switzerland, 29 November 1992.

[IB93]   John Ioannidis and Matt Blaze, "Architecture and
         Implementation of Network-layer Security Under Unix",
         Proceedings of USENIX Security Symposium, Santa Clara, CA,
         October 1993.

[IBK93] John Ioannidis, Matt Blaze, & Phil Karn, "swIPe: Network-Layer
         Security for IP", presentation at the Spring 1993 IETF Meeting,
         Columbus, Ohio.

[Ken91] Kent, S., "US DoD Security Options for the Internet Protocol",
         RFC 1108, BBN Communications, November 1991.

[Ken93] Kent, S., "Privacy Enhancement for Internet Electronic Mail:
         Part II: Certificate-Based Key Management", RFC 1422,
         BBN Communications, February 1993.

[KB93]   Kohl, J., and B. Neuman, "The Kerberos Network Authentication
         Service (V5)", RFC 1510, Digital Equipment Corporation,
         USC/Information Sciences Institute, September 1993.

[MS95]   Metzger, P., and W. Simpson, "IP Authentication with Keyed
         MD5", RFC 1828, Piermont, Daydreamer, August 1995.

[KMS95] Karn, P., Metzger, P., and W. Simpson, "The ESP DES-CBC
         Transform", RFC 1829, Qualcomm, Inc., Piermont, Daydreamer,
         August 1995.

[NS78]   R.M. Needham & M.D. Schroeder, "Using Encryption for
         Authentication in Large Networks of Computers", Communications
         of the ACM, Vol. 21, No. 12, December 1978, pp. 993-999.

[NS81]   R.M. Needham & M.D. Schroeder, "Authentication Revisited",
         ACM Operating Systems Review, Vol. 21, No. 1., 1981.

[OTA94] US Congress, Office of Technology Assessment, "Information
         Security & Privacy in Network Environments", OTA-TCT-606,
         Government Printing Office, Washington, DC, September 1994.

[Sch94] Bruce Schneier, Applied Cryptography, Section 8.6,
         John Wiley & Sons, New York, NY, 1994.

[SDNS]   SDNS Secure Data Network System, Security Protocol 3, SP3,
          Document SDN.301, Revision 1.5, 15 May 1989, published
          in NIST Publication NIST-IR-90-4250, February 1990.

[VK83]   V.L. Voydock & S.T. Kent, "Security Mechanisms in High-level
          Networks", ACM Computing Surveys, Vol. 15, No. 2, June 1983.

[ZDESZ93] Zhang, L., Deering, S., Estrin, D., Shenker, S., and
          D. Zappala, "RSVP: A New Resource ReSerVation Protocol",
          IEEE Network magazine, September 1993.

DISCLAIMER

   The views expressed in this note are those of the author and are not
   necessarily those of his employer. The Naval Research Laboratory has
   not passed judgement on the merits, if any, of this work. The author
   and his employer specifically disclaim responsibility for any problems
   arising from correct or incorrect implementation or use of this
   design.

AUTHOR'S ADDRESS

   Randall Atkinson
   Information Technology Division
   Naval Research Laboratory
   Washington, DC 20375-5320
   USA

   Phone: (202) 767-2389
   Fax: (202) 404-8590
   EMail: atkinson@itd.nrl.navy.mil

```
Network Working Group                                          IAB
Request for Comments: 1984                                    IESG
Category: Informational                                August 1996
```

IAB and IESG Statement on Cryptographic Technology and the Internet

Status of This Memo

> This memo provides information for the Internet community. This memo
> does not specify an Internet standard of any kind. Distribution of
> this memo is unlimited.

July 24, 1996

> The Internet Architecture Board (IAB) and the Internet Engineering
> Steering Group (IESG), the bodies which oversee architecture and
> standards for the Internet, are concerned by the need for increased
> protection of international commercial transactions on the Internet,
> and by the need to offer all Internet users an adequate degree of
> privacy.

> Security mechanisms being developed in the Internet Engineering Task
> Force to meet these needs require and depend on the international use
> of adequate cryptographic technology. Ready access to such
> technology is therefore a key factor in the future growth of the
> Internet as a motor for international commerce and communication.

> The IAB and IESG are therefore disturbed to note that various
> governments have actual or proposed policies on access to
> cryptographic technology that either:

> (a) impose restrictions by implementing export controls; and/or

> (b) restrict commercial and private users to weak and inadequate
>   mechanisms such as short cryptographic keys; and/or

> (c) mandate that private decryption keys should be in the hands of
>   the government or of some other third party; and/or

> (d) prohibit the use of cryptology entirely, or permit it only to
>   specially authorized organizations.

We believe that such policies are against the interests of consumers and the business community, are largely irrelevant to issues of military security, and provide only a marginal or illusory benefit to law enforcement agencies, as discussed below.

The IAB and IESG would like to encourage policies that allow ready access to uniform strong cryptographic technology for all Internet users in all countries.

The IAB and IESG claim:

The Internet is becoming the predominant vehicle for electronic commerce and information exchange. It is essential that the support structure for these activities can be trusted.

Encryption is not a secret technology monopolized by any one country, such that export controls can hope to contain its deployment. Any hobbyist can program a PC to do powerful encryption. Many algorithms are well documented, some with source code available in textbooks.

Export controls on encryption place companies in that country at a competitive disadvantage. Their competitors from countries without export restrictions can sell systems whose only design constraint is being secure, and easy to use.

Usage controls on encryption will also place companies in that country at a competitive disadvantage because these companies cannot securely and easily engage in electronic commerce.

Escrow mechanisms inevitably weaken the security of the overall cryptographic system, by creating new points of vulnerability that can and will be attacked.

Export controls and usage controls are slowing the deployment of security at the same time as the Internet is exponentially increasing in size and attackers are increasing in sophistication. This puts users in a dangerous position as they are forced to rely on insecure electronic communication.

TECHNICAL ANALYSIS

KEY SIZE

It is not acceptable to restrict the use or export of cryptosystems based on their key size. Systems that are breakable by one country will be breakable by others, possibly unfriendly ones. Large corporations and even criminal enterprises have the resources to break many cryptosystems. Furthermore, conversations often need to be protected for years to come; as computers increase in speed, key sizes that were once out of reach of cryptanalysis will become insecure.

PUBLIC KEY INFRASTRUCTURE

Use of public key cryptography often requires the existence of a "certification authority". That is, some third party must sign a string containing the user's identity and public key. In turn, the third party's key is often signed by a higher-level certification authority.

Such a structure is legitimate and necessary. Indeed, many governments will and should run their own CAs, if only to protect citizens' transactions with their governments. But certification authorities should not be confused with escrow centers. Escrow centers are repositories for private keys, while certification authorities deal with public keys. Indeed, sound cryptographic practice dictates that users never reveal their private keys to anyone, even the certification authority.

KEYS SHOULD NOT BE REVEALABLE

The security of a modern cryptosystem rests entirely on the secrecy of the keys. Accordingly, it is a major principle of system design that to the extent possible, secret keys should never leave their user's secure environment. Key escrow implies that keys must be disclosed in some fashion, a flat-out contradiction of this principle. Any such disclosure weakens the total security of the system.

DATA RECOVERY

Sometimes escrow systems are touted as being good for the customer because they allow data recovery in the case of lost keys. However, it should be up to the customer to decide whether they would prefer the more secure system in which lost keys mean lost data, or one in which keys are escrowed to be recovered when necessary. Similarly, keys used only for conversations (as opposed to file storage) need never be escrowed. And a system in which the secret key is stored by a government and not by the data owner is certainly not practical for data recovery.

SIGNATURE KEYS

Keys used for signatures and authentication must never be escrowed. Any third party with access to such keys could impersonate the legitimate owner, creating new opportunities for fraud and deceit.

Indeed, a user who wished to repudiate a transaction could claim that
his or her escrowed key was used, putting the onus on that party.   If
a government escrowed the keys, a defendant could claim that the
evidence had been forged by the government, thereby making
prosecution much more difficult.   For electronic commerce, non-
repudiation is one of the most important uses for cryptography; and
non-repudiation depends on the assumption that only the user has
access to the private key.

PROTECTION OF THE EXISTING INFRASTRUCTURE

In some cases, it is technically feasible to use cryptographic
operations that do not involve secrecy.   While this may suffice in
some cases, much of the existing technical and commercial
infrastructure cannot be protected in this way.   For example,
conventional passwords, credit card numbers, and the like must be
protected by strong encryption, even though some day more
sophisticated techniques may replace them.   Encryption can be added
on quite easily; wholesale changes to diverse systems cannot.

CONFLICTING INTERNATIONAL POLICIES

Conflicting restrictions on encryption often force an international
company to use a weak encryption system, in order to satisfy legal
requirements in two or more different countries.   Ironically, in such
cases either nation might consider the other an adversary against
whom commercial enterprises should use strong cryptography.   Clearly,
key escrow is not a suitable compromise, since neither country would
want to disclose keys to the other.

MULTIPLE ENCRYPTION

Even if escrowed encryption schemes are used, there is nothing to
prevent someone from using another encryption scheme first.
Certainly, any serious malefactors would do this; the outer
encryption layer, which would use an escrowed scheme, would be used
to divert suspicion.

ESCROW OF PRIVATE KEYS WON'T NECESSARILY ALLOW DATA DECRYPTION

A major threat to users of cryptographic systems is the theft of
long-term keys (perhaps by a hacker), either before or after a
sensitive conversation.   To counter this threat, schemes with
"perfect forward secrecy" are often employed.   If PFS is used, the
attacker must be in control of the machine during the actual
conversation.   But PFS is generally incompatible with schemes
involving escrow of private keys.   (This is an oversimplification,
but a full analysis would be too lengthy for this document.)

CONCLUSIONS

As more and more companies connect to the Internet, and as more and more commerce takes place there, security is becoming more and more critical. Cryptography is the most powerful single tool that users can use to secure the Internet. Knowingly making that tool weaker threatens their ability to do so, and has no proven benefit.

Security Considerations

Security issues are discussed throughout this memo.

Authors' Addresses

Brian E. Carpenter
Chair of the IAB
CERN
European Laboratory for Particle Physics
1211 Geneva 23
Switzerland

Phone: +41 22 767-4967
EMail: brian@dxcoms.cern.ch

Fred Baker
Chair of the IETF
cisco Systems, Inc.
519 Lado Drive
Santa Barbara, CA 93111

Phone: +1-805-681-0115
EMail: fred@cisco.com

The Internet Society is described at http://www.isoc.org/

The Internet Architecture Board is described at
http://www.iab.org/iab

The Internet Engineering Task Force and the Internet Engineering
Steering Group are described at http://www.ietf.org

Index